BECOMING BLACK POLITICAL SUBJECTS

BECOMING BLACK
POLITICAL SUBJECTS

*Movements and Ethno-Racial
Rights in Colombia and Brazil*

TIANNA S. PASCHEL

PRINCETON UNIVERSITY PRESS
PRINCETON AND OXFORD

Published by Princeton University Press,
41 William Street, Princeton, New Jersey 08540
In the United Kingdom: Princeton University Press,
6 Oxford Street, Woodstock, Oxfordshire OX20 1TW
press.princeton.edu

Jacket Art by Iléa Ferraz.

Library of Congress Cataloging-in-Publication Data

Names: Paschel, Tianna S., author.
Title: Becoming black political subjects : movements and ethno-racial rights
    in Colombia and Brazil / Tianna S. Paschel.
Description: Princeton : Princeton University Press, [2016] | Includes
    bibliographical references and index.
Identifiers: LCCN 2016007389 | ISBN 9780691169385 (hardcover : acid-free
    paper)
Subjects: LCSH: Blacks—Colombia—Politics and government. |
    Blacks—Brazil—Politics and government. | Blacks—Race
    identity—Colombia. | Blacks—Race identity—Brazil. | Identity
    politics—Colombia. | Identity politics—Brazil. | Colombia—Politics and
    government—1974– | Brazil—Politics and government—1985-2002. |
    Brazil—Politics and government—2002–
Classification: LCC F2299.B55 P37 2016 | DDC 305.896/0861—dc23 LC record available at
https://lccn.loc.gov/2016007389

British Library Cataloging-in-Publication Data is available

This book has been composed in Sabon Next LT Pro

Printed on acid-free paper. ∞

Printed in the United States of America

10 9 8 7 6 5 4 3 2 1

CONTENTS

LIST OF ORGANIZATIONS

ACRONYM/ ABBREVIATION	PORTUGUESE/ SPANISH	ENGLISH	COUNTRY
ACABA	Asociación Campes- ina del Baudó	Peasant Association of the Baudó River	Colombia
ACADESAN	Asociación Campes- ina del Bajo San Juan	Peasant Association of the Lower San Juan River	Colombia
ACIA	Asociación Camp- esina Integral del Atrato	Peasant Association of the Atrato River	Colombia
AFRODES	Asociación de Afrodesplazados	Association of Displaced Afro- Colombians	Colombia
AMUNAFRO	Asociación Nacional de Alcaldes de Muni- cipios con Población Afrodescendiente	National Association of Municipalities with Afro-Colombian Populations	Colombia
ANC	Assembleia Nacional Constituinte	National Constituent Assembly	Brazil
ANC	Asamblea Nacional Constituyente	National Constituent Assembly	Colombia
APN	Agentes do Pastoral Negro	Black Pastoral Agents	Brazil
CEAP	Centro de Articu- lação de Populações Marginais	Center for the Artic- ulation of Marginal Populations	Brazil
CEERT	Centro de Estudos de Relações de Trabalho e Desigualdades	Center for the Study of Labor Relations and Inequality	Brazil

ACRONYM/ ABBREVIATION	PORTUGUESE/ SPANISH	ENGLISH	COUNTRY
CEN	Coletivo de Entidades Negras	Collective of Black Entities	Brazil
CERD		UN Committee on the Elimination of Racial Discrimination	International
Cimarrón	Cimarrón: Movimiento Nacional de Derechos Humanos de Comunidades Afrocolombianas	Cimarrón: National Movement for the Human Rights of Afro-Colombian Communities	Colombia
CNOA	Conferencia Nacional de Organizaciones Afrocolombianas	National Conference of Afro-Colombian Organizations	Colombia
COCOMACIA	Consejo Comunitario Mayor de la Asociación Campesina Integral del Atrato	Regional Community Council of the Peasant Association of the Atrato	Colombia
COCOMOPOCA	Consejo Comunitario Mayor de la Organización Popular del Atrato	Regional Community Council of the Popular Organization of the Atrato	Colombia
CONEN	Coordenação Nacional de Entidades Negras	National Coordinator of Black Organizations	Brazil
CUT	Central Única dos Trabalhadores	Unified Workers' Central	Brazil
ECLAC		UN Economic Commission on Latin America and the Caribbean	International
GTI	Grupo de Trabalho Interministerial para a Valorização da População Negra	Interministerial Working Group for the Valorization of the Black Population	Brazil
IDB		Inter-American Development Bank	International

ACRONYM/ ABBREVIATION	PORTUGUESE/ SPANISH	ENGLISH	COUNTRY
ILO		International Labour Organisation	International
IPCN	Instituto de Pesquisa de Cultura Negra	Institute for Research on Black Culture	Brazil
MNU	Movimento Negro Unificado	Unified Black Movement	Brazil
OBAPO	Organizaciones de Barrios Populares	Organization of Popular Neighborhoods	Colombia
OCN	Organización de Comunidades Negras	Organization of Black Communities	Colombia
PCdoB	Partido Comunista do Brasil	Communist Party of Brazil	Brazil
PCN	Proceso de Comunidades Negras	Black Communities' Movement	Colombia
PT	Partido dos Trabalhadores	Workers' Party	Brazil
SEPPIR	Secretaria de Políticas da Promoção da Igualdade Racial	Secretary for the Promotion of Racial Equality Policies	Brazil
SINBA	Sociedade de Intercambio Brasil-África	Society for Brazil-Africa Exchange	Brazil
TEN	Teatro Experimental do Negro	Black Experimental Theatre	Brazil
UNEGRO	União de Negros pela Igualdade	Union of Blacks for Equality	Brazil

BECOMING BLACK POLITICAL SUBJECTS

CHAPTER ONE

POLITICAL FIELD ALIGNMENTS

In 1991, black farmers and miners left the rural areas of Colombia's Pacific Coast, making their way to the capital city of Bogotá. They took with them marimbas, drums, and songs about rural life and culture with the intention of serenading the delegates to the National Constituent Assembly. Their *serenatas* served one purpose: to convince those elected to draft Colombia's new constitution that the state should grant black communities specific rights. Ultimately, they succeeded, and the country's 1991 constitution recognized that black people, like indigenous peoples, were a distinct "ethnic group" whose right to collective territory was to be legally protected. The constitution also mandated the adoption of the Law of Black Communities (1993), which recognized the rights of rural black communities to ethnic education, alternative development, natural resources, political participation, and local autonomy. This legislation profoundly disrupted the way that the Colombian state had imagined the nation for nearly a century, as racially mixed and culturally homogeneous.

Colombia's neighbor, Brazil, had reformed its constitution along similar lines just three years before when it recognized the land rights of indigenous peoples and descendants of runaway slaves. However, Brazil's more transformative ethno-racial reforms came about a decade later with a wave of policies designed to "promote racial equality." This happened in August 2001, when black Brazilian activists flew to Durban, South Africa, as part of one of the largest delegations to the United Nation's Third World Conference against Racism.[1] In contrast to Afro-Colombians who carried with them symbols of cultural difference, Brazil's black activists traveled equipped with official statistics on racial inequality and discrimination in their country. They had one main objective: to pressure the Brazilian state to grant the country's black population reparations in the form of affirmative action policies.[2] The strategy worked. In December 2001, then-president Fernando Henrique Cardoso gave an historic speech in which he stated, "The Brazilian state recognizes the painful consequences that slavery has caused in Brazil and it will continue with the task of repairing such damage through policies that promote equal opportunity."[3] He added that the best way to address this issue was through both "universal and affirmative action policies for Afro-descendants." Subsequently, government agencies and nearly a hundred of Brazil's most prestigious universities implemented unparalleled race-based affirmative action policies with the goal of proactively addressing racial inequality and discrimination.

These political changes in Colombia and Brazil disrupted prevalent state discourses, which had denied the existence of racism and downplayed these countries' cultural heterogeneity for decades. Nationalist narratives in these cases had been based on the notion of *mestizaje*—the idea that biological mixture and cultural hybridity between European, indigenous, and African peoples—had given way to a racially egalitarian and homogeneous society. The official state discourse was that these countries had overcome their sordid histories of slavery and colonization to create racial paradises of sorts. As such, the state, and society more generally, often dismissed those who thought otherwise. Black activists were often accused of importing racism from elsewhere, and in rare cases, the state repressed such ideas outright.[4] However, this began to change radically in the late 1980s, as states throughout Latin America recognized black and indigenous rights as well as adopted policies aimed at bringing about ethno-racial equality. These reforms shook the very foundation upon which nationalism was built in these countries.

In this book, l examine these political transformations in Colombia and Brazil. More specifically, I analyze the process through which blackness became legitimated as a category of political contestation in the eyes of the state and other powerful political actors. In order to do so, I examined archives and conducted ethnographic fieldwork over nearly eight years in the style of what scholars across disciplines have called "political ethnography" (Auyero 2006; Baiocchi and Connor 2008; Schatz 2013). While this approach to ethnography relies on participant observation, it is more fundamentally about being immersed in political communities in ways that lead to a more textured analysis of political processes.[5] Embedding myself in the very political processes I was studying helped to generate a productive analysis that moved beyond simple "categories of state, civil society, and social movements," as Baiocchi and Conner (2008, 139) have noted. In the methodological appendix, I explain my methods in greater detail and also explore how being an African American woman affiliated with elite U.S. universities shaped my experience in the field.

I first ask: Why did the Colombian and Brazilian states go from citizenship regimes based in ideas of the universal and formally unmarked citizen to the recognition of black rights? I argue that in both cases they did so in the face of pressure from black social movement organizations. However, while these movements were essential to the making of black political subjects, they were small and under-resourced networks of activists. They also had very few political allies and were unpopular with, and largely unknown to, the masses. In fact, social movement scholars might debate the extent to which they were movements at all. Even if we assume they were in fact movements, we are still left with many questions about why activists were able to reshape state policy and discourse in such drastic ways. Their success runs counter to the ideas that have been cultivated for decades that massive, disruptive movements as well as those with strong political allies and favorable public opinion are more likely to bring about the changes they desire.[6]

Yet the story I weave together here is still fundamentally about how black social movements in Colombia and Brazil did succeed—against all odds—in bringing about specific legislation for black populations as well as substantive changes in popular discourse. In addition to analyzing the strategies they used to do so, I also examine how their embeddedness in a complex field of local and global politics often blurred the very definition of what a social movements is. In this vein, I argue that the only way to understand the making of black political subjects in Colombia and Brazil is to take as a point of departure the idea that these movements, like many movements around the world, operate within the material and discursive boundaries of multiple fields of contestation.

The two fields in which black movements were embedded in these cases were the field of domestic politics, and something I call the global ethno-racial field. These fields (a term I borrow from Bourdieu) were composed of local and global discourses of race, nation, and rights as well as a plethora of political actors, including state officials, academic "experts," environmentalists, international human rights advocates, development workers, capitalists, and other social movement actors. I show how black movements in Colombia and Brazil successfully pressured their respective states to adopt ethno-racial reforms because they acted strategically in the context of this consolidated global ethno-racial field oriented around multiculturalism, indigenous rights, and anti-racism, which converged with profound changes in the domestic political fields of these countries. I contend that by mobilizing around these political field alignments, black movements in Colombia and Brazil overcame significant ideological and material odds to ultimately transform citizenship regimes previously based on homogeneity and formal colorblindness.

The second question I seek to answer is: Why have black rights taken such distinct forms in different countries in Latin America? Nearly every country in the region has adopted some type of ethno-racial policies over the last three decades. However, unlike previous scholarship I do not see these reforms all as making up a singular "multicultural turn."[7] Instead, I argue that it is more useful to view these changes as constituting two distinct moments of interplay between domestic and global politics. The first of these, I suggest, began to unfold in the late 1980s with the shift to what Van Cott (2000) called "multicultural constitutionalism." In this period, Latin American states reformed their constitutions in ways that recognized the "pluri-ethnic" and "multicultural" character of the political community while at the same time they extended specific rights to indigenous peoples and in some cases to black populations. In countries that did include blacks in this multicultural alignment, the black political subject that emerged was defined by a discourse of cultural difference and autonomy that was very much entangled with concerns about the struggle and well-being of indigenous peoples.

About a decade later, Latin American states initiated a new wave of ethno-racial reforms aimed at combating racial discrimination and bringing about racial equality. This included establishing national holidays celebrating black history and culture, creating state institutions aimed at combating racial discrimination, including new kinds of ethno-racial questions on national censuses, and the passing of anti-discrimination legislation. Unlike the multicultural policies of the 1980s–1990s, blacks—rather than indigenous peoples—were the presumed subjects of these new reforms. I examine how both of these rounds of reforms played out in two of the most important cases in the region, Colombia and Brazil.

Last, I explore the broader social and political consequences of these shifts. By the time I embarked upon fieldwork in 2006, I did not find the kind of silencing of racial critique that previous scholars found to be so prevalent in this region. Instead, both the Colombian and Brazilian states talked openly about racism and ethno-racial policies.[8] Moreover, rather than be seen as divisive, black identity was considered a legitimate political category. Yet while these governments had dramatically shifted their discourse around ethno-racial issues, many questions remained unresolved. Who would be the beneficiaries of these policies? How would blackness be defined in these contexts where ethno-racial categories were notoriously so blurry? Did people have to be rural and culturally distinct, reside in "black regions," or trace their ancestry back to runaway slaves to qualify for multicultural rights? Would having a black ancestor be enough to qualify one for affirmative action at a university?

Further, given that both Colombia and Brazil are notorious for their gaps between laws on the books and actual state practices, did these reforms actually matter on the ground? I show how the institutionalization of ethno-racial rights and policies not only reconfigured the state, it also reshaped the terms—both the conditions and language—of the black movement itself. In the wake of what were inevitably partial victories, what developed were entangled relationships between black movement actors and the state, as well as contentious debates within these movements over questions of authenticity, representation, and political autonomy. All of these political dynamics shaped how deep these reforms actually went.

FROM RACE MIXTURE TO BLACK RIGHTS

Throughout most of the twentieth century, elites, ordinary citizens, and visitors shared a view of Latin America as a region of racial harmony. Such an idea made some sense when you situated these cases in a global context. In a world of Jim Crow, apartheid, and ethnic cleansing, Latin America—with its high levels of mixing, its lack of racially exclusionary laws, and its low levels of ethno-racial conflict—seemed exceptional. These characteristics were especially pronounced when contrasted with the racist regimes of the United States up until the 1960s or South Africa until the 1990s (Freyre 1933; Pierson 1942; Bourdieu and Wacquant 1999; Fry and Maggie 2004; Magnoli 2009).[9] To some observers, even slavery took a more benevolent form in places like Brazil than it did in the United States (Tannenbaum 1947; Harris 1956; Hoetink 1967).

Latin American state officials echoed this sentiment, often presenting their countries on the world stage as models of racial egalitarianism. As one Brazilian diplomat suggested before the United Nations in 1978, "even though there is a multiplicity of races that live within our borders, racial problems simply do not exist in Brazil."[10] State officials in both countries argued that the prevalence of race mixture, and a tradition of colorblind legalism, and universal citizenship had made racial conflict disappear. A Colombian diplomat captured this idea well in a 1984 report to the UN Committee on the Elimination of Racial Discrimination (CERD): "The legal and social organization of Colombia has always guaranteed racial equality and the absence of discrimination [against] any element of the population."[11] This statement channeled a deeply entrenched nationalism based on *mestizaje*. Also implied in these narratives was that countries like Colombia and Brazil had overcome the stain of slavery and colonization, something their neighbors to the north had not.

During the colonial period, European colonists, enslaved Africans, and indigenous peoples did, in fact, intermix more in Latin America than they did in English colonies. While this might suggest that these differences were cultural in nature, scholars have argued that they were more likely the result of vastly different demographic and political dynamics in these different regions (Degler 1971; Telles 2004). Whereas English settlers came to the United States fleeing religious persecution with their families in tow, Portuguese and Spanish colonists were men largely migrating alone and often with the idea that they would make a fortune in the New World and return home. There is no doubt that, in some cases, African and indigenous women entered into some consensual concubine relationships with European men in colonial Latin America (Stolcke 1989). However, many of the encounters that produced these mixed-race nations also entailed violence and coercion, something that narratives of *mestizaje* often obscure (Stolcke 1989; Caldwell 2007).

Nevertheless, the most significant distinction between Latin America and the United States was not the amount of race mixture per se, but where this mixture figured into the law and into the nationalist project. The United States increasingly outlawed miscegenation over the course of the eighteenth and nineteenth centuries, while Latin American countries not only allowed mixture, they often celebrated it. Under *mestizaje* nationalism, the *mestizo* ("mixed person") became the quintessential national subject, and indigenous and black populations often stood at the center of the symbolic nation. Moreover, rather than formalize racial exclusion via state institutions, elites in Latin American states extended formal citizenship to subordinate groups, even though these groups continued to be marginalized informally.[12]

Yet *mestizaje* was never simply an elite-centered state project (Wade 2005; Chaves and Zambrano 2006). Rather, it was an ideology built through both top-down and bottom-up processes and one that became meaningful for people on the ground. Among other things, *mestizaje* strongly shaped racial and national identities (Wade 2005; Alberto 2011). Beyond identifying with the idea that everyone was mixed, Latin Americans often felt deeply that their societies were indeed racially egalitarian and not stratified by race.

Nevertheless, like any nationalist project, this one was plagued with irreconcilable internal contradictions. First was the irony of constructing a raceless nation through the deeply racialized process of mixing "races." The second problem had to do with the silences inherent to such a project. While most Latin American countries can be said to have three roots—European, indigenous, and African—they included these ancestries in the discourse of the *mestizo* nation selectively (Wade 1997). In Mexico, for example, elites developed a national identity based on the idea of a *mestizo*, or white/indigenous mix, which conveniently left out the fact that in the early part of the seventeenth century, Mexico imported more enslaved Africans than any other country in the world (Andrews 2004).

Beyond the issue of invisibilization was that of hierarchy. Even when countries celebrated both indigenous and African "culture" and "blood"—as Brazil and Venezuela did—they still emphasized their evolution toward whiteness (Wright 1990; Wade 1997; Telles 2004). They expressed this in many ways, including nationalist narratives that exalted a valiant and noble indigenous past while emphasizing the industriousness and capacity that came with their European heritage. In this way, narratives of nation painted a past that was indigenous/African, and the future was inevitably whiter, more European. The project also entailed intentional processes of cultural genocide and violent assimilation.[13] Ultimately, though, these ideas were not drummed up solely within Latin America, but rather reflected increasingly "scientific" thinking in Europe in the early part of the twentieth century (Stepan 1991; Skidmore 1993; De la Fuente 2001; Fitzgerald and Cook-Martín 2014; Loveman 2014). Such conceptions equated European culture and blood with modernity and portrayed Africans and indigenous peoples as inherently backward.

A final tension came from the persistence of ethno-racial inequalities, a phenomenon that was greatly at odds with the idea that these countries were racially egalitarian. Latin American states did not always collect ethno-racial data in their national censuses, as the collection of such data ran counter to the ideal of the culturally homogeneous and racially mixed nation (Loveman 2014). However, the availability of new data has given much empirical evidence that these societies continue to be stratified by race, language, and skin color.[14] For example, we know that today indigenous people are much more likely than nonindigenous people to live in poverty and to work in the informal sector; their children are also more likely to work than their nonindigenous counterparts (Hall and Patrinos 2006). In Brazil—the only country besides Cuba to consistently collect data on blacks and mixed-race people over the last century—whites had higher incomes, higher levels of education, and better health outcomes than non-whites (Telles 2004). Furthermore, in 2005, black Colombians were nearly twice as likely to be impoverished; their infant mortality rate was twice as high, and they had much shorter life expectancy than the rest of the population (Barbary and Urrea 2004; Rodriguez et al. 2008).

Given these many contradictions, scholars have argued that rather than build racially egalitarian societies, Latin American elites simply created a more hegemonic and durable form of racial domination than their counterparts had in the United States or South Africa (Hanchard 1994; Marx 1998; Winddance Twine 1998; Winant 2001; Goldberg 2002; Sawyer 2006). According to these accounts, nationalist discourses of race mixture—insomuch as they relied on the logic of colorblindness and the silencing of racial critique—have often served to mask the reality of continued racism and structural inequality. It comes as something of a surprise then that nearly every Latin American country would change course so dramatically with respect to ethno-racial questions beginning in the late 1980s. In some cases, this shift also meant that state officials would recognize the persistence of racism within their societies for the first time in their histories.

MULTICULTURAL CONSTITUTIONALISM

Over the last few decades, Latin America underwent a number of radical transformations from authoritarian regimes to democratic ones, from interventionist to neoliberal economic policies and from citizenship regimes based on *mestizaje* to regimes that recognized the pluri-ethnic nature of their societies. The last shift is best captured in the plethora of Latin American constitutions that recognized the specific rights of indigenous peoples, and, in some cases, black communities as well. These reforms went beyond symbolic recognition and promised to guarantee these groups the rights to collective territory, natural resources, and alternative development. If fully implemented, they also threatened to restrain unfettered capital and thus to profoundly change the hegemonic model of development operating in these countries at the time.

Many Latin American states also mandated overhauling national education curricula to include the study of indigenous and black history. In some cases, they also passed affirmative action policies, in the areas of education and even in political office. These policies had the potential to challenge dominant narratives of race and nation, and in cases like Brazil, of radically changing the color of the middle class. They also meant that Latin American states had to institutionalize new types of ethno-racial political subjects through changes to the law and with the collection of ethno-racial statistics.[15] In this period, states throughout the region began to institutionalize new forms of political participation as well as create new state bureaucracies. In some cases this entailed reforming existing institutions such as those that had been charged since the 1950s and 1960s with "Indian affairs." In others, states created from scratch new national, regional, and state-level agencies to guarantee ethnic rights and to coordinate the implementation of these new policies. This all amounted to a reconfiguration of Latin American states' orientation toward ethno-racial questions, and arguably their very model of citizenship.

While this transition constituted a significant shift in the "Indian question"—from trusteeship to formal autonomy, from veiled assimilation to cultural pluralism—it represented a much more decisive break with the past for these countries' black populations. Indeed, throughout Latin America, blacks and indigenous peoples had very different legal statuses vis-à-vis citizenship regimes. Whereas many countries had treated unassimilated indigenous people as "savages" or "uncivilizable" de facto sovereigns within their borders, they largely treated blacks in legal terms as ordinary citizens, presumed fully assimilated into the *mestizo* nation (Wade 1997). So while the move from *mestizaje* to multiculturalism did constitute a real change for indigenous communities, for blacks it represented a colossal shift. It marked the first time they would begin to engage with the state not only as individual citizens, but also as the subjects of collective rights.

The adoption of specific policies for black populations throughout Latin America, then, presents a profound challenge to how we have long thought about the role of race and ethnicity in political life in this region. In the decades leading up to the reforms, neither scholars who defended *mestizaje* nor those who challenged it predicted these kinds of transformations. This is, in part, because neither expected social movements or policies based on black identity to have much traction in these cases, albeit for very different reasons. While *mestizaje* advocates saw race-based movements and rights as having no place in these already racially egalitarian societies, scholars who critiqued *mestizaje* often argued that such ideologies had made the development of oppositional racial consciousness nearly impossible and large-scale black mobilization unlikely.[16] So how do we explain the emergence of ethno-racial rights in Latin America over the last few decades, and particularly the inclusion of black populations in these reforms?

EXPLAINING ETHNO-RACIAL POLICY IN LATIN AMERICA

One possible cause might be found in international factors.[17] Throughout Latin America, multicultural reforms happened on the heels of devastating neoliberal reforms that increased poverty and inequality. These policies also intensified land dispossession and prompted state intervention in indigenous communities that had previously been somewhat autonomous (Yashar 2005). Hale (2002) has argued that these worsening conditions catalyzed the domestic and transnational indigenous mobilization that led to multicultural reforms. Moreover, international factors may have had the same impact as they have had in other rights-based struggles in Latin America. Namely, the international may have expressed itself through the diffusion of international norms around human rights, through the direct influence of international actors, or by the use of transnational strategies among ethno-racial movements in these countries.[18]

Beyond the empirical question of how international factors mattered in the adoption of specific policies for black populations in Latin America is the normative question of how we should understand such influence. Were international forces positive in that they ushered in more egalitarian citizenship regimes where those based in *mestizaje* had failed? Alternatively, was international influence pernicious? Was the move to ethno-racial policy the result of U.S. cultural imperialism, and thus, profoundly at odds with local realities, as Bourdieu and Wacquant (1999) have argued?[19]

In this book, I approach these questions head on. In so doing, I do not assume that particular international dynamics or actors are at play a priori, but rather, I treat this as an empirical question. Through careful archival analysis and the use of ethnographic methods, I ask a number of specific questions about the role of international factors. For instance, were U.S. scholars and foundations so powerful, and how exactly did they change racial discourse in Brazil so dramatically? Moreover, if the United States exported racial discourse and policy to these countries, how do we account for all of the variation in the region? Additionally, why would U.S. foundations and academics have so much influence in Brazil but not its neighboring countries? In relative terms, Brazil is more economically powerful, has a far more developed academic sector, is infamous for its entrenched culture of insularity, and has historically been far less susceptible to U.S. influence than the rest of Latin America. More importantly, the assumption that particular models were either exported or diffused from one place to another fails to explain a question that is at the center of this book: Why have black populations become institutionalized as culturally distinct rural political subjects in some cases and as culturally integrated urban populations, defined by their experience of systematic racial discrimination, in others?

It is precisely this variation in the extent and nature of ethno-racial reforms in Latin American countries that has led some scholars to locate their seeds not in the international, but in domestic political processes, particularly in black mobilization (Grueso et al. 1997; Martins et al. 2004; Telles 2004; Hooker 2005; Asher 2009).[20] While these accounts are convincing, they defy nearly everything we know about social movements. In neither Colombia nor Brazil did black movements have the characteristics—resources, organizational strength, mobilizational capacity, elite alliances, or favorable public opinion—that we would have expected them to have to bring about these major political changes.[21] How, then, were they ultimately so successful? Before I address this puzzle, I want to say more about why my comparative framework is best suited for taking it on.

WHY COLOMBIA? WHY BRAZIL? WHY COMPARE?

In some ways, Colombia and Brazil are obvious choices for an analysis of black rights in Latin America. Aside from being among the first in the region to enact multicultural constitutions that recognized black communities, they also have the first and third largest Afro-descendant populations in the Americas (Telles 2007).[22] According to Brazil's 2010 census, 54 percent of the country's 190 million people identified as either *preto* ("black") or *pardo* ("brown"). While the "official" state count of Colombia's black population varies widely from 1.5 to 26 percent of the population, the figure most widely used comes from the 2005 census in which 10.6 percent of Colombians identified as Afro-descendant.[23] As a result, policies aimed at Afro-descendants stood to apply to many more people in Colombia and Brazil than they did in other countries in the region.

More interestingly, however, are the reforms the Colombian and Brazilian states actually underwent. *Mestizaje* began to lose ground as a state project throughout Latin America as countries began adopting ethno-racial

TABLE 1.1: ETHNO-RACIAL LEGISLATION IN LATIN AMERICAN COUNTRIES

	1987–1998[1]	2001–PRESENT
Cuba	No specific legislation for indigenous or black populations	
Dominican Republic		
El Salvador		
Argentina	Recognition of indigenous rights	
Chile		
Costa Rica		
Mexico		
Panama		
Paraguay		
Peru		
Uruguay		
Venezuela		
Bolivia	Recognition of rights for subsets of black population	
Ecuador		
Guatemala		
Honduras		
Nicaragua		
Colombia		Robust racial equality policies
Brazil		

[1] Bolivia (2009) is one of the only countries where these changes were incorporated outside this period.

legislation in the 1980s. Even so, there was a great deal of variation in the degree and type of reforms. First, countries differed with regard to who was included in and who was excluded from ethno-racial reforms (Hooker 2005). Table 1.1 outlines some of these important differences. Of the nineteen countries in Latin America, nearly all recognized the rights of indigenous peoples (column 1) and about half also recognized specific sectors within the black population, typically rural and geographically concentrated communities like those on the Atlantic Coasts of Central America and the Pacific Coast of Colombia (column 2).[24] After this initial round of multicultural reforms of the 1990s, countries throughout Latin America began to adopt a series of reforms aimed at racial equality, most of which happened in the wake of the 2001 Third World Conference against Racism held in Durban, South Africa.

If we take these temporal and substantive distinctions between these multicultural and racial equality policies seriously, Colombia and Brazil are particularly interesting cases both for their similarities and their differences. While many countries in Latin America underwent both rounds of reforms, Colombia and Brazil adopted the most comprehensive policies. Brazil's first recognition of black rights involved guaranteeing black rural communities—namely *quilombo*, or "maroon," communities—the right to territorial and cultural rights.[25] Some fifteen years after the signing of a new constitution, the Brazilian state began to adopt affirmative action policies that were unparalleled in Latin America. During this period, the government also began to proactively address racial inequality across a number of policy areas, including health and education. As it expanded such policies, it did so in the language of promoting racial equality.

Similarly, the first wave of reforms for black populations came just after Colombia's 1991 constitutional reform. After passing the Law of Black Communities in 1993, the state began to aggressively implement multicultural policies. In so doing, officials typically defined black communities as rural communities living on Colombia's Pacific Coast. As such, the 1990s and early 2000s marked a period of contention as black urban organizations attempted to expand existing legislation to include urban blacks, and those living outside of the Pacific Coast. Partly in response to this pressure, the Colombian state began to flirt with broadening the legal definition of blackness through a number of constitutional court rulings, the 2005 census, and a number of policies with the stated aim of "equal opportunity" for "Afro-Colombians."

Despite similar trajectories, Colombia and Brazil are interesting cases of ethno-racial legislation because of their differences. As the images of Afro-Colombians with marimbas and Afro-Brazilians with statistics in hand underscores, the dominant discourse of black rights in Colombia has been one of collective territorial rights, rural black communities, and the "right to difference," whereas "racial equality" and a focus on urban black populations saturated Brazil's political field. In Colombia, this black political subject has come to be embodied in the figure of the rural black farmer from the Pacific Coast, whereas in Brazil it is personified in urban disenfranchised blacks.

It was these differences that first led me to this research project. I was interested in comparing these two countries with similar nationalist narratives and that had adopted ethno-racial legislation, but where very different conceptions of a black political subject had taken hold. This comparative approach gives me analytic leverage that examining a single case would not have.[26] First, it allows me to uncover these two overlapping discourses of blackness that have become institutionalized. Making this distinction between state policies that seek to protect the culture of ethnic minorities (the right to difference) and those that emphasize the need to combat racism (the right to equality), is important not only for understanding the nature of this region's ethno-racial reforms, but also their causes. I argue that these different emphases have less to do with demographic realities of the two countries and more with how blackness was politicized in each case. Finally, in comparing these two canonical cases, I am better able to tease out the relative importance of domestic and international dynamics in the shift to black rights in Latin America more generally.

POLITICAL FIELD ALIGNMENTS AND THE MAKING
OF BLACK POLITICAL SUBJECTS

This book examines two interrelated phenomena that I argue constitute the making of black political subjects. First, I analyze how the state and other powerful political actors came to see blackness as a legitimate political category, however incomplete and fraught, in Colombia and Brazil. I take as a point of departure the idea that black identities—and the movements based on those identities—do not automatically flow from slavery or anti-black racism. I draw on theorists who avoid these essentialist accounts of race as well as purely instrumentalist ones. Ethno-racial identities do not simply appear out of thin air either. Instead they often have some historical, material, and even cultural basis. In this sense, I treat ethno-racial identities as Murray Li (2000) does in her work on indigeneity in Indonesia, as "contingent products of agency and the cultural and political work of articulation" (151). This anti-essentialist way of thinking about identity and political struggle also recognizes that identity is itself inherently multiple. People are never exclusively or singularly black, but rather inhabit many social locations simultaneously (Cohen 1999; Collins 1999; Wright 2004).

This book is not about a politicized black consciousness that always existed, nor is it about a sudden "awakening" of black consciousness among the Brazilian and Colombian masses. Rather, it focuses on the circumstances that allowed for a unified discourse of a black political subject to be "forged" or "made," as cultural theorist Stuart Hall has proposed we examine (Hall 1986). Following this call, I analyze the local and global political processes through which Colombians and Brazilians have come to articulate these politicized black identities over the last few decades.

Very early on in my fieldwork, as I sifted through the archives and spoke with key political actors, I knew that black activists would be the main protagonists of this work. They showed up prominently in the historical records of the constitutional reform process in each country, and they also cropped up often in my interviews with politicians, state bureaucrats, and academics involved in these political processes. In fact, black activists seemed to not only be the main catalysts for including black populations in ethno-racial reforms but also critical actors in the implementation process. Despite this, I saw firsthand the collective identity challenges and abysmal resources that continued to plague these organizations. In the context of Colombia's internal war, I also witnessed many black activists who had become my close friends receive death threats; some of them were assassinated for defending the very rights that motivated this study.

Why Brazil and Colombia recognized black rights becomes even more baffling if we consider the material implications of such policies. In granting indigenous and black rural communities the rights to land and precious natural resources like gold, platinum, and silver, these policies not only threatened to reconfigure economic power but also challenged models of development based in accumulation, extraction, and urbanization (Escobar 2008). In Brazil, policies also had the potential to transform patterns of inequality through access to higher education.[27] Thus, several powerful groups in each society had much at stake in debates around black rights. More specifically, affirmative action directly undermined Brazil's white middle class, which depended on prestigious public university slots to reproduce itself. For those who presumed they were the true owners of the land that was to be titled under legislation for *quilombo* communities, these policies threatened their most prized commodity. Relatedly, in Colombia, black rights undermined the bottom lines of mining companies that for decades had used Colombia's Pacific Coast as their profit wonderland. Moreover, by reserving two congressional seats for black communities, the Colombian government threatened to shake up, even if only slightly, political party competition in the country.[28] Given these high stakes, why did Colombia and Brazil adopt policies for black populations? What role did different actors, local and global, play in this process?

I argue that in the absence of extensive resources or massive mobilization, and with serious ideological constraints, black movements in both Colombia and Brazil were at the center of these important political transformations. I suggest that in order to understand their centrality, we must first take as a point of departure a more flexible definition of social movements. In my first visit to Colombia's Chocó region, Zulia Mena—a long-time Afro-Colombian activist and winner of one of the first congressional seats reserved for black leaders—invited me to stay at her home in the city of Quibdó. As she prepared dinner for us, I asked if she considered the black mobilization that was instrumental in bringing about ethnic reforms in Colombia to be a grassroots movement. She responded:

> Mobilizing a community that's hungry to take up a cause that goes beyond their stomach isn't easy. It's important to have that in mind . . . that this has been a struggle that comes from a place of good intentions, but that the great majority of the Afro-Colombian community has not participated directly in it. It is a progressive movement, the kind you see in history, those great movements that are made up of small groups that create social change. In the end, their efforts are able to serve that broad population (interview, Zulia Mena, August 2006).

Zulia's candidness stood out from the over hundred interviews and thousands of informal conversations I had in Colombia and Brazil in preparation for this book. In contrast, the black activists with whom I spoke were much more likely to characterize their organizations—and the movement more generally—as grassroots, and massive, even if they admitted that there were many challenges to mobilization. In this, they often highlighted certain critical, though extremely rare, moments of street protest—the sit-in at the Haitian embassy in Colombia in the early 1990s, the 1995 Zumbí March for Citizenship and Life in Brazil—rather than their use of bureaucratic strategies, transnational activism, legal mobilization, or efforts to lobby Congress. In responding in this way, activists often privileged the exciting moments of disruptive protest and ignored the more banal, bureaucratic, and less spectacular ways that I will argue activists actually did achieve change in these cases.[29]

In contrast, and more in line with the analysis that Zulia offered that day in her kitchen, I adopt a more malleable definition of social movements. I draw on Charles Tilly's (1999) definition of social movements as a "sustained challenge to power holders in the name of a disadvantaged population living under the jurisdiction of those power holders by means of repeated public displays of that population's worthiness, unity, numbers, and commitment" (257). Even while this definition emphasizes the "sustained" and "public" nature of contention, like Zulia, it does not imply that social movements have to be particularly massive, or even engage primarily in street protest, to count as movements, or to bring about change.

With this definition in mind, I treat black mobilization in Colombia and Brazil over the last three decades as constituting a social movement. I suggest that it is only when we situate these movements within a larger constellation of politics—that involves state actors as well as a myriad of different nonstate political actors, local and global—that we are able to explain how they overcame such incredible odds. In this way, I follow the recent shift in the social movement scholarship away from the state-centric idea of "political opportunity structures" and toward an examination of how context, arena, or fields made up of a plethora of actors shape social movement politics (Ray 1999; Jasper and Goodwin 2011; Jasper 2012; Fligstein and McAdam 2012).

This perspective is part of the political fields approach that I develop, which draws loosely on Bourdieu's idea of fields as well as theories of transnational activism. Bourdieu has long thought about politics in terms of fields, which he saw as made up of a set of forces and defined by the "struggles aimed at transforming the relations" among those forces (Bourdieu 1991, 171). In contrast to some social movement accounts, I do not see state actors and political elites as the creators of a structure of opportunities for movements. Rather, I treat them as one of many actors (albeit powerful ones) within these complex fields of politics.[30] What is more, within any field, the struggle is not only about control over material resources like state power but also over how the "distinctively political game is organized" and who has the "legitimate use of symbolic power" to define the fundamental categories of representation within the field (181). In this sense, I understand social movement politics not only as a process of contentious mobilization, but fundamentally as one of meaning making. In so doing, I do not assume that collective identity and cultural frames simply exist a priori. Rather, I am interested in understanding the construction and legitimation of the very political categories that traditional social movement accounts have often taken as a given.

I also understand political fields to never fully be contained within national borders. Rather, I argue that a degree of permeability allows discourses to interpenetrate and actors from political fields outside the nation-state to have influence. In the case of contestation over ethno-racial rights in Colombia and Brazil, the political game was and continues to be organized at the intersection of a national political field and a more recently consolidated global ethno-racial field. This makes sense when we consider that political struggles in the Global South today are deeply globalized. It follows, then, that resistance to hegemonic understandings of ethno-racial hierarchy and exclusion would also take on a similar character.[31]

I advocate for a translocal approach to understanding the political field, one that gleans insights from scholars of transnational politics. Transnational activism has played a significant role in the emergence of social movements, and in accounting for their effectiveness (Keck and Sikkink 1998; Evans 2000; Kay 2005; Tarrow 2005; Tsutsui and Shin 2008; Merry 2009).[32] Dynamics outside the boundaries of the nation-state—including discursive opportunities that international institutions help to create, the diffusion and translation of global policy norms, and transnational organizing—can all play a critical role in local social movement politics. Scholars have developed concepts such as "international regimes," "global regimes," and "transnational governance structures" to delineate these otherwise intangible webs of international actors and cultural norms that so deeply influence local politics.[33] Additionally, they have identified the different mechanisms and sets of actors that mediate this diffusion.[34]

Building on this work, I identify the contours of what I call "global political fields," made up of international institutions, transnational networks, global norms, and transnational repertoires of action. This way of understanding global political fields assumes that the field, or arena of politics, is not only defined by a set of people and institutions but is also fundamentally about symbolic power. Indeed, political fields—much like Tania Murray Li's (2000) idea of "spaces of recognition" or David Scott's (2004) "problem-spaces"—can be oriented around specific issues (for example, women's rights, nuclear proliferation, environmental issues, ethnic rights), and they range from incipient to highly consolidated.[35] As we will see in the cases of ethno-racial rights in Colombia and Brazil, the more consolidated the global field, the more likely it was to matter for local struggles.

Most relevant to ethno-racial rights in Brazil and Colombia was a global ethno-racial field that emerged in the last half of the twentieth century. Several crises around the globe—including World War II, apartheid in South Africa, and ethnic cleansing in Yugoslavia—prompted a reconsideration of the role the international community should play in domestic ethno-racial conflicts (Kymlicka 2007). In addition, indigenous mobilization and nongovernmental organizations (NGOs) specializing in ethnic issues around the world—and in Latin America in particular—helped to initiate a global trend toward thinking about collective rights in ways that did not contradict entirely the liberal framework of human rights (Williams 1990; Felice 1996; Van Cott 2002; Dersso 2010).

In the end, though, the networks, institutions, and cultural practices that made up this global ethno-racial field—or any global field of power for that matter—were rarely self-evident. Rather, global fields tend to articulate themselves in more visible ways in the context of international events like the Third World Conference against Racism held in 2001. As was the case with other international events of this kind, mobilization by activists in the region as well as maneuverings of sympathetic allies within international institutions both played a substantial role in bringing these conferences about (Lennox 2015). These conferences were not only important because they consolidated and physically embodied an otherwise dispersed and unintelligible field. They also served to construct and institutionalize a particular language of ethnic rights, to legitimate expertise around an issue, to solidify transnational alliances to pressure states to make reforms, and, finally, to create legal instruments that were later "vernacularized"—as Merry (2009) terms it—into local struggles.

The political fields in which black movements operated in the 1980s were not only made up of national political elites but also included indigenous activists, transnational human rights workers, environmentalists, anthropologists, and development specialists. Likewise, the discourses that permeated this field were not only local histories and narratives of race and nation, but also global discourses that increasingly linked democracy with anti-racism and multiculturalism. Fields, then, are not only about contestation over material power but also about the power of representation, who defines the language of the debate, and who legitimates categories. In the case of ethno-racial legislation in Colombia and Brazil, symbolic power came just as much from within these nations as from outside. The fact that in Latin America, race/ethnicity has come to be understood as the root of a number of social problems that require state action is as much about domestic political struggles as it about the formal embrace of "multiculturalism" and "social inclusion" by institutions like the United Nations, the International Labour Organisation (ILO), the World Bank, the Inter-American Development Bank (IDB), and the Economic Commission on Latin America and the Caribbean (ECLAC). One need only analyze the text of recent ethno-racial legislation—which closely resembles international conventions much more than domestic law—to see the embodiment of such symbolic power. This all underscores the need to understand the fields in which debates around black rights occurred in Colombia and Brazil over recent decades as simultaneously local and global.

Nevertheless, we must be careful not to conclude that consolidating the global ethno-racial field automatically led to domestic reforms in these cases. The fact that countries like the Dominican Republic and others in the region have not adopted such legislation underscores this. Indeed, being enmeshed in this global ethno-racial political field was no guarantee that the Colombian and Brazilian states would recognize ethnic rights, or that such legislation would venture beyond indigenous populations to include black populations. Rather, I will argue that the making of black rights in these cases required two additional ingredients: radical changes in power relations in the domestic political field; and the existence of black movements poised to take strategic advantage of these changes. I call this convergence of local and global changes "political field alignments."

Political Field Alignments

Global policy norms, transnational activism, and geopolitical dynamics all have profoundly shaped the nature of, and conditions of possibility for, ethno-racial rights in Latin America. However, multicultural reforms in this region have included black populations to varying degrees. This fact calls for a closer examination of why global political fields may have shaped

TABLE I.2. POLITICAL FIELD ALIGNMENTS

	EMERGENT GLOBAL ETHNO-RACIAL POLITICAL FIELD (1960S–EARLY 1980S)	CONSOLIDATED GLOBAL ETHNO-RACIAL POLITICAL FIELD (LATE 1980S–PRESENT)
STABLE DOMESTIC POLITICAL FIELD	Stasis	Misalignment
FRACTURED DOMESTIC POLITICAL FIELD	Domestic transformation	Alignment

domestic struggles more in some cases than they did in others. I argue that political field alignment provides a useful lens through which to understand these dynamics.

Political fields align when the conditions of possibility in global political fields and domestic political fields converge. At such moments, actors articulate and legitimate political struggles that may have otherwise remained at the margins. In table 1.2, I offer a schematic for understanding the alignments that brought about the articulation of ethno-racial rights in Latin America. The first column indicates the relationship between domestic and international politics during the period (1960s–early 1980s) in which global discourses and institutions around anti-racism, multiculturalism, and indigenous rights were incipient. At that time, the field was still not fully consolidated and the most powerful international institutions still showed little interest in multiculturalism. While a consensus was emerging about how to protect indigenous communities in institutions like Cultural Survival, such discussions were not yet consecrated in the form of international legal norms with real symbolic power. Likewise, international institutions dedicated to ethno-racial rights had not yet developed the specific mechanisms necessary for effective transnational activism around these issues. In this sense, this emergent global ethno-racial field had yet to produce the material and symbolic power that it would have in domestic struggles in later decades.

Before the late 1980s, black political organizations in Latin America had to rely nearly exclusively on the conditions of possibility within their domestic political fields, which were characterized by deeply uneven power relations and hegemonic discourses of *mestizaje*. This led to stasis in nearly every Latin American country prior to the 1980s.[36] However, in cases like the Dominican Republic, where the national political field experienced few changes in power relations in the 1990s, ethno-racial reforms did not occur, even with the consolidation of the global ethno-racial field. This mismatch—between changes in this global political field and persistent limited conditions of possibility within the national political field—created a situation of misalignment.[37]

Rather, in nearly all cases in Latin America, state recognition for black populations required both changes in the national political field and the consolidation of the global ethno-racial field. The kinds of domestic changes needed to radically shift state discourse and policies were often on the scale of what Sawyer (2005) calls "state disequilibrium." In Colombia and Brazil, ethno-racial recognition occurred, as it did throughout much of the region, in the context of widespread popular unrest, the intensification of civil war, and crises of state legitimacy. This disequilibrium led to constitutional reform processes as well as a number of other significant transformations in state institutions, all with the goal of furthering democratization.

Where domestic and global dynamics aligned and black activists mobilized, black recognition was much more likely to happen. However, what ultimately mattered was not the size of these movements but how effectively they mobilized around these alignments, as well as how they conceptualized their struggle. The language of black mobilization and the nature of their claims were especially important because this alignment of political fields did not happen all at once. Instead, I argue that these reforms unfolded in two distinct moments of political field alignment, the multicultural alignment and the racial equality alignment. In each a very different conception of the black political subject became institutionalized.

Multicultural Alignments, Racial Equality Alignments

Existing scholarship tends to collapse policies as collective ethnic rights and race-based affirmative action into a singular "multicultural turn." In contrast, I conceptualize such ethno-racial policies as consisting of two types that I argue were produced through two distinct historical moments: the multicultural alignment and the racial equality alignment. Table 1.3 offers a heuristic—albeit a somewhat crudely drawn one—for thinking about the differences between these two alignments.

First, each alignment focused on a different ideal subject of rights. Whereas the state rooted the policies of the late 1980s and early 1990s in the idea that it needed to protect the culture and autonomy of blacks and indigenous peoples as an ethnic group, it based later policies on the notion that it had a responsibility to combat racism and ensure overall racial equality. While indigenous peoples were the original ideal subjects of the former, blacks were the prototypical beneficiary of the latter. In fact, the idea that the multicultural legislation of the 1990s would also cover certain subsets of the black population came through a contentious process. In the few cases where Latin American political elites could even conceive of specific rights

TABLE 1.3. MULTICULTURAL AND RACIAL EQUALITY ALIGNMENTS

	THE MULTICULTURAL ALIGNMENT (1980S–1990S)	THE RACIAL EQUALITY ALIGNMENT (2000S–2010S)
Types of Reforms	Territorial rights, political autonomy, language rights	Equal opportunity laws, affirmative action policies
Legal/Moral Justification	To protect the culture and identity of minority groups	To combat systematic racial inequality
Type of Claim	Right to difference	Right to equality
Relevant International Norm	ILO Convention 169	CERD, Durban Plan of Action
Subject	Indigenous peoples, rural/geographically specific black populations	General black population typically with an emphasis on urban issues
Type of Groupness	"Ethnicity" (culture)	"Race" (phenotype)
Expertise	Anthropologists, and to a lesser extent historians	Sociologists/demographers, and to a lesser extent economists
Dominant Discourse	Colombia	Brazil

for black populations in the constitutional reform processes of the 1980s and 1990s, they spoke exclusively in the language of protecting "cultural difference" and local autonomy.

Consequently, only certain segments of the black population qualified. In all countries where they were recognized, it was rural and geographically concentrated black communities that were able to make a somewhat plausible claim to cultural distinction (Hooker 2005). In a sense, certain black populations became "indigenous-like" in the eyes of the Latin American multicultural state, or at the very least, "blackness increasingly look[ed] like indianness," as Wade (1997) has noted.[38] However, as I will show in later chapters, even when multicultural reforms eventually included specific black populations, activists still found it difficult to convince the state and other key actors that they were indeed a culturally distinct group. This framing of blackness as indigenous-like contrasted with the reality of the urban black population, which was more numerous than rural and geographically concentrated blacks in nearly all cases, and which was understood as fully assimilated into the dominant culture (Wade 1997; Barbary and Urrea 2004; Paschel 2010).[39]

In contrast to the multicultural alignment, black populations—not indigenous peoples—were the natural subjects of the racial equality alignment.[40] These two alignments also relied on different types of expertise. Whereas with the multicultural alignment, anthropological expertise was used to authenticate cultural difference, the racial equality alignment was premised on the expertise of sociologists, typically those specializing in inequality. Another key distinction was that in both Brazil and Colombia, at each moment of alignment, different kinds of black organizations were often at the forefront of the struggle. In the multicultural alignment, incipient rural black organizations took center stage, while urban black organizations that had been mobilized for decades, and that used the language of racism and racial equality, were pushed aside.

The tables turned with the racial equality alignment a decade later, when black urban organizations succeeded in pressuring the Brazilian state, and to a lesser extent the Colombian one, to adopt policies aimed at racial integration and black mobility. These differences between the multicultural and racial equality alignments also played out with the taking up of different international norms. Rural black movements in Colombia and Brazil tended to see International Labour Organisation Convention 169 (1989) on Indigenous People and Tribal Groups as foundational. Approved in 1989, it outlined the language of indigenous rights that best reflected the kinds of demands that indigenous communities around the world were making on their respective states: the right to territory, sovereignty, natural resources, and prior consultation.[41] Urban black movements, on the other hand, often saw themselves as fighting against racism and for racial equality. As such, they looked to the Convention on the Elimination of Racial Discrimination (CERD) and the Durban Plan of Action for leverage.

The flattening out of these two historically specific moments of ethno-racial reforms in Latin America, as well as the conflation between the different logics embedded in them, is most evident when we use a comparative lens.[42] This is because the logic of the multicultural alignment became much more saturated in the political field of Colombia, whereas the language of the racial equality alignment tended to dominate the black movement's and the state's discourse in Brazil. *Becoming Black Political Subjects* compares these two alignments both within and between these two significant cases of ethno-racial reforms in Latin America. Doing so allows me to consider why the logic of the multicultural alignment gained so much sway in Colombia and not in Brazil, while the opposite was true of the racial equality alignment. There is no obvious reason why this would be the case. Perhaps Colombia's black population was largely rural and Brazil's mostly urban. In fact, about 70 percent of the Afro-descendant population in both countries reside in urban areas.[43]

Similarly, one might speculate that black Colombians retained more distinctively African cultural practices than Brazilians did. If anything, the reverse was true. In fact, Brazil is arguably the country in the Americas with the highest degree of African cultural retention, from African-based religions like Candomblé to African influence in Brazilian Portuguese and in the country's culinary traditions (Freyre 1933). Furthermore, over the last decades, black movements in both countries have made claims using both the language of racial equality and that of cultural difference. So what accounts for these differences? I argue that the Colombian state tended to institutionalize the logic of cultural difference and Brazil the logic of racial equality for two reasons: the different ways in which blackness figured into each country's nationalist imaginary and differences in the articulations of black movements in each case.[44]

Thus far I have talked exclusively about the making of black political subjects defined as the political process that led to the adoption of specific legislation for black populations. However, this book is also about the making of black political subjects in a second sense—that is, through the everyday, ongoing, and often ambiguous political practices that have unfolded in the wake of these policies. I ask how do black activists navigate this new political moment where they no longer confront states that are deaf to ethno-racial issues, but rather states that have institutionalized black rights, formalized black participation, and incorporated activists themselves. I suggest that these dynamics of institutionalization are directly related to the more fundamental question of whether these moments of alignment have actually brought about material change in the lives of people on the ground. In taking on this question, I show how the making of black political subjects was also accompanied by a process of their unmaking. Indeed, just as the Brazilian and Colombian states began to adopt ethno-racial legislation, the increasing institutionalization and fragmentation of black organizations—as well as the emergence of reactionary movements—intervened to both refashion and restrict such rights.

ORGANIZATION OF THIS BOOK

In the rest of this book, I trace the making of black political subjects in Colombia and Brazil over the last two decades. In chapter 2, I use mainly secondary literature to analyze the historical context of the domestic fields in which black movements emerged. My aims are twofold, to highlight the magnitude of this shift from *mestizaje* to black rights and also to begin to explain why different conceptions of blackness became institutionalized in each case. In this chapter, I also situate the two states' ideologies of race-making within a broader political field. In chapter 3, I draw on archives and interviews to better understand the ideological terrain of the political fields of Colombia and Brazil during the period directly preceding the multicultural alignment. In addition, I show how black activists organized—as blacks but also around other political categories—in a field dominated by ideas of what Goldberg (2002) calls "racelessness."

Chapters 4 and 5 develop my concept of political field alignment by examining the political processes that led to the initial recognition of black rights in Colombia and Brazil in the 1980s and 1990s and the subsequent adoption of policies in the 2000s and 2010s. In chapter 4, I analyze the multicultural alignment. In it, I draw on interviews with key actors as well as constitutional assembly transcripts to examine the conditions under which each state recognized specific black populations in their new constitutions. Chapter 5 turns to the racial equality alignment, where I analyze how and why the Colombian and Brazilian states passed laws, including affirmative action and other policies more explicitly focused on promoting racial equality. I argue that while black movements had pushed for these kinds of policies since at least the 1980s, their efforts were emboldened at the beginning of the twenty-first century by international events. Because the multicultural alignment became the dominant way of framing black rights in Colombia, I pay more attention to that case in chapter 4, while the Brazilian case is the main focus of chapter 5. Taken together, these chapters suggest the need to complicate the notion of the multicultural turn at the same time they strongly challenge the idea that blackness became politicized in these countries as a result of U.S. imperialism.

In chapters 6 and 7, I engage in a more ethnographic examination of the making and unmaking of black political subjects. Chapter 6 reveals the ways in which black activists and organizations navigate these new political fields where state institutions have enshrined particular types of black political subjects. In both countries, recent legislation required the state to create internal spaces to guarantee black political participation and to ensure the full implementation of newly adopted legislation. I analyze the nature of these state structures and the ways in which black activists and their organizations have become institutionalized within them. In chapter 7, the final empirical chapter of the book, I examine the extent to which the Colombian and Brazilian states have actually implemented ethno-racial reforms. I argue that the dynamics of black movement institutionalization that I explored in the previous chapter, as well as the emergence of powerful reactionary actors—including transnational mining companies, armed groups, white/*mestizo* landowners, and the white urban middle class—have made implementing ethno-racial policy in these countries a difficult task.

I show how this reconfiguration of the political field helps to make sense of this unmaking of black rights in these cases.

Finally, in chapter 8, I move toward a broader discussion of the contributions this book offers to the study social movements and to scholars of race and ethnicity. In it, I argue that when we theorize up from noncanonical cases—like the ones I examine here—it forces us to move toward more globally embedded accounts of both race making and social movement politics. At the same time, these cases also push us toward conceptualizing "blackness," "social movements," and "power" in much more complex ways.

A NOTE ON ETHNO-RACIAL TERMINOLOGY

Before continuing, I want to clarify the ethno-racial terminology I use throughout the rest of this book. Those familiar with Latin America know one cannot take ethno-racial categories for granted in this region. Among other things, scholars have highlighted the existence of an elaborate racial/color continuum in these countries, rather than finite and clearly demarcated racial groups. However, because this study analyzes the making of new black political subjects within a specific realm—that is, within social movements and the Colombian and Brazilian states—I did not encounter the same kinds of ethno-racial ambiguity that scholars who have examined how race is made through everyday social practices have found. In fact, in the research sites where I did my work, only a few ethno-racial categories emerged as important.[45] Thus, I pay more attention to how the various actors involved in these political processes used ethno-racial terms—including how Brazilian and Colombian law conceived of these categories—than how these terms mapped onto the categories used in everyday social praxis. That is not to say that I was uninterested in the relationship between political and social processes; I do touch on this at different points in the manuscript.[46]

Relatedly, I tend to use the term "black" rather than "Afro-Colombian" or "Afro-Brazilian."[47] When I first got to the field I found that while international agencies, professionalized black organizations, and, increasingly, the state tended to use these interchangeably, the activists I knew rarely used these terms.[48] Black movements in both Colombia and Brazil had long struggled to promote a sense of "black" identity rather than "Afro-descendant identity." That said, things began to change while I was conducting research as more and more actors began using some variation of "afro." At important moments actors did contest the boundaries around these different categories. I highlighted these moments of contestation when they did emerge.[49]

Ultimately, my goal in this book is to do what qualitative social science research does best, which is to understand social processes in ways that take seriously the meaning and categories that people themselves use to make sense of their worlds. In the cases I explore here, this means developing a deep understanding of how activists, intellectuals, and state officials understood the political fields in which they were embedded.

Translating ethno-racial categories from Spanish and Portuguese into English is always complicated, especially since Brazilians use two words that both translate to "black" in English: *preto* (the color black; this term refers to the darkest Brazilians); and *negro* (a more political term for racial identity that includes both *pretos* and *pardos*, or mixed-race Brazilians).[50] I translate the word *negro* to "black" whether I am talking about the Colombian or the Brazilian context. While I also translate *preto* to "black," I highlight the occasions in which political actors use that term as something distinct from *negro*. More generally, when an appropriate English equivalent exists, I use it and the Spanish or Portuguese word interchangeably (for example, *mulato* and mulatto, or *pardo* and brown). When there is no English equivalent—as is the case with the Spanish word for those of mixed European and indigenous ancestry, *mestizo*—I leave the word in its original language.

My use of the terms race and ethnicity also merits some discussion. I prefer to use the term "ethno-racial" so as not to reify what I consider a problematic and analytically slippery distinction between race and ethnicity.[51] The idea that race and ethnicity capture very distinct types of difference is pervasive in the academic literature as well as common sense understandings. Yet we know that both "race" and "ethnicity" are often used to refer to perceived biological and cultural differences. Further, the boundaries around each are socially constructed and both have been used to justify hierarchy, violence, and atrocities rooted in often essentialist ideas of human difference.[52] In my refusal to make this analytic distinction, I am acutely aware of the fact that ethno-racial difference can at certain times be more marked and experienced more viscerally in the body than at others; I just don't believe that this requires us to continue to operate with the idea that race and ethnicity, or race and culture, are entirely distinct social phenomena.

That said, the distinction between blackness as culturally defined (think ethnicity) and blackness as racially defined (think phenotype, biology, ancestry) is very important to the political processes I examine here. I show how the idea that these definitions constitute different kinds of groupness has led states, academics, activists, and international experts to, at crucial moments, treat this blurry distinction between race and ethnicity as a very real difference. I also show how this has had material consequences for the people who are thought to inhabit these different types of difference. While I use the term "ethno-racial" throughout this book, I am still interested in the political and material consequences of the use of the terms "race" versus "ethnicity."

Finally, I refrain from using quotation marks around the words "race," "ethnicity," and "ethno-racial" not only because it would annoy some readers, but more importantly because I believe doing so would be redundant. Many of the categories that social scientists use are socially constructed (including categories such as "gender," but also more seemingly "real" concepts such as "class" or "the state"). This social construction is precisely what makes these topics interesting. However, one unintended consequence of placing quotation marks around the term "race"—but not other words like "ethnicity"—is that scholars ultimately reify these other socially constructed categories. Rather than fixate about quotation marks, I believe that our more fundamental aim should be to simply do the kind of constructivist work that the quotation marks are meant to do.

CHAPTER TWO

MAKING *MESTIZAJES*

The project of building a modern nation-state with an imagined homogeneous national community was a difficult, and often violent, task everywhere. In Latin America, political elites also had to grapple with the legacy of colonization and slavery. More than ten times the number of enslaved Africans went to Latin America as to the United States (Andrews 2004). In many countries in the region, those who were enslaved greatly outnumbered the free population (Andrews 2004). Thus, Latin American elites had to confront the extreme social hierarchies that persisted from the colonial period, as well as the fact that the populace was largely indigenous, descended from enslaved Africans, or the result of mixture between these groups and European migrants. This demographic reality is important when one considers that nation building in these countries began at the end of the nineteenth century, precisely at the moment in which scientific racism and a global eugenics movement to "better the human race" through heredity emerged. As a result, independence in this region was as much about declaring independence from the Spanish and Portuguese empires as it was a struggle for legitimate entrance into modernity.

In newly independent Latin America, elites were especially concerned with developing political and economic institutions and constructing a culture that exemplified modern liberal ideals.[1] These same elites also had to grapple with their own blood, so to speak, which was often the result of mixed ancestry. Examining the role the eugenics movement played in the nation-building project in Latin America, Stepan (1991) argues that science was often a double-edged sword for elites in this region. Advancing in science signaled modernity. However, "scientific" reasoning ultimately led many European thinkers to see Latin American nations as degenerate because of their racial composition, mixture, and even climate. This "mongrelization" meant that Latin American nations were destined to perpetual backwardness, at best, and subject to neocolonial occupations, at worst. Indeed, the United States, for example, used racialized discourse to justify imperialism and the occupation of a number of Caribbean countries at different points throughout the nineteenth and twentieth centuries (Helg 1990; Suárez Findlay 1999; De la Fuente 2001). In so doing, they often invoked racist notions of these places as backward and childlike nations of mongrels needing protection (Helg 1990). While the United States did not challenge the political sovereignty of larger countries like Brazil in the same way, their capacity for development was still called into question using a similarly racist logic (Andrews 2004; Loveman 2014). Domestic factors, then, were not the only ones that shaped the development of Latin American nationalist discourses or institutions (Loveman 2014). Rather, these external threats put pressure on elites to develop nationalist narratives based on principles of modernity and progress that were themselves deeply entangled with ideas about ethno-racial difference.

Latin American political elites and intellectuals began to experiment with a different model of the nation: *mestizaje*. Rather than view race mixture as an impediment to national progress, they appropriated a particular branch of scientific racism, Lamarckian eugenics, that considered both biological and cultural/environmental factors important in the march toward human improvement (Stepan 1991). This offered a way for Latin American elites to reconcile the project of modernity with their own entangled histories and demographic realities. Both cultural and biological assimilation were central to the creation of this new superior race, even while the specific imaginaries in each country were somewhat distinct. In Mexico, for example, nationalist thinker José Vasconcelos spoke of "the cosmic race," while Gilberto Freyre in Brazil often wrote about the "the Brazilian race." Similarly, Venezuela was imagined as "café con leche" or "coffee with milk," while Panamanian elites described the nation as a *crisol de razas* or a "melting pot of races."[2] The idea in all of these was that race mixture would give way to a culturally and biologically homogeneous people that were stronger than any of their individual roots.

Yet, like all nationalist projects, *mestizaje* was writ with contradictions. To begin with, the focus on race mixture was itself a pragmatic response to the impossibility of Latin America becoming another Europe. Just decades before developing nationalist narratives based on race mixture, Latin American states widely adopted policies that sought to whiten the population through immigration from Europe (Skidmore 1993; Andrews 2004). Beyond giving European immigrants access to citizenship, legislation often included recruitment campaigns as well as provisions that offered subsidies to immigrants. These policies aimed not simply to whiten the population but, more fundamentally, to deblacken and/or deindigenize them (Andrews 2004).[3]

By the 1920s, however, most Latin American states had abandoned explicit whitening policies and replaced them with ethno-racial ideologies that embraced cultural mixture and interracial sexual reproduction. While this marked a substantive shift, it did not mean that states had left behind the kind of racial thinking that placed Europeans and whiteness at the top of the social racial hierarchy and "pure" Africanness and indigeneity at the bottom. According to these new ideologies, the nation was still moving toward a whiter and inevitably a less-African and less-indigenous future.[4]

Though, precisely what *mestizaje* meant across countries in Latin America did vary.[5] Colombia and Brazil illustrate this point particularly well. Whereas Colombian political elites developed a regionalized nationalism that discursively erased blacks, elites in Brazil produced a more centralized nationalist discourse that relied heavily on the symbolic inclusion of African culture. Moreover, while Brazil considered the mixed nation to literally and figuratively reside in each Brazilian's blood and culture, Colombia's ethnically distinct geographic regions were thought to aggregate up to form a mixed-race nation.

Nationalist projects in Colombia and Brazil were also embedded in radically different political fields. Brazilian nationalism developed most fully as the country experimented with authoritarian rule. While Colombia was nominally democratic, beginning in the late 1950s an intense and protracted internal conflict between leftist guerilla groups, the state, and, later, right-wing paramilitary groups heavily shaped the field of Colombian politics. As I will argue in more detail later, these differences in the Colombian and Brazilian political fields not only set the stage for contestation between black movements and their respective states but also affected which version of multiculturalist and anti-racist discourse became institutionalized in each case.

BRAZIL: RACIAL DEMOCRACY AND THE POLITICAL FIELD

Brazil stands out as the paradigmatic case of *mestizaje* ideology in Latin America. It had one of the largest and longest lasting slave economies in the Western Hemisphere, yet it was thought to have overcome the stain of racialized slavery and colonization to build a truly multiracial, egalitarian society. In this way, Brazil exemplified the major tenets of *mestizaje*: the lack of formal racial exclusion, and the recognition and valuing of race mixture. However, Brazil's version of *mestizaje*—more commonly known as "racial democracy"—has at least two unique features. First, unlike many of its neighbors in the Andean region and the Southern Cone, African culture and blackness was central to its national identity. Second, the Brazilian state had an unusual capacity to actually disseminate nationalist ideologies across its vast territory.

From Whitening to Racial Democracy

Upon independence, Brazil's race problem was particularly pronounced, due to both its size and demographics. In 1890, two years after the country abolished slavery, the overwhelming majority of Brazilians (66 percent of the population) were nonwhite (Skidmore 1993, 46). The "racial problem" also touched close to home for some elites, many of whom were of some mixed ancestry themselves. Consequently, the whiteness of Brazil's white population was always of a precarious kind. While most of the country's economic and political elites were white according to Brazilian standards, their ancestry, places of birth, cultural practices, and even their ability to tolerate Brazil's tropical climate made them suspect vis-à-vis newly consolidated ideas of science and human improvement coming out of Europe. More fundamentally, Brazilian elites' hybridity called into question their capacity for civilization. Accordingly, the emergent concept of race was one of Brazil's major impediments to national progress. If the country did not aggressively study and resolve this problem, it would have likely been relegated to indefinite backwardness.

In such a context, creating a racially advanced Brazilian nation was just as prominent in the minds of elites as economic development and the construction of a rational state and modern political system (Skidmore 1990; Stepan 1991; Loveman 2014). These elites would have to construct a discourse around race and nation that reconciled their racial past and present with the future to which they aspired. In the late decades of the nineteenth century, the Brazilian state began to proactively improve the nation in more than one sense of the word. This included adopting policies that recruited and offered jobs and land subsidies to European immigrants beginning in the 1880s.[6] At the time, labor for Brazil's growing economy was in short supply, particularly in the southeastern part of the country where the central government had been investing heavily. What is more, population growth was a key geopolitical concern, especially for a country of Brazil's size.

Notwithstanding these motivations, the primary aim of such immigration policies was to whiten the country both by increasing the raw numbers of whites and by mixing immigrants with the existing Brazilian population (Loveman 2014). This is perhaps more clear when you examine the immigration legislation passed in the same period that restricted immigration according to race (Skidmore 1993). In Brazil's 1891 constitution, for example, the government prohibited the entry of "Africans," while also limiting the immigration of Asians to 3 percent of the Asian-descendant population already in Brazil (Skidmore 1993; Pereira 2013). In addition to infusing the nation with European blood, these migrants were supposed to bring with them the culture of the "better" or "superior" races.

This goal was not a covert one left for conspiracy theorists to drum up. Rather, Brazilian nationalist thinkers and state officials often made explicit, public calls not only to whiten the population but also to "deblacken" it (Loveman 2014). For instance, in Oliveiro Vianna's introduction to Brazil's 1920 census, he argued that "the best European races, who distribute themselves among the mass of our population" were "influencing powerfully the reduction of the index of blackness (*nigrescência*) of our people" (Loveman 2014, 149). In part to measure if they were moving toward the racial horizon they envisioned, Brazil and Cuba were the only countries in Latin America to consistently include a question on the Afro-descendant population on the national census (Nobles 2000; Telles 2004; Loveman 2014).

While political elites tried this whitening-though-immigration strategy throughout Latin America, it was particularly successful in Brazil. Of the some 10 to 11 million Europeans who arrived in Latin America between 1880 and 1930, 90 percent went to Brazil, Argentina, Cuba, or Uruguay (Andrews 2004). In the 1890s, the peak of this wave in Brazil, 1.2 million Europeans immigrated to the country; another 2 million people did so over the next decades (Telles 2004, 30). This was a large influx given that in that same period there were only about 5 million whites in Brazil. In the end, though the white population remained relatively small, the "index of blackness" did decrease and the percentage of whites increased steadily through the turn of the century.[7]

Beyond immigration, Brazil also adopted a number of policies at the level of the city, state, and national governments that, while not always explicitly racial, did have racial undertones (Azevedo 1987; Borges 1993). As Borges (1993) notes, "a wide range of imperial and republican social policies—of regulation of prostitution, sanitation of ships, factories, and barracks, licensing of domestic servants, sports and physical education, universal military service—were also justified in terms of protecting the race from contamination or regenerating its health" (249). In this period, the issues of health and degeneracy were largely inseparable from pseudo-scientific ideas of racial difference.

These policies did not simply emanate from the minds of Brazilian elites. Rather, whitening as a state project had its roots in increasingly consolidated "scientific" thinking on race and modernity. By the early twentieth century, Brazil had become an important site in the eugenics movement, sponsoring regional and international conferences and training scientists in the latest thinking and methods related to the science of improving the human race. Yet while the dominant strand of eugenics in Europe stressed biological determinism, Brazilians latched onto a branch that also saw cultural and environmental factors as important for determining the "quality" of the race. One of the most prominent Brazilian thinkers of the time was Raimundo Nina Rodrigues, a wealthy medical doctor and criminologist from Brazil's Northeast region. Rodrigues not only worked as a medical doctor with his own practice, he was also a professor at the prestigious Medical School of the Federal University of Bahia. He also conducted ethnographic studies on the religious beliefs of nonwhites as well as on the link between crime and what he called "racial degeneracy" (Stepan 1991; Borges 1993). Among other things, Rodrigues was known for attending African-based religious ceremonies as part of his research, something rare for scientists at the time but characteristic of the emergent field of anthropology. Rather than defend these cultural practices, Rodrigues argued that they were directly linked to criminality and psychiatric deviance that would eventually lead to the downfall of the Brazilian nation. In this sense, he was deeply concerned that rather than moving toward whiteness, Brazil (and especially its Northeast region) was becoming increasingly blacker, in terms of both "blood" and "culture."

Yet while Rodrigues unapologetically endorsed the idea that Africans were inferior, he was torn over the question of where race mixture, and particularly the mulatto, fit into the project of improving the Brazilian race. Rodrigues's own mixedness may have been what drove this ambivalence, as Telles (2004) has argued. While he was considered white in his social world in Brazil's northeast region, he was of mixed ancestry. Thus, as Rodrigues questioned the fate of his racially mixed country, many of the European scientists that he admired, including Italian craniologist/criminologist Cesare Lombroso, likely considered him degenerate (Borges 1993; Telles 2004).[8] Furthermore, Rodrigues was sick most of his life during a time when eugenicists linked illness directly to heredity and racial difference.

Rodrigues's biography tells us a lot about elite anxieties around race and national identity. It also underscored the infeasibility of pure whiteness as Brazil's racial horizon. The fact that many in Brazil's elite class were not quite white in the eyes of European eugenicists made the study of heredity and human improvement awkward in Brazil, to say the least (Stepan 1990; Telles 2004; Alberto 2011). Moreover, by the 1920s, it was clear that while the large influx of European migrants did in fact make the country less black, it was not necessarily becoming white; rather, it was, as Andrews (2004) put it, "browning." In that period, it became increasingly apparent that Brazil was destined to be a mixed nation.

Settling for Racial Mixture

These contradictions of whitening policies, paired with the rise of Nazi Germany and the slow decline of scientific racism in Europe, shifted the terms of the debates around race and nation in Brazil. In this context, the idea that racial mixing was positive—rather than an obstacle to modernity—took hold (Stepan 1991). By the late 1920s, and as elites around the world began to question eugenics, the Brazilian state also abandoned their affirmative action–like policies for European immigrants. Those restrictions on citizenship and subsidies for European immigrants had stood out as exceptions in a broader citizenship regime that included everyone, at least on paper. In this period, a different model of nationhood—one based in race mixture—gained sway. This new nationalist narrative simultaneously helped to calm elites' anxieties about the future of Brazil as it also gave popular classes a sense of connectedness to the national project.

Gilberto Freyre is widely regarded as the father of Brazil's version of *mestizaje*, or racial democracy. While thinkers had been proposing a view of Brazilian society that embraced racial mixture, rather than white purity, since at least the 1880s, Freyre popularized these ideas. His landmark work, *Casa Grande e Senzala*, published in 1933, became the main lens through which the Brazilian nation would imagine itself.[9] A student of Franz Boas—a pioneer in thinking about race as socially, rather than biologically, constructed—Freyre established himself as a major critic of the dominant thinking about race and degeneracy that had prevailed in Brazil for decades. He proposed that over time the Brazilian people would become not degenerate but one homogeneous race with the virtues of Europeans, Africans, and indigenous peoples combined.

Racial democracy in Brazil was different from *mestizaje* discourses in much of the rest of Latin America in that it centered on African culture.[10] Indeed, discourses of race mixture in the region often highlighted the mixture of European and indigenous heritage, but in many cases they marginalized, or completely ignored, African roots. In contrast, Freyre and other Brazilian intellectuals argued that African culture was just as important as Portuguese or indigenous culture in the making of the Brazilian people. He often used the verb "Africanize" as nearly synonymous with "Brazilianize" in his work.[11] Further, Freyre argued that this hybridity of culture and ancestry had led to an egalitarian society that was at the center of Brazilian people's moral superiority. As Freyre himself put it, "Hybrid from the beginning, Brazilian society is, of all those in the Americas, the one most harmoniously constituted so far as racial relations" (Freyre 1986, 83). This blending of Brazil's three different cultural traditions created not only a harmonious Brazilian culture but also a distinctive and superior "Brazilian race."

While Freyre's understanding of race and nation diverged from the deterministic views of thinkers like Nina Rodrigues, Freyre was equally as essentialist. He challenged the idea of racial hierarchy as he continued to hold onto the idea that races had a particular essence.[12] This can be seen throughout Freyre's work but is particularly acute in an article published in the UNESCO magazine, the *Courier*, in 1952. In it, Freyre described to an international audience the many virtues of Brazil's race mixture:

> Brazilian quadroon or octoroon girls have a special charm that harmonizes peculiarly with the forms and colours of the tropical land-

scape. It is rarely attained by completely white girls or girls with only a touch of Indian blood. And it is common, now, in Brazil to observe, in even the whitest Brazilian girls, a sort of subtle or indirect imitation of this type of feminine beauty or grace, as in the Negro's rhythm of walking, and her grace in dancing and smiling.[13]

Thus, while Freyre valued African culture, he largely folklorized it. Rather than providing Brazilian people with intellect or innovation, in his view, African culture provided the drums, the food, and the sexual freedom that he referred to as "contagious" in his work. In this sense, Freyre replaced an essentialism based on hierarchy and determinism with a more celebratory and malleable variety.

Nevertheless, Freyrian ideas claimed an equality of races by valorizing the contribution of not only the European elements of Brazilian society but also its African and Indian roots. As Freyre famously said, every Brazilian carries with him the "birthmark of the aborigine or the negro, in our affections, our excessive mimicry, our Catholicism which so delights the senses, our music, our gait, our speech, our cradle songs, in everything that is a sincere expression of our lives, we almost all of us bear the mark of that influence." (Freyre, 1986, 278). Freyre elevated these non-European cultures and replaced the idea that whiteness was the ultimate end goal of Brazil's nationalist development with the notion of Brazilians as a mixed "tropical race." Even so, Freyre continued to reify the link between whiteness/Europeanness and progress/modernity (Skidmore 1990; Hanchard 1994; Marx 1998; Nobles 2000).

While this is implicit in much of Freyre's work, it becomes more explicit in his discussion of "advanced" and "backward" races. For example, Freyre held that what defined Brazilian society was the "practical cultural reciprocity that results in the advanced people deriving the maximum of profit from the values and experiences of the backward ones" (Freyre 1986, 83). Thus, if Brazil's African ancestry gave the country its flavor and its sensorial and physical aptitude, its Portuguese roots were responsible for the country's intellect and industriousness. In this way, racial democracy was not a complete rupture with the whitening project of Brazil's recent past, but instead as a refashioning of it.[14]

Like all nationalist narratives premised on mixing, racial democracy in Brazil was also a deeply gendered project (Wade 2000; Caldwell 2007). The preceding quote by Freyre underscores this with little subtlety. Perhaps more than any other country in Latin America, Brazil's ideas of race mixture entailed producing and reproducing the nation through interracial sexual intercourse.[15] To sexually mix was, as Freyre put it, a way to be "patriotically Brazilian."[16] While Brazilian culture certainly did exist as an amalgamation of African, Indian, and European culture, for Freyre, these different roots were always also thought to exist in the "blood" of each individual Brazilian.[17] Racial democracy was also gendered in another way. Freyre believed that indigenous and black women had a very specific role to play in Brazilian society: nursing, feeding, teaching, passing down rich cultural traditions and sexual development (Caldwell 2007). In this sense, nonwhite women were essential to the reproduction of the symbolic nation and in the self-realization of the intended national subject—the elite white Brazilian male (Caldwell 2007).[18]

Reimagining slavery as the root of Brazil's unique racial egalitarianism was also central to the idea of racial democracy. According to this view, Brazil's cordial and less oppressive system of slavery had led to high rates of miscegenation, which had, in turn, produced a kind of inclusive and racially egalitarian society. This account recast slave masters not as villainous but as benevolent. It reimagined their relationship with their slaves as symbiotic rather than exploitative. At times, Freyre even suggested that slaves were better nourished than their masters, further advancing the idea that slavery was simply not as horrific in Brazil as it was elsewhere (Freyre 1986, 50).[19]

These accounts were not entirely wrong. There were major differences in the slavery systems in Brazil and the United States, to cite one oft-used comparison. Recently arrived enslaved people in Brazil often found themselves on plantations with others from the same African ethnic groups. Also, enslaved people could marry, have their families legally recognized, sue people in court, and even buy themselves out of slavery (Degler 1971). Nevertheless, while Brazilian manumission rates[20] were high, enslaved people in Brazil died young at much higher rates than in the United States. They were often worked to death, quite literally, but they also committed suicide at much higher rates than in the United States (Degler 1971; Telles 2004). The large number of slave rebellions in Brazilian history also serves as a reminder that manumission was not a viable option for every enslaved person in Brazil. However "cordial" or "symbiotic" slavery may have been, people risked their lives time and time again to escape from it (Degler 1971; Schwartz 1974; Telles 2004). However, racial democracy ideologies in Brazil, in great part, depended on these romanticized narratives of slavery.

As the Brazilian nation came into its own, serious ruptures and transitions from authoritarian to populist regimes and back defined the political field. Racial democracy ideals became most crystalized into state institutions in Brazil under authoritarian rule—first with Getúlio Vargas's dictatorship (1930–1945) and later under the military authoritarian regime (1964–1985).[21] African culture received unprecedented national recognition, as Alberto (2011) contends, but it also had to be "carefully controlled and circumscribed—within a few discrete areas of cultural life (that is, music, carnival, or religion)" or to a "particular space or region" (115). This meant the institutionalization not only of racial egalitarianism but ultimately of what Goldberg calls racelessness, or colorblind ideologies that led to a si-

lencing of discussions about racial hierarchy and inequality. This racelessness would become a defining feature of Brazil's political field well into the
1980s.

Racelessness, Nation, and Authoritarian Regimes

The development of *mestizaje* projects was highly entangled with attempts at state building in Latin America. Prominent thinkers like Freyre
in Brazil and Vasconcelos in Mexico not only crafted ideas about the nation
within insular intellectual circles, they also acted as the architects of the
state's own nationalist projects. In some cases, they even served as high-level
bureaucrats and legislators, which allowed them to institutionalize their visions of their countries through centralized state institutions.[22]

Nevertheless, there was still a colossal gap between these nationalist narratives and everyday reality. After independence, Brazil quickly emerged
as one of the most unequal countries in the world, a designation it continued to bear throughout most of the twentieth century. In 1920, Brazil's
Gini coefficient was 0.83, where 0 measures perfect income equality and 1
represents the highest possible income inequality (Luna and Klein 2014,
123). These disparities were at once economic and political, and they also
mapped directly onto both regional and color hierarchies.

As Brazil grew throughout the early twentieth century, it did so in extremely uneven ways that were anything but naturally given. In 1930, for
example, 25 percent of Brazil's population lived in the Northeast region,
but that region accounted for only 10 percent of the country's wealth (Baer
1964). Stark ethno-racial inequalities existed in part because nonwhites
were concentrated in these less industrialized regions and in rural areas.
In 1940, while 59.3 percent of whites were literate, 29.3 percent of *pardos*
and only 20.9 percent of *pretos* could read and write (Andrews 1992). Even
in more industrialized parts of the country, not everyone experienced economic growth in the same way. In the state of São Paulo, for instance—
where blacks made up 12.2 percent of the working age population—they
represented only 3.2 percent of professionals (Andrews 1991). The differences in business ownership were even starker.

These extreme disparities posed a serious challenge for Brazilian elites,
who had to manage such inequalities, if only for reasons of curbing potential dissent. The solution was to develop a model of what Holston (2008)
calls "differentiated citizenship," or the simultaneous existence of formal
membership and the lack of "substantive distribution of the rights, meanings, practices, and institutions that membership entails to those considered citizens" (197). In so doing, the Brazilian state emphasized ideologies
of universal inclusion that "effectively blur—in the sense of making less
appreciable—its massively inegalitarian distribution of rights and resources"

(275). This governance strategy was explicitly entangled with the development of racial democracy, which took its fullest form as a state project under authoritarian rule. In 1930, a military coup backed by a coalition of political and economic elites from regions not traditionally represented in the national government brought Getúlio Vargas to power.[23] When he took office, his agenda was a decidedly nationalist one. He wanted to bring about national unity and widespread economic development as well as project Brazil's power abroad (Levine 1998; Skidmore 1999). More specifically, Vargas sought to secure state control of the petroleum industry, develop a centralized education system, and take steps to bring about regional integration. In order to reach these goals, he had to win the support of the masses. While Vargas was white and a member of the landed elite of Brazil's most European state of Rio Grande do Sul, he became known for embracing the country's working classes and celebrating its African roots. This was so much the case that he became affectionately known as "The Father of the Poor" (Levine 1998). More concretely, Vargas increased wages, expanded social welfare, invested heavily in the industrial sector, and privileged domestic industries and labor over foreign imports and immigrant workers.

Vargas also wanted to build a nation that was politically centralized and cohesive. He created federal ministries, attempted to reconfigure traditional patronage relationships, and prioritized the construction of a unified national culture. All of these were monumental tasks not only because Brazil was one of the world's most economically unequal countries but also because it was one of its most massive and populous ones. Also, at the time and arguably still today, each region in Brazil was like an entirely different country. Whereas the Northeast was extremely poor and had a large non-white population, the much whiter Southeast was emerging, in that period, as the industrial and financial capital of the country.

A central part of Vargas's project to unite the nation was recognizing and valorizing many aspects of Brazilian culture that were formerly marginalized, stigmatized, and in some cases, prohibited. This included investing in and standardizing Brazil's popular celebration of carnival around the country and embracing formerly banned capoeira (an African-based martial art) and Candomblé (an African-based religion) (Andrews 2004; Alberto 2011).[24] In so doing, Vargas opened up unexplored space for Afro-Brazilian culture to be valued as central to the nation. He also incorporated this message into his political discourse and enshrined it in a new set of federal institutions as part of his effort to create a modern and centralized Brazilian state. For questions of race and nation, the most important of these was the Federal Ministry of Education and Public Health, established in 1938.[25] Vargas invested heavily in the construction of nationhood by having the Ministry consciously cultivate the idea of "Brazilianness" both internally and globally. More concretely, the Ministry built national museums and monuments, preserved historic landmarks, standardized the educational curricula, and funded popular culture like soccer and carnival (Williams 2001).

All of these policies made Vargas an incredibly popular figure among the poor and working classes. Furthermore, his strategy to nationalize aspects of the economy and halt European immigration showed his commitment not only to Brazilians, but also to black Brazilians. Andrews (2004) notes, this was because "more than any other group in São Paulo, they [Afro-Brazilians] were the ones who had borne the brunt of immigration, who had been most jarringly shunted aside as the state was 'Europeanized'" (Andrews, 1991, 152). Indeed, because Vargas's populist politics came on the heels of whitening policies and massive European immigration, they necessarily had racial undertones. For many black workers in this period, Vargas's use of the word *nacional* was nearly synonymous with *preto* and *pardo* (Alberto 2011).

Yet, Vargas's policies often acted as a double-edged sword. The celebration of African culture and of the working classes came with serious restrictions, especially after 1937, when an imminent military coup led him to move further to the right, and to more repressive governance technologies. While Africans and their descendants were front and center of the nation in a symbolic way, they continued to occupy the lower rungs of Brazil's socioeconomic ladder. They also had very little political power. Additionally, though Vargas had promised the poor that they would achieve economic prosperity, the country remained drastically unequal. Between 1920 and 1950, Brazil's Gini coefficient remained constant. More disturbingly, Vargas became the architect behind Brazil's now infamous urban spatial order that placed the poor and working classes in the periphery and the middle class at the center of the city (Holston 2008).

His populism also came with the serious condition of regulation and the demobilization of potential social unrest. Vargas nationalized unions and cracked down severely on autonomous organizing by labor. He also banned political parties, including the first and only black political party in Brazil, the Brazilian Black Front.[26] This logic of control was also at the center of his cultural policy. While Vargas did successfully integrate African culture and the working classes into carnival, they could only take part if they participated in what Alberto (2011) calls a "controlled nationalist ritual" (115). Carnival themes and songs had to be cleared by the state for their potential subversiveness, and carnival schools were institutionalized into formal patronage relations with the state. Thus, the cost of inclusion under Vargas was the silencing of race and class-based dissent.

These policies also became the archetype for how future authoritarian governments would deal with the question of race and nation. Brazil's image as a happy, soccer-playing, racially mixed paradise often obscures the fact that it experienced the longest military authoritarian rule in South America (Alvarez 1990). The military regime—which held power from 1964 to 1985—also had the distinction of institutionalizing racial democracy into the Brazilian state in unprecedented ways. It was under this authoritarian government that racial democracy was consecrated into the state (Telles 2004). In this period, the idea that race mixture was the foundation of Brazil's strength as a nation pervaded state institutions from educational curricula to the discourse of state officials (Alberto 2011). More importantly, the state used both its symbolic power and military might to limit discussions about racism and racial inequality in Brazil. After 1967, for example, the regime also outlawed and surveilled many leftist groups, including black organizations, which the state argued were inciting racial conflict and importing racism from the United States (Alberto 2011). In this sense, racelessness was not only a defining feature of Brazil's civic culture, it was institutionalized into the state apparatus itself.

COLOMBIA: *MESTIZAJE* AND THE POLITICAL FIELD

In some ways, the project of *mestizaje* nationalism in Colombia was similar to that of Brazil. Like their Brazilian counterparts, Colombian elites developed discourses of race mixture in the wake of colonization and a system of economic development that relied on the labor of enslaved Africans. Over several decades, both countries also adopted immigration laws aimed at whitening their majority nonwhite populations. In 1960, in one of the rare instances in which the central Colombian state did collect ethno-racial statistics, the overwhelming majority of Colombians were identified as mixed: 47.8 percent were identified as *mestizo* and 24 percent as *mulato*. This led census officials to conclude, "Very few countries give less importance to race than this one. Whites, blacks and Indians live together and mix without any fuss; and this indifference has been and continues to be so much the case that in the national statistics gathering these [ethno-racial] questions have been totally ignored."[27]

Nevertheless, *mestizaje* in Colombia and racial democracy in Brazil developed amid different demographic and political realities, which dramatically shaped the nature of these projects. First, whereas in Brazil most enslaved Africans worked on large plantations close to the country's political and economic capitals, in Colombia, they also labored mostly in the mining industry in isolated regions of the country (Uribe 1963; Appelbaum 2003).[28] Second, while Brazil institutionalized racial democracy throughout its vast territory through powerful, authoritarian state institutions, the Colombian state had little interest in, or capacity for, such an undertaking. These differences—as well as others rooted in geography—created a peculiar brand of regionalized nationalism in Colombia. Another key difference was that whereas blackness was embraced in Brazil, in Colombia it was the source of deep ambivalence.

Regionalized Mestizaje, *Regional* Mestizajes

In the early twentieth century, much like the rest of Latin America, Colombia underwent a shift from ideologies of white supremacy to discourses of *mestizaje* that still contained remnants that valued Europeanness above indigeneity and Africanness. Colombia also developed a considerable eugenics movement made up of scientists, medical doctors, and politicians (Stepan 1991). In 1922, the Colombian Congress passed Immigration Law 114, which sought to "better the ethnic conditions, both physical and moral" of the country and also prohibited the entrance of those who would be "inconvenient" for the nation.[29] Despite this law, and other legislation that offered land grants to immigrants, Colombia was not very successful in recruiting European immigrants, especially when compared to Brazil or Argentina (Andrews 2004; Cárdenas and Mejía 2006). This, paired with the changing tide of racial discourse in Latin America more generally, led to debates within Colombia about the feasibility of a nationalism based on whitening.

In such debates, no singular intellectual emerged as the "father" of *mestizaje* in Colombia as Gilberto Freyre did in Brazil. Even so, both intellectuals and political elites saw race as an important issue in envisioning the future of the Colombian nation (Wade 1993, 16). The two nationalist thinkers who figured prominently in these debates in Colombia were Luis López de Mesa, a prolific writer and the minister of education (1934–1935), and former Colombian president Laureano Gómez (1950–1953) (Wade 1993; Wade 2003; Castillo 2007). Whereas Gómez felt that the Colombian nation was damned to inferiority because of its race mixture, López de Mesa argued that the country could actually overcome that fate. Despite these differences, both sides converged in their belief that Europeans were morally, intellectually, and aesthetically superior (Wade 1993, 16).

Over time, the idea that race mixture was the source of the country's degeneracy shifted to one where mixture was seen as a solution to overcoming the black and Indian elements of the Colombian nation. Though in contrast to Brazil, where blackness was imagined to be at the center of the nation, the national imaginary of a homogeneous, *mestizo* Colombia largely excluded blacks from the national discourse. Rather, the mixture of European and Indian blood came to signify what it was to be Colombian. While the "explicit derogation of blackness" was rare, as Wade (1993) notes, it was common to "encounter the celebration of mixedness alongside silence about blacks" (17). In this framework, Africans were seen as an unassimilable group whose savageness, "sensual vigor," and intellectual limitations were impediments to the development of the Colombian nation (Green 2000, 119). In part because of this, blacks and mulattos were largely erased from both historical and popular narratives of the Colombian nation (Appelbaum 2003; Mosquera 2004; Sanders 2004; Múnera 2005).

Certainly, in early twentieth century Colombia, white and *mestizo* elites considered both indigenous peoples and blacks inferior. However, they treated these groups in distinct ways when thinking about the "evolution" of the Colombian nation. As early as the nineteenth century, Colombian elites had the goal of solidifying the nation through whitening the population, incorporating Indians, and ignoring the country's black population. This is clear in the 1789 memoir of Pedro Fermín de Vargas, an intellectual and leader of Colombia's independence struggles:

> We know from much experience that among animals, breeds become better when they mix, and although we can say that this observation is also true of humans from the half-breed categories in the castes, the result of mixing Indians and whites are "stepping stones." Consequently, this evidence shows that through our nation's legislation, we can easily achieve a society in which Indians are extinguished and confused for whites.[30]

As Vargas's vision of the country's future suggests, *mestizaje* in Colombia was very much about the mixing of Spanish and indigenous blood and culture, and as such, the near erasure of African culture and contemporary black Colombians.

Rendering invisible a group that represented more than 10 percent of the population may seem like a difficult task. However, this marginalization was facilitated by their regional concentration on Colombia's two coasts and outside of the centers of national political power (Wade 1993; Green 2000; Appelbaum 2003; Sanders 2004).[31] As Sanders (2004) notes, "blacks and mulattoes—especially in discourse, if not in reality—were pushed to the margins of the Colombian nation and state, isolated geographically and ideologically from the rest of the polity" (195). In addition, the Colombian state was weak, with little presence outside Colombia's major cities, which further contributed to the invisibility of blackness within the national imaginary.

Yet while black Colombians largely disappeared from the state's official national discourse, they did persist both in state institutions and society in the form of region as a proxy for race.[32] Colombia developed what Wade (1993) calls a "cultural topography of race" whereby racial hierarchies persisted in Colombian society in forms highly entangled with, and coded in, region (Wade 1993; Green 2000; Appelbaum 2003). In this, Colombia's highlands were widely considered the place of beauty, industriousness, and whiteness, while its coasts were associated with laziness and hypersexuality.[33] Such entanglements between race and region not only reflected a symbolic national imaginary but also an underlying material reality in which black Colombians found themselves disproportionately in the poorest of regions. To be sure, the states that were largely abandoned by the state were also the ones with higher concentrations of black Colombians, such as the Chocó. Today, these areas remain the poorest in the country. Nevertheless, these regional inequalities are often naturalized, seen as a reflection of moral and intellectual differences between the people who inhabit them rather than as a consequence of racialized state policies.

Thus, regionalism became a powerful language for understanding blackness and articulating the racial order in Colombia (Wade 1993). Even today, while many Colombians might consider it inappropriate to say that "blacks" are lazy, ugly, stupid, or corrupt, suggesting that *Chocoanos* —people from the Chocó, a state where 74 percent identify as black—have these qualities is not equally wrong. While doing fieldwork in Bogotá, I constantly heard these stereotypes about the Chocó, mainly from working-class whites and *mestizos*. Typically, people made such comments while trying to guess which region of Colombia I was from.[34] Because I am African American and Colombians saw me as black, people would typically guess that I was either from the southern Pacific Coast or the Atlantic Coast, two regions known for having a black population. However, neither region was seen—as the Chocó was—as the space of original or pure blackness. When I would ask why they hadn't guessed the Chocó, countless cab drivers, doormen, shopkeepers, and friends of friends would explain to me that my facial features were "too refined" (*finos*) or my skin color too light for me to be from the Chocó. These were meant, of course, as compliments, that I was supposed to graciously accept. A few times, this digging into my national/regional roots led to a diatribe about the Chocó that was extremely racialized, even though the speaker never mentioned race or blackness directly.[35] These frequent exchanges signaled not only that racial meanings in Colombia were often transposed onto region but also that this imbrication allowed expressions of racism to permeate everyday interactions in socially acceptable ways.

This linking of race with region has its origins in the late nineteenth century (Appelbaum 2003; Restrepo 2007). In examining debates between nationalist thinkers in this period, Restrepo (2007) suggests that what these diverse intellectuals shared was the idea of an "inescapable 'geography of races' that saw a correlation between the characteristics of particular places (zones, climates, physical and natural environment) and the dispositions of particular racialized groups" (59). The mix between the blood and culture of "superior" and "inferior" races, which preoccupied elites elsewhere, mapped directly onto the Colombian territory in unique ways. In this sense, Colombia's imagined race mixture could be said to be more about culture and geography than about imagined notions of "mixed blood," even though the latter was still important to its construction. This created an underlying tension between the idea of a Colombia made up of individuals who blend its different ancestral and cultural roots and that of an aggregated Colombian nation constituted of its discrete, culturally distinct regions. The common expression *juntos pero no revueltos*, or "together but not scrambled," comes to mind as a useful way to make sense of *mestizaje* in this case.[36]

Colombia's version of *mestizaje* was a highly regionalized project in another way. Beyond the mapping of race onto the country's regions, distinct variants of *mestizaje* developed in different regions in ways that reflected the local realities (Wade 2003; Sanders 2004; Chaves and Zambrano 2006). Scientific racism of the late nineteenth century interacted with the region's own local history of racism (Sander 2004). These localized *mestizajes* were also evident as local governments adopted whitening policies aimed at luring European migrants to their areas. As Appelbaum (1999) underscores:

> In Cauca, lawmakers, large landowners, and other leading citizens at the state and local level often expressed disdain for their own rural poor, especially Afro-Caucanos and Indians. Businessmen and politicians longed to replace their unsatisfactory local population with migrants whom they regarded as more productive. Since Cauca did not attract Europeans in large numbers, elite Caucanos turned instead to migrants from neighboring states, mainly Antioquia (634).

In some cases, Colombian governors even passed local legislation that, like the national policies, offered land grants to European migrants and also banned Asian migration (Appelbaum 1999).

It was in this context of a weak Colombian state that regional *mestizajes* emerged. Colombia stands out as one of the few in Latin America never to endure long periods of dictatorship. This lack of an overtly repressive state apparatus, paired with the difficult geographic terrain of the country, meant that the Colombian state developed with limited territorial reach and even less centralized authority.

In addition, the country's internal conflict between the military and a number of armed rebel groups that began in the late 1950s and continues today testifies to the fact that the Colombian state has never commanded a monopoly of violence across its territory (Centeno 2002). In fact, in nearly every area, including that of education, the administrative and coercive reach of the Colombian state has historically been limited (Centeno 2002). It is no surprise, then, that the Colombian state never quite developed a centralized cultural policy arguably until the 1990s, when multicultural reforms took hold. Rather, questions of cultural preservation, collective national memory, and identity were often relegated to suboffices within other ministries, including the under-resourced Ministry of Public Instruction (later called the Ministry of Education).[37] We know from Brazil and Mexico that national cultural institutions can serve as important sites in the construction and diffusion of *mestizaje* ideology.

The weakness of Colombia's state institutions had direct implications for the project of *mestizaje*. First and foremost, it meant that *mestizaje* in Colombia was simply not as developed or hegemonic as in other cases in the region. For instance, Green (2000) argues, Colombian "elites never openly embraced the idea of a *mestizo* nation as official ideology" and "were less sophisticated in their attempts at hegemony" than other countries like Brazil (116). At the turn of the century, Colombian elites were increasingly concentrated in particular regions in the country. This fact, paired with Colombia's harsh topography, fostered the development of unintegrated regions (Green 2000). Though *mestizaje* was far from institutionalized in Colombia, it was still an important framework that shaped identity formation and social practices in much of the country (Wade 1993; Appelbaum 2003; Wade 2005). In the end, while ideas emanating from Bogotá did not completely constrain local understandings of race and nation, they did very much inform them.

CONCLUSION

Concerns about race mixture were at the center of broader debates around nationhood and modernity in both Colombia and Brazil. At the turn of the twentieth century, elites in these countries struggled with the implications of scientific racial determinism for the future of their nations. The dominant idea that Latin American countries could get rid of their less-desirable indigenous and African elements over time was replaced with *mestizaje*, a nationalist project that might be understood as settling for a more attainable racial horizon. This ideology was an effort not to achieve whiteness, but to move closer to it.

While *mestizaje* in Colombia and Brazil are similar in many ways, I have also highlighted several key differences. First, whereas in Brazil centralized authoritarian state entities institutionalized and disseminated ideologies of race mixture, Colombia's approach was much more piecemeal and decentralized. Colombia lacked a cohesive nationalist *mestizaje* project with the same ideological weight as the one that authoritarian regimes in Brazil developed. Second, blackness fit differently into each country's nationalist imaginary. While *brasilianidade* centered on African culture, *colombianidad* often included blackness in ambivalent ways. Indeed, blackness was never officially recognized in Colombia to the same degree it was in Brazil, where the cultural practices once associated with enslaved Africans—feijoada, samba, Candomblé, capoeira—all became institutionalized within the state and solidified as the quintessential symbols of the Brazilian nation.[38] This difference was in part because of how regions figured into Colombia's version of *mestizaje*.

However, to say that *mestizaje* was regionalized in Colombia is not to ignore similar processes of regionalization in Brazil. In both countries certain regions came to be racialized as black and as inferior to the rest of the nation. Even so, the regions that came to be associated with blackness in Brazil have had a very different place in the symbolic nation. For example, while Colombia's Chocó is understood as "outside" the Colombian nation, Brazil's Northeast—which is similarly understood as the country's black region—is very much at the center of the imagined nation. It is simultaneously seen as backward, as the homeland of its celebrated African roots, and the home of the country's first capital city.

There are other key differences between narratives of race and nation in the two countries. Whereas *mestizaje* came to be articulated in Brazil primarily in the idea of a racially mixed modal Brazilian citizen, in Colombia it was an aggregated citizenry made up of its distinct cultural and regional parts. To borrow from colloquial metaphors, if Brazil was a melting pot, Colombia was a quilt. As I will argue in the following chapters, these differences in the relationship between blackness, region, and national identity help to explain why the language of black cultural difference had such resonance in Colombia's version of ethno-racial reforms, while in Brazil the idea that blacks simply needed socioeconomic equality to match their symbolic inclusion became the dominant narrative.

Nevertheless, *mestizaje* narratives in the two cases did converge on one dimension: the discursive erasure of racial critique. In both Colombia and Brazil, *mestizaje* ideologies brought with them the idea that the prevalence of race mixture at once produced, and evinced, a society in which race was not a problem. Even while dominant nationalist discourse was full of contradictions, the political fields of both Colombia and Brazil came to stigmatize critique of the ethno-racial order as irrelevant and as inherently unpatriotic. This ideological constraint, however, did not mean that discourses of race mixture were completely hegemonic or static over time. Rather *mestizaje* was a "multifaceted, fluctuating and contested terrain," as Chaves and Zambrano (2006, 7) remind us. I now turn to a discussion of such contestation. More specifically, I analyze the black political organizations that emerged in the 1970s and 1980s as a window into the nature of the political fields of Colombia and Brazil on the eve of multicultural reforms.

CHAPTER THREE

BLACK MOVEMENTS IN
COLORBLIND FIELDS

The idea that every Colombian is more or less *mestizo* and every Brazilian is at least a little African is similar to the widespread notion that all Americans are middle class. Beyond obscuring the very real ways that these societies are, in fact, differentiated along class and ethno-racial lines, these commonly held beliefs often serve to depoliticize such inequalities. This is, in part, because myths of homogeneity make it difficult for those on the bottom of a social hierarchy to develop an oppositional consciousness. In fact, in such ideological contexts, critiquing inequalities is often seen as divisive, as waging racial or class warfare.

Even in the absence of formal ethno-racial exclusion, in Colombia and Brazil a system of informal ethno-racial hierarchy developed. While the boundaries around ethno-racial categories were sometimes blurry, these informal systems of racial classification were still highly entangled with social norms that valued whiteness over blackness and indigeneity (Telles 2004; Wade 2005). In this, the symbolic value of particular categories did not always match material realities. For example, in Brazil, despite the fact that *pardos* and *pretos* tend to have similar outcomes on a number of socioeconomic measures, suggesting that they may be systematically disadvantaged when compared to whites, they have rarely understood themselves as the victims of racialized oppression (Degler 1971; Wade 1993; Wade 1998; Telles 2004; Bailey 2009).[1]

Racial ambiguities paired with the fact that class inequalities were arguably more salient than racial inequalities in the every day lives of ordinary people made mobilization around blackness particularly difficult. The task that black activists faced, then, was to mobilize people around identities that were both blurry and to a great extent secondary to class and national identities. What is more, for many would-be beneficiaries of their struggle, *mestizaje* had created the possibility of imagining an egalitarian and unified nation of which they were a part.

In such a context, black movements in Colombia and Brazil were weak not because of outright state repression but because they were embedded in a political field in which both the state and society dismissed such mobilization as misguided and antithetical to the nation.[2] Furthermore, because black organizations often framed the problem they faced as racism, they were especially susceptible to the critique that they were being unpatriotic and divisive. This also meant that they were often accused of being racists themselves, guilty of importing racial discourses from the United States (Hanchard 1994; Telles 2004; Alberto 2011).

In this chapter, I examine the ways in which black activists in Colombia and Brazil navigated this formally colorblind ideological terrain. In it, I look at the trajectories of black movements by drawing on secondary literature as well as the oral histories of black activists, focusing primarily on the two decades before recent ethno-racial reforms. In so doing, I hope to give texture to the many theoretical accounts of black consciousness in these political and ideological contexts. At the same time, I seek to underscore the unlikelihood that, only a decade later, the Colombian and Brazilian states would adopt a host of ethno-racial policies. In so doing, I make the analytic distinction between two different kinds of politics that might otherwise be conflated: mobilizing *while* black and mobilizing *as* blacks. This distinction, I contend, is important for understanding not only the articulation of black movements but also the subsequent institutionalization of black political subjects in each case.

MOBILIZING WHILE BLACK, MOBILIZING AS BLACKS

Struggles within a political field are a contestation over material power as much as symbolic power. As Bourdieu (1977) noted, "Every power which manages to impose meanings and to impose them as legitimate by concealing the power relations which are the basis of its force, adds its own specifically symbolic force to those power relations" (4). In both Colombia and Brazil, the language of *mestizaje* acted to obscure a set of power relations that were heavily inflected with a logic of race and racial hierarchy. As such, the rule that governed the fields of political struggle in these countries was a type of colorblind liberalism that formed the basis of what Hanchard called "racial hegemony."

In such a context, some Colombian and Brazilian activists did organize explicitly around black identity, while others mobilized around other political identities: as peasants, as women, as workers, as students. In order to understand the adoption of multicultural and racial equality reforms in Colombia and Brazil, we must examine not only the emergence of black political organizations in the 1970s–1990s but also the increasing politicization of black identity among activists involved in these other struggles. I realized early on that many of the activists I interviewed and spent time with had become politicized around other political categories before explicitly mobilizing around blackness. While one might recast these earlier instances of mobilization of black people as black mobilization, I argue that doing so would be to confound two distinct phenomena. When black people engage in movements that articulate the struggle primarily in terms other than ethno-racial identity—even if most of the people in such movements identify as black—we might call this *mobilizing while black*. In contrast, when movements frame their struggle primarily in terms of black identity and typically—though not always—as a fight against racism, we should understand this as *mobilizing as blacks*.

The question of political subjectivity is central here. Marxists have distinguished between the working class constituting a "class-in-itself" versus a "class-for-itself." For Marx, a class-in-itself simply meant that structural conditions had produced classes defined in material terms, based on their relation to the means of production. He distinguished this from the notion of a class-for-itself, by which he meant that classes acted consciously in ways that sought to further their collective interests.[3] This distinction led many scholars to think through the conditions under which the working class could develop the consciousness to go from being a class-in-itself to a class-for-itself. They also often argued that when structural conditions had produced this proletariat class but that class still failed to act collectively, they suffered from a kind of false consciousness (Lukács 1971, 76).

In a similar vein, race theorists have argued that racial domination in raceless contexts like Brazil produced a sort of false consciousness among the racially dominated classes (Hanchard 1994; Marx 1998; Goldberg 2002). The ethnographic and demographic evidence suggested that race played some role in structuring and stratifying social and economic relations in these countries. More specifically, it suggested that these societies had developed a durable de facto ethno-racial hierarchy that placed blacks at the bottom of the material and symbolic social order. Nevertheless, while these material conditions had arguably produced blacks as an (ethno-racial) class-in-itself, they did not mean that blacks also constituted a class-for-itself. Doing the latter required activists to overcome tremendous ideological constraints.

While I find the distinction between class in and of itself useful for understanding the politicization of blackness in Colombia and Brazil in recent decades, I reject the idea that false consciousness applies here for at least three reasons. First, while some Colombians and Brazilians certainly believed that class rather than race stratified their societies, others were painfully aware of the weight of racial hierarchy. Yet rather than confront it outright, many ordinary people often internalized it (Burdick 1998; Twine

1998; Sheriff 2005). In so doing, they sought a kind of racial mobility either over the course of their life, or over generations by "improving the race" (Wade 1993; Telles 2004; Telles 2007; Viveros Vigoya 2016). As Wade (1993) contends, if they married "lighter," "their offspring [had] an even greater chance of avoiding discrimination directed at blacks and mulattoes" (7). Whitening, then, must be understood as a strategy to navigate these racially stratified societies. In fact, people who engage in whitening might be hyper-aware of ethno-racial hierarchy, even if they do not challenge it directly (Viveros Vigoya 2016). This is the second reason I believe false consciousness is not appropriate in this context: hyper-awareness of the social order is very different from a lack of awareness. Put another way, while choosing ethno-racial mobility may indicate a lack of politicized black identity, it does not preclude a consciousness of racial hierarchy.

Third, equating a lack of racial mobilization with false consciousness ignores the political agency of people who identify as black and assumes that only a particular kind of explicitly race-based mobilization counts as anti-racist. Anti-racist mobilization may, instead, take multiple forms. Important examples include Afro-Cuban intellectuals and activists like Rafael Serra, who had an anti-racist praxis but chose to organize primarily along nationalist lines, and Afro-Colombian political leader and thinker Diego Luis Córdoba, who organized around regional identity and under a socialist platform.[4]

Moreover, the question of consciousness itself is complex for people who live at the intersection of various hierarchical systems, among them those based on race, class, gender, and sexuality. Did black women who organized against patriarchy necessarily lack racial consciousness, or had they simply chosen to focus primarily on the struggle against patriarchy? I see domination and hierarchy—as well as the identities that emerge from them—as inherently intersectional.[5] As such, black people are never singularly black in the same way that workers are never singularly workers.[6] Rather, their identities, experiences, and political organizing reflect the fact that they simultaneously occupy positions within several entangled social hierarchies.

Recent scholarship on Colombia and Brazil has underscored the intersectional nature of black mobilization (Carneiro 2003; Asher 2007; Rodrigues 2010; Perry 2013; Melo 2015). In so doing, they have called on us to reimagine what black mobilization looks like, as Perry (2013) does in her ethnography of a black women–led neighborhood association fighting against land dispossession in the city of Salvador da Bahia. In it, Perry uncovers how local organizing around space in the neighborhood of Gamboa de Baixo is deeply infused with an anti-racist praxis. We find a similar rethinking of black politics in Robin D.G. Kelley's (1994) study of resistance and consciousness among poor and working class African Americans.

With this in mind, I do not tell the story of black political organizing in Colombia and Brazil as a total transformation from a complete lack of black consciousness to an exclusive embrace of it. Rather, it is useful to think of black political movements as emerging out of a complex process of what Stuart Hall calls articulation. Indeed, despite the persistence of racial hierarchies that put blacks in Colombia and Brazil at the bottom of the symbolic and material social hierarchy, neither black subjectivity nor its politicization was inevitable. Alternatively, the lack of explicit black mobilization at particular historical moments did not necessarily suggest a complete lack of black consciousness either.

A better approach to understanding black political subjectivity, I suggest, is to examine the historical conditions under which blackness became increasingly central to political struggles in the two cases. In this chapter I do this by examining the trajectories of black mobilization in the decades leading up to ethno-racial legislation in each country.[7] I argue that black movements in Colombia and Brazil came to be articulated through two paths, both of which were important to the later recognition of black rights. The first was through the emergence of black organizations rooted in black identity and committed to issues of race since their inception. The second road was more indirect: black activists and organizations mobilizing around other political issues increasingly articulated their struggle as based on blackness. In this, many black activists in both countries went from mobilizing as women, students, peasants, and workers to organizing as *black* women, *black* students, *black* peasants, and *black* workers.[8] In Colombia, this mobilization also happened in a context of an internal conflict where regional identities were particularly salient and heavily imbricated with race.

THE ARTICULATION OF BLACK MOVEMENTS IN BRAZIL

Mobilizing around black identity in Brazil dates back to the early part of the twentieth century. However, it has tended to ebb and flow in ways that reflect Brazil's struggles with democracy and authoritarianism.[9] Early on, São Paulo emerged as an important site of such black organizing (Leite 1992; Butler 1998; Cardoso Simões Pires 2006; Alberto 2011; Pereira 2013). It was home to black civil society organizations, or associations of "men of color" or "classes of color," and the hub of Brazil's burgeoning black press (Alberto 2011). Between 1910 and 1920, São Paulo saw the founding of many of Brazil's largest and longest running black newspapers, including *Baluarte, O Menelik, O Alfinete, O Clarim d'Alvorada, A Liberdade,* and *O Elite* (Alberto 2011). More than any other place in Brazil, blacks in São Paulo created what Hanchard (1994) calls the "Afro-Brazilian public sphere," an alternative political space outside mainstream politics (Hanchard 1994). Such early black movements typically emerged among middle-class and upwardly mobile blacks in cities like São Paulo. Perhaps more than any other group in Brazil, this sector could feel the contradictory discourses of racial democracy. Despite living in Brazil's wealthiest region, they felt the marks of their color in the form of glass ceilings in the workplace and social boundaries between them and their white colleagues (Andrews 1991; Alberto 2011).

Black mobilization in this period culminated with the founding in São Paulo in 1931 of the Brazilian Black Front, which also circulated the newspaper, *A Voz da Raça*. The organization sought to raise consciousness by speaking to the issues most pertinent to blacks across the country. Beyond socioeconomic mobility, the organization also sought to achieve the full integration of black Brazilians into the political life of the country. They had a great deal of success, quickly developing a membership base not only in São Paulo but also in cities throughout the country (Andrews 1991). This was particularly clear in 1936 when the organization became an official political party. However, just one year later, the government banned it—along with all other political parties—when a military coup led populist President Getúlio Vargas to become more authoritarian. At that time, the Front went underground and survived only until 1938 (Alberto 2011).

The next major attempt to build a massive black political organization came just a decade later in Rio de Janeiro with the founding of the Black Experimental Theatre (TEN). The organization aimed to combat racism where they argued it was most pervasive: in the theater, television, and education system (Alberto 2011, 215). Its focus signaled the centrality of culture to practices of racism and to the formation of a collective black identity. Organizing around culture was also a strategy to fight against racism without seeming overtly political. After all, the TEN emerged during the height of state-promulgated racial democracy, when Gilberto Freyre had become more and more involved in politics and President Vargas had already made racial democracy central to his populist project.[10]

The organization drew on the "repertoires of contention" (to borrow Tilly's term) that the Black Front had established decades earlier. Following these strategies, the TEN started *Quilombo*, a nationally circulating journal that included articles written by its founder, Abdias do Nascimento, as well as other thinkers. The newspaper also included exchanges about the situation facing blacks in the Caribbean, Africa, France, and the United States (Guimarães 2005). While the TEN was ostensibly much less political than the Black Front, the Brazilian state saw the very attempt to organize around black identity and in autonomous black spaces as a threat. The organization received invitations to participate in a number of international events, but the regime did not allow them to go (Alberto 2011). When a military coup shook the country in 1964, the TEN, along with many other civil society organizations, disbanded (Hanchard 1994); Abdias do Nascimento went into exile in the United States.

Military Dictatorship and the Black Brazilian Movement

The Brazilian state had long seen organizing around black identity and denouncing racism as fundamentally anti-patriotic. However, this was particularly the case under the military dictatorship of 1964–1985. This regime was not only the most adamant about preserving the idea of racial democracy but also the most repressive. Consequently, the late 1960s and early 1970s marked another downturn in black organizing in Brazil (Hanchard 1994; Alberto 2011). Yet even while organizing was largely quelled in this period, mobilization did not dissipate entirely. Rather, a number of underground organizations emerged throughout Brazil as well as in similarly authoritarian contexts throughout the Southern Cone (Alvarez 1990). Wherever they occurred, they planted the seeds for later democratization efforts. Like all movements in abeyance, these leftist organizations in Brazil had to adapt organizationally and culturally to the new political climate in which they found themselves (Taylor 1989). A repressive military regime meant that rather than organize explicitly as political organizations, many activists organized in spaces that were, at least on their face, apolitical or cultural in nature.[11] This included organizing within neighborhood and slum-dweller associations, community health clinics, and soup kitchens, as Alvarez (1990) notes.

This period of state repression in Brazil also marked the emergence of clandestine leftist anti-dictatorship groups made up of students and other militants. Some of the black Brazilian activists I interviewed had begun their militancy in these organizations. One such leader was Reginaldo Bispo, born in São Paulo to parents from Bahia. He became an important leader in the black movement in the late 1970s with the founding of the Unified Black Movement or Movimento Negro Unificado (MNU). Previously, he had been involved in a number of leftist organizations, where he had begun to formulate his own political views based in a Trotskyist variant of Marxism. Before the MNU, Bispo had participated in three local black political organizations: the Federation of Afro-Brazilian Entities of the State of São Paulo, the Black Community of Campinas, and the theater group Evolution. He explained how many black activists like himself had been simultaneously involved in class-based and race-based mobilization. "I entered in a period in which we were already in a process of overcoming, but the first initiative was a sector of the [International] Workers League, which was a Trotskyist organization that had a great deal of penetration among young blacks from São Paulo, in the capital" (interview, Reginaldo Bispo, April 2010).

Bispo's trajectory was common for black Brazilian activists who later figured prominently in the movement that led to racial equality policies in the 2000s. For instance, activist Flavinho Jorge moved to the city of São Paulo from a small town some 300 kilometers away. He overcame many obstacles that migrants typically face and became the first in his family to go to college. There, at the Pontific Catholic University (PUC), he became politicized. In the 1970s, PUC's campus became a place where Flavinho began to meet people involved in clandestine groups, some armed, others not. He explained that he joined a subversive theatre group on campus, where he "began to have an understanding of politics" (interview, Flavinho Jorge, May 2010). Flavinho co-founded a student organization called the Blacks of PUC and emerged as a leader within the student movement locally and nationally. In this role, he also helped to organize the famous 1977 march, the first open student protest against Brazil's military regime. For Flavinho, it was a dynamic time because clandestine groups, like the ones he participated in, were coming out of the shadows and opposing the authoritarian state head on. Flavinho later became involved in the building of the Workers' Party (PT) and was central to building its anti-racism platform.[12]

Other activists told similar stories of their own transitions from leftist organizing to creating black leftist organizations. Edna Roland, for instance, explained that she became involved in the black movement relatively late in her political trajectory. "My militancy in the black movement began in the mid-1980s, precisely during the period of redemocratization. I didn't live the period of the 1970s [in the black movement]. I was confronting the dictatorship in organizations that had political party ties, in the clandestine organizations that I belonged to" (interview, Edna Roland, August 2010). Similarly, Gilberto Leal noted, "my history of militancy is a long one that started when I was young. In reality, I started out with political mobilization in the socialist left in the period before the end of the military dictatorship. . . . After, I became absorbed by the militancy and the specific issue of the black population" (interview, Gilberto Leal, November 2009).

The 1970s–1980s marked an articulation of black identity as leaders like these began a process of further politicization. Black identity would become increasingly important, even as it existed alongside their identities as workers and militants of the left. All of these articulations were also embedded in a rapidly changing Brazilian economy that sometimes exacerbated racial inequality (Alvarez 1990; Telles 2004). These political transformations, as well as sociocultural change, were all important for the articulation of the contemporary black Brazilian movement. However, rather than create one singular black movement, what came to be articulated was one with ideological tensions, organizational diversity, and deeply entrenched issues of sexism. I now turn to an overview of each of the major tendencies within this complex configuration of organizations that we might call Brazil's black movement.

Black Cultural Organizations

The 1970s marked the emergence of decidedly black cultural movements in popular neighborhoods throughout Brazil. In Rio, a movement often called "Black Rio" or "Black Soul" had emerged and was deeply influenced by the music and aesthetics of black power in the United States. In this period, deejays began to play James Brown and other funk music as black Brazilians invented their own hybrid ways to dance to it. These *bailes black*, or "black clubs," quickly spread to São Paulo, which had been the epicenter of explicitly black social spaces (*clubes negros*) for most of the twentieth century. In this period, the streets of São Paulo, and particularly the city center, became a space for the articulation of a more global black identity (Hanchard 1994).

At the same time, more explicitly political organizations also emerged in this same part of the country.[13] These organizations were typically small and engaged in a wide range of political activities including organizing study groups, offering Afro-Brazilian and African history classes in popular neighborhoods, producing newspapers and journals, and ultimately, engaging in protest against racial discrimination. These more explicitly political black organizations were not completely disconnected from the cultural movements that were also happening around them. Indeed, the *bailes black* were a space for recreation and fun, at the same time they were also where black militants met each other and formed other type of black movement organizations (Contins 2005).

In the 1970s, culture was particularly central to the black movement in Brazil's North and Northeastern region, where black organizations took the form of formal cultural institutions aimed at fortifying black consciousness. In this, Salvador da Bahia emerged as the center of a black cultural revival made up primarily of black carnival groups, or *blocos afros*. The first *bloco afro*, Ilê Aiyê, was founded in 1974—in a neighborhood appropriately called Liberdade, or Freedom—in response to continuing racial discrimination in Salvador's carnival (Guerreiro 2000). This group, known for elaborate African costumes and powerful drums affirming negritude, set the stage for what would become a cultural renaissance in Salvador, a revival that would eventually lead Bahia's state apparatus to institutionalize African-inspired aesthetics. After Ilê came many other *blocos*, including the internationally renowned Olodúm. The leaders of these cultural institutions saw a direct link between consciousness-raising through cultural events and the denunciation of racism.

For example, founded in 1979 in the city of São Luis, the Center of Black Culture's mission was to "raise political and cultural consciousness with the goal of recovering ethno-cultural identity as well as the self-esteem of black people, making possible actions that contribute to the promotion of [black people's] organization in search of citizenship, combating all forms of intolerance caused by racism and promoting the rights of the black population in Maranhão" (Sloan 2007). Some of these efforts—which had emerged in different forms throughout the country in the same period—culminated in the founding of the MNU, the most important black political organization in contemporary Brazil (Covin 2006).

The Making of the Unified Black Movement (MNU)

On July 7, 1978, activists from a number of Brazilian cities organized a public demonstration in São Paulo in response to two disturbing incidents: the case of Robson Silveira da Luz, a black worker accused of stealing fruit from a market and later murdered by the police; and discrimination against four black men who were not allowed to play volleyball at the Clube de Regatas Tietê in São Paulo. The demonstration led to the founding of the Unified Black Movement against Racial Discrimination (Mitchell 1998; Covin 2006; Alberti and Pereira 2007).[14] The MNU was the culmination and aggregation of local mobilization in cities like Rio, São Paulo, Salvador, and Belo Horizonte. The organizational and ideological base included the Institute for Research on Black Culture (IPCN), founded in 1974 from the Society for Brazil-Africa Exchange (SINBA). Because IPCN had developed organizational and physical infrastructure, it served as an important nexus in the construction of this new national black movement. The Inter-American Foundation gave the initial grant to IPCN to build their headquarters and was subsequently kicked out of Brazil (Davis et al. 2011)

Activists like Amauri Mendes and Yêdo Ferreira of IPCN joined Lélia Gonzalez, Milton Barbosa, and many other black activists organizing around anti-racism in São Paulo and Belo Horizonte to eventually create the MNU in 1978. The MNU was different from previous black mobilization in several ways. First, it was arguably the first attempt at consolidating all black organizations throughout the country into a national movement. Previously, aside from local grassroots groups, organizations based in São Paulo or Rio tended simply to expand to the rest of the country with varying levels of success. Second, the MNU came from a much different ideological tradition. Whereas the ultimate goal of the Brazilian Black Front of the 1930s and the Black Experimental Theatre of the 1940s was full integration into the political and sociocultural life of the country, MNU founders had a much more radical proposal. Indeed, while the MNU's stated goal was to fight for a "real racial democracy," many of the MNU's founding members had a separatist political orientation, and many were skeptical of political integration (Covin 2006).[15]

While still far from a large-scale movement, the organization had become by the mid-1980s the most important black political organization in the country (Covin 2006). They had achieved a small grassroots base in many of Brazil's major cities, including places like Salvador da Bahia, where a more culturalist movement had already taken hold. In this, the MNU was perhaps the most important grassroots mobilization effort in Brazilian history. They confronted daily the fact that many of the people they encountered did not identify with racialized struggles, or even identify as black. As a result, much of the MNU's work sought to build a strong collective identity among marginalized black Brazilians and to denounce systematic racism in every part of Brazilian society.

For many of the activists I interviewed—most of whom hailed from popular neighborhoods in the "suburbs" or "periphery" of Brazil's major cities— the MNU was their first encounter with their own racial consciousness.[16] Hamilton Borges, an activist who was involved in the MNU in Bahia for some time, talked about first encountering the MNU when he was facing a difficult moment in his own life:

> Luiza Bairros, Luiz Alberto, and all of them did work in the community. They did grassroots work in communities to confront police violence, to question incarceration. I inherited this. I became a member of the MNU. . . . The MNU held courses on political education, about Pan-Africanism, the history of Africa, the history of blacks in America, as well as other areas of white peoples' knowledge, like philosophy. The MNU had a permanent classroom and I was educated there. Not in the university, not in the student movement, not in the political party (interview, Hamilton Borges, November 2009).

At the time, MNU members were, as Hamilton put it, "obligated to mobilize within communities, to mobilize in the places where the majority of us were."[17] He added that through these "grassroots nucleuses"—which met in community centers, local work sites, schools, and members' homes—the MNU sought to build a strong collective identity among young and marginalized black Brazilians while at the same time denouncing structural and everyday racism in Brazilian society.

Nevertheless, just as the democratization process began to unfold in the mid-1980s, the MNU began to fracture. As the organization's name suggests, its founders originally attempted to construct a unified national black movement. This meant that it had to somehow reconcile the political diversity within its ranks. When faced with the possibility of constructing a viable left political party, many activists within the organization began to rethink the strategy of critiquing racism from outside formal politics (Covin 2006). As political parties were legally allowed to form, and as the MNU marked its tenth anniversary, many activists went into official politics and became extremely active in emergent parties, particularly the Workers' Party (PT). After much internal debate, the leadership of the MNU also decided to put up candidates for congressional seats throughout the country. In this period, a number of black leaders involved in autonomous black political organizations were also active in leftist political parties like the Workers' Party, something Johnson (2008) calls the "dual strategy."[18]

After winning congressional seats in Bahia and elsewhere, many MNU members became disillusioned with electoral politics. MNU activists felt that MNU-leaders-turned-congress-members had, instead of infiltrating the state with a radical black agenda, become coopted by political parties and entrenched in a state that cared little about racial issues. In the mid-1990s, part of the MNU's leadership decided to reestablish itself as autonomous from political parties and the state, while others were still convinced that the dual strategy was the best one. By that time, it was too late to fix an organization whose membership had dwindled significantly and that was still deeply divided over the question of political autonomy (Covin 2006).

CONEN, UNEGRO, and Party Politics

Amid these debates, another kind of black political organization sprang up. As the MNU struggled with internal tensions, a number of militants who had been involved in emergent leftist political parties began to create semi-autonomous black organizations with close ties to parties. The first of these was the Union of Blacks for Equality (UNEGRO), founded in 1988, followed by the National Coordinator of Black Organizations (CONEN), which was created at the First Meeting of Black Entities held in São Paulo in November 1991. While the discourse of CONEN makes it far from explicit, the organization was founded as an alternative to the MNU, which had been divided over the issue of formal politics.

These new forces within the black movement were convinced that working from within political parties and state institutions was the only way to get the Brazilian state to take up the struggle for racial justice (Johnson 1998; Covin 2006). As such, CONEN's main objective was to develop a unified front of black activists on the left to occupy the state apparatus and bring the racial justice debate to formal politics. While CONEN included black organizations aligned with left and left-center political parties, there was what Flavinho called a "hegemony of black people who were militants in the PT." This "hegemony" of the Workers' Party within CONEN allowed for a kind of political coherence. However, as most of CONEN's activism revolved around PT officials' elections and taking stances in support of the PT administration, their closeness to the PT also led some to question whether CONEN and the PT were one and the same. In later chapters, I will show how these entanglements between CONEN and the PT helped institutionalize a racial equality agenda within the Brazilian state, while at the same time they made it more difficult to pressure for further reforms.

The Emergence of the Black Women's Movement

In the late 1980s, the black Brazilian movement not only diverged around political party affiliation but also splintered off in another direction. Early in my field research in Brazil, I naïvely asked activists in black women's organizations how they began their militancy in the "black movement." Many of them responded as Vilma Reis did. She maintained, "The experience of the movement of black women, for me it isn't the experience of the black movement" (interview, Vilma Reis, June 2009). Other black feminists corrected me, saying, "Oh, you mean the black women's movement?" These activists wanted to make an important ideological and historical distinction. As Edna Roland, one of the founders of the black feminist organization Speak Black Woman!, explained, organizations that we typically understand as "the black movement"—as well as state institutions like the Conselho do Negro in São Paulo—were in fact "fundamentally masculine" (interview, Edna Roland, May 2010). Black women fed up with both overt and subtler forms of sexism within male-dominated black organizations began to build spaces within and outside mainstream black organizations where black women could organize autonomously. Their critique of the male-run black movement was multilayered. Women who had worked within "mixed organizations"—or organizations made up of both men and women—found the sexism palpable. Organizing separately meant that women could take leadership positions in ways that they could not in male-dominated organizations. Consequently, they could fully develop their voices as militants.

Moreover, black feminist activists had fought for years to make the case that the mainstream movement's political platform should pay more attention to the unique ways that racism and gender hierarchies differentially affected black women. They raised many issues, including violence against black women, state-led sterilization campaigns, the exploitation of domestic workers, and the negative portrayals of black women within popular culture (Morrison 2003; Caldwell 2007; Rodrigues and Prado 2010). If male-dominated black organizations addressed these issues at all, they often relegated them to the margins. This marginalization mirrored the ways in which a Brazilian women's movement dominated by white, middle-class women treated issues affecting black women (Alvarez 1990; Carneiro 2003).

In response to what Cohen (1999) calls secondary marginalization, black women in cities throughout Brazil began to create their own organizations in the 1980s. The first significant group was Maria Mulher, which some thirty women active in the black movement, the women's movement, and the labor movement founded in 1987 in Porto Alegre. These women were originally a chapter of a global network of NGOs called S.O.S. Racism, which was founded in France in 1984. In its Brazilian branch, the organization provided legal and psychosocial services for victims of racism as well as other services aimed at "ensuring the rights and dignity of human life."[19] A year later, in 1988—amid the constitutional reform process and celebrations of the centennial of the abolition of slavery in Brazil—black women activists from throughout the country met in Valença, for the First Meeting of Black Women. In an interview, Vilma Reis argued that this was the most important event in the articulation of a black women's movement in Brazil. That same year, Geledés, one of the most important black Brazilian organizations, was founded in São Paulo. A plethora of others followed, including the Coletivo de Mulheres Negras da Baixada Santista, Casa de Cultura da Mulher Negra, Grupo de Mulheres Negras Mãe Andrés, Grupo de Mulheres Negras de Espírito Santo, Coletivo de Mulheres Negras de Belo Horizonte and Criola. It was also in this period that Nzinga: Coletiva de Mulheres Negras emerged, an organization where prominent black leader Lélia Gonzalez organized, even as she continued her militancy in the MNU (Caldwell 2007).

It is no surprise that many black women's organizations were founded directly after Valença, a historic and decisive moment in which black women activists chose a third path between white feminist spaces and black male spaces, threatening both movements in the process. In fact, white activists in the women's movement saw the Valença meeting as inherently divisive, as Ribeiro (1995) notes. This charge of divisiveness happened in part because many of the black women activists who started black women's organizations (though not all) began their political trajectories in either the male-dominated black movement or the white-dominated women's movement. This meant that the same activists developing the black women's movement had previously tried for years to etch out space for black women's issues within the broader women's movement. A few months before Valença, for instance, many black women had attended the Ninth National Feminist Meeting, where the conflict between them and white middle-class feminists was palpable (Ribeiro 1995). The House of Culture of Black Women—an organization active in this period—included on its website some text from a document black women activists wrote at that meeting:

> And we cannot consider ourselves an inferior subtopic anymore. We are a huge percentage of the feminine population that organizes against the

discrimination against women. However, we are alone. We are alone when it comes to more serious discussions like the absurd social and economic marginalization that confines us to restricted spaces because of our color.[20]

While interactions like Valença were contentious, black women activists did eventually convince the white middle-class-dominated feminist movement to take up some of the issues they raised. Domestic workers' rights, which became central to the mainstream women's movement in Brazil in the 1980s, is a case in point.

Notwithstanding this success, black feminist activists still felt that they needed their own autonomous space outside both the feminist movement and the black movement (Ribeiro 1995; Caldwell 2007; Rodrigues and Prado 2010). Their experiences within the former, though difficult, gave black women activists like Nilza Iraci of Geledés what some of them referred to in interviews as *acúmulo político*, or "political experience." Their involvement in organizing within the broader women's movement would allow them to form NGOs and later to effectively use transnational strategies. Although their involvement in the women's movement was often contentious, it gave black women activists access to funding that mixed-gender black organizations could not obtain. When I asked Jurema Werneck of Criola why most of the black organizations that received international funding in the 1990s were black women's and black feminist organizations, she explained:

> How did we achieve that? Because we are part of the women's movement. Here in Brazil, the '80s was the decade of women, and we tagged along to the end of that trajectory of the strengthening of the [political] representation of women. We caught the end of that, a small part of it. . . . The women's movement was really strong, not the black women's movement. The difficulty was visible. But we were able to get some of what was left (interview, Jurema Werneck, October 2009).

Jurema added that black women's organizations like Maria Mulher, Geledés, and Criola also tended to have women among them who had the "kind of labor market skills" that only the middle class commanded. They were women with university training who often went "in and out of the women's movement," she added. While some activists in the black women's movement had been involved in organizations with black men, others followed different trajectories. This was the case with Cidinha da Silva, who entered Geledés as a professional interested in combating patriarchy and racism through a formalized organization. Ultimately, many black feminist and black women's organizations took the form of NGOs, in part because of the background of the black women involved in them, but also due to the NGO-ization of the black movement and of Brazilian civil society more generally (Alvarez 1999).

The NGO-ization of the Black Brazilian Movement

Whereas in the 1970s black organizing in Brazil took the form of attempts at grassroots mobilization, by the 1980s the tide had changed toward black NGOs (Guimarães 2001; Telles 2004). In addition to Geledés, Fala Preta, Maria Mulher, and Criola, a number of mixed-gender black NGOs emerged in this period, including the Center for the Articulation of Marginalized Populations (CEAP) (1989); the Center for the Study of Labor Relations and Inequality (CEERT) (1990); and the Steve Biko Cultural Institute (1992). While the substantive focus of these organizations varied, they shared some organizational characteristics that set them apart from earlier groups. First, they were made up primarily of professional paid staff rather than volunteer activists. As Jurema Werneck of Criola explained, "This was the first time they paid us for the work that we were doing" (interview, Werneck, October 2009).

The second difference between these new black NGOs and previous black political organizations was the question of advocacy. In this period, NGOs focusing on racial inequality—much like NGOs focused on other issues—began to produce publications aimed at policy circles as well as hire lawyers to engage in legal mobilization. This strategy would later prove important in the adoption, design, and implementation of state policies directed at the black population. The final distinctive characteristic of these organizations was the new relationship they had with black people on the ground. The NGO model required that black organizations move away from grassroots mobilization and toward providing services, away from contentious engagement with the state and toward collaboration (Treviño González 2009; dos Santos 2009). Rather than creating activists, then, black NGOs funded by international foundations produced program beneficiaries just as they also produced practical information about racial issues for these beneficiaries, and to engage in advocacy. Of course, this new relationship with the grassroots did not preclude raising the consciousness of the beneficiaries of their funded programming. However, it did mean a significant change in the nature and goals of black movement action.

This NGO-ization was only possible because of broader geopolitical changes. Brazil's military regime had previously banned all international foundations from Brazil in the belief that they threatened to undermine the dictatorship's goal to have a self-sustaining country, while also fueling discontent.[21] When the government let international foundations back into

Brazil in the mid-1980s, it fundamentally restructured civil society in the country (Lavalle and Bueno 2011). Indeed, the shift toward NGO-ization was not unique to the black movement but was symptomatic of a broader shift in Brazil's political field prompted by "the incentive provided by the growth of international funding for philanthropy" (Guimarães 2001, 17). Black women's organizations led this trend because of the professionalized profile of many black women activists involved in them. This NGO-ization of black activists and their organizations also coincided with the Unified Black Movement's shift toward political party involvement. Taken together, these transformations within the black movement meant a shift away from serious attempts to mobilize the masses. As a result, the success of Brazil's black movement no longer depended on the difficult task of fully consolidating a collective black identity or resonating deeply with the masses.[22] Instead, the task was to convince those in power—both within the state and within political parties—that race was an important issue needing serious political attention and resources.

As they won allies and began to resonate in a variety of institutions, black activists also shifted their discourse away from denunciation and toward more proactive language that emphasized addressing racial questions. As Ivanir dos Santos, the founder of the black NGO CEAP, noted in an interview, "In reality, the movement was really against racism; it wasn't about proposing things. One thing is a movement that is about denouncing, which is important, and about contestation. In the 1970s, 1980s, and the mid-1990s we were a movement of contestation" (interview, Ivanir dos Santos, October 2009).

The structural and ideological transformations within the MNU as well as the emergence of black NGOs like CEAP, Geledés, and political party–affiliated organizations such as UNEGRO and CONEN amounted to a serious reconfiguration of both the architecture and the strategies of the black movement. Instead of being made up of voluntary organizations that denounced racism through grassroots action, the bulk of black Brazilian organizations that existed in the late 1990s were formalized, professional organizations that proposed specific changes in state policy.

In the end, this trend toward professionalization and institutionalization was a double-edged sword. On the one hand, these black NGOs were at the forefront of the political process that led to affirmative action in Brazil, which suggests that NGO-ization was arguably a more effective strategy for pressuring the Brazilian state to make reforms. On the other, it meant a moving away from grassroots mobilization and consciousness raising that could have cultivated widespread support for policies like affirmative action decades later. Moreover, the professionalization of Brazil's black movement may have led to its pacification, to its moving away from the serious issues that motivated its emergence—including racialized state violence by the police and death squads especially against black youth (Smith 2013).

THE ARTICULATION OF BLACK MOVEMENTS IN COLOMBIA

The articulation of Colombia's black movement in recent decades happened under historical and political conditions very distinct from those in Brazil. Despite the fact that some forms of black resistance in Colombia can be traced back to the colonial period—including the establishment of the hemisphere's first maroon society in 1519—more explicit forms of ethnoracial resistance largely faded out in the post-independence era. In this sense, mobilization by Colombia's black population around ethno-racial identity has been a much more rare and recent phenomenon than in Brazil. Throughout the twentieth century, when black Colombians did engage in struggles, they often did so around class or region rather than mobilize as blacks (Appelbaum 2003; Helg 2004). Thus, in order to understand the articulation of Colombia's black movement in the 1990s, we must first examine these earlier modes of organizing, which in many cases morphed into what we today understand as Colombia's black movement.

One of the earliest instances of such organizing by black Colombians was the rise in the 1930s–1940s of a political movement known as Cordobismo, named after its charismatic founder, Diego Luis Córdoba, a political philosopher and congressman. Its strongest following was among the urban poor and middle classes in the Chocó, where Córdoba was himself from (Wade 1993). Córdoba became politicized while studying at the University of Antioquia and would eventually declare himself a socialist (Wade 1993). While Rausch (2003) has characterized Cordobismo as an "Afro-Colombian" movement, I contend it is better understood as a leftist liberal movement with a strong regional identity. Only if we understand any politics in which black people engage as black politics can we cast Cordobismo as a black movement. At the center of Córdoba's thinking—which was institutionalized in the Democratic Action Political Party he founded in 1933—was the need to expand the education system, particularly among the poor, and to integrate the Chocó more fundamentally into the Colombian nation. Himself an educated black congressman from a well-off family, Córdoba likely experienced different forms of racial discrimination. As such, he made important interventions in debates about racial inequality, discussing the need for equal opportunity for *Chocoanos* and for blacks throughout the country (Rausch 2003). Even so, the pillars of his political project were never explicitly racial integration or black uplift, even if that was implied.

In a similar vein, newspapers of the Chocó in this first half of the twentieth century did have content that sometimes resembled that of the black press in Brazil. However, newspapers like the *Antorcha del Chocó* were primarily concerned with regional integration, respect, fraternity, and the nation. In this, they largely expressed such ideals through a regional lens rather than an ethno-racial one, even while they did so in a context in which being from the Chocó was deeply entangled with blackness. Nevertheless, mobilizing as *Chocoanos* was not substantively the same as mobilizing as blacks. In the decades that followed, more explicitly ethno-racial movements did emerge. However, rather than arise in the country's "black region" of the Chocó, these movements developed in more unexpected places such as Cartagena, a region associated with mixedness and ambiguous blackness, as well as Antioquia, a region prized for its whiteness and industriousness.

Black Urban Intellectual Movements and the Struggle against Racism

Colombian writer Manuel Zapata Olivella was born in the small town of Lórica on Colombia's Atlantic Coast, though his family moved to Cartagena when he was a small child. He was a renaissance man of sorts, a medical doctor, an anthropologist, a novelist, and an activist, among other things. In the 1970s, he became one of the first Colombians that we know of to organize explicitly around racial identity, raising visibility about racism as well as highlighting the contributions of blacks to Colombian society. In 1974, Zapata Olivella founded the Colombian Foundation for Folkloric Research, which in addition to doing cultural productions and consciousness-raising, organized the First Congress of Black Culture of the Americas, held in Cali in 1977 (Wade 1998).[23] The event included participants from the United States, other Latin American countries, and the African continent.[24] Another influential Colombian activist in this period was Amir Smith-Córdoba, a sociologist and founder of both the Center for the Investigation and Development of Black Culture and the newspaper *Black Presence*. He deployed a mobilization strategy designed to agitate the public to think seriously about racism in all its forms, including internalized racism. As Wade (1998) holds, Smith-Córdoba "gained notoriety for selling his newspaper in the city center and loudly addressing people whom he regarded as black calling out 'Hola, negro.'" (313).[25] While this strategy was likely off-putting for many Colombians, it may have been particularly the case in Cartagena where race mixture had been prevalent and where very few people identified as black.

Both Zapata Olivella and Smith-Córdoba focused their writing and organizing on questions of black consciousness, culture, and politics, and they aimed to integrate blacks fully into Colombia's social, economic, and political life. While both were largely unsuccessful in mobilizing the masses, they did inspire later organizations like Movimiento Cimarrón, which would also emphasize equality and racial integration as well as the contributions the black population made to the country's history and development. Juan de Dios Mosquera was one of the many college educated black Colombians in attendance at the 1977 Congress in Cali. Directly following this important transnational event, he, along with other young black Colombians, created the Soweto Study Group, named after the South African township that was at the center of the anti-apartheid uprisings. The group, which consisted mostly of young students, became more politicized through reading works by Malcolm X, Fanon, Cabral, and Martin Luther King (Wade 1998). In 1982, Soweto's leaders decided to move beyond a study group and build a national organization called Cimarrón. As they did so, they did not leave behind the intellectual aspect of the project. In many ways, the organization served as a school of black consciousness, and many of the most important black activists in the country received their political education there. From its inception, the organization was largely an urban, intellectual movement highly influenced by the civil rights movement in the United States and the anti-apartheid struggles in South Africa. While some of the founders were originally from the Pacific Coast of Colombia, Cimarrón's activities were mainly in Medellín, Pereira, and Bogotá, with some activities in rural communities along the Atlantic Coast (Wade 1998).

The organization's main objective was to recapture the history of the African presence and contributions to Colombian society as a way of developing a common identity among black Colombians. While another important goal of Cimarrón was to denounce racism, racial discrimination, and inequality, the organization was mainly intellectual and cultural in nature. Its founder, Juan de Dios Mosquera Mosquera, was a teacher, and most of its activities reflected his strengths. Members read and produced material on the importance of black people in the making of the Colombian nation and tried to raise consciousness among black Colombians and the general population alike around this heritage. In this sense, Cimarrón's approach was not targeted at the state but rather at society.

Cimarrón's move toward a more explicitly political agenda in the mid-1980s came with its own problems. First, the group had to contend with an ideological context that not only denied the existence of racism but considered any discussion of race to be itself racist. Second, members had to face growing tensions within the organization around whether they should continue to focus on urban black populations or expand into rural areas on the Pacific Coast and elsewhere. This brought with it more fundamental questions around whether the problems facing blacks in Colombia should be resolved through policies of social and political integration or autonomy.

While Cimarrón began as an urban movement, their consciousness-raising work in cities like Quibdó caught the attention of young activists like Rudecindo "Yuya" Castro and Chonto Serna, who were both migrants from villages along the remote Baudó River in the Chocó. Yuya was enamored by the political discourse of Cimarrón at the time and eventually became the president of the Chocó branch of the organization. He explained his perspective on mobilization at the time:

> With him, [Chonto Serna] as members of Cimarrón we said, "We have to take the thinking of Cimarrón to the countryside." But the brother, Juan de Dios, said that was not the [right] strategy, he said that the struggle and the vindication had to be in the cities. So if I'm here and I'm seeing that the cultural identity in the rural areas is stronger than in the city, well, I strengthen the rural areas . . . but since we couldn't, we split [with Cimarrón] (interview, Rudecindo Castro, October 2008).

As tensions grew, Cimarrón divided into two lines, one urban and one rural. However, by 1985, many rural black activists had left the organization. More than a question of geography, the splintering of Cimarrón was more fundamentally about irreconcilable ways of seeing the black struggle. While Yuya, who at the time was a technology engineer living in the city of Quibdó, had been convinced that racism and discrimination against urban black populations was a problem, he also saw black rural movements as the space of the real black struggle.

As contestation over land in the Chocó between capitalists and local communities became increasingly contentious, Cimarrón Chocó turned toward these issues, which they saw as more immediate and more important. Chonto—who along with Yuya and others helped to form the Peasant Association of the Baudó River (ACABA)—explained that they had to distance themselves from Cimarrón because it refused to acknowledge that the struggle should be "territorial" (interview, Chonto Serna, March 2009). Implicit in many of these debates was the fact that Cimarron's political project, based as it was on principles of racial integration, uplift, and modernization, was somewhat incompatible with rural black movements. This tension was apparent in an interview with Juan de Dios Mosquera, who talked about the organization's challenges in the early years:

> And so the conclusion we reached in Cimarrón was that there was no consciousness here [in Colombia]. There was no mobilizing, there was no leadership. There wasn't even any acknowledgement of our humanity, no recognition that our people were in the jungle and haven't even awakened to the twenty-first century.

As this quotation illustrates, there was often a lot of slippage between Cimarrón leaders critiquing the deeply entrenched ideas of Colombia's black rural population as backward, and actually reproducing such ideas. It is no surprise, then, that urban-based black movements like Cimarrón put forth a counter-conception of Colombia's black population that highlighted their contributions to the progress of the Colombian nation. These ideas of black uplift and the conversion of black rural people into "normal" Colombians were in direct tension with the views of the Chocó branch of Cimarrón in the late 1980s. The latter felt that the organization should build the movement around the struggle for land, the preservation of black rural life, and local autonomy.[26] Ultimately, these tensions between rural and urban blackness within Cimarrón proved irreconcilable; the Chocó branch eventually left Cimarrón to work more closely with the ethno-territorial movement unfolding there and throughout Colombia's Pacific Coast.[27]

Amid these issues, Cimarrón changed its name to the National Cimarrón Movement for the Human Rights of Afro-Colombian Communities. By the end of the 1980s, the organization had also shifted its strategies. After losing the Chocó contingent of the organization, it became clear that Cimarrón could not reach its goals if it did not move more decidedly into the political arena. The special report from the Seventh Annual National Executive Council Meeting, held in 1990, captures this sentiment:

> In the last few months, we have been very successful in the diffusion of the culture of the black community of Colombia. . . . This Seventh Executive Committee meeting in Medellín is important in that it shows that we have been able to consolidate the organizing efforts of the National Black Community. In this meeting, we approved strategies for 1990 that include the necessity to adopt a more political profile . . . we think that the socio-economic and political situation needs a greater effort. If we can just create consciousness and unity in order to conquer spaces within our society, we will be more in line with the *new times* (Cimarrón, 1990).

Although it is not exactly clear what they meant by "new times," these words foreshadowed dramatic changes both within Colombia's black movement and in the broader political field. The country was embarking upon a constitutional reform process that presented a huge political opening for black organizations to push for policy reforms. However, not Cimarrón but an emergent ethno-territorial movement—made up in part by defectors of Cimarrón—led this charge and became the main protagonist in this political moment.

The Catholic Church and the Making of an Ethno-Territorial Movement

The black organizations that emerged in the 1970s and early 1980s in Colombia, Brazil, Peru, and throughout the region had a decidedly urban focus. However, by the late 1980s, such groups represented only one branch of the black movement in this region. As Cimarrón organized black youth in cities like Buenaventura and Pereira, black peasants were beginning to organize primarily in the Chocó region. In much the same way that peasant associations came to articulate their struggle as indigenous peoples' movements in the 1960s and 1970s (Yashar 2005), black rural movements throughout Latin America began to make claims more squarely in the language of ethnic rights just a decade later. This was in great part due to the role of the Catholic Church in politicizing grassroots communities in both indigenous and black areas, in the Andean region and beyond.

Colombia is the quintessential case of this articulation (Grueso et al. 1998; Restrepo 2004; Hooker 2005; Castillo 2007). The movement based in black identity that emerged in the mid-1980s in the Chocó set the pattern that other Colombian regions followed. In this period, missionary groups helped start a number of peasant associations along the various rivers that run through the Chocó, including the Rio Atrato, Rio San Juan, and Rio Baudó. The first of these was the Peasant Association of Atrato (ACIA), created amid deep concerns about and contestation over land. Nevaldo Perea of ACIA (now named COCOMACIA) explained why the association was born:

> Corporations were robbing the territory, and the government had hidden Law 2 of 1959 that declared the Pacific, the entire Pacific from top to bottom, they declared it national empty lands [state preserves]. So since they were national empty lands everyone came here and they took whatever they wanted. Everybody came and they just took things. They came from Antioquia, from Valle, from Risaralda, from every corner of the world they came to take what [the Chocó] has (interview, Nevaldo Perea, June 2009).

The intensification of capitalist expansion served as the main catalyst for organizing peasants in this region. Communities had no guarantee of land and they were afraid they would be forcibly displaced; with the help of missionary groups, they began to try to stave off these market forces (Grueso et al. 1998). Beyond ACIA, nearly all the organizations that emerged in the Chocó in this period—the Peasant Association of the Lower Atrato (OCABA), the Peasant Association of the Lower and Middle San Juan (ACADESAN), the Peasant Association of the Higher Baudó (ACABA), among others—initially talked about their struggle in terms of defending "the traditional territory of the Pacific."[28]

The Catholic Church was extremely important in the emergence of this peasant movement not just in Colombia but also in the rest of Latin America (Wade 1998; Khittel 2001; Restrepo 2004). As Restrepo (2004) highlights, by the 1980s, the core mission of the Church in Colombia and around the world was to organize the people through grassroots mobilization. This was particularly the case in the Chocó, where Claretian missionaries in the tradition of liberation theology began to develop political consciousness around land and a critique of capitalism. Zulia Mena was one of the many activists politicized through her involvement with the Diocese of Quibdó. She explained how organizing began:

> More or less around 1980 we began to be concerned. As of '83 we started to conduct workshops in peasant communities, the first of which was in the Atrato [river] in a community called Buchadó. Father Gonzalo de la Torre, who is a Claretian priest, but one who is from here in Chocó, was there. There was a priest from Germany, Uli, and then there was me, the three of us. I had just left school. I was almost 16 years old. Over there in the Atrato we gave the first workshop of peasant organizing. They had been doing five-day workshops designed to raise the consciousness among the people (interview, Zulia Mena, August 2006).

Sor Angel Mosquera, who was also politicized through the Catholic Church, highlighted that after disputes over land between a Dutch company and local communities, the Church became increasingly involved in organizing: "[The Church] saw that there's the need to develop a consciousness among the people, consciousness of their black identity and indigenous identity. Of course, there had already been some similar work done with indigenous people" (interview, Sor Angel Mosquera, March 2009).

The Church's efforts to raise the consciousness of black rural communities along Colombia's Pacific Coast were successful. In fact, nearly every activist I interviewed who had been involved in peasant organizations began his or her political trajectory in the Church. This included activists who have since distanced themselves from the Church, like Zulia Mena. The influence of the Church was also obvious because of the involvement of people like Father Emigdio and Father Sterling and nuns like Sister Aida, who were all key figures in black mobilizing since early on. Sister Aida was involved in the founding of ACADESAN and explained that in addition to consciousness-raising, the Church also offered financing that made it possible for peasant associations to scale up their organizing efforts (interview, Hermana Aida, February 2009).

These peasant organizations would eventually become what we now understand as the black rural or ethno-territorial movement in Colombia. However, they were not always explicitly ethno-racial. They were instead a nascent movement based in regional and class-based identities, even while they were made up almost entirely of black peasants.[29] Indeed, in the early years, these movements were first and foremost about defending the territory of the Pacific Coast, even if they were aware that they were also black and living in a black region. It was only later that these implicitly black peasant organizations from Colombia's Pacific Coast underwent a laborious process of articulation, and more specifically of ethnicization (Restrepo 2001). As Restrepo (2001) suggests, "more than awakening an ethnicity that had always silently been there, hiding, waiting for the right moment to make itself heard in the consciousness of the local peoples, we witnessed an arduous task unfold on multiple levels for the production of such ethnicity" (43). In this sense, the politicization of blackness as an ethnic group was a "new way to imagine the population" (Restrepo 2001, 43). The constitutional reform process catalyzed the ethnicization of black identity not only in the eyes of the Colombian state but also within the movement. While land continued to be important to the struggle, affirming ethnic identity became increasingly central to how these communities articulated their claims (Wade 1998; Restrepo 2004; Oslender 2008).

However, what developed within these peasant organizations is best understood as an intersectional struggle. As Oslender (2008) maintains, "It was there that the first direct ties between the notions of a peasant identity and blackness were articulated, and also where territory was combined with the political expression of the specific relations of black peasants" (27). These peasant movements converged with other mobilizing under way in other regions: civic strikes in Tumaco and the north of Cauca, organizing in Palenque on the Atlantic Coast. Together, these efforts would ultimately constitute Colombia's black ethno-territorial movement.

This constellation of disparate organizational processes solidified during the constitutional reform process of the early 1990s. Whereas Cimarrón continued to fight against racial discrimination and for the full integration of black Colombians in society, this new ethno-territorial movement made claims in the language of cultural difference and political autonomy. As I elaborate in detail in the following chapter, one of the defining features of this new black rural movement was the distance they maintained from urban black organizations like Cimarrón. In fact, these two tendencies within Colombia's black movement—urban black organizations that fought for the right to equality and integration, and black peasant associations that fought for the right to difference and autonomy—would prove a perpetual source of conflict within the movement, as well as between these movements and the Colombian state.

SYMBOLIC POWER AND ANTI-RACISM AS RACISM

Despite serious ideological and organizational differences between the contemporary black movements of Colombia and Brazil, activists in both countries faced the challenge of mobilizing around issues most of society saw as taboo and divisive. As a result, when black people in these two countries did begin to organize as blacks, and particularly when they did so by talking specifically about racism and racial inequality, they were often met with the full ideological force of racelessness. The idea that race was inconsequential to social life had a kind of symbolic power that made it difficult to articulate an anti-racist discourse. While such discourses of racelessness were not institutionalized into Colombia's political field in the same way they were in Brazil, statements by Colombian representatives in UN meetings in the latter half of the twentieth century reveal that they did represent the Colombian nation as devoid of ethno-racial divisions. Indeed, *mestizaje* was still a powerful organizing principle in Colombian society. Yet in both countries, ideas of racial difference and hierarchy permeated everyday life—in the media, in popular culture, in interpersonal relations, in decisions about marriage—but critiquing this situation was considered inappropriate and even unpatriotic.

Perhaps more powerful than a repressive state was the resistance among political elites and ordinary black citizens to the notion that race was a problem in their respective societies. In both cases, whites/*mestizos* were not the only ones who refused to talk critically about racial hierarchies. The very people who activists argued were racialized as inferior—blacks and mulattos—also shunned talk of race and racism. When I asked activist and former congresswoman Zulia Mena why the black movement in Colombia had not been particularly massive, she said the history of colonialism and slavery made people reluctant to identify as black:

> Nobody wants to be black because the imagery of what it means to be black comes at a serious cost. So everyone wants to whiten themselves as a way out, as a way to survive, to be recognized. As some would say, marrying a white person, or someone who was a little more mulatto was to "better the race." And even today it is still said among ignorant people (interview, Zulia Mena, August, 2006).

Zulia added, "Instead of condemning a black person because they have whitened," we have to understand it as "a form of resistance," as a way to "survive in a system that is so strong, so intelligent, so racist."[30] This refusal of people to identify firmly with blackness, is not merely the result of racial fluidity in this region or a kind of false consciousness. It suggests instead a constant awareness and internalization of racial hierarchy, which only sometimes exists alongside a public disavowal of this hierarchy. This has created a kind of "absent presence of race," a contradiction that allows for the reproduction of racial hierarchy and privilege.[31]

These ideological constraints to organizing around black identity figured prominently in my interviews with black activists in Colombia and Brazil.

This was true in the narrative of Amauri Mendes, a black Brazilian activist who was instrumental in the founding of three important black movement organizations: SINBA, IPCN, and later the MNU. In the early 1970s, every Saturday, Amauri made his way on the train to the main avenues of Rio de Janeiro's working-class and poor neighborhoods in the Baixada Flumi-nense, carrying a megaphone, a table, and written material. Among these materials was the newspaper of the Brazil-Africa Exchange (SINBA), an or-ganization that he, along with several others, had founded in 1974 to ad-dress racism in Brazilian society. The organization also sought to link their efforts to anti-colonial struggles on the African continent. Amauri ex-plained how he and his comrades in SINBA did this for nearly three years:

> We would get there and put up a stand and yell to agitate people . . . and this was something we would do because the idea was to take the message of the struggle against racism to the masses. . . . Many peo-ple hadn't heard about this. "How strange," [they thought] and they would leave. After a second time, and a third time, there were various people that would come up to us and say, "You guys are the ones that were here last week, right?" . . . Others would say, "They aren't doing anything over there, just blowing hot air!" Or, "That's not right. [Rac-ism] doesn't exist here." Sometimes they were black, sometimes they were white, but the majority of people that stopped were black. . . . They were light-skinned black mixed people, dark-skinned mixed people who could have identified as black, people who were darker than me. I'm on the light side. So people of my complexion or lighter in Brazil, they could dodge blackness, you know? . . . Because being black was much more devalued than it is today, they were ashamed of being black. We would tell them that. We would say, "We shouldn't be ashamed of being black." And we would say this with a megaphone in our hand, shout it. It was a way to . . . well, we would sort of verbally attack people, at least that's how many people felt, attacked (inter-view, Amauri Mendes, October 2009).

Amauri's recounting of his experience organizing around blackness and against racism highlights a number of similarities between the struggles of Co-lombian and Brazilian black activists in the 1970s–1980s. First, given the ideo-logical context in which they were embedded, activists in both cases deployed similar strategies, circulating newspapers and trying to raise awareness about racism in public spaces. Moreover, as activists in both countries explained to me, they felt the ideological impediments to their organizing on an everyday basis as they encountered the black and brown masses who saw the struggle against racism as incompatible with their own identities and as a nonissue in their societies. In the most extreme cases, mobilizing around black identity and against racism opened activists up to the charge of being racists themselves, guilty of importing U.S.-style racism into their respective countries.

YOU ARE THE RACISTS!

The experiences of Amauri Mendes in Brazil and Amir Smith-Córdoba in Colombia show the many parallels between the political and social fields of Colombia and Brazil in this period. Racelessness had begun to function as what Goldberg (2002) calls a "civic religion" of sorts. These two activists' work was emblematic of the black political organizations that emerged in both: small organizations made up mainly of lower middle class blacks from urban areas who were determined to challenge racism and black marginalization. In doing so, they tried to mobilize people, one person at a time, against incredible ideological odds: indeed, anti-racism was recast not only as taboo but as itself racist. In the case of Brazil, the inverting of anti-racism into racism had deep historical roots. As Alberto (2011) notes:

> The problem with *negro* theater, *negro* newspapers, and *negro* clubs, to critics like these, was not just that they undermined the idea that Brazil was truly a society without racism and therefore without need for social transformation. Perhaps more ominously, groups or publications built around distinctly *negro* racial identities threatened the increasingly widespread idea of a unified Brazilian identity blessed by the absence of racial divisions (196).

Thus, beyond making people feel uncomfortable, black activists in both countries had to face charges that they were the racists.[32]

The subtext of this claim that black activists were dividing the Brazilian nation was that they were also importing race-talk, and even racism, from the United States. In the 1960s, at the same time the military regime removed the race/color question from the national census, military and naval intelligence labeled a number of black organizations as "black racist groups." They argued that these groups promoted a kind of "black racism" that was—in a Brazilian context—designed to "foment racial disaggregation" (Alberto 2011, 270). By talking about the Brazilian nation as primarily defined by its race mixture, or *mestiçagem*, the military dictatorship effectively prohibited race as legitimate grounds for identity formation or political claims making.

The state was not the primary impediment to organizing an effective black movement: Brazilian society also largely saw black political organizations as racist. One case in point was Ilê Aiyê, the Afrocentric carnival group, or *bloco afro*, that emerged in the 1970s in Bahia. At the time, people who wanted to march with a particular carnival school in Salvador had to fill out an application that typically asked for a photo and information on what neighborhood they lived in. This was widely known to be a discriminatory practice used to ensure that elite carnival groups could weed out the less desirable who had somehow managed to save enough money to join their groups (Guerreiro 2000). While this was about class, it was also heavily intertwined with racial discrimination as schools also used applicant photographs to guarantee that only *gente bonita*, or "beautiful people" (a euphemism for white, middle-class people), would be approved. Groups like Ilê Aiyê offered a radical critique of such practices and a challenge to Brazil's purported racial democracy more generally.

Over time, the group would come to be part of Salvador's cultural landscape and be known for their African aesthetics and lyrics that celebrated blackness. However, in the beginning they were heavily criticized for their lyrics, their dress, and their policy of allowing only black people to parade with them. In February 1975, the largest circulating newspaper in the state, *A Tarde*, published an article titled "Racist Carnival Group Hits a Low Note." It read:

> Carrying posters with expressions such as "Black World, Black Power, Black for you," etc., the carnival group Ile Aiyê—nicknamed the "Carnival Group of Racism"—performed an ugly spectacle in this year's carnival. Because racism is prohibited in this country, we have to hope that the members of Ilê Aiyê come back in a different way next year, in a way that reflects the natural liberation and instinct of carnival. We are happy that we do not have a racial problem. That is one of the great prides and happiness of the Brazilian people, the harmony that reins in the divisions between different ethnicities.[33]

It was common for the state, the media, and the broader Brazilian population to interpret groups like Ilê who raised awareness about racism and promoted a positive image of blackness as racist. While Bailey (2009) has argued that the recognition of racism was much more prevalent in Brazilian society than we once thought, the assertion of black pride and the explicit denunciation of racism were still largely shunned (Hanchard 1994). As the preceding newspaper article suggests, such expressions were considered racist and fundamentally unpatriotic.

Explicit critiques of racial inequality were also seen as racist in neighboring Colombia. Afro-Colombian activist Ivan Sinisterra discussed how difficult it was for Cimarrón to organize in the early years precisely because of this disconnect between the way that black activists and other people understood Colombian society. "Cimarrón was the movement that began to discuss and raise visibility about racism as a conflict that affects our lives. Everyone would tell us that we were the racists, even our own people! They would compare and say 'in the United States, they hit you, they kill you, not here! Here, we are equal'" (interview, Ivan Sinisterra, March 2009). Juan de Dios—also of Cimarrón—echoed this sentiment: "We started by studying, learning, and understanding Afro-Colombian history, to value things like Africanness, and we created a method for studying it. There was nothing like this at the time. Everyone would tell us that we were the racist ones for organizing as *afros*" (interview, Juan de Dios Mosquera, July 2006).[34]

The idea that critiquing racism was incompatible with, and even an act against, the Colombian nation had deep roots.[35] Discourses of *mestizo* republicanism in Colombia, much like racial democracy in Brazil, amounted to a state of racelessness that allowed for the silencing of debate about historic or contemporary forms of racism. As such, racial critique was often relegated to the private sphere (Lasso 2007).

In both cases, this happened with the complicity of the state. Latin American states are hardly reservoirs of the kind of symbolic power that Bourdieu (1999) spoke of when he argued that state embodies the highest concentration of symbolic power (63). Their inability to build national militaries capable of interstate war, to maintain a monopoly on the legitimate use of violence, to manage their sometimes-vast territories—as well as their lack of capacity to measure, tax, or provide services for their populations—have led scholars to characterize Latin America as a region of weak states (Centeno 2002). Yet while the state capacity of Latin American states was and continues to be lacking, their ability to construct nationalist identities that did penetrate their societies has been quite remarkable. By the early twentieth century, political elites throughout the region had invested in the project of imagining the nation, both by solidifying nationalist doctrine and creating ministries of education and culture (Centeno and Ferraro 2013). Thus, while the fiscal and military capacity of Latin American states was lacking, they still can be said to possess a great deal of symbolic power.

In both explicit and implicit ways, Latin American elites used such symbolic power to construct an ideological context in which ethno-racial identity was not only an illegitimate political category but a fundamentally unpatriotic one. In the face of these challenges, black activists in Colombia and Brazil looked outward to anti-racist struggles in the United States, Africa, and other parts of Latin America in order to sustain their movements.

PAN-AFRICANISM AND THE GLOBAL DIMENSIONS OF BLACK STRUGGLE

Activists did not fight racism in Colombia and Brazil in a vacuum. Rather, the discourses, strategies, and even aesthetics of the organizations signaled the inspiration they found in struggles for decolonization in Africa and the civil rights and Black Power movements in the United States. As a result, the activists with whom I spoke often constructed ideas of a global black community facing a set of issues that were not unique to a particular nation. As Hanchard (2003) rightfully argues, these movements should be seen as constructing an "imagined community" that is at once "multinational, multilingual, ideologically and culturally plural" (22). In Brazil, this kind of black transnationalism has its origins in the 1920s with organizations like the Brazilian Black Front and the many black Brazilian newspapers that sustained dialogue with the black press in the United States (Leite 1992; Hanchard 2003; Pereira 2013).

There is no denying that U.S. black movements greatly influenced black movements in Colombia and Brazil. This took many forms, including the use of organizational names that referenced struggles in other sites of the African Diaspora as well as the use of visual references to Malcolm X, Martin Luther King, Angela Davis, and the Black Panthers. These nods to struggles elsewhere also expressed themselves in the form of aesthetics. The use of the "afro" hairstyle, popularized by U.S. black artists and activists in the 1970s and appropriately called a "black power" (in English) in Brazil up to this day is merely one example of this. Even so, activists emphasized how these diasporic political connections were never simply about influence from North to South. Nor were they exclusively references to black movements in the United States (Pereira 2013). As Reginald Bispo of the MNU in Brazil explained, "After observing from a distance news about the struggle for liberation and decolonization in Africa, when I was 14 or 15 years old, and about the struggle for civil rights in the United States, I had special sympathy for Malcolm X and the Black Panthers that helped me to define my vision related to things" (interview, Reginaldo Bispo, November 2010). Bispo ultimately chose a path of black Trotskyism, which was very much a product of the local processes of politicization under way in São Paulo and Brazil more generally.

Anti-colonial struggles on the African continent and the writings of African and Caribbean intellectuals were also an important source of inspiration for black activists in both Colombia and Brazil. This is particularly evident in the names of the organizations that were founded in this period, including the Brazil-Africa Exchange Society (Brazil) and the Soweto Study Group (Colombia).[36] When I asked Juan de Dios Mosquera why he named the organization after Soweto, he explained, "The struggle in South Africa influenced us a lot, the debates they had within the movement in South Africa and the Negritude movement also influenced us, Amilcar Cabral, Aimé Césaire, also Frantz Fanon. The process of decolonization in Africa influenced us a lot" (interview, Juan de Dios Mosquera, July 2006). It was only fitting, then, that Afro-Brazilian activist Amauri Mendes named his first son after Amilcar Cabral, and, in a similar fashion, Afro-Colombian leader Ivan Sinisterra named his son after Malcolm X.

While many of these linkages were symbolic in nature, there were key moments of tangible exchange, as was the case with the 1977 First Congress of Black Culture of the Americas in Cali, Colombia, as well as the first meetings of the Pastoral Afroamericana held in Buenaventura, Colombia (1980), and Esmeraldas, Ecuador (1983). Additionally, as Pereira (2013) reports, Stokely Carmichael of the Student Nonviolent Coordinating Committee (SNCC) and later of the Black Panther Party visited Brazil in 1988. He was received by the Institute for Research on Black Culture (IPCN), which was the epicenter of such transnational exchanges. As activist Ruth Pinheiro put it, it was an institution that had a relationship with the whole world. "So if I knew someone was arriving [from outside Brazil], I would take them to IPCN" (interview, Ruth Pinheiro, October 2009).

This solidarity that black activists in Brazil and Colombia felt with black people around the globe came from a belief not only that they had a shared history but also that they continued to face some of the same problems.[37] As black Colombian activist Dionicio Miranda of San Basilio de Palenque—one of the first maroon societies in the western hemisphere—explained:

> We believe that regardless of where the diaspora is, our well-being is linked. We are all Afro-descendants, Afro-descendants from the United States, Afro-descendants from Colombia, Afro-descendants from Uruguay, from Peru, from Panama, from Brazil, etc. I mean we are facing the same challenges in society, in the nations in which we find ourselves immersed (interview, Dionicio Miranda, October 2008).[38]

Many of the activists I interviewed in Colombia shared this view. In so doing, they subscribed to an idea of black politics as inherently global because of both the global nature of anti-black racism and the shared realities of socioeconomic and political marginalization of blacks throughout the western hemisphere.[39]

Yet even while activists in Colombia and Brazil saw similarities between the material realities of black populations in their countries and elsewhere, they were also very much aware of differences. As a result, they navigated a fine line between being inspired by U.S. black movements without importing their logic wholesale, between learning lessons from the strategies they used, without assuming that such strategies would have equal resonance in Colombia or Brazil. Juan de Dios Mosquera—who was very much inspired by U.S. civil rights and who was often accused of importing such discourses into Colombia—talked about the delicate balancing act involved:

> So those texts allowed us to understand Malcolm X, Martin Luther King, the Black Panthers, the Black Power Movement, that whole move-

ment. The black revolution in the United States allowed us to have a vision . . . but we said we cannot apply the concept of racism from the United States and that struggle here because this is a different context. We have to create a vision, an understanding of here, one that is enriched with [the experience of black movements in] the United States, but also with South Africa, which also influenced us (interview, Juan de Dios Mosquera, July 2006).

This difference was rooted in state *mestizaje*, which black activists in Colombia and Brazil saw as mystifying racism in their societies. The particularities of this ideological context, they argued, required them to approach racial inequality and racism in ways distinct from those employed in places like the United States, where racism was explicitly institutionalized. Indeed, the very fact that activists were engaged in a kind of mobilization that aimed to convince people to identify as black reflected their local realities of racial fluidity and whitening logics. In the end, though, it was precisely these diasporic connections that opened black activists in both Colombia and Brazil to the critique that they were importing racism from the United States.

CONCLUSION

It is not surprising that black Colombians and Brazilians did not always organize their political struggles primarily or exclusively around ethnoracial identity. It also makes sense that black identity wasn't always the most politicized identity among blacks, given that class and gender inequalities were also heavily structuring their lived realities.[40] It was more expected that they would engage in what Scott (1990) called infrapolitics, or "the circumspect struggle waged daily by subordinate groups" that lies beyond visible and recognizable forms of resistance. In the ideological contexts of Colombia and Brazil, would-be activists had to navigate a formally colorblind political field dominated by the idea that critiquing racial inequality was unwarranted at best and racist at worst.

Even so, the 1970s and 1980s marked the emergence of a contemporary black movement made up of diverse organizations in both countries. In this chapter, I have argued that this articulation happened through several overlapping political processes. On the one hand, there were urban organizations primarily concerned with questions of race and racism. On the other, black activists involved in student, peasant, and women's struggles came to see blackness as a salient political identity. When they came to articulate their struggle as decidedly black, they did not necessarily leave behind the political identities and banners for which they had fought previously. In fact, many of the organizations that brought about racial equality policies might be called intersectional, like the black peasant associations that proved critical to the adoption of Law 70 in Colombia and the black feminist organizations that promoted affirmative action and racial equality policies in Brazil.

Nevertheless, at the end of the 1980s, political elites and society writ large in Colombia and Brazil continued to understand black political organizations as illegitimate, divisive, and unpatriotic. These countries' political fields continued to be dominated by the idea that racial critique was antithetical to democracy, rather than something that could possibly deepen it. Even if the activists I discussed here had not yet achieved the substantial social and political change they hoped for, they were still very important to the trajectory of black organizing in both countries. I will argue in the following chapters that these same black organizations were central to the adoption of ethno-racial legislation a few years later, against all odds. In the years leading up to these reforms, both Brazil and Colombia's black movements remained small, isolated entities with very little impact on popular understandings of race and identity and even less political traction. Yet, beginning in the late 1980s, things began to change dramatically. Not only did blackness become a legitimate category of political struggle in the eyes of the state, but the black movement in each country became increasingly incorporated into formal political institutions and state bureaucracies in unprecedented ways. How do we explain these transformations?

In the next two chapters, I grapple with this paradoxical shift from the illegitimacy of black political movements to the institutionalization of black political subjects in the law, state bureaucracies, and political discourse in these two cases. I show how three important changes produced the conditions of possibility for making ethno-racial claims on the Colombian and Brazilian states. First were changes in the strategies of black movements. Here, I have charted the articulation of a politicized black identity through multiple paths. While this was a necessary step in the making of black rights, so too was the movements' shift toward making more concrete demands on the state. The second important factor was the consolidation of a robust set of international institutions, global discourses, and norms that I argue constitute a global ethno-racial political field. The third and final factor had to do with changes in the domestic political field in each case. Indeed, the consolidation of a global political field oriented around ethno-racial issues would not have had the impact it did on ethno-racial policy in Colombia and Brazil in the 1990s had it not converged with dramatic changes in the political fields of these countries, producing what I call the "multicultural alignment."

CHAPTER FOUR

THE MULTICULTURAL ALIGNMENT

An element of mystique often crept into my conversations with key actors about the constitutional recognition of black communities in both Colombia and Brazil. When I interviewed activists, academics, and state officials who were directly involved, they typically described the recognition as a "huge, unexpected goal," a fluke, and used terms like "undercover," "low-key," and "unperceived." They even suggested that Transitory Article 55 in Colombia's 1991 constitution—which mandated the 1993 Law of Black Communities—had somehow "passed under the radar." In Brazil, the first Afro-Brazilian Senator and long-time advocate for racial equality within congress, Benedita da Silva, used similar language:

> The chapter [on *quilombos*] that was most discussed was land reform. That was the big chapter, and within that land reform they discussed the issue of indigenous lands. *Quilombos*, well, they didn't give them much attention. And that's how we were able to put it in there, and it is in the constitution: land for the descendants of *quilombos*. That is black lands. But I believe that it passed because they didn't have. . . . Well, at that moment they were so eager [to deal with] the indigenous issue that they didn't even feel it happen (interview, Benedita da Silva, February 2014).

Black Brazilian activist Flavio Jorge echoed this sentiment by suggesting that nobody, not even those in the black movement, had a real sense of the "dimension" of the *quilombo* issue at the time of constitutional reform. He explained that "the very ignorance of congress members, of the legislators at that time, made it so that [the *quilombo* land titling] law was approved" (interview, Flavio Jorge, May 2010). Other activists explained how the provision must have been included when the constituents were dead tired.

Implicit, and sometimes explicit, in this recounting was the sense that in neither case did political elites fully grasp what was at stake in recognizing such rights. The archival record substantiates this perspective. Nowhere in the constituent assembly transcripts does the relatively short debate around *quilombo* territorial rights reflect a deep understanding of their magnitude or geographic reach.[1] As Arruti (1998) notes when considering Provisional Article 68, which recognized *quilombo* rights, it seemed that state officials thought they were dealing with an insignificant number of *quilombos*, no more than twenty throughout Brazil (29). The fact that both the Brazilian and Colombian states have since either slowed down or scaled back titling also suggests that political elites did not quite know what exactly they were getting into. Yet, as Benedita da Silva also highlighted, the state had to confront the reality of these reforms once they were written into constitutions. "It was only after the fact that they saw what was in the constitution. At the time of implementation, we would go to battle it out with them and say, 'No, no, no, we have to implement this chapter because, look, here it says. . . . It's right there.' They didn't even realize it!" (interview, Benedita da Silva, February 2014).

How could legislators not pay attention to something as important as rights to land and natural resources? In Colombia, the magnitude of these reforms is particularly clear. The recognition of collective territory for indigenous peoples and black communities meant the biggest agrarian reform in that country's history.[2] Were the political elites involved in the constitutional reform process simply ignorant about what was at stake in granting territory to these communities, as some have suggested? If not, how else do we explain such monumental gains?

I argue this *golazo*[3] depended in part on the global field in which these ethno-racial reforms emerged. These transformations in how Latin American states approached ethno-racial questions happened amid the emergence of a global ethno-racial field made up of institutions, discourses, norms, and transnational strategies, all oriented around multiculturalism with a specific interest in the plight of indigenous peoples around the world. In table 4.1, I map out in some detail the key elements of the ethno-racial political field and particularly those elements that became increasingly salient in discussions around multiculturalism and racial equality in Colombia and Brazil. I do not intend the table to provide a comprehensive genealogy of the global ethno-racial field, nor do I mean it to be an exhaustive list of the actors that constitute that field. Instead, I aim to make the concept of global fields somewhat less abstract by introducing some of the key actors and elements that will emerge more prominently in the rest of this chapter and book.

POLITICAL FIELD ALIGNMENT AROUND MULTICULTURALISM

The political field in which Brazil and Colombia's black movements were embedded in the 1980s–1990s was dominated not only by each country's white/*mestizo* political elites but also by emergent norms around multicul-

TABLE 4.1. GLOBAL ETHNO-RACIAL POLITICAL FIELD

	SUPRA-NATIONAL	CIVIL SOCIETY
Institutional Aspects of the Field	*International Institutions (ECLAC)*	*Transnational Networks Alianza Estratégica*
	Gender, Ethnicity & Health Unit of Pan-American Health Organization (PAHO) Inter-Agency Consultation on Race in Latin America and the Caribbean (IAC) Office of the High Commissioner for Human Rights UN Committee on the Elimination of All Forms of Racial Discrimination United Nations Development Programme (UNDP) UNESCO United Nations Permanent Forum on Indigenous Issues (UNPFII) World Bank Social Development Unit	The Amazon Basin Dwellers' Federation Cultural Survival Fondo Indígena Ford Foundation Inter-American Institute of Human Rights International Human Rights Law Group (Global Rights) International Work Group on Indigenous Affairs (IWGIA) Mexican Solidarity Network (Zapatista) Pastoral Indígena/Afro Southern Education Foundation Transafrica Forum Washington Office on Latin America (WOLA)
Cultural Aspects of the Political Field	*Global Discourses/Norms*	*Transnational Repertoires of Action*
	Convention on the Elimination of All Forms of Racism (CERD) (1963) Durban Plan of Action (2001) ILO Convention 169 (1989) UN Declaration on the Rights of Indigenous Peoples (2007)	Accountability politics* Informational politics* Leverage politics* Symbolic politics (Pan-Indigeneity, Pan-Africanism)*

*Taken from Keck and Sikkink (1998)

turalism, international law, and questions of democratization. While do-mestic politics opened the possibilities for making new kinds of claims on the Colombian and Brazilian states, such demands were legible for several reasons that speak to the power of international influence. First, there was a global trend toward recognizing "collective rights" in ways that did not contradict the framework of liberal constitutions (Van Cott 2002). This al-lowed black populations to claim collective rights within the legal frame-work of the new constitutions being consolidated. Second, international actors and institutions began to think very differently about democracy and social inclusion. Perhaps most importantly, international conventions were influential in Latin America (Van Cott 2002). In fact, they often acted as blueprints for including provisions for indigenous peoples in new constitu-tions throughout the region.[4]

Latin America's increasing adoption of multicultural policies in the last few decades links directly to the human rights revolution and the develop-ment of global policy norms around racial equality in the post–World War II period (Kymlicka 2007). While this process took full shape in the 1980s, it really began as early as the 1960s with a number of specific international initiatives. These included the creation of the Working Group on Indige-nous Populations (1982) and the Program on Indigenous Peoples within the UN High Commissioner's Office for Human Rights.[5] In 1993, the UN Gen-eral Assembly declared 1995–2005 the "First International Decade on the World's Indigenous Peoples." All these efforts aimed to create mechanisms within international institutions to guarantee the rights of indigenous peo-ples, especially where their respective states were unwilling to recognize such rights (Williams 1990; Van Cott 2000). This emergent global ethno-racial field was made up not only of agencies, such as the UN, which shifted their focus to indigenous rights, but also of new international institutions like the Fondo Indígena (1992), created with the explicit goal of address-ing these issues. These institutions and others, like Survival International, which had existed for decades, joined to constitute a web of transnational advocacy around indigenous rights.

The World Bank also began incorporating indigenous-specific program-ming through its Latin America and Caribbean Region's Environment Di-vision in the late 1980s; later, it made such programming a key component of its Social Development Unit. In order to do this, rather than hire only economists, the World Bank also began to contract with anthropologists who specialized in indigenous culture. The World Bank intended its new focus on indigenous communities to be a departure from its previous pol-icies aimed at universal "poverty reduction," which, somewhat ironically, had worsened the lives of indigenous peoples around the globe (Dwyer 1990; Brysk 2000). Structural adjustment and other austerity policies as well as large-scale development projects had displaced and dispossessed indigenous communities throughout Latin America. In part because of this pressure, these institutions began to change their policies. Among other things, the World Bank—alongside other international institutions—began to give aid to Latin American governments throughout the 1990s to demarcate and title collective ethnic territories.[6] The motives of such programs were likely multiple. Among other things, by investing in social inclusion, these programs sought to show a softer side of these institutions.

This was possible, in part, because of the work and negotiations within the World Bank of people like anthropologist Shelton "Sandy" Davis. Sandy was one of the first anthropologists to join the bank and quickly became known within the bank and the DC policy community as the "staunchest advocate" for indigenous peoples.[7] Before joining the bank, Sandy became known in academia for his commitment to "public-interest anthropology" for his work with indigenous communities in Brazil's lowlands.[8] As one of his colleagues explained:

> I was thrilled in 1987 when Sandy agreed to join the very first Social and Environmental Division of LAC [the Latin American and Caribbean Region]. We fielded the Bank's strongest social science team at the time, namely Sandy and Maritta Koch-Weser. Between them they forcefully implemented the Bank's Indigenous Peoples Policy, such that a year or so later the Brazilian Government told us that LAC had financed more than half of all Brazil's Indigenous Reserves![9]

Such policies, though, were not without their ambiguities. The World Bank's new focus on indigenous and black rural communities also often existed alongside other policies that continued to be devastating for these groups.

Beyond the World Bank, nearly every major development institution in the Western Hemisphere also turned their attention to ethnic rights. In so doing, they too focused almost exclusively on the plight of indigenous peoples. This included special units and programs within the Inter-American Development Bank, the Economic Commission for Latin America and the Caribbean (ECLAC), the Organization of American States (OAS), the Pan-American Health Organization (PAHO), and the Inter-American Foundation, all in the 1980s–1990s. With these institutions came international conventions and global policy norms that became important legal instruments for indigenous, and later black, communities in Latin America. The OAS, for example, started a working group in 1989 that was charged with drafting the American Declaration on the Rights of Indigenous Peoples. It was finally approved in September 1995. The most significant legal instrument of this kind, however, was ILO Convention 169 on Indigenous and Tribal Peoples. More generally, the global diffusion of policy norms from the United States and Western Europe around multiculturalism and human rights were important in the recognition of indigenous rights in Latin America (Van Cott 2007).

However, if we look more closely, this is far from a story of influence from North to South. International development and human rights institutions began to take an interest in collective ethnic rights, and particularly indigenous rights, in great part as a response to pressure by movements around the globe. Indigenous movements, in particular, had accused these institutions of marginalizing their issues for decades (Williams 1990; Hale 2002). Rather than simple diffusion, the emergence of indigenous rights in international legal discourse was a "direct response to the consciousness-raising efforts of indigenous people in international human rights forums" (Williams 1990, 665). Beginning in the late 1980s, indigenous organizations garnered international support by making their voices heard in highly publicized domestic events—state crises in Ecuador, public inauguration of the North American Free Trade Agreement—as well as international forums like the quincentenary celebrations of the "discovery" of Latin American countries, United Nations meetings, and the Nobel Peace Prize ceremony in 1992 (Hale 2002, 485). International institutions and norms that came as a result of indigenous mobilization would have serious implications on how black populations were understood and ultimately included in the new constitutions of Colombia and Brazil.

Much like the international institutions I mentioned earlier, transnational advocacy networks dedicated to ethnic rights emerged in response to growing threats against the livelihood of indigenous communities. As early as the 1960s, a number of new transnational advocacy networks began to develop. They were followed by international institutions like Cultural Survival (1972), the International Work Group on Indigenous Affairs (IWGIA, 1968), and later the Fondo Indígena (1992) and the Mexican Solidarity Network (1998), as well as pan-indigenous networks like Pastoral Indígena (1969) and the Amazon Basin Dwellers' Federation (COICA, 1984). Furthermore, human rights organizations like the Inter-American Institute of Human Rights and the Washington Office on Latin America (WOLA) also turned their attention to indigenous rights.

The global ethno-racial field consists of these material features, including the institutions that make it up and the actors involved in contestation within it. The field is also discursively constituted. In other words, it is a terrain of ideological struggle, a space in which the very categories of representation are contested. This conceptualization of fields is akin to what David Scott (2004) calls a "problem space," "an ensemble of questions and answers around which a horizon of identifiable stakes (conceptual as well as ideological-political stakes) hangs" (4). The global ethno-racial field can be thought of as a problem space initially oriented around questions of cultural protection and the rights of indigenous peoples and only later around the plight of Afro-descendant populations. This discursive space—concretized in international norms and conventions along with the other aspects of the political field—had serious symbolic power in domestic debates around constitutional reform in both Colombia and Brazil.[10] As Murray Li (2004) has suggested in her work on indigeneity in Indonesia, "There are moments in which global and local agendas have been conjoined in a common purpose, and presented within a common discursive frame" (326). This may be particularly true in cases like Colombia where the state is especially weak (Centeno 2002), and where symbolic power is just as likely to come from outside than from within the nation. Thus, rather than thinking of such ideas as imposition, imperialism, or contamination of an otherwise contained national field, I find it more useful to think of them as part of a widespread process of articulation and alignment.

In this chapter, I analyze archival material in order to uncover the process that led to the recognition of specific rights for black communities in Brazil and Colombia's recent constitutions.[11] More specifically, I look at the making of Provisional Article 68 in Brazil and Provisional Article 55 in Colombia, both of which grant black people ethnic and territorial rights. Given the limited ability of black movements in both countries to mobilize the masses, I examine the important interactions among black activists, political elites, and local and international "experts" on ethno-racial questions, as well as global discourses that were central to understanding this shift. While these constitutional reform processes did provide key political openings for black activists in Colombia and Brazil, constitutional reform itself was not enough to guarantee the adoption of specific rights and policies for black populations. Instead, black movements in both countries had to seize upon a multicultural alignment that involved the convergence of these constitutional reform processes and the consolidation of a global ethno-racial field.

In this multicultural alignment, only certain kinds of blackness would fit into the category of the multicultural subject, while others would remain either illegible or deemed incompatible with this push toward further democratization. Indeed, the black subject identified in multicultural constitutions throughout Latin America did not include the general black population, but specific subsets like *quilombos* in Brazil and black rural communities on the Pacific Coast of Colombia. In both cases, this specific recognition happened despite the fact that black organizations pushed for policies aimed both at specific rural black communities and the black population more broadly. In this way, this first wave of institutionalizing black political subjects was about both the opening of possibilities for the adoption of unprecedented multicultural reforms in each country and the closure of other types of claims—namely, those of racial equality.

THE MULTICULTURAL ALIGNMENT IN BRAZIL

Brazil's constitutional reform came as part of a relatively slow process of democratic transition after twenty years of repressive military dictatorship. Such democratization, which has come to be known in Brazil as the *abertura,* or "opening," lasted some sixteen years. It happened as the result of both internal military and political party dynamics, as well as growing pressures of democratization from below. It culminated with the country's first free elections and the 1988 constitution (Hagopian 1990; Mainwaring 1999).

While scholars have rightfully questioned the depth of this initial phase of democratization in Brazil, it undeniably entailed a radical redefinition of the Brazilian nation and particularly of the relationship between the state and civil society.[12] The constitutional reform process began in July 1985 and took nearly three years. The first step was when President Jose Sarney named the Provisional Commission on Constitutional Studies, a body of business leaders, congress members, union leaders, and academics that became known as the Arinos Commission.[13] Among the fifty members of the commission there were only two women, and Helio Santos was the only black Brazilian. A number of newspaper articles published at the time noted this racial and gender imbalance, while others tended to downplay it with headlines like "Minorities Seek to Occupy Space," "Blacks Have a Representative," and "Feminists Will Be Heard."[14] Also on the commission was Gilberto Freyre, the nationalist thinker known as the father of racial democracy, whom I discussed in previous chapters.

However, amid a crisis of leadership, Ulysses Guimarães, president of Brazil's Chamber of Deputies and a vocal opponent of the dictatorship, named another, more representative commission to begin the process of constitutional reform. This led to the election of 594 congress members to Brazil's National Constituent Assembly (ANC) who were charged with writing Brazil's new Magna Carta beginning in 1986.[15]

The National Constituent Assembly and Ethno-Racial Rights

Among the candidates to the ANC was the long-time activist Abdias do Nascimento, who ran on an anti-racism platform. In August 1986, *Folha de São Paulo* published an article titled "Blacks and the Constitutional Reform: Hoping for Racial Democracy" highlighting Nascimento's candidacy:

> The priorities of Abdias do Nascimento, also a candidate from the Democratic Labor Party, turns to blacks. He proposes an act of compensation "for blacks chained up in Africa and dumped into Brazil"

in the constitution. He also proposes the introduction of an item condemning racism and guaranteeing blacks an equality of rights and opportunities in relation to whites. Abdias is also asking for the recognition of black religions and the introduction of the History of Africa in the educational curricula.[16]

While Abdias did not win a seat on the ANC, Afro-Brazilian constituents Carlos "Caó" Alberto, Paulo Paim, and especially Benedita da Silva—Brazil's first black woman senator—became some of the main voices of antiracism and black inclusion in this process.[17]

Equally as important, just as the constituents geared up for what would be a nearly two-year task, black political organizations throughout Brazil began to organize around the constitutional reform process. They focused their efforts on constructing a united platform and lobbying allies within the ANC like Benedita da Silva. The height of such mobilization happened in August 1987, when the movement held the National Convention of Blacks for the Constituent Assembly in Brasília. The Unified Black Movement (MNU) organized the meeting, though they intended to bring together the entire black movement and develop a unified, coherent platform and set of demands for the new constitution. As such, MNU leaders invited 580 black movement organizations.[18] In the end, a little over 200 people participated in the convention, including representatives from local MNU chapters, representatives of about a dozen other black organizations, labor union activists, as well as people representing political parties and neighborhood/*favela* associations. Representatives of state agencies like the Council for the Black Community of São Paulo (CCDN) and the National Council on Women also attended.

Ultimately, participants representing sixty-three entities consecrated their demands by signing a final declaration that made clear on whose behalf they were advocating. It explained: "*Negros* encapsulates all of those that have phenotypic or genetic characteristics of the African People that were brought here for the purposes of slave labor."[19] These activists' conception of *negro* contrasted with Brazil's dominant discourses of race mixture and racial ambiguity, in which whites often invoked their African heritage, or *pé na cozinha*, often to subvert racial critique.[20] The declaration emphasized phenotype rather than culture and made an implicit demand for reparations for the violence committed under the slave system rather than claiming cultural protection; the language Afro-Colombian activists used in their constitutional reform process just three years later was radically different.

The August manifesto also outlined a set of critiques of the constitutional reform process itself as an inherently nondemocratic and exclusionary space:

> We are conscious of the fact that the 1987 Constituent Assembly will not include the democratic participation of Brazil, since the "group" that is charged with creating our new Magna Carta is a product of alliances between the elites that have always dominated, and consequently, have determined the economic and cultural destiny of the nation.

Nevertheless, the activists convened in Brasília that August made a strategic decision to participate in the constitutional reform process rather than boycott or otherwise delegitimize it. This was made explicit in the declaration: "As blacks, we understand that as a politically defined ethno-social group within this immense multi-ethnic country of Brazil, we need to collectively bring our needs to the debate." The way they did this, though, was not through disruptive protest as we might expect, but through lobbying. This included delivering the declaration to each of the subcommissions within the constituent assembly, pressuring individual constituents to take on the issue, and even collaborating directly with constituent Benedita da Silva's office.

The declaration read like a manifesto; it included a section on rights and guarantees as well as subsections on police violence, health and quality of life, women, youth, education, culture, work, international relations, and land rights for *quilombos*.[21] Surprisingly, the National Constituent Assembly conducted a great deal of discussion around many of these issues. Though, only two of these demands were ultimately included in Brazil's 1988 constitution: racism was criminalized, and *quilombos* were guaranteed territorial rights. Of all of the demands, why were these two ultimately included? *Quilombo* rights were a relatively new black movement demand and had been included in the August declaration only after much negotiation within the black movement (interview, Luiz Alves, June 2010). To understand the inclusion of these provisions—as well as the exclusion of others—I analyze the transcripts of the Subcommission on Blacks, Indigenous Peoples, the Disabled, and Minorities and draw on interviews with a few key people involved in the constitutional reform process.

The Subcommission on Blacks, Indigenous Peoples, the Disabled, and Minorities

The ANC involved months of philosophical and political debates among legislators, intellectuals, and civil society representatives about what Brazil's new version of democracy should look like. Reading the ANC transcripts, one can sense optimism bordering on romanticism about the possibilities of transcending the many entrenched social cleavages and deep political and economic problems that the country faced. The fact that these discussions about redefining the Brazilian nation took place against the backdrop of the centennial of abolition presented the black movement with both ironies and opportunities to discuss historic injustice and ongoing racial inequality and discrimination in the country. The structure of the ANC was complex. It included a total of twenty-four subcommissions organized in eight commissions, made up of three subcommissions each. The some 600 constituents had to choose among the subcommissions, with many dedicating their time to one or two of them. Political parties, particularly those with fewer representatives, like Brazil's Workers' Party, had to be strategic about how they divided their constituents across these many areas. While ethno-racial issues were cross-sectional and arguably relevant to many of the subcommissions, such debates were largely relegated to the Subcommission on Blacks, Indigenous Peoples, the Disabled, and Minorities, which I will refer to as the subcommission. This subcommission was under the Commission on Social Order, and it held sixteen official meetings between April 7 and May 25, 1987.[22]

It was clear from the outset that the subcommission would face an uphill battle. For starters, it was a hodgepodge commission set up to deal with a plethora of issues related to all of Brazil's "others": blacks, indigenous peoples, those living with disability, and other minorities. Moreover, the marginalization of these groups in society matched the marginalization of the subcommission in the constitutional reform process. So few of the ANC's constituents chose to participate in the subcommission that the first few sessions did not have enough people to hold an official meeting. Even when things moved forward, those present sensed that the subcommission was still very marginalized. As one member reflected, "We are participating in a subcommission, that based on its actual composition, based on the topic that we debate here, is relegated to being a second fiddle," adding, "part of our mission is to give this subcommission the weight that shows how important it is."[23]

This relegation to "second fiddle" was in part because, in addition to lacking the necessary number of constituents, there was little representation from the political parties with the most political weight. The most significant parties within the ANC were part of the *Centrão*—a voting bloc made up of centrist parties like the Democratic Movement Party of Brazil (PMDB), the Liberal Front Party (PFL), and the Social Democratic Party (PSD)—none of which were well represented in the subcommission. The frustration of those constituents present was apparent throughout their meetings. One constituent commented on what he saw as the "impotence" of the subcommission. He also expressed doubts about whether the subcommission really had the "political conditions to advance on these issues within the Constituent Assembly."[24]

These doubts were not unwarranted. To be sure, many ANC members saw issues related to minorities as peripheral to the more central constitutional debates happening in the constitutional reform process around political rights and economic policy. As a result, the commissions on these issues had extraordinarily high levels of constituent participation. The Sub-commission on Blacks, Indigenous peoples, the Disabled, and Minorities' lack of political weight led to much ambiguity about its mandate and poten-tial impact. Would its work ensure that the constitution was not explicitly exclusionary or discriminatory, or was its purpose to include measures that sought to address inequalities? How could they fight for the inclusion of specific protections for blacks, indigenous peoples, and those living with disabilities in the context of a universal constitution? Furthermore, to what extent was the subcommission supposed to coordinate with, and even lobby, the other subcommissions around these issues? Notwithstanding these questions, subcommission members moved forward, calling on activ-ists and academics to help inform their recommendations to the Commis-sion on Social Order, and ultimately, their recommendations to the plenary.

Anthropological Expertise

The constituent members who made up the subcommission were self-selected among the few who cared about these issues. Yet even among those sympathetic to protecting minority groups in the constitution, there was some contention over racial issues, especially when invited speakers spoke from personal experience. The consensus seemed to be that, while activists were important to hear, the voices of academic experts would be especially important. This preference for a certain kind of objective, scientific exper-tise was implicit throughout the subcommission, but it was made explicit by constituent José Carlos Sabóia:

> In addition to other speakers from movement organizations and other institutions, we need to bring an anthropologist to see what he has to say about minority issues, what it means to be marked in society, what it means to be disabled and be considered a second or third class citi-zen, what it means to have a nationality, to have a different ethnicity from the majority of the Brazilian population, which is the case with Indians.[25]

Sabóia added that the presence of intellectuals working on these issues would give the subcommission a much-needed "philosophical, theoretical, and political foundation." He warned that without this expertise, they were doomed to create what he called a "mediocre" proposal. Another ANC member suggested a number of researchers who "understand very well the question of minorities." This included Peter Fry, an anthropologist who later became a vehement critic of affirmative action policies in Brazil, as well as future first lady and anthropologist, Ruth Cardoso, who was public in her opposition to race-based quotas some fifteen years later. The constituent also recommended historian Decio Freitas, who had written on Brazil's maroon leader, Zumbí dos Palmares, and who he described as "having the best work on blacks in Rio Grande do Sul."[26]

In fact, constituents invoked academic expertise throughout the meetings and expressed anxieties about the subcommission's legitimacy and seriousness. Even in the final hours of the constitutional process, as constituent assembly members celebrated the work that they had done, one member brought into view the reality of a more serious battle to come:

> My worry is a little more urgent: it is about how we are going to sensitize, how we are going to challenge the white consciousness of our noble assembly members who are not all white. How are we going to make it such that the Brazilian population, this mosaic that is represented to varying degrees among the assembly members, understand this basic question? How are we going to construct democracy and democratic institutions? . . . Here I think the role of the *anthropologist* is more important than that of the *Indian* [emphasis mine].

This assessment had some foundation. Anthropological expertise would, in the end, legitimate multicultural subjects in constitutional reform processes throughout Latin America. Anthropologists played an even more critical role in implementing ethno-racial policy. After the constitutions were signed, both the Brazilian and Colombian states began to demarcate and title collective territories for black and indigenous communities, anthropologists would take on the task of certification and cultural authentication (French 2009; Farfán-Santos 2015).

Anthropologists came to occupy these powerful positions of legitimation in part because of the nature of the discipline itself. As Brysk (2000) notes, "anthropology's raison d'être was the celebration of human difference," and as such, anthropologists had symbolic power in these constitutional reform spaces.[27] Further, anthropologists working in and on Latin America also had developed strong ties with the pan-indigenous movement since at least the 1960s (Brysk 2000).

Given that the subcommission privileged certain kinds of knowledge, the black movement and their allies were strategic about which activists they invited to speak. Lélia Gonzalez, a well-known leader of the Unified Black Movement (MNU) and an accomplished anthropologist, was the first of a number of black activists to appear. Introducing her, constituent Benedita da Silva said, "We have here one of the brightest anthropologists that blacks have had in the history of Brazilian society, Lélia Gonzalez, who will give her presentation on the theme 'Blacks and their Situation.'" Lélia had cofounded the MNU and still held a leadership position within the organization. Yet both she and da Silva emphasized her anthropological expertise in the topic. This move to depoliticize also happened with other activist-scholars whose academic credentials—rather than their years organizing within the black movement—were highlighted in order to legitimate them in this space. Ultimately, the subcommission invited about a dozen academics, including anthropologists, psychologists, historians, and sociologists, many of whom spoke on their own behalf. However, those representing the Institute for Anthropological Research of Rio de Janeiro as well as the Brazilian Association of Anthropology (ABA) took an official institutional position on indigenous rights. The president of the ABA, Manoela Carneiro da Cunha, opened her discussion by talking broadly about the concepts of "minorities" and "minority rights." However, she spent the rest of her time speaking exclusively about the situation facing indigenous peoples, including land struggles and invasion by domestic and foreign capital. There was no mention of any other group.

No academic institution made an official statement on black Brazilians and their inclusion in the 1988 constitution. Even so, the subcommission did invite a number of academics and activists to speak directly to the "situation" facing black Brazilians. Despite the many issues they raised, however, nearly all the debate revolved around two issues: the criminalization of racism and "isonomy," or equality before the law.

Criminalizing Racism, Defining Equality

There was a surprising amount of discussion among constituent members and invited speakers about the prevalence and nature of racism in Brazilian society. This discussion revealed an acute awareness that Brazil's racial issues were unlike the racism in countries like the United States and South Africa. Florestan Fernandes—a pioneer in the study of racial inequality in Brazil and an ANC member—suggested, "Our prejudice is not open and systematic, it is masked and diffuse. It is an indirect prejudice which allows blacks and whites to live together under false appearances."[28] It was precisely this mystified nature of Brazilian racism that led some black activists to advocate for constitutional provisions that went beyond formal equality. Indeed, despite the fact that the Arinas law had criminalized racism since 1951, it had not been effective either in deterring racism or in diminishing racial inequality.[29] As a result, the subcommission agreed to include a more effective provision on the criminalization of racism in Brazil's new constitution.

The subcommission members also had a much forgotten debate around affirmative action–like policies.[30] In contrast to the discussions about criminalization, those around affirmative action proved particularly contentious. On April 28, 1987, Lélia Gonzalez of the MNU gave a powerful speech that set the tone of the subcommission's discussions around black rights. She offered a bold indictment of historic and ongoing racism in Brazil and called for isonomy:

> In this moment where we are discussing constitutional reform, we cannot pretend to effectively construct a society where the principle of *isonomy* is concretized. We cannot create lies that hide the fact that there is a great threat to the construction of a Brazilian nation. Without the *crioléu*,[31] without blacks, there is no constructing a nation in this country!

Gonzalez was likely responding to Attorney General Octavio Blatter Pinho, who had introduced the term "isonomy" to the subcommission and traced the word's etymology back to ancient Greece. She also highlighted the informal ways in which formal equality disguises ongoing racial injustices. Yet while the word isonomy appeared more than forty times thereafter, the concept itself took on different meanings throughout the subcommission proceedings. While some ANC members saw isonomy as a fundamental question of access and equal opportunity, others argued that the constitution needed to institutionalize proactive affirmative-action-type policies. The first concrete proposal for quotas came from ANC member José Carlos Sabóia of Maranhão, who called for them in public and private schools as well as the labor market.[32] Sabóia had also been a vocal advocate for indigenous rights within the subcommission and argued that while such policies would be a real "shock" to Brazilian society, they were an important way of addressing racism in a much more "explicit" way.[33] Other ANC members also expressed support for racial quotas. For instance, Domingos Leonelli argued that even under conditions of formal equality, "the subjective element of appearance and other markers typically disfavors blacks, and not just blacks, but people of other ethnic origins in our country."[34] Beyond expressing support, others vowed to take concrete actions. Helio Costa, for instance, stated early on that he was prepared to present a proposal that included not just affirmative measures but "quotas" more specifically.[35]

However, opposition to affirmative-type policies came from unlikely people, including some of those who recognized Brazil's deep-seated racial inequalities. Two Afro-Brazilian activists affiliated with the Council for the Black Community of São Paulo (CCDN) were particularly vocal in their disapproval of quotas. After debates heated up and newspapers had begun to cover the contentious issue, the subcommission invited Ricardo Dias of CCDN to talk. After emphasizing that he was representing Brazil's "black movement," he said the following:

> We discussed this and other questions in the Council for the Black Community of São Paulo in some heated debates. We came to the

conclusion that isonomy, my friends, is nothing more or less than equality of treatment for the black man and for the black culture that he represents, and an equality of conditions when compared to the other cultures that form the Brazilian nation. That is what isonomy is.[36]

Dias went on to argue that "isonomy in terms of labor is nothing more and nothing less than ensuring black men the right to work, to occupy the positions he's prepared to occupy." The major cause of racial inequality in the workplace, he added, was the lack of training among blacks. This is why he was worried about quotas. Blacks were simply "not prepared to fill these spaces."[37]

While Lélia Gonzalez did not specify exactly what isonomy might look like in terms of policy, her address made clear that formal equality was not enough. She said "continuing forward with a paternalistic logic of telling us that everything is going to be okay, but when the time comes, you close all doors such that blacks, with all of their historic competence, won't be able to access the labor market, won't be able to organize in political parties."[38]

After the subcommission recessed to work on the draft proposal, the prospect of affirmative action quickly disappeared, in part because the members feared political and public backlash. While the press had largely ignored the subcommission's session, they did cover the quotas proposal heavily. In fact, this media coverage generated a great deal of hate mail for the subcommission. In one meeting, Benedita da Silva read one such letter addressed to the rapporteur:

> Alceni, I just read the racist, ridiculous, and inflammatory proposal of Benedita da Silva to guarantee slots in the workplace for blacks. An opening for 20 spaces where 70 whites apply and 20 blacks apply, and if we say that the average grades of whites is 7.5 and the average for blacks is 6.5, is that not racism? In this case, all of the blacks would be approved, even though they have lower scores than the whites. It is ridiculous, medieval, elitist! . . . I'm Bahian and I'm the great-grandson of a black woman. I am a white man with hair like a Brillo pad. In my case could I consider myself black to get this advantage from the project of the honorable Ms. Silva? This is not viable for Brazil because of the strong [racial] mixture.

Interestingly, Benedita had not actually been the one to introduce this idea to the subcommission.[39] In fact, perhaps strategically, she did not even hold a leadership position within the subcommission at all, nor did she talk about quotas at any point in the official meetings. However, because Benedita was black, racial quotas were ascribed to her rather than to the nonblack members who had actually introduced them into the debate a number of times.

Beyond backlash from the public, constituents also feared that other ANC members would feel strongly that racial quotas were incompatible with Brazil's future universal democracy. Subcommission members had to consider the political viability of the provisions they proposed. For instance, while Sabóia said that he supported quotas, he questioned if the subcommission had the "political force necessary to include a constitutional principle of that magnitude."[40] Some saw this lack of political leverage as a consequence of the myth of racial democracy itself, which constrained the types of proposals the commission could make. How would they sell quotas to constituents who had pride in what they saw as Brazil's racial egalitarianism?

There were also other impediments. As one commissioner suggested, the lack of a massive grassroots black movement to push from outside the ANC gave the subcommission little leverage.[41] In the end, it did not include racial quotas in its proposal to the plenary, despite lots of debate and support for them. The very opposite was true of land rights for communities made up of the descendants of escaped/freed slaves, or *quilombos*. While the guarantee of territorial rights for *quilombo* communities never came up in the official subcommission meetings, it was included in their final proposal and, more importantly, in the new constitution as Provisional Article 68. How do we explain this?

Quilombos *and Indigenous Rights*

The recognition of *quilombo* rights in Brazil's 1988 constitution presents somewhat of a puzzle. While a number of activists brought up the issue of *quilombos* early on in the subcommission, it was always in the symbolic sense. They often evoked historic forms of black resistance, particularly the example of Quilombo dos Palmares, one of the earliest and longest lasting maroon societies in the Americas.[42] Their use of the *quilombo* as a symbol of black resistance mirrored that of earlier activist-thinkers like Abdias do Nascimento, who in the 1970s developed the idea of *quilombismo* as a political ideology, not a basis of concrete claims-making on behalf of contemporary black populations. In this way, historic *quilombos* served black movements in both Colombia and Brazil as important symbols of black resistance (Arruti 2000), though the movements rarely demanded that the state address the contemporary realities of those living in *quilombos* in the present.[43] Only through Brazil's constitutional reform process did this important symbol of black resistance came into direct conversation, and even tension, with political projects centered on *quilombo* rights and the rights of black rural communities more generally.[44]

Paradoxically, the only time *quilombos* appeared in the proceedings of the subcommission as living communities with their own struggles and political claims was on the very last day, when the group read its final proposal.

In it, the subcommission proposed that the state "guarantee the titling of definitive properties of land to the descendants of *quilombo* communities." In the absence of serious discussion, how did this transpire?

We cannot understand this inclusion of *quilombo* rights without examining the rise of indigenous movements and the increasing centrality of indigenous rights to the international human rights community. The indigenous movement in Brazil had been mobilized for some time around constitutional reform. Most of this organizing happened through the Union of Indigenous Nations (UNI), a national organization founded in 1980, which also included important academic allies like the Brazilian Association of Anthropology (ABA). By the mid-1980s, the UNI had constructed a unified platform focusing on the rights to territory and self-determination, and had agreed on a very specific set of demands about the recognition of indigenous rights in the 1988 constitution (Carneiro 1985; Lacerda 2008).

Furthermore, just as political elites in Brazil began to reimagine the nation through this constitutional reform process, the growing international human rights community was consolidating norms around the question of indigenous rights. Anaya (2004) notes that the 1971 United Nations study titled the "Problem of Discrimination against Indigenous Populations" was particularly important for making indigenous rights central to the UN platform.

Much of the debate within Brazil's ANC was insular, focusing on the legacy of Brazilian law and the democratic virtues of Brazilian culture. Even so, international law also entered into these debates at critical moments. One such time was captured in an article written by the then-president of the Brazilian Association of Anthropology (ABA), Manoela Carneiro da Cunha, who also spoke before the subcommission. Published in the *Folha de São Paulo* newspaper on May 5, 1987, the op-ed was an attempt to make the legal and moral case for the recognition of indigenous rights to territory and autonomy. In addition to mentioning the guarantee of indigenous rights in all of Brazil's previous constitutions, Carneiro da Cunha also cited international norms: "We demand that the new constitution maintain the recognition of these territories, which has basis not only in the legal traditions of Brazil, but in international law. Such is the case of the International Labor Organization's Convention 107 [on Indigenous and Tribal People], to which Brazil is a signatory."[45] She went on to cite the UNESCO San José declaration to make the case for indigenous rights to autonomous development and natural resources.[46]

While Carneiro's plea—and international norms around multiculturalism more generally—made indigenous peoples the ideal subjects of these rights, the underlying imperative to protect and preserve the culture of "traditional" ethnic communities was also relevant to *quilombo* communities. In fact, some of these communities had already been organizing around precisely such claims to traditional territory (interview, Luiz Alves, June

2010). By the time the ANC deliberations began in 1985, struggles for territorial rights for *quilombos*—or what some called *terras de pretos* or black lands—were also well under way, particularly in the North and Northeast (Alberti and Pereira 2007; Bernardo Gomes 2009; Pereira 2013).

The first mention of *quilombo* territorial rights appeared in an amendment introduced by constituent Abigail Feitosa of Bahia after the subcommission had already agreed on a draft proposal. A member of the socialist party and an advocate for agrarian reform, Feitosa introduced two amendments: the first proposed to make November 20 a holiday commemorating the death of fugitive slave leader Zumbí dos Palmares, and another guaranteed land rights for *quilombo* communities. While the subcommission did not include the former in its final proposal, it did include the latter. This happened, in part, because a sector within the black movement had been lobbying constituents behind the scenes. The Center of Black Culture (CCN) of Maranhão had taken the lead in making the case for territorial rights not only to constituents but also within the black movement itself. As Luiz Alves of CCN explained to me in an interview, "We were the ones to bring up the issue of land and *quilombos*, it was us! At that time I said, 'Look, I'm from a *quilombo*, I was born in a *quilombo*, and there is a struggle for land there. Over there [on the land] we have everything.'" (interview, Luiz Alves, June 2010). CCN also made the case to MNU activists and others during the Brasília Convention in 1987. In this way, the constitutional reform process in Brazil marked a shift within the black movement from understanding *quilombos* in purely symbolic terms to conceptualizing a black political project situated in *quilombos* and a subject defined in terms of territorial rights.

While the umbrella platform of the black movement included *quilombo* rights, there was no guarantee the ANC would take them seriously. As such, during the months leading up to the constitutional reform, activists from CCN and other organizations from the North and Northeast began to lobby constituents. Ivan Costa, also of CCN, explained this strategy to Bernardo Gomes (2009) in an interview:

> The national movement was already discussing and taking proposals from everywhere in Brazil to the new Constituent Assembly in 1987. It was then that the Center of Black Culture (CCN) of Maranhão together with the Center for the Defense of Blacks of Pará (CEDENPA) took proposals related to the rights of black rural communities. For that, we had to articulate with the black movement of Rio de Janeiro because the majority of federal constituent members from both Maranhão and Pará were a part of the landed elite (189).

Costa further explained that because the black movement of Maranhão and Pará knew that their regional representatives would not advocate for black rural communities' land rights, they turned to Afro-Brazilian constituents Benedita da Silva and Carlos "Caó" Alberto to make the case within the assembly (Bernardo Gomes 2009).

When I asked constituent Benedita da Silva how *quilombo* rights figured into the constitutional reform process, she said:

> In reality, we had a much bigger discussion in the constituent assembly around the ethnic question. To the extent we talked about land, the debate was always about the indigenous population because of the long tradition they have, the fact that it was them that were here [first] and only after came the colonizers to occupy indigenous spaces. So the discussion came through there, not through *quilombo* lands (interview, Benedita da Silva, February 2014).

Thus, while lobbying by black political organizations did figure into the inclusion of *quilombo* rights in Brazil's 1988 constitution, these activists' efforts were also aided by changes in what McCammon et al. (2007) call the "discursive opportunity structure." Indeed, by the late 1980s, a discursive infrastructure had been built around indigenous territorial rights in Brazil, in the region, and, perhaps more importantly, at the international level. To the extent that *quilombos* were understood as having similar claims to culture, tradition, and territory, they were also recognized.

Blacks and the Final Draft of the 1988 Constitution

The subcommission's final proposal was at once bold and watered down. It included a general section called "rights and guarantees" that laid out some general principles of recognition, respect, anti-discrimination, and equality of opportunity. This was followed by specific recommendations on blacks, indigenous peoples, the disabled, and minorities. The section on blacks included six recommendations: the mandating of specific educational curricula at all levels, the criminalization of racism, the designation of holidays "of high significance to the various ethnic groups," the breaking of diplomatic relations with countries that violate human rights,[47] and finally, the guarantee of "permanent titles of the land occupied by the descendants of *quilombos*."

Proposals were further narrowed in the subsequent steps of the constitutional reform process, first in the Commission on Social Order and later through the plenary and "systematization" stages. This narrowing occurred even though constituents made additional proposals during these stages. For instance, in one plenary meeting, Senator Paulo Paim highlighted the need to make the teaching of African history mandatory. He also made a heartfelt plea to the constituents to deal with issues of racial profiling and the criminalization of black youth. This demand—while also central to the platform of black movement organizations like the MNU—continued to be pushed aside even as the Brazilian state moved toward racial equality policies a little over a decade later (Smith 2015).

The final text of the constitution did include some of the recommendations of the Subcommission on Blacks, Indigenous Peoples, the Disabled, and Minorities, and it emphasized equality throughout the text, including in areas of education and the labor market. However, this equality was juxtaposed in Brazil's magna carta with an underlying inequality based on region and class rather than race.[48] While the 1988 constitution did criminalize racism, it did not recognize or address issues of racial inequality in any meaningful way. This absence of policies to address racial inequality was not, as some have suggested, about the constitution being an inadequate venue to address these questions.[49] In fact, if we turn to the examples of gender and disability, we see that Brazil's constitution went a step beyond formal equality. It reserved a percentage of public jobs for disabled people and guaranteed women protection in the labor market through "specific incentives."[50]

In the end, two constitutional articles were specific to black Brazilians, both related to *quilombos* and both included in the Temporary Constitutional Provisions rather than the text of the constitution itself.[51] The first article recognized *quilombo* communities and documents as sites of national heritage, and the other guaranteed collective land rights to the descendants of *quilombos*. It stated: "Final ownership shall be recognized for the remaining members of the *quilombo* communities who are occupying their lands; the state shall grant them the respective land titles."

The ultimate shape that ethno-racial rights in Brazil took in the constitution was the result of several factors, including strategic lobbying by the black movement and the building of alliances with legislators within the ANC. In addition, the imperative to protect the culture of rural *quilombo* communities also resonated with an increasingly pervasive multicultural logic within the region and around the globe. Thus, ethno-racial rights in Brazil's 1988 Constitution can be read both as a major gain and as profoundly limited. While the document did guarantee collective land rights for *quilombo* communities, it also made invisible many of the other black movement demands for effective and full citizenship.

This tension was also reflected in the subcommission's language, which often bifurcated into two separate policy discussions: indigenous rights and territory on the one hand, racism and racial inequality on the other. The latter was almost exclusively understood as a problem facing *negros*, not indigenous peoples. This may be why neither subcommission constituents nor activists mentioned indigenous people when discussing isonomy or affirmative action. In this way, *quilombos* occupied an ambiguous space.

They did not fit easily into either discourse, though they were ultimately included—within a culturalist logic—in language similar to that used in relation to indigenous people.

At the MNU convention of 1987, black Brazilian organizations called for a set of policies, including the criminalization of racism, land rights for *quilombo* communities, the rupture of diplomatic relations with apartheid regimes, and affirmative action–like policies. Ultimately, the constitution provided only for *quilombo* rights and the criminalization of racism. In so doing, it recognized only individualized, not structural, racism and established a law that would prove too harsh to be effective at prosecuting racism.[52]

A similar process unfolded in Colombia just a few years later when a wide range of black movement claims would be left out of the 1991 constitution, with the exception of territorial rights for some rural black populations. The similarities between the two cases raise many questions about whether this narrowing of black rights emerged purely from domestic processes. In what follows, I will show how the multicultural alignment in these countries, and arguably throughout Latin America, required the deracialization—or what Restrepo (2004) calls the "ethnicization"—of blackness.

THE MULTICULTURAL ALIGNMENT IN COLOMBIA

Just two years after Brazil adopted its new constitution, Colombia began its own process of further democratization through constitutional reform. The 1980s were politically unstable in Colombia. The country was still embroiled in a protracted and violent civil war between the Colombian military and armed leftist guerilla groups that had started in the 1960s. Moreover, since the central state had been historically weak, regional inequalities were large, and many areas still remained outside the state's reach. Even so, up until then Colombia's internal conflict largely took place in remote rural areas away from the country's economic and political center.

That changed with the emergence of a number of urban guerilla groups. The geographic proximity of these groups to the central state apparatus, and their use of new forms of political violence, posed new threats to the Colombian state (Dugas 1993). The M-19, or April 19 movement, perhaps the most important of these groups, emerged in response to the 1970 presidential election, which was marred with charges of fraud and, which effectively shut the left out of electoral politics. This movement, made up of a wide cross section of Colombian society, including many students, became most known for their unorthodox tactics, including unprecedented political violence. This culminated in 1985, when the M-19 seized the Supreme Court, leading to a standoff with the military in which twelve Supreme

Court justices were killed (Carrigan 2009).This political violence converged with the emergence of an array of class-based movements around the country as well as the rise of Colombia's notorious drug cartels. These "non-civil-society" groups, as well as a failed attempt to reform the political party system, contributed greatly to what has been called the "crisis of legitimacy" of the Colombian state in the late 1980s (Dugas 1993). In this, the state faced increasing pressure to respond to, and more specifically, to demobilize urban guerilla groups like the M-19. This political volatility prompted the state to launch a constitutional reform process beginning in 1990 (Dugas 1993; Van Cott 2002; Agudelo 2004; Castillo 2007). As in Brazil, constitutional reform in Colombia became a space for debate about other important concerns, among them gender equality, divorce, the plight of the disabled, and ethnic rights.

The 1991 Constitutional Reform Process

In 1990, the Colombian government began to sponsor meetings across the country to ensure a participatory constitutional reform process, to activate civil society, and to restore confidence in a government that was losing legitimacy. After 80 percent of Colombians voted for constitutional reform, the state held popular elections for representatives to the National Constituent Assembly (ANC), which was charged with representing constituents in the drafting of Colombia's new constitution (Van Cott 2000). This process opened space in the political sphere for a number of voices that had not been at the forefront of pressuring for constitutional reform, among them the voices of black Colombians concerned with land dispossession and institutionalized racism.

Meanwhile, another kind of political opening occurred in the global political field. Norms around multiculturalism and ethnic rights were diffusing throughout the globe, and Colombia's neighboring countries, including Brazil, particularly around indigenous rights. Despite the fact that Colombia is one of the oldest democracies in Latin America, it had lagged behind the region in recognizing the specific rights of ethnic and indigenous groups. This fact also figured into the calculations of National Constituent Assembly members (Sánchez 1993; Van Cott 2006), who often referred to international and regional norms, at least in making the case for indigenous rights. After reading the provisions on indigenous peoples in the constitutions of Nicaragua, Panama, Brazil, and Venezuela, Francisco Rojas Birry, one of the two indigenous members of the ANC, stated, "This is not something new, we aren't making things up here; to the contrary, we are elevating the level of the constitution, so that Colombia can do the same as other countries have in recognizing special titling for indigenous peoples" (ANC Minutes, June 10, 1991). The point here was that modern democracies had modern constitutions that recognized the specific rights of indigenous peoples. It followed that if Colombia wanted to be advanced or developed, it would have to do the same.

These changes in international norms were important but not sufficient to bring about the adoption of multicultural policies in Colombia. What is more, there was no guarantee that, once translated into the Colombian context, these norms would actually include black populations. In this sense, rather than seeping into countries, these changes in political culture and norms in the global political field aided local political struggles for recognition (Van Cott 2006; Kymlicka 2007). In Colombia, indigenous leaders and their allies had begun organizing around rights to ancestral territory and political autonomy since at least the 1970s. As the constitutional reform process became more imminent, these activists began to lay the groundwork for having indigenous rights and multiculturalism recognized in the new constitution itself. Miriam Jimeno, an anthropologist, expert on indigenous movements, and one of the main advocates for multiculturalism in Colombia's constitutional reform process explained in an interview that activists and intellectuals collaborated: "The Constitutional reform process is not what initiated [indigenous] mobilization. It was the other way around. The Constitutional Reform process was the result of a process of at least two decades of previous work by indigenous communities, of some black activists, some intellectuals, some of which had worked on black communities" (interview, Miriam Jimeno, August 2006).

Thus, while indigenous peoples' claims to land, political autonomy, and collective rights were rooted in local histories and struggles, they also drew heavily on international discourses of indigeneity that were being solidified in the same period. However, whereas indigenous people were considered the ideal subject of multicultural policies, black populations were not (Hooker 2005). Indeed, black Colombians were not automatically included in Colombia's move toward a multicultural model of citizenship. Rather, they had to prove themselves fit for such rights through a combination of discursive and material strategies (Paschel 2010).

In addition to organizational challenges, Afro-Colombian activists faced policymakers and government officials who opposed legislation in favor of Afro-Colombian interests because they felt it would create interethnic conflict in an already war-torn country. Afro-Colombian activist Libia Grueso of the Black Communities' Movement (PCN) noted that "the left, conservatives, and liberals all thought the same" when it came to including black communities in the constitution: none offered their support (interview, Libia Grueso, July 2006). ANC member Cornelio Reyes was one of the most vocal opponents of what would become Provisional Article 55 for black communities. He argued that including Afro-Colombians in the constitution would create a system of "apartheid" in Colombia that did not previously exist. He added that advocating for special rights for Afro-Colombians was a sure way to "divide the country more than it is already divided" (ANC minutes, May 15, 1991). Other ANC members asserted that even though the "black ghetto, poverty, and isolation" existed, the task at hand was to "promote better integration of these communities" (ANC Minutes, May 15, 1991).[53] Though members recognized that in some respects Afro-Colombians and indigenous peoples faced similar conditions, these populations were thought to inhabit a different kind of difference, resulting in policies of difference and multiculturalism for indigenous peoples and policies of racial integration for black populations. In the face of opposition from the ANC and ideological and regional differences among black movement organizations, activists achieved inclusion in the constitution by launching an effective campaign that included lobbying and forming alliances both with indigenous leaders within the ANC and with other black organizations.

Since Afro-Colombians were not successful in getting a candidate elected to the ANC, Francisco Rojas Birry—an indigenous leader from the Pacific Coast of Colombia with connections to traditional black organizations in the Chocó—became the main advocate for Afro-Colombians in the ANC.[54] Before being elected, he had pledged to run on a "multiethnic" platform and to fight for both indigenous and Afro-Colombian rights.[55] It made sense that the Chocó would be the epicenter of organizing around land rights for black communities, since many of the black peasant associations that I mentioned in the previous chapter were created there in the early and mid-1980s. Rojas Birry's representation also proved strategically important: indigenous leaders were part of a center-left bloc led by the M-19, and although M-19 did not originally support rights for black communities, it agreed to support all the indigenous delegates' proposals in exchange for their support of the M-19 platform. This strategic bloc wielded great power, because it represented more than one-third of the ANC. All proposals had to gain a two-thirds majority vote in order to pass (Van Cott 1996; 2002).

While a strong advocate within the ANC was important, black Colombians also deployed other tactics consistent with traditional accounts of black social movements. They orchestrated sit-ins, organized marches, formed strategic alliances with other Afro-Colombian and indigenous organizations, and created the Black Telegram Campaign, which resulted in 25,000 telegrams to policymakers demanding Afro-Colombians be included in the constitution (Grueso 2000; Agudelo 2005; interviews).[56] Through these actions, a diverse group of organizations advocating for ethno-racial rights for Afro-Colombians came together to form the Organization of Black Communities (OCN), which was central to this process.

Whereas opposition to Afro-Colombian provisions had hinged on arguments that the indigenous and black populations faced separate issues, Rojas

Birry argued that these issues were linked. On April 30, 1991, he presented a proposal to the ANC titled "The Rights of Ethnic Groups," in which he outlined provisions for indigenous peoples, black communities, and other ethnic groups. The fact that one of the two indigenous leaders in the ANC spearheaded this legislation added to its legitimacy. But approval of the proposal was not ensured. As one leader of the organization OBAPO explained to me, "There was no response . . . so we mobilized by municipality and sent telegrams to the president so that he had no choice but to respond to us" (interview, OBAPO leaders, July 2006).[57] In its final hours of deliberation, the ANC included an article on black communities in the constitution as Provisional Article 55 (AT55). As a provisional article, it was left somewhat undefined, and it mandated further legislation to develop specific policies. Its provisional nature suggests the reluctance of ANC members to recognize indigenous and black populations in similar ways (Arocha 1998).

Despite activists' attempts to include a broader definition of black communities, the article recognizes only those communities "which have come to occupy uncultivated (empty) lands in the rural zones adjoining the rivers of the Pacific Basin, in accordance with their traditional cultivation practices and the right to collective property over the areas which the same law must also demarcate."[58] As in Brazil, the inclusion of an article for black populations should be considered the fruit of strategic action, in this case by Afro-Colombian activists and their allies. Even so, it cannot be understood without considering the unique political context in which this *golazo* was scored. First, while black activists lobbied, formed alliances, and occasionally protested, such mobilization occurred within the context of state disequilibrium in the form of serious (and even armed) pressure to quickly resolve issues of political exclusion as well as changes in policy norms around multiculturalism.

Second, while issues of ethnic pluralism were significant, they were far from the center of the constitutional reform process. Transitory Article 55 was discussed only briefly and approved in the final hours of the ANC. In the end, the inclusion of AT55 in the reformed constitution of Colombia was a major feat; however, it should be considered a milestone in a longer struggle for constitutional recognition. Though AT55 mandated legal change, very unfavorable circumstances surrounded its implementation. Generally speaking, there was a considerable gap between the adoption and implementation of legislation in Colombia. In addition, state officials raised questions about AT55's feasibility, heightening activists' fears that it would become *letra muerta*, or unenacted legislation.[59] Consequently, the strategic organizing that took place between the passing of the constitution and the later approval of the Law of Black Communities (Law 70) was essential. Between 1991 and 1994, the *El Tiempo* newspaper reported over thirty regional and national Afro-Colombian or "black community" conferences, as well as some small protests. The same newspaper had not published a single article explicitly on black mobilization in 1990. Many of the black Colombian activists I interviewed said the black movement gained strength in the critical period after the 1991 constitution. During this time, the movement shifted more firmly away from making claims based on the right to equality and toward fighting for the right to difference.

The Special Commission on Black Communities

The 1991 constitution stipulated that the government create a special commission to develop a law for black communities within two years. In addition to government officials, it was to include "representatives elected by the communities involved." By May 1992, the government had chosen committee members but taken little action, fomenting activists' fears that it would exclude them from the process. Six of the Afro-Colombian representatives to the Special Commission issued a letter to various state agencies demanding the installation of the commission (letter dated May 19, 1992), and in July 1992 President Gaviria complied. Nevertheless, the commission's status was not secure. In November, the Afro-Colombian commissioners issued another letter threatening to suspend all activities and participation in the Special Commission if the state did not offer a "political or financial guarantee" for the development of Provisional Article 55.[60] The Special Commission included representatives from six government agencies as well as twelve representatives from Afro-Colombian communities, chosen from four of Colombia's thirty-two states, all on the Pacific Coast. Most of the Afro-Colombian representatives were activists from organizations that had participated in the constitutional reform process, and many of them had already begun to develop discourses of ethnic rights.

Cimarrón, the urban-based movement that had emerged in the early 1980s, was virtually pushed out of the formal political process during the negotiations around Law 70 (Wade 2009). In an interview, Juan de Dios said that this process not only nearly "killed" his movement but also opened the door for the proliferation of black organizations, many of which only existed on paper (interview, Mosquera, July 2006). The marginalization of Cimarrón was also evident in a letter the organization sent to Miriam Jimeno, executive secretary of the Special Commission, demanding the names of the Afro-Colombian representatives and asking to be kept in the loop about meeting proceedings. Cimarrón's exclusion from Law 70's drafting process, while surprising, makes sense within the context of the policy norms being solidified in that period. Cimarrón's framing—racial inequality and the need for racial integration—did not fit the idea of multicultural citizenship. Indeed, the 1991 Constitution included black communities in cultural and ethnic terms, with a specific focus on the Pacific Coast. Further, by the time the Special Commission took shape, there was little space for movements working on racism and urban black issues in these discussions. While Cimarrón did not participate directly in the Special Commission, many people who did had gone through Cimarrón's training; some had broken off from the organization precisely around the issue of territorial rights. I have argued elsewhere that the black movement's shift away from discourses of racial justice to a more ethnic and cultural framing should be understood as both cause and consequence of the adoption of multicultural policies for black Colombians (Paschel 2010).

Anthropological Expertise and the Special Commission

In addition to black Colombian representatives, the Special Commission also included representatives from government agencies, among them representatives of the Colombian Institute for Agrarian Reform and the Colombian Institute of Anthropology (ICAN), a semi-autonomous state institution. The role of academics in this case was most apparent in the state's decision to ask ICAN to act as the commission's technical secretariat. Though ICAN was just one of six government agencies involved, because of its symbolic power, it played a more powerful role than the other agencies in the debates around what would become the Law of Black Communities. Although policymakers and government officials were a fundamental part of the constitutional reform process and subsequent legislation, when faced with important decisions about specific provisions, they often deferred to and relied on expert knowledge from the academic sector. These academics brought with them expertise and strong perspectives on the question of rights for Afro-Colombians. Opposition to legislation for Afro-Colombians came from all directions, but academics were among the most critical opponents, acting as powerful agents in legitimizing and delegitimizing the use of particular frames. The power of anthropologists associated with ICAN and the absence of systematic research on black communities within the academy led to contentious debates that highlighted the relationship between material inequalities perpetuated by the state and symbolic marginalization reproduced by the academy. Debates within the Special Commission were often tense. Miriam Jimeno, who was at the time both executive secretary of the Special Commission and the director of ICAN, issued a two-page briefing in 1994 that said, "It took more than eight months of debate, discussion, antagonism, and accusations to reach a common ground." Similarly, in an interview, Jimeno asserted that many months were "wasted" because of the "strong reproach" of some Afro-Colombian activists, which sometimes included accusations of racism. She admitted that, at times, the line between the state and anthropologists associated with ICAN was blurred, resulting in what the latter perceived as personal attacks. Many of the black activists I interviewed argued that it was the intellectuals affiliated with ICAN who presented serious obstacles in these debates. As activist Libia Grueso contended, "The fact is that the academy and anthropologists, above all, are indigenists, they've always had the power and authority" (interview, Libia Grueso, July 2006). Similarly Rudecindo "Yuya" Castro explained to me that ICAN was "the institution that defines everything here in terms of the ethnic and cultural. It is the arm of the state that says if something is law or not. . . . And when ICAN says that you are not an ethnic group, nobody pays any attention to you" (interview, Rudecindo Castro, October 2008).[61]

Whereas policymakers critiqued Article 55 and subsequently Law 70 in fear that they would create a system of apartheid, anthropologists argued that black people, unlike indigenous peoples, were not a distinct ethnic group. According to some anthropologists, an ethnic group has a collective identity and culture distinct from those of the nation. Although these same anthropologists within ICAN had advocated for rights for indigenous peoples, they challenged the notion that black Colombians deserved similar recognition. Consequently, most of the debates in the Special Commission were not about specific legislative provisions but rather involved the interrogation of black Colombians as an ethnic group.[62] Perhaps the single most important illustration of the role that intellectuals played in defining the terms of the Law 70 debates occurred in the Special Commission session titled "Concepts of Cultural Identity in Black Communities."

On November 20, 1992, ICAN invited leading anthropologists to a forum designed to conceptualize cultural identity in black communities in preparation for the official Special Commission meeting on the same topic. Convening over twenty prominent Colombian anthropologists, the meeting aimed to establish "the criteria and possible obstacles to black cultural identity" (Commission Meeting Notes, November 20, 1992). These "criteria" were salient in that they would later set the tone for activists' strategies within the Special Commission; these strategies centered on challenging and stretching the bounds of traditional culture and identity as the basis of collective land rights. This was not the first time that activists faced such resistance from anthropologists. In the mid-1980s, the Peasant Association of Atrato (ACIA) and other organizations in the Chocó had demanded that the state title a large area of land in the Medio Atrato region. The activists first attempted to make a squatter rights claim, demanding individual titles. In so doing, they then tried to leverage international law such as ILO Convention 107 to make the claim that they were traditional African communities (Khittel 2001). Many activists from the Chocó talked with me about this moment, including Yuya Castro, who said, "In Medio Atrato, which was about 800,000 hectares at that time, it wasn't possible because the white anthropologists said that we weren't an ethnic group and we didn't have the legitimacy to make that type of claim" (interview, Rudecindo Castro,

October 2008). Nearly a decade later, Yuya and other activists found themselves fighting the same kind of battle, to be considered an ethnic group that merited its own right to territory, among other rights.

Academics' strong reservations about conceptualizing blacks as the subjects of ethnic rights can be explained, in part, by the fact that many of them were specialists on indigenous peoples rather than black communities. Until the early 1990s, anthropology in Colombia focused almost exclusively on indigenous populations, with the exception of a handful of anthropologists who studied black Colombian communities (de Friedemann 1974; de Friedemann and Arocha 1988; Arocha 1998). Moreover, and as Wade (1997) contends, in Colombia and throughout Latin America, "the study of blacks and Indians . . . has, to a great extent, been divided into, on the one hand, studies of slavery, slavery-related issues and 'race relations' and, on the other, studies of Indians" (27). In the discussions that led to Law 70, scholars used classic frameworks still dominant in anthropology in Colombia. They defined the "other" in terms of culture and identity, and they considered these criteria to be the basis upon which multicultural rights should be recognized. Beyond this, when evaluating black communities, these same anthropologists considered indigenous peoples the prototype of a group that deserved multicultural rights. As such, they tended to see black communities' struggle as an imitation of indigenous peoples' struggle. As Jaime Arocha, one of the first anthropologists to focus on black communities in Colombia, explained, "The argument of these anthropologists was that this legislation made no sense because these people didn't have particular identities and that instead, they [black communities] opted for an opportunistic stance, cloning the indigenous model" (August 14, 2006).

Given this, the few anthropologists who had been researching black communities and working closely with activists felt that the best way to guarantee black rights was not to copy the indigenous model—as some charged they were doing—but instead to "deracialize" the perception of blacks. In other words, in this moment, it was more important for black Colombians to emphasize their culture, traditions, and knowledge of the environment than their groupness based on racial discrimination or marginalization. This deracialization of Afro-Colombians was likely a necessary step toward guaranteeing that they would benefit from multicultural policies (Pedrosa 1996; Restrepo 2004; Wade 2009).

Insofar as indigenist anthropologists would concede that black Colombians were a group at all, they identified this groupness as based on racism, not on ethnicity (read as culture and identity). As a result, they conceived of Afro-Colombians' challenges as very different from indigenous struggles and as an inadequate basis for multicultural rights. In the Special Commission meetings, for instance, one intellectual argued that "the focus of attention of the black community has been the struggle against racial segregation, whereas the indigenous struggle has been the recognition of collective human rights (territory, language, etc.)" (Commission Meeting Notes, November 20, 1992).

Academic production and ethnic struggles merged so thoroughly in this political field that interviewees had a hard time distinguishing the intellectual project of indigenist scholarship from the indigenous movement itself. Even anthropologist Miriam Jimeno said, "The indigenous movement started in the 50s if you start with when the anthropologists began to write and collect data and see 'the difference'" (interview, Miriam Jimeno, August 2006). She explained that the anthropologists' ideological project of "constructing difference" was an important part of, and perhaps a precondition for, the articulation of a viable indigenous movement. This was true not only in Colombia and earlier in Brazil but throughout Latin America more generally.[63] In Colombia, anthropologists' discursive and political orientation required black activists to shift their efforts and strategically appropriate strict ideas of what it meant to be an ethnic group. The activists understood that ethnic difference was the criterion that led to multicultural rights, and they challenged the dominant ideology that indigenous peoples were the only legitimate ethnic group in Colombia. For example, Commissioner Silvio Garcés argued that the most imperative task at hand was to make sure that the law gave "normative legal recognition of the black community as an ethnic group" (Commission Meeting Notes, November 20, 1992). Similarly, Grueso argued that the main purpose of the Special Commission was not to develop a law for Afro-Colombians but rather to determine whether they "were an ethnic group or not" (interview, Grueso, July 2006).

In this period, black leaders' main strategy was not necessarily to organize mass protests but rather to intervene in centralized political processes, which included convincing indigenist anthropologists to endorse the idea that Afro-Colombians were an ethnic group deserving collective rights.[64] Indeed, while some black organizations from the Pacific Coast had already begun to articulate their claims in the language of ethnicity before the 1991 constitutional reform, some of their explicit discursive distancing from Cimarrón—which persists today—may have stemmed from the lack of legitimacy of ideas of anti-racism and racial equality in debates about multicultural policies. As a result, activists appropriated anthropologists' criteria and at the same time maintained that it was important to discuss identity and culture on black communities' own terms. In so doing, they highlighted the unique and dynamic nature of black identity and culture, and they linked the problems in identifying this culture to the lack of research on these communities.

In both meetings and impromptu mobilizations, black Colombian activists also filled in the gaps by bringing maps, marimbas, drums, songs, and knowledge of the biodiversity of the Pacific Coast in order to prove their ethnic distinction. As black Colombian activist Zulia Mena asserted, bringing the cultural traditions of the Pacific Coast and performing serenades in Bogotá was extremely important in proving that Afro-Colombians could exercise a "right to difference" (interview, Zulia Mena, August 2006). Such manifestations served the dual role of constructing a particular type of black Colombian culture while also demarcating an ethnic boundary by distinguishing these traditions from mainstream Colombian culture. Moreover, in order to bolster claims of cultural difference, activists asked policymakers and intellectuals if they were familiar with the rivers and animals in their communities. They would ask: "Do you know how to play this instrument?" "Do you know this song?" "Can you identify this river on the map?" (interview, Zulia Mena, August 2006).

In the end, their efforts proved successful when the Law of Black Communities was decreed on August 27, 1993. Since Afro-Colombians, particularly those on the Pacific Coast, were already included in the constitution in cultural and ethnic terms, between 1991 and 1993 black community representatives worked mainly within the framework of global multiculturalism, even if they stretched the boundaries of that concept.[65] In doing so, they may have unwittingly undermined their attempts to expand the legal concept of black communities beyond the rural zones of the Pacific Coast during that period and for decades to come. Activists had made many attempts during Special Commission meetings to expand the idea of black communities. For example, one of the black activists on the commission, Silvio Garcés, argued that "the reach of this article must not be limited to the riverine communities of the Pacific Coast. . . . You can't deny the territorial rights of our black community in this country" (Special Commission Minutes, October 2, 1992).[66] Despite these efforts, the process of constructing the Law of Black Communities led to the reproduction of a limited and geographically specific notion of blacks as rural and as from the Pacific coast that persists within state institutions today.

Rather than evidence of a lack of concern about urban issues among black activists involved in this process, this can be read as a result of two important factors. First, these activists struggled to make sure that Law 70 actually came to fruition. In the end, they made tacit agreements with the state rather than insist on their true aspirations around black rights. Second, and more importantly, concern for the plight of indigenous people put discursive constraints on ideas of multiculturalism and consequently on discussions of black rights; the black political subjectivity that Law 70 institutionalized reflects those constraints.

The black Colombian movement of the early 1990s juggled two largely incongruent notions of black communities: the ethno-territorial approach was rooted in ideas of distinct ethnic identity, history, and geography; the other approach was much broader and included urban black populations and areas beyond the Pacific Coast. Despite this incongruence, the discourse of ethnic difference became the only legitimate way of talking about black rights in Colombia. I will show later how black communities that sought to access Law 70 could do so only inasmuch as they could convincingly show that they were traditional black communities with a distinct culture, history, and identity. The very discussion of a more expansive notion of blackness—one that might include Colombia's urban black population, estimated to be more than two-thirds of the total black population—risked delegitimizing altogether the concept of black communities as ethnic others.[67]

CONCLUSION

In the years leading up to both countries' constitutional reform processes, black movements in Colombia and Brazil were still relatively small and under-resourced. They also continued to face tremendous ideological barriers that made it difficult to mobilize the masses *as* blacks. In neither case did activists overcome these hurdles entirely. Instead, they were successful because they took strategic advantage of the multicultural alignment. More specifically, they made claims on the state amid dramatic changes in their domestic political fields—including a crisis of state legitimacy and constitutional reform processes—as well as the emergence and consolidation of an influential global field that linked development and democracy with multicultural protections. In the end, the black movements in both countries achieved considerable gains, among them collective land rights for black rural communities in their countries' new constitutions. As we will see later, however, such recognition was no guarantee that these states would actually make good on their promises.

Further, constitutional recognition of black communities in Colombia and Brazil only partially addressed a more foundational issue, the systemic marginalization of blacks and their uneven inclusion into the political, social, and economic life of each country (Barbary and Urrea 2004; Hooker 2005; Ng'weno 2007b). Indigeneity, defined almost exclusively in terms of land and culture, became the prism through which both indigenous people and black communities were granted rights in Colombia, and in Latin America more generally. Rather than a full frontal attack on anti-indigenous or anti-black racism in Colombia and Brazil, multiculturalism was—as Van Cott (2000) aptly put it—a "friendly liquidation of the past." For this very reason, some have even characterized this shift from *mestizaje* to multiculturalism as a slight of hand that kept *mestizaje*'s very premise—that cultural diversity had produced an egalitarian and harmonious society—intact.

What's more, this narrowing of black rights into the logic of multiculturalism happened amid tense and extremely uneven negotiations between activists, constituent assembly members, intellectuals, and globally circu-lating discourses of democracy and multicultural citizenship. In Colombia, the making of a black political subject defined strictly in cultural terms also reflected black organizations' strategic decision to "ethnicize" the black struggle (Pedrosa 1996; Restrepo 2004; Paschel 2010). Indeed, emergent Afro-Colombian organizations integral to the passing of the Law of Black Communities did not explicitly formulate their struggles in terms of race or racial discrimination. Carlos Rosero of the Black Communities' Movement articulated it best: "Racism and racial discrimination are all a part of the assertion of the right to equality. . . . We fight for the right to difference" (interview, Carlos Rosero, June, 2006). Similarly, Libia Grueso also of PCN argued that activists demanded not "programs to not be excluded" but the "right to territory" (interview, Libia Grueso, July 2006).

This distinction—between equality and difference—was often overly po-liticized within Colombia's black movement and a perpetual source of con-flict between urban and rural movements that may have otherwise formed necessary and long-lasting political alliances. Yet while the dichotomy be-tween equality and difference may be overdrawn (Scott 1988), Libia Grueso may have been onto something when she said that the two ideas represent fundamentally "distinct ways of thinking." In the debates around equality and difference in Colombia, what was at stake was not only what kind of political subject black Colombians would be institutionalized but also where blacks fit in the country's plans for economic development. Whereas those fighting for equality demanded symbolic inclusion in nationalist narratives and their piece of the country's economic and political power, those fighting for the right to difference seemed to question the very premise of such a project. Rather than demand jobs and social mobility, they defended their right to tra-ditional economic practices, among them subsistence farming and mining.[68]

Ultimately, these black rural folk and their advocates inside and outside Colombia's black movement succeeded in defending their rural way of life and in claiming territoriality, autonomy, and difference-based inclusion. Their counterparts in other parts of the region, such as Nicaragua, Honduras, and Brazil, did the same and were also included in new constitutions as the sub-jects of multicultural rights (Hooker 2005). In this sense, the first round of ethno-racial policies adopted in the 1980s and 1990s throughout Latin Amer-ica can be understood as a series of alignments and misalignments. More spe-cifically, the success of black rural and geographically specific communities, and the corresponding policies aimed at protecting their culture, have to be understood alongside the misalignment of policies aimed at a less geograph-ically specific black population. Organizations like Cimarrón in Colombia and the MNU in Brazil that had since the 1970s mobilized discourses that emphasized racial discrimination, racial inequality, and the need for in-tegration did indeed mobilize around the constitutional reform process.

However, the multicultural alignment is ultimately a story of their defeat and of the triumph of a culturally and territorially defined black political subject.

This misalignment of claims to racial equality highlights the strength of the analytic approach I have developed here. Even after these constitutional reforms happened, some scholars argued that when black movements made demands on their states, they did so in a language very different from that of indigenous peoples (Yashar 1999; Van Cott 2000). Van Cott (2000), for instance, held that "despite their legal equality, blacks endured social discrimination, were under-represented in political office, and were trapped in rural or urban poverty. For the most part, where they have mobilized politically qua blacks it has been to demand equality, rather than recognition as a distinct group" (49). Similarly, Yashar (1999) argued that the politicization of black identities "has been largely limited to urban movements and has resulted in types of political demands that are different from those voiced by indigenous movements in Latin America" (78). While such accounts tend to minimize the presence of black rural organizations, these scholars are right in highlighting that the dominant narratives of black organizations in the decades leading up to constitutional reform had emphasized equality rather than difference. Black urban activists had been the first to organize *as blacks*, beginning in the 1970s in Colombia and as early as the 1910s in Brazil. Yet these actors were not ultimately the protagonists who achieved black rights in the 1980s–1990s. This was in part because they made claims to integration and equality rather than the claims to ethnic difference and autonomy that eventually became consecrated in constitutions throughout Latin America.

In this chapter, I have shown how black activists in both Colombia and Brazil actually lodged a robust set of demands with their respective states during this period of political instability and reform.[69] On the one hand, urban-based movements in both countries made claims to inclusion and equality and fought for inclusionary affirmative action-type policies. On the other, rural black movements came to articulate their demands in the discourse of difference and autonomy in ways that mirrored the emergent requirements of global multicultural citizenship; at the same time, their discourse reflected the similarities between their material realities and those of indigenous communities. Indeed, both groups were concerned with territory and the imminent threat of dispossession posed by a number of actors, including domestic and foreign capital. Yet in both countries, the process of constitutional reform systematically narrowed these demands such that black rights took on a much more specific character of cultural protection and geographic concentration. In this way, the inclusion of cultural rights for black rural populations in the reformed constitutions of Colombia and *quilombos* in Brazil did not reflect the diverse set of demands the black movement made on these states in this period.

This disciplining of black rights resulted from the nature of a multicultural alignment, in which indigenous people were the quintessential subject of such rights. The adoption of multicultural reforms throughout Latin America, and certainly in these two cases, would not have been likely without the solidification of a global ethno-racial field in the 1980s. The institutions, legal norms, and logics that made up this field made it easier for both indigenous peoples and black populations to make certain kinds of ethno-racial claims on their respective states. Also, the alignment of this field with drastic changes in domestic politics gave anthropologists a great deal of symbolic power, influence that would first impede black rights and later help black activists couch their claims more squarely in the language of difference.

Conceiving of the black political subject exclusively as "black communities" on Colombia's Pacific Coast and as *quilombos* in Brazil had its limitations (Barbary and Urrea 2004; Hooker 2005; Ng'weno 2007a). This conception presumed the urban black masses were culturally assimilated and as a result largely disqualified from multicultural citizenship. According to the new multicultural logic, it was not historic injustice or ongoing ethno-racial oppression but rather the need to protect the nation's cultural diversity that justified recognition of rights. This is why, in addition to recognizing the land rights of *quilombo* communities, the Brazilian constitution vowed to "protect the expressions of popular, Indian, and Afro-Brazilian cultures." Similarly, the Colombian constitution guaranteed the protection of the "ethnic and cultural diversity of the Colombian nation." While all liberal constitutions promise to protect the life and liberty of all citizens, this was a very specific kind of cultural protection. In both cases, too, academic knowledge, and anthropological expertise in particular, was central to the construction of this multicultural subject.

It would be another decade before the Colombian and Brazilian states revisited the question of ethno-racial legislation that specifically addressed black populations. In the 2000s, the Brazilian state, and the Colombian state to a lesser degree, began to adopt a set of policies, including affirmative action, predicated on the idea that there was racism, or at the very least racial inequality, in society. I see these not as a simple extension of previous multicultural policies but rather as constituting a different approach entirely; they also occurred at a distinct historical moment that I call the racial equality alignment. This new racial equality approach did not displace entirely the multicultural logic. Instead, over the last decades Colombia and Brazil institutionalized overlapping, and sometimes competing, logics of black rights. Though, as we will see in the following chapter, despite the passing of similar legislation for *quilombo* communities in Brazil, the logic of cultural difference never quite permeated the Brazilian political field in the same way, neither among activists nor state actors.

CHAPTER FIVE

THE RACIAL EQUALITY ALIGNMENT

The articulation of local and global mobilization and discourses led to the construction of a particular kind of black multicultural subject in Colombia and Brazil in the 1980s–1990s. Yet in neither country did this multicultural alignment quell a number of other serious issues looming in the background. During the constitutional reform processes, black activists raised issues around racial discrimination and inequality in employment, education, health, and policing. None of the constitutional provisions adopted in the 1980s–1990s, nor the subsequent legislation, directly addressed this uneven incorporation of black populations into the social and economic life of these countries. Instead, the Colombian and Brazilian states—as well as others throughout Latin America—institutionalized territorial rights for a segment of the black population defined in cultural and geographic terms (Hooker 2005). This emphasis on ethnic territory, while extremely important, did not easily map onto urban and majority white/ *mestizo* cities, where most black Brazilians and Colombians lived. What would collective territory actually mean in cities like Rio de Janeiro or Medellín? Can we think about "traditional culture" or "ancestral land" as happening in these urban spaces, or is that a contradiction of terms? This also raised the question: had state multiculturalism set discursive constraints on black movements' ability to make these other kinds of claims on the state?[1] In other words, did institutionalizing a black political subject defined by cultural difference undermine a racial equality or racial justice agenda?

In the early 2000s, just a decade after many Latin American states adopted multicultural constitutions, governments in the region initiated a new round of ethno-racial reforms that seemed to reconcile some of these contradictions. They created national holidays around black history, identity, and culture; they included questions on their national census to count their Afro-descendant populations—sometimes for the first time since the colonial period; and in some cases, they passed anti-racism legislation. In addition, many states in the region had created national-level state entities with the mandate of combating racial and other forms of discrimination.

While this shift was widespread in Latin America, Colombia and Brazil stand out for having experimented with more proactive racial equality policies including affirmative action.

In this chapter, I analyze this new round of reforms, much of which happened in the wake of the 2001 Third World Conference against Racism in Durban, South Africa. Unlike the cultural and territorial rights granted to subsets of the black populations in the 1990s, these new policies were broader and wrapped in the language of racial equality and inclusion. The categories of political contestation also seemed to change in this period from "black" to hyphenated national categories such as "Afro-Brazilian," "Afro-Colombian," and "Afro-Peruvian." In this way, the new wave of reforms represented a considerable departure from the multicultural policies adopted throughout Latin America just a decade before. In fact, these new policies were precisely the kind that urban black organizations like the MNU in Brazil and Cimarrón in Colombia had demanded for decades. At the same time, these new racial equality policies still fell incredibly short of meeting all of the historic demands of black movement organizations in each country. Even so, they did mean the institutionalization of a black political subject defined not exclusively by culture but rather by their experiences with systematic discrimination and disadvantage. I call this shift, or widening, of the discourse around ethno-racial policies in Latin America in the 2000–2010s the racial equality alignment.

Although both Colombia and Brazil moved in the direction of racial equality policies—as did many countries in Latin America—the shift in Colombia was much more timid. By the 2000s, the idea that black communities were multicultural subjects—defined by their cultural distinction from the rest of the nation—had become deeply entrenched in Colombian law, in state institutions, and in the black movement itself. Once consecrated in the 1991 constitution, the Colombian state spent the next decade institutionalizing the concept of black communities as a distinct ethnic group. Under the continual pressure of black organizations, they adopted the Law of Black Communities, which led to massive land titling for black rural communities on the country's Pacific Coast, as well as the institutionalization of a number of *etno-educación* initiatives in school curricula throughout the country. The state also created the Office on Ethnic Affairs within the Ministry of the Interior to coordinate the implementation of Law 70. This "ethnicization of blackness," as Restrepo (2004) rightfully called it, had permeated Colombia's political field, not only in the language of black activists, but also state actors and academics. Accordingly, when discussions around racial equality policies began to emerge in Colombia in the late 2000s, they created serious tensions with existing discourses of blackness as cultural difference. Even in the context of new policies aimed at bringing about racial equality, a multicultural logic continued to be the dominant discourse governing black politics in Colombia.

In contrast, Brazil's flirtation with the brand of multiculturalism that became so prevalent in Colombia was brief. While the Brazilian government did create the Cultural Palmares Foundation in 1988 to address *quilombo* issues, the "black rights as cultural rights" archetype associated with the multicultural alignment quickly faded into the distance as the state began to adopt racial equality reforms just over a decade later. In this, neither the Brazilian state nor black activists fought to make *quilombo* rights, or cultural definitions of blackness, all-encompassing. Instead, the discourse of racial equality began to dominate Brazil's political field.

This difference, I suggest, was not because the black populations of Colombia and Brazil were inherently different. Rather, the way movements in each country politicized blackness affected how deeply certain ideas of a black political subject permeated their political fields. Of course, historical constructions of race and nation, and particularly ideas about where blackness fit into the imagined nation, shaped this process of politicization. The idea of blacks as a cultural other was a hard sell in both countries but especially in Brazil, where blacks were presumed to be fully incorporated into the nation. As I discussed in chapter 2, since the early twentieth century, political elites in Brazil had crafted a narrative of Brazilianness in which African culture and ancestry was central. The problem facing Brazil's black population, then, was not invisibility or the need for symbolic inclusion into the nation. Rather, the rhetorical inclusion of blacks into Brazilian nationalism needed to be matched by their full social, economic, and political inclusion. In Colombia, on the other hand, blackness occupied an ambiguous and geographically specific space within the national imaginary. This idea was only reinforced with the 1991 constitution and Law 70. This fact, paired with the understanding that Colombia's regions were culturally distinct, meant that a discourse that defined blackness—and particularly blackness from the Pacific region—as cultural difference had more resonance than in the Brazilian context.[2]

Beyond national imaginaries, academic scholarship in the decades leading up to ethno-racial reforms also reflected these different ways of understanding blackness vis-à-vis the Colombian and Brazilian nations. Colombian anthropologists documenting the culture of black rural communities were among the few academics researching black Colombians in the 1980s (de Friedemann and Arocha 1982; de Friedemann and Roselli 1983; de Friedemann and Arocha 1988). It was only in the 2000s that this scholarship began to seriously analyze urban populations and racial inequality (Barbary and Urrea 2004). This is in stark contrast with the abundant research produced since the 1950s or even earlier on blacks in Brazil. While such scholarship included important works on African culture in Brazil (Bastide 1971), sociologists and anthropologists focused on racial inequality produced the main current of research on black Brazilians (Costa Pinto 1952; Fernandes 1965; Hasenbalg 1979; Gonzalez and Hasenbalg 1982; Hasenbalg and do Valle Silva 1988). In this sense, academic knowledge about black populations in Colombia helped to produce an idea of blackness as rural and culturally distinct, whereas scholarship on contemporary black populations in Brazil reproduced the idea of blackness as urban and defined by experiences of inequality and discrimination. All of this helped to constitute a "regime of recognition"—to borrow a term from Murray Li (2000)—that preconfigured the kinds of black political subject that came to be articulated in Colombia and Brazil, both within each state's apparatus and within black movements themselves. Even so, such a regime was far from immutable. The political shifts in both countries in the 2000s reveal the importance of ongoing political contestation in the making of black political subjects.

POLITICAL FIELD ALIGNMENT AROUND RACIAL EQUALITY

The shift in Colombia and Brazil toward the making of a black political subject defined in terms of racial inequality—as opposed to cultural difference—was directly linked to discursive changes in the global ethnoracial field. In the 1990s, this field consisted of actors researching, advocating for, and creating international norms around protecting indigenous peoples' cultural rights. However, this changed substantially in the 2000s as these same actors, as well as new ones, began to focus on issues of ethnoracial inequality. This change reconfigured international institutions to involve a broader set of actors interested in questions of social inclusion. It also entailed the emergence of new institutions and norms designed specifically with black populations in Latin America in mind.

Previously, the region's black population had been largely invisible to the ethnic agenda developing within key international institutions (Davis et al. 2011). This began to change in the early 2000s. One of the first important efforts in this regard was the World Bank's June 19, 2000, meeting about race and poverty, which included representatives of a number of international institutions, donor agencies, academics, and activists from Latin America. The meeting resulted in the founding of the Inter-Agency Consultation on Race in Latin America (IAC), a consultative group of institutions based in Washington, DC, among them the World Bank, the Inter-American Development Bank, the Ford Foundation, the Inter-American Foundation, and the Inter-American Dialogue, which acted as the IAC secretariat.[3] Like previous institutions founded to address the plight of indigenous peoples, the IAC emerged as a direct response to the demands of civil society groups. In the late 1990s, black activists from throughout Latin America began to pressure international institutions to focus their programming on the region's black population. They argued that the institutions that had been working on questions of social inclusion had further marginalized black communities. This exclusion, they held, was evident in the difficulty they had in accessing funding from these institutions (Davis et al. 2011). Responding to this pressure, major international institutions that had focused their ethnic policies on indigenous populations—like the ones that made up the IAC—began to focus on the plight of black populations and social inclusion more broadly. When these institutions did finally develop programming for black populations, or Afro-descendants, they did so using the language of racial equality. Rather than protect the culture of these "vulnerable" groups, the new language of social inclusion was about combating racial and gendered discrimination and inequality.

Over the course of the early 2000s, the IAC institutions held meetings in Washington as well as large international conferences in Latin America around questions of racial equality.[4] The most notable were the Todos Contamos, or "Everyone Counts," conferences held in Cartagena in 2000 and in Lima in 2002, designed to get Latin American states to collect ethnoracial statistics (Davis et al. 2011; Loveman 2014). These efforts coincided with preparations for the Third UN World Conference against Racism to be held in Durban, South Africa, in 2001, a conference that would prove particularly important to the shift toward racial equality in Latin America, and to the making of affirmative action in Brazil. Just as the UN Decade of Indigenous Peoples in the 1990s brought a coherence to the global ethnoracial field oriented around multiculturalism, events like the Todos Contamos, Durban, and its Preparatory Conference in Santiago converged with domestic changes to produce a new opening for otherwise small and under-resourced black movements.

The reorientation of the global ethno-racial field toward black populations and racial equality also coincided with the formalization of transnational ties and strategies among movements, including black movements, in Latin America. Unlike the previous multicultural alignment, the racial equality alignment required activists to leverage geopolitics and to use transnational strategies. As I discussed earlier, in the 1970s and 1980s, activists in both Colombia and Brazil felt deep solidarity with anticolonial struggles on the African continent and the U.S. civil rights and Black Power movements. In the late 1990s, these largely symbolic diasporic connections began to morph into tangible transnational ties with black organizations and other transnational actors interested in the plight of black communities and human rights more generally.

While all this played an important role in the making of racial equality policies in both Colombia and Brazil, it did so in different ways in the two countries. In Brazil, the presence of a sympathetic President Fernando Henrique Cardoso aligned with preparations for the Durban Conference, creating a domino effect of racial equality policy reforms, among them affirmative action in government and in universities. Though similar transnational dynamics propelled the Colombian state to consider policies to address racial discrimination and inequality in the late 2000s, this shift was fraught. In it, discussions about racial equality policies ran up against deeply institutionalized multiculturalist policies as well as ongoing tensions within black Colombian movement over how to define the subject of black rights and policies.[5]

PROMOTING RACIAL EQUALITY IN BRAZIL

In 1995, on the 300-year anniversary of the death of fugitive slave leader Zumbí dos Palmares, Brazil's black movement mobilized tens of thousands of people to march on Brasília. In this protest—known as the Zumbí March against Racism and for Citizenship and Life—activists called for a shift in the state's position on racial issues and demanded concrete policies for black populations in the areas of education, health, employment, and justice. Officially, the long-established MNU organized the march, but black NGOs and activists working within unions and leftist political parties like the Workers' Party (PT) also had a central role.[6] In the end, the march drove then-president Cardoso to recognize publically that the country was not a racial democracy but instead suffered from pervasive racism and racial inequality, a first in Brazil's history. What is more, Cardoso promised to take concrete steps to address this inequality through policy reforms. His first step was to create the Inter-Ministerial Working Group for the Valorization of the Black Population (GTI), a national committee made up of high-level government officials and Afro-Brazilian leaders charged with conducting research and designing anti-racist government policies.

While this historic Zumbí mass mobilization succeeded in pressuring the state to make symbolic statements, it did not lead to actual reforms (Telles 2004). By 1999, the Cardoso administration had yet to implement any of the concrete actions the GTI recommended in its 1995 report. Ivair Alves dos Santos, an Afro-Brazilian member of Cardoso's administration and a long-time advocate for race-based policies, discussed his difficulty in the late 1999s in pushing to convert the GTI's recommendations to actual policy. He explained, "Nobody believed in these issues that I was talking about. . . . I talked and talked and I kept hitting the ceiling" (interview, Ivair Alves dos Santos, May 2010). That ceiling had a lot to do with Cardoso's centrist party, which largely saw racial issues as either irrelevant or as a Workers' Party issue (interview, Gilberto Sabóia, March 2010). Cardoso himself and some of his key advisors were committed to adopting racial equality policies (Htun 2004). However, as pressure mounted from both inside and outside his administration, there was still serious opposition within his party. Ultimately, the Zumbí March resulted only in symbolic gestures. However, what did catalyze the adoption of racial equality policies was the convergence of these domestic dynamics with preparations for the 2001 Durban Conference.

It is nearly impossible to talk about the adoption of affirmative action policies in Brazil without discussing the Durban Conference. In fact, nearly all legislation passed from 2001–2015 related to promoting racial equality in the country cites Durban as legal justification. One of the many examples of this is Decree 4886 of 2003, which instituted Brazil's National Policy for the Promotion of Racial Equality. It stated as its normative justification the Durban Plan of Action and the Third World Conference against Racism, "in which governments and civil society organizations from around the world were called to elaborate global measures against racism, discrimination, intolerance, and xenophobia."[7] The law also alluded to statements Cardoso made throughout the late 1990s: "Considering that in order to finally break from the limits of rhetoric and solemn declarations, it is necessary to implement affirmative action, and create an equality of opportunities, translated into tangible, concrete and well-articulated measures."[8] In this sense, Durban was the needed bridge between symbolic rhetoric and actual policy reforms.

Nevertheless, those involved in the Durban Conference did not immediately see its importance.[9] Ivair Alves dos Santos, for example, expressed his initial skepticism about the impact this UN conference could have on racial policy in Brazil. Ivair was close to President Cardoso and had been advocating for racial equality policies for years within Cardoso's Social Democracy Party. However, he explained, as preparations went on, the magnitude of the conference grew exponentially. In fact, recent reforms are incomprehensible if you do not analyze the Durban Conference. He summed it up in the following way: "There is before Durban and after Durban. . . . From there, everything changed" (interview, Ivair Alves dos Santos, May 2010). Nearly all the activists I spoke with talked about Durban as a "critical juncture" or, as one activist put it, as a moment that "divided the waters."[10]

Scholars have also underscored Durban's importance in bringing about racial equality policy in Brazil (Htun 2004; Telles 2004). However, I argue that to understand the magnitude of the Durban Conference we must situate it in the context of the Brazilian government's decades-long investment in being the model of race relations in the world, particularly within the UN. In the remaining part of this section on Brazil I first analyze these geopolitical dynamics, drawing on official statements Brazilian diplomats made in the UN between 1978 and 2002. I then discuss the actual Durban

Conference using interviews with activists, diplomats, and scholars central to the process. Afro-Brazilian activists—fully aware of the Brazilian states' projection abroad of the country as a racial paradise—saw Durban as an opportunity to expose the contradictions between this image and the reality on the ground. As was the case during the multicultural alignment, it was not a massive black Brazilian movement but a small group of activists using institutionalized strategies that led to actual policy reforms.

Projecting Racial Paradise

As early as the turn of the twentieth century, visitors from around the world, among them prominent African Americans, began to travel to Brazil and write about the country's harmonious race relations. Even the well-known theorist of race W.E.B. DuBois argued that Brazil did not suffer from the same burden of racism as the United States (Hellwig 1992).[11] The Brazilian state also consciously produced and reproduced this image of Brazil as a racial paradise. One of the first examples of Brazil's racial project within the UN apparatus came even before the UN began to work systematically on anti-racism.[12] In 1950, UNESCO commissioned a large multicity study on Brazilian race relations to be carried out by prominent social scientists from Brazil and elsewhere, including Florestan Fernandes, Costa Pinto, and Roger Bastide.[13] The studies were intended to offer a more harmonious model of race relations in a world scarred by apartheid, the Holocaust, and World War II. However, scholars researching São Paulo and Rio de Janeiro largely concluded that there was a de facto racial hierarchy and pervasive racial inequality, while those researching the Northeast largely reaffirmed ideas of racial democracy (Telles 2004).

In September 1952, UNESCO reported the results in their internationally circulated magazine, the *Courier*. Despite mixed findings, the general tone of the report still indicated that Brazil had created a multiracial harmonious society. A featured article by the father of racial democracy himself, Gilberto Freyre, concluded, "Brazil remains an exemplary nation, destined because of this to play an important role in the building of a world in which mutual respect between races will become an established universal."[14] So while these studies were circulated in Brazil as evidence that racial inequality did in fact exist (Telles 2004), they were packaged internationally as proof that Brazil was the model of race relations to be followed. Brazil's history of colonization and slavery, which it was thought to have overcome, was key to its appeal as a model for countries with similarly sordid pasts. As such, in UN meetings on anti-racism, Brazil was constantly juxtaposed with the racist, intolerant, and cruel regime of apartheid in South Africa.[15]

In promulgating Brazil's image in a world of apartheid, racism, and ethnic cleansing, Brazilian diplomats did not paint the country as an organic racial democracy. Instead, they emphasized the racially mixed and egalitarian nature of Brazilian culture as well as the Brazilian state's proactive approach to combating racism. This was especially true after Brazil criminalized racism in the 1988 constitution. This dual nature of Brazil's message about its racial character was clear in a UN meeting on November 30, 1999 where diplomats discussed the approaching Durban Conference. "Under Brazilian legislation, racism is a crime for which there is no bail or statute of limitations. Any kind of racial discrimination is punishable by law. . . . Brazil is proud to be a melting pot of cultures, all of which have contributed to building a tolerant, multi-ethnic society."[16] Diplomats not only emphasized the inherent cultural features of Brazilian society that promoted racial egalitarianism but also highlighted the government's leadership in criminalizing racism and ensuring equality in the country, at least formally.

In some instances, though not always, this meant that Brazilian officials did recognize that the country had to cope with the residue of slavery:

> Today [in Brazil] it is recognized that democracy means equality for all. Governments must set an example by scrupulously enforcing nondiscriminatory policies. . . . It is the responsibility of States to prohibit and put an end to discrimination within their territory. . . . For Brazil, a country made up of people of different races and ethnic origins, diversity is a valuable asset in achieving the nation's goals. Nevertheless, Brazil still had to cope with a legacy of social problems largely resulting from injustices perpetrated during colonial times and the early stages of independence.[17]

Even though Brazilian diplomats acknowledged historic injustices, they often failed to recognize that ongoing racism and discrimination was a problem in Brazil. Instead, statements like these, as well as many others made well through the 1990s, painted the picture of a multiracial, multi-ethnic society that, as one diplomat put it, "had always been at the forefront of the struggle against racism and racial discrimination."[18]

In addition, Brazilian diplomats were also extremely active in the UN's efforts to combat racism. They participated actively in monitoring compliance with the Convention on the Elimination of Racial Discrimination (CERD), and they showed leadership during the UN decade against racism campaign. Further, Brazil was one of the first countries to speak within the UN about the significance of a Third World Conference against Racism. In one meeting, a Brazilian diplomat said that her government planned to take an active role in convening the conference, in part because Brazil was proud of its "harmonious coexistence among people of different religious, racial, and cultural backgrounds." She added that the conference should also be "action-oriented" and "come up with concrete commitments and measures to counter racial discrimination and intolerance, wherever they occurred. It must send a clear message that was understood by the public at large."[19] In fact, as I will discuss later, the Durban Conference's new format—which contrasted with the previous two World Conferences against Racism that were small meetings mostly of government officials—was particularly important for the Afro-Brazilian movements' success there. Yet while the Brazilian government's interest in leading anti-racism efforts within the UN may have been rooted in their genuine belief that Brazil was a model of racial tolerance, their goal may also have been geopolitical in nature, given the Brazilian government's active quest for a permanent seat on the UN Security Council. That aim put a spotlight on Brazil as preparations for the Durban Conference developed (Telles 2004).

Fully aware of both the image diplomats projected about Brazilian race relations and Brazil's ambitions within the UN, Afro-Brazilian activists began to mobilize around the conference relatively early (Telles 2004). In many ways, the conference was exactly the opportunity the movement needed to exert pressure on the Brazilian state to make good on the promises it had made, most recently with the failed GTI of 1995. As Htun (2004) notes, the conference also reenergized Afro-Brazilians working within Cardoso's administration, many of whom had lost momentum and hope about implementing race-based policies.

In March 2000, Brazil stepped up to host the Regional Conference of the Americas, the first of four regional preparatory conferences held around the world before the Durban Conference to take place the following year. However, just a month later, the Brazilian government rescinded its offer after scandals emerged around the country's celebrations marking 500 years since the "discovery" of Brazil. Images flooded the national and international media of Brazil's military police violently repressing peaceful protestors, among them students as well as indigenous and black activists.[20] In the international press, this state violence was often juxtaposed with the popular image of Brazil as a racially mixed and harmonious society. So even as Brazilian diplomats cited a lack of financial resources as the reason Brazil would not host the regional conference, activists speculated that they withdrew because they feared more protest and unwanted international attention.

However, many of the activists I spoke with said the 500-year debacle and the refusal to host was a blessing in disguise as it further widened the political opening of Durban. I asked Ivanir dos Santos of the Center for the Articulation of Marginalized People why he thought organizing around the Durban Conference was so effective. He responded: "At first it wasn't. . . . The thing that helped us was the moment in which the Brazilian government refused to host the regional conference" (interview, Ivanir dos Santos, October 2009). Government officials also admitted that Brazil's 500-year celebration was a pivotal moment in the Durban process. Ambassador Gilberto Sabóia, who was a central figure in the Brazilian delegation to Durban, explained this to me in an interview:

> The 500-year celebration was really poorly done. It ignored the contribution of indigenous peoples. It was as if everything had started with the Portuguese. And the people that I met in the Ministry for Human Rights and other sectors, they said: "Look, Ambassador, if we don't succeed in doing this conference and doing something during this administration that really promotes the true advancement of blacks in Brazil, the moderate [black] leaders are going to be replaced by the more and more radical ones that are emerging among the youth (interview, Gilberto Sabóia, March 2010).

What these events signaled to black Brazilian activists was that the state had much at stake in upholding the country's image in the international arena as a racial paradise.

In the absence of Brazilian leadership, the Chilean government agreed to host the regional meeting of the Americas. In October 2000, just two months before the regional conference, the Chilean government held a small meeting of regional experts in its capital, Santiago. In addition to government officials, they invited twelve experts on discrimination and intolerance to present background papers to help frame the regional conference and Latin America's participation in the Durban Conference. Edna Roland, co-founder of the black feminist organization Fala Preta (Speak, Black Woman!) was charged with presenting the background document on Afro-descendants in the Americas. Roland's presentation painted a picture of sharp racial inequalities and racism in Brazil and the region as a whole. This was one of the first of many moments in the preparations for Durban where Brazilian diplomats had to face black activists who contradicted the picture they had painted for decades of race relations in Brazil. For example, despite the fact that the GTI had not been successful in implementing any concrete policies, the Brazilian government highlighted the important work that group was doing to address racial inequalities in the country. Roland disagreed: "While positive changes have taken place in Brazil, the government has not been able to implement many of the recommendations of the Inter-Ministerial Working Group (GTI) and particularly those that would have a real impact on the living conditions of Afro-Latinos."[21]

Roland's rebuttal was important, given that the statements made by Brazilian diplomats had previously gone unchecked in international forums like the one in Santiago. The presence of black Brazilian activists in these elite transnational spaces, however, made it nearly impossible for Brazilian officials to maintain the picture of harmonious and egalitarian race relations in their country. Instead, in such venues, black Brazilian activists offered radically different accounts than their white diplomat compatriots did, and the activists often backed up their stories with solid statistics (Telles 2004). Such events gave activists an unprecedented opportunity to negotiate with high-level government officials.

Their efforts were successful at the Santiago regional conference in December 2000. Brazil was one of many Latin American governments that signed on to the final Santiago Program of Action, which recognized that racism and institutionalized discrimination were problems in their countries. Among other things, the Santiago declaration called for reparations for slavery as well as "strategies, programs, and policies that can include affirmative action measures to favor the victims of racism, racial discrimination, xenophobia, and other forms of discrimination that impede the effective enjoyment of civil and political rights."[22] Because the Santiago conference was specific to the Latin American experience, and because of the actual language in the document, many Afro-Latin American activists saw, and continue to see, the Santiago Declaration as even more important than the Durban Program of Action.

The National Committee on Durban

Upon returning from the Santiago Regional Conference of the Americas, Cardoso signed a Presidential Decree creating a national committee charged with preparation for the Third World Conference against Racism. The committee had two objectives: (1) to consult with the president on formulating the Brazilian government's position for regional and international negotiations during the world conference; (2) to promote—in cooperation with civil society organizations—seminars and other activities designed to develop a deeper understanding of, and to disseminate information about, issues related to the world conference, especially those topics relevant to the Brazilian reality.[23] He appointed a number of government officials to the committee, including Afro-Brazilian senator Benedita da Silva as well four black activists from established black NGOs. Edna Roland, who impressed diplomats in Santiago, acted as a quasi-member of the committee.

High-level government officials were willing to listen to the recommendations of activists in the National Committee, and in some cases the officials even charged the activists with formulating the Brazilian government's position and policies. This was especially the case with Roland, who actually represented the Brazilian delegation in negotiations with other countries in Durban (interview, Edna Roland, May 2010, and interview, Minister Gregori, March 2010).[24] The influence they had in Durban was indispensable, they inserted more binding language, and specific policies, into the Brazilian government's official statement. Alberti and Pereira (2006) show

how the inclusion of one phrase in the document that became the Brazilian delegation's official statement at the Durban Conference set the ball rolling for affirmative action policies in Brazilian universities. That phrase was "quotas in the university for blacks."

NGOs and Transnational Mobilization

During preparations for Durban, it was not clear whether the National Committee was actually serious about adopting and implementing specific policies for black populations. Some activists were skeptical, seeing it as coopted by the Brazilian state. For them, it was a more effective strategy to lobby the state from outside and through transnational networks, first in Santiago and later in Durban (Martins et al. 2004; Telles 2004). Black Brazilian activists created strong transnational advocacy networks with other black organizations throughout Latin America and the Caribbean. They held regional meetings to develop a strategy for Durban and, most importantly, they approached donor institutions to ensure a strong presence at both the Santiago and Durban conferences (interview, Jurema Werneck, October 2009).[25]

In so doing, these activists appropriated established repertoires that professionalized civil society organizations around the globe had developed (Keck and Sikkink 1998). In Brazil, leveraging these kinds of UN conferences had already emerged as a viable strategy to influence state policy (Fernandes 1994). Afro-Brazilian women activists heading initiatives in Durban had already attended and organized around the 1994 Population and Development Conference in Cairo and the Fourth World Conference on Women in Beijing in 1995. Indeed, in the 1993 national Brazilian civil society conference called "Our Rights for Cairo," at least twenty-five activists in attendance represented black women's organizations. [26] They participated and helped draft the document that later became the basis of negotiation between the women's movement and the Brazilian state. Participation in these conferences gave black feminists a leg up for Durban organizing at the same time it gave them proof that their efforts could lead to changes in state discourse and policy reforms.[27]

Black women's organizations mobilized at the local and national level in the months preceding Durban. In 2000, they founded the Articulation of Black Brazilian Women's Organizations (AMNB), which was made up of twenty-four organizations from around the country with the goal of "establishing the adequate conditions for the participation of this segment [black women] in the process of mobilization and development of the Third World Conference Against Racism, Xenophobia and Related Intolerances."[28] These same black women were central to regional efforts like the Strategic Afro-Latin American Alliance (Alianza), founded in San José, Costa Rica, in

September 2000. Made up mostly of black activists representing NGOs in various Latin American and Caribbean countries, the network's main goal was to organize around Durban as a way of pressuring Latin American states to collect data on ethno-racial inequality and to adopt specific policies for black populations (Telles 2004; Martins et al. 2004).

The Afro-Brazilian feminist NGO Geledés sought out and oversaw international funding for Alianza members to participate in both the Santiago and Durban conferences. Ultimately, they secured a grant from the Ford Foundation and consequently managed the participation of the Latin American black organizations in Durban (interview, Werneck, October 2009). As such, Geledés, along with another Afro-Brazilian women's NGO, Criola, became a nexus of national and international organizing around the Durban Conference. In addition, the partnerships Afro-Brazilian activists developed with U.S.-based institutions such as the Southern Education Foundation and the International Human Rights Law Group were also important (Telles 2004). However, such efforts were significantly undermined when the U.S. government launched an effective boycott of the conference amid accusations that it was anti-Israel and anti-Semitic.[29] The withdrawal of the United States and its allies left a vacuum of government and civil society leadership upon which Afro-Brazilian activists were able to capitalize. Black Brazilian activists became the nexus of regional civil society efforts, and this further elevated them to a status of legitimate interlocutors with the Brazilian government in Durban negotiations.

While Brazilian diplomats in Santiago initially ignored activists from Geledés and other NGOs, arguing that they had adequately consulted the black movement through the National Committee, they eventually changed their tune. In a sense, Afro-Brazilian NGOs were too visible for the Brazilian government to ignore. As a result, in Santiago and later in Durban, Afro-Brazilian activists outside the National Committee succeeded in having daily meetings with the heads of the Brazilian delegation as well as with other important diplomatic staff (interview, Jurema Werneck, October 2009; interview, Gilberto Sabóia, March 2010; Sabóia and Porto 2001). The goal of these meetings was to hold the Brazilian government accountable for the positions they had promised to take in the meetings of the previous day.

In addition, the Alianza network also devised a strategy whereby they collectively lobbied governments to support the inclusion of specific policies into the official Santiago document, and later the Durban Plan of Action. Speaking about this tactic, Minister Jose Gregori, the head of the Brazilian state delegation to Durban, said, "Durban was the triumph of black Brazilians. . . . So, even if governments were against Durban at the beginning, they would eventually have to collide with black Brazilian activists. In Durban, [black activists] found the place to affirm their struggle" (interview, Jose Gregori, March 2010). The minister added that the work of the Afro-Brazilian movement, and particularly of Afro-Brazilian women, allowed him to push the racial equality agenda within the Brazilian delegation as well as other delegations. Through these transnational processes, Brazilian activists emerged as the main articulators of regional civil society mobilization, which gave them more momentum and clarity in their negotiations with Brazilian diplomats.

As Brazilian activists made their way to South Africa for the Durban Conference, the Brazilian government was already poised to make strong statements about their commitment to adopt "affirmative measures" to address racial inequality in Brazil.[30] Afro-Brazilian activists both in and outside the National Committee had been central to shaping this official position.[31] The Brazilian state had already signed on to the Santiago document. They had also sponsored meetings throughout the country, including the National Meeting on Racism and Racial Discrimination that included 1,700 participants (Sabóia and Porto, 2001). Moreover, as the state delegation embarked upon its trip to South Africa, it expressed its intent of exerting diplomatic pressure on other governments to include the language of "reparations," "affirmative action," and statements acknowledging the transatlantic slave trade as a "crime against humanity" in the Durban Program of Action.

Somewhat ironically, in responding to pressure by black activists, the Brazilian state was ultimately able to reinforce its image as a leader in the struggle against racism both at home and globally. Minister Gregori recounted to me a moment in Durban where Brazilian diplomats and activists were all cloaked in a Brazilian flag singing the national anthem. He explained, "We worked a lot on the Durban Conference for reasons that don't have to do with Brazil, exactly. . . . It helped us, Brazil, emerge in that world of people, with everybody happy, everybody singing, everybody understanding each other, in the context of this dispute between Palestinians and Jews, those things that almost foreshadowed 9/11." Indeed, by promising to adopt concrete policies to ameliorate racial inequality and discrimination, Brazilian officials were also showing the world that Brazil, in contrast to much of the rest of the world, was one happy, tolerant democracy.

Beyond symbolic gestures, in the days leading to and the months after Durban, the Brazilian state began to adopt what would become an avalanche of racial equality policies. A few months before Durban, officials announced the creation of the first government affirmative action program in the Ministry of Agriculture and upon returning from Durban, Cardoso announced an affirmative action program in the foreign service (Itamaraty).[32] However, Brazil eventually adopted the bulk of its affirmative action and racial equality policies under President Lula. The process was largely decentralized, happening both through state legislation, as was the case with the first affirmative policy at the State University of Rio de Janeiro (UERJ,

2001). The policies spread like wildfire through state legislatures and university councils throughout the country. By 2008, 62 of Brazil's 236 public universities had adopted some form of affirmative action (Paixão et al. 2010). Beyond affirmative action, the Lula administration passed legislation creating the National Secretariat for the Promotion of Racial Equality (SEPPIR) in 2003 as well as a number of pieces of legislation aimed at moving toward racial equality in nearly every area, including health, education, and social welfare policy.

Yet while Durban did certainly initiate a sort of domino effect in terms of racial equality policies in Brazil, black activists within the Workers' Party (PT) also played an important role in this process. Many activists close to Lula's administration had dedicated many decades to assuring that racial issues would become a key component of the administration's policy. Indeed, some activists from organizations like CONEN were involved in the Durban Conference preparation but did not actually go to the conference because they were deeply entrenched in Lula's presidential campaign. For them, far too much was at stake to risk leaving just months before the election season (interview, Flávio Jorge, May 2010). In the end, the combination of the Durban momentum and this party activism led to the wave of racial equality policies in Brazil.[33]

THE PARTIAL MOVE TO RACIAL EQUALITY IN COLOMBIA

Whereas Durban was essential to the making of racial policy in Brazil, the conference's effect on Colombia's political field was less clear and slower to materialize. Afro-Colombian activists did participate in Durban, as well as the regional preparatory conference in Santiago (interview, Dorys Garcia, February 2009). Different factions within the movement were also active in transnational activist networks that effectively mobilized around Durban including Afro-América XXI, the Network of Afro-Latin American and Caribbean Women, and Alianza. What is more, the Colombian government signed on to the robust Santiago Declaration in 2000. Even so, upon returning from Durban, the state did very little to make good on the promises contained in the declaration.

By the early 2000s, the idea of black communities as a subject of multicultural rights was firmly institutionalized into the Colombian state, through the Office on Ethnic Affairs as well as the state agencies charged with agrarian reform, and even in the census bureau. While the Brazilian government dragged its feet on *quilombo* land titling, the Colombian government was titling collective black territories relatively quickly, all with the purpose of protecting cultural difference. More generally, the 1990s and early 2000s were heavily marked in Colombia by a shoving of all black issues into the discourse of ethnic difference such that blacks in rural and urban areas, those with and without "legitimate" claims to cultural distinction all had to make demands on those discursive grounds. All of this made discussions of Durban, and racism and racial equality more generally, somewhat out of place in Colombia's new political field.

When the Colombian state did start to talk in the language of equality and anti-racism it was not until the mid- to late 2000s. When the discourse of ethno-racial politics began to emerge, it came in direct conflict with the multicultural model that had been consolidated over the previous decades. In what follows, I examine Colombia's timid shift toward discourses of racial equality. In so doing, I also analyze the discursive and material conflicts that this new round of reforms created between ideas of urban blackness and rural blackness.[34] I do this by analyzing two moments in Colombia where these tensions were particularly acute: the 2005 census debates and the 2012 Equal Opportunities Bill.

The 2005 Census and the Tentative Shift to Racial Equality

The size of Colombia's black population has been a point of contention between and among black activists, state bureaucrats, and academics. While little data existed before the 1990s, more recently there have been a number of "official" state estimates, which have ranged from 1.52 percent to 26 percent.[35] This variation is due, in part, to the fact that Colombia historically did not include a race question on its national census. Between 1905 and 2005, only four of Colombia's eleven national censuses included a question aimed at counting its black population.[36] In all four cases, the criteria the state used as well as the percentage of individuals that identified as black varied radically, from about 6 percent in both 1912 and 1918 to 1.5 percent in 1993 and 10.5 percent in 2005. Scholars have found similar variation over time in other Latin American countries and have shown that variation to reflect reclassification as well as shifts in social understandings of the boundaries around particular ethno-racial categories (Carvalho et al. 2004; Loveman and Muniz 2007). However, in Colombia this variation is also rooted in substantial differences in the ethno-racial question itself. Radically different conceptions of blackness have been embedded in different Colombian census and household survey questions (Barbary and Urrea 2004). Moreover, behind each estimate of the black population lies a complex and contentious political process (Paschel 2013).

The ethnic question in the 1993 census was deeply rooted in a cultural understanding of the black population. It read, "Do you belong to an ethnic group, indigenous group, or black community? If so, which one?" The idea that one could belong to a specific black community as one might belong to an indigenous group proved incompatible with the complex ways that different sectors within the Afro-Colombian population—particularly those in majority white/*mestizo* cities—understood themselves. In the end, less than two percent of the population identified as black, a number slightly smaller than those that identified as indigenous.

This culturally specific definition of blackness resulted directly from the political process I described in the last chapter, a series of contentious debates and compromises between urban and rural black movement organizations and between them and the state. However, by the late 1990s, many government officials and activists agreed that the 1993 census had grossly undercounted the black population (Barbary and Urrea 2004). In this new context where black communities were the legal subjects of particular rights and where previous data was unreliable, much was at stake with the ethnic question in Colombia's 2005 census.

Before Colombia's National Statistics Administration (DANE) began preparations for the 2005 census, another state agency, the Department of National Planning, pledged it would include an appropriate ethnic question. Specifically, it vowed in one report to "include a question of ethnic belonging and territoriality in the next census"[37] and in another "to develop indicators and instruments to permit a greater knowledge and evaluation of the socioeconomic and cultural conditions [of the black population]."[38] In addition, the Colombian state had made international commitments to collect ethno-racial statistics. Throughout the 2000s, DANE officials participated in a number of high-level international meetings organized by the Economic Commission on Latin America and the Caribbean, the World Bank, the Pan-American Health Organization, the Inter-American Development Bank, and the United Nations (Telles 2007; Del Popolo 2008). Perhaps most importantly, they served as regional leaders in organizing the first international "We All Count" conference in Cartagena in November 2000. The meeting gathered government officials, activists, and bureaucrats from multilateral institutions with the goal of "identifying strategies to promote the capturing of ethnic and cultural diversity in the censuses of Latin America and the Caribbean."[39]

In a speech two years after the Todos Contamos meetings, the vice president of the World Bank called data collection one of the "four areas in which the World Bank as an active member of the IAC, [was] making progress toward reducing disparities between Afro-descendant and other populations." He also applauded Colombia's census bureau for its efforts to compile "reliable statistics" on race and ethnicity. Indeed, DANE was one of the most proactive government institutions in Latin America working on these issues. A number of international agencies had granted DANE funds precisely to develop the ethnic question on the 2005 census. This international stage was particularly important to the Colombian government, as a report on the 2005 census process revealed. It emphasized DANE's "international recognition" for hosting the Todos Contamos Conference and for involving communities in collecting ethnic statistics.[40]

In Colombia, and Latin America more generally, much of the debate between bureaucrats and black activists around collecting ethno-racial statistics happened in these international forums (Telles 2007; Del Popolo 2008; Loveman 2014). International developments allowed Afro-Colombians not only to insist that ethno-racial data be collected but also to participate in the process. Among many other things, black Colombian activists demanded that the state collaborate with representatives of black organizations to develop the appropriate census question, ensure through pilot studies that the population understood the question, and finance "national socialization campaigns" to make sure that the Afro-Colombian population would be fully counted this time.[41]

To this end, beginning in 2004, DANE officials met with representatives of the National Commission on Black Communities, a body of black representatives elected by black organizations and tasked with representing the movement in official negotiations with the Colombian state. The state also signed Resolution 786, which laid out DANE's specific obligation to collect ethnic data in the census and mandated the creation of the National Afro-Colombian Board (JAN), which was to work closely with DANE to hold workshops throughout the country to raise awareness about the ethnic question on the census.

In addition, a number of national organizations formed a coalition, the Afro-Colombian Working Group for the 2005 General Census, which consisted of national and regional urban and rural black organizations and would also play a central role in shaping this process.[42] While such coalitions were rare and often short-lived within the Afro-Colombian movement, the importance of this census had arguably made such alliances necessary. Activists across these sectors were worried that state officials would use the census results to roll back policies for black communities.[43] They articulated this concern in a letter they sent to President Uribe in October 2004 after the director of DANE, with whom activists had reached specific agreements, resigned. The letter cited domestic and international mandates that obligated the Colombian state to collect ethno-racial data, and outlined the agreements DANE and activists had made. The letter ended: "Finally, Mr. President, we are absolutely convinced that the results of the next census will have profound repercussions on the life of the country, on our communities, and on public policies that are designed to overcome the structural racism that we live."[44]

In response, DANE held a series of workshops with Afro-Colombian activists throughout the country to find the census question that would adequately capture the Afro-Colombian population and to devise a plan to raise awareness about the question before the actual census. This culminated with the First National Conference to Raise Awareness about Afro-Colombian Populations in the Census (DANE 2007). Participants' use at the conference of mixed-race categories such as *mulato* and *zambo* (of mixed African and indigenous descent), and the awareness that different regions defined these categories differently, raised questions about where one should draw the line around blackness/Afro-Colombianness.

The Black Communities' Movement (PCN)—which was at the forefront of organizing around the census—reported that before the conference two things had already been negotiated. First, the census would include two separate questions, one related to culture and the other to phenotype. Second, rather than using only the term "black" (*negro*), the census questionnaire would also include a number of popularly used categories which were often understood to be associated, if not synonymous, with black, among them *mulato*, *moreno*, and *trigueño* (PCN 2006). However, competing ideas about race, culture, and regional differences continued to surface as census officials defined blackness in more restrictive terms and a new coalition of urban and rural Afro-Colombian organizations advocated for broader definitions of the black population.

The Beautiful Faces Campaign of 2005

Equally as important as getting the question right was the national campaign to encourage people to identify as black/Afro-Colombian. Like activists throughout Latin America, those in Colombia saw the census as an important opportunity to counteract what they saw as internalized racism. As a result, they sought to encourage people to embrace their blackness/Afro-Colombianness through the Beautiful Faces of My Black People Campaign. Inspired by a song of the same name that Afro-Puerto Rican singer Ismael Rivera recorded in 1978. The campaign included posters, radio, and television commercials and had the goal of getting a more accurate—and what they thought would be a higher—count of the Afro-Colombian population.

Given prior agreements, the movement saw this type of consciousness-raising or "socialization" campaign as at least partially the obligation of the Colombian government.[45] While the production and most of the organizing around the campaign fell on the shoulders of the movement itself, DANE's division of marketing and diffusion did eventually partner with them. According to DANE, the campaign commercial aired on both regional and national stations through the National Television Commission.[46]

The Beautiful Faces commercial was about 30 seconds long. With images of people of various skin tones, urban Afro-Colombians as well as farmers and people in traditional clothes, and music in the background that was not easily identifiable with any specific region in the country, the commercial's message was clear: they were all Afro-Colombian. "I am *negro, morena, mulata, zamba*. I am Afro-descendant. I count. *Palenquero, raizal, mulato, negra*, I count. Afro-descendant, *morena, negra*. I'm *zambo, raizal*. I count. *Palenquero, negro*." It ended with the confident words of Maria Eugenia Arboleda, a famous Afro-Colombian actress who said: "My people, in this census, count yourself!" followed by the some fifteen Afro-Colombians featured in the commercial exclaiming in unison "Proud to be Afro-Colombian."[47] The most interesting aspect of the Beautiful Faces campaign was the shift from organizing around the category "black" or "black communities" to the broader term "Afro-Colombian." This was clear not only in the commercial but also in a public statement the campaign organizers issued on November 23, 2005: "This campaign is a proposal to achieve a higher number of blacks, mulatos/as, morenos/as, zambos/as, Afro-descendants, Afro-Colombians, palenqueros, raizales, in other words, everyone that feels black-African blood run through their veins, even if it is only a drop, to identify themselves when they respond on the [census] form."

However, getting more people to identify as black/Afro-Colombian in this census than in the previous one required a less culturally specific definition as well as the inclusion of mixed-race categories. As such, rather than understanding the black population as bound by culture and space, as the 1991 constitution did, the campaign called people to understand their blackness as a shared history rooted in Africa and defined by "one drop of black blood." In this sense, the movement adopted a hypo descent approach to blackness/Afro-Colombianness reminiscent of the one-drop rule in the United States.[48]

The category of "Afro-Colombian" that emerged was likely a compromise between the broader notion of blackness that urban organizations like Cimarrón had advocated for decades and the more culturally and geographically specific definitions that rural organizations from the Pacific coast adopted (Asher 2009; Paschel 2010). The constitutional reform process had exacerbated tensions between urban and rural organizations, but organizing around the 2005 census was a rare moment in which groups like Cimarrón joined with a wide range of rural black groups, including PCN, to present a united front in negotiations with the state. In so doing, they advocated for a conception of group membership that could encompass urban blacks, those outside of the Pacific coast, and even those of mixed ancestry. While activists in the movement still differed on many points, they continued to pressure the state to include categories like *moreno* and *mulato* on the census. Meanwhile census officials continued to view the question through an exclusively ethno-cultural lens. As a result, tensions remained between that notion and the idea of a black population defined by both culture and ancestry/physical traits.

Ultimately, DANE included in the census not the two questions that they previous agreed on, but a hybrid one. It read: "According to your culture, community, or physical traits . . . you recognize yourself to be" and gave the following six choices: (1) Indigenous, (2) Rom [Gypsy], (3) From San Andres and Providencia, (4) Palenquero de San Basilio, (5) Black, *mulato*, Afro-Colombian, or Afro-descendant, and (6) None of the above.[49] Interestingly, this question reflects both the state's previously institutionalized definition of blackness as culturally specific and a more racially defined notion that included "physical traits." Unlike in the 1993 census, it also included a mixed-race category. Even so, the fact that whites and *mestizos* were considered "none of the above" suggests a very ethnic conception of groupness. Indeed, within the logic of Colombia's 2005 census, those who were not indigenous, Afro-descendant, or Gypsy were presumed to be simply Colombians, culturally unmarked, *colombianos normales*, if you will.[50] This conception of ethno-racial difference would be inconceivable in Brazil. There, the state had collected such statistics throughout the twentieth century according to "racial" or "color" categories, rather than "cultural" ones.[51] Every Brazilian was thought to be part of the national culture, they simply occupied different descriptive categories like white, brown, black.

Yet even as Colombian census officials began to describe "Afro-Colombian" in more ethno-racial terms—by both phenotype and culture—tensions over the definition lingered. DANE's report outlining the census results underscores this ambivalence. It defines "Afro-Colombians as:

> People of African descent who possess cultural characteristics that make them a unique human group. They share a tradition and preserve their own culture in such a way that reveals an identity that distinguishes them from other groups, regardless of whether they live in rural areas or the city. They are also known as the black population, Afro-descendants, among other names.[52]

To be sure, this definition of Afro-Colombian moves beyond the spatial confines of the concept of "black communities" institutionalized in the 1991 constitution and Law 70. Nevertheless, *afrocolombianidad* is still defined by cultural distinction from "other groups," rather than by the many other potential bases of ethno-racial difference including ancestry, phenotype, or shared identity based on experience. Further, this purely cultural definition of Afro-Colombian was somewhat inconsistent with the actual census question, which included "physical traits" alongside "community" and "culture." This ongoing tension reveals state officials' discomfort with the idea of noncultural definitions of rights; it also echoes the multicultural logic embedded in the 1991 constitution and the Law of Black Communities.

In this way, the Colombian state's understanding of blackness continues to reflect these prior struggles between state actors and black activists (Asher 2009; Paschel 2010).

In the end, Afro-Colombian activists moved beyond one of the deepest fissures in their movement, namely the different definitions of blackness that urban and rural black leaders have held since the early 1990s, as well as their distinct diagnoses and prognoses of the problems facing them. Even so, a number of factors undermined their efforts. As PCN put it in their official evaluation of the census, "Despite all our efforts, DANE committed a permanent and avoidable set of errors that resulted in many Afro-Colombians being made invisible yet again" (PCN 2006, 3). First, some ethno-racial categories that were prominent in the commercial, including *zambo* and *moreno*, were notably omitted from the census form. This disjuncture likely undermined the campaign's effectiveness, particularly in the regions, such as the Atlantic Coast, that use omitted categories (Mosquera et al. 2009).[53] Moreover, DANE decided to have heads of household fill out the ethno-racial question for the entire family, and the census omitted the question altogether in some regions. The movement also feared that commercial was not as widely disseminated as DANE officials claimed (PCN 2006; Mosquera et al. 2009).

Ultimately, nearly 4.3 million people, 10.5 percent of Colombia's population, identified as black, Afro-Colombian, *mulato*, *palenquero*, or *raizal*. This was much lower than the 26 percent figure that Afro-Colombian activists typically use; however, it was still much higher than the 1.5 percent reported in the 1993 national census. At their core, these numbers reflect a political process in which black Colombian organizations shaped "official" ethno-racial categories. In so doing, they moved beyond blackness as culturally defined and geographically specific, and toward the notion of blackness as rooted in culture, shared history, and phenotype.

In so doing, Colombia inched toward conceptions of blackness that looked more like dominant understandings of blackness in Brazil. For decades, Brazil's state institutions and its black movement had defined blackness through experiences with discrimination. To the extent that ambiguity or contestation existed around census categories there, it was around where mixed-race people figured into racial categories in Brazil. These tensions manifested most clearly around Brazil's 1990 census when the black movement proposed a collapsing of the black and brown category into a singular *negro* category, with no success (Nobles 2000). At the center of such debates was not whether browns were culturally similar to blacks but rather whether they experienced the same kinds of systematic disadvantage that blacks did. This idea of blackness as defined by discrimination had long existed in Brazil. Indeed, nearly a century before, explicit black organizing took the form of social and political clubs of *homens de cor*, or "men of color." As such, the dominant grammar of black struggle in Brazil in that period, and over the next century, came to be about color, race, and inequality rather than about culture and distinction.[54]

These different conceptions of blackness were very much in flux in Colombia in the 2000s. Rather than a full-blown racial equality alignment, what the country experienced was an awkward shift toward the language of the right to equality, in a political field in which the idea of the right to difference was already firmly planted. Could black populations be both urban and rural, need both integration and autonomy? In the 2000s, the Colombian state shifted its ethno-racial categories and discourse in ways that emphasized the need for racial equality and anti-racism. However, this widening of state discourse was linked to the emergence of a new branch of Colombia's black movement, the *afro-derecha*, or black right.

Equal Opportunity Laws and the Right to Racial Equality

In May 2009, Colombia's Office of the Vice President teamed up with USAID, Cimarrón, and scholars like Claudia Mosquera to launch the first National Campaign against Racism. In a video they produced featuring Afro-Colombian hip-hop group Chocquibtown, they emphasized the need for racial equality and respect and the need to stop racial discrimination against Afro-Colombians. It takes place in a classroom of mostly black children, and starts with a young black boy with his hand raised. He says, "I want to be an airplane pilot!" and then a young black woman says, "I want to go to the university." Finally, a black man in a suit says emphatically, "I can be a bank manager!"[55] In July 2012, the Observatory against Discrimination and Racism (OCDR) was created within the Ministry of the Interior[56] with the goal of "collecting and analyzing information as well as documenting and monitoring the dynamics and practices of racism and discrimination that are present in Colombia."[57]

The campaign and the founding of OCDR were part of a larger trend toward state discourses of anti-racism and racial inequality in Colombia. Just months before OCDR began its work, the Colombian Congress passed a bill making racism and other forms of discrimination a punishable crime, as Brazil did with its 1988 constitution.[58] The law mandated that discrimination based on race, nationality, gender, or sexuality be punished with a fine equivalent to between ten and fifteen months' worth of a minimum-wage salary as well as twelve to thirty-six months in prison. However, many people, including black activists, critiqued the law as impractical.

What is more telling about this law is who advocated for it. The law was not a result of movement pressure or a push from Afro-Colombian Congress members but an initiative of the Christian political party, MIRA.[59]

Despite much vocal opposition within Congress and without strong support from black political organizations, MIRA used the limited political power it had to push it through. Soon after the law passed, MIRA launched a political ad featuring a well-dressed black couple getting ready for work in a nice apartment. The man narrates: "Thanks to the Anti-Discrimination Law, my partner and I have jobs, and our quality of life has drastically improved. Thank you, MIRA for saying no to discrimination in the country." The commercial ends with an explicit call to action: "Vote MIRA in the Senate and Lower Chamber regional races!" To be clear, MIRA's political motivations do not necessarily undermine the legislation's importance. However, the direct link the commercial makes between criminalizing racism and social mobility for Afro-Colombians assumes that the law—unlike its predecessor in Brazil—will actually be effective in stamping out racism.

In contrast to the criminalization approach, the Equal Opportunities Bill set out to do precisely that. Proposed in September 2012, the legislation calls for affirmative action throughout Colombia and across a number of areas. Unlike in Brazil, where affirmative action policies were initiated through a decentralized process, this bill sought to adopt them in one big sweep as well as reach beyond the limited spaces where Law 70 has been implemented. The political process behind this legislation and the discourse embedded in it reveal the awkward shift that both the Colombian state and the Afro-Colombian movement have made in the language of black rights.

The Equal Opportunities Bill

On the National Day of Afro-Colombian History and Culture in May 2011, President Juan Manuel Santos promised in a speech to propose a law that would settle Colombia's "historic debt" to its Afro-Colombian population by providing its members with equal opportunities.[60] Rather than couch this proposed law in the language of multiculturalism or the right to identity, he cited inequality statistics, including Afro-Colombians' higher rates of illiteracy and forced displacement. In so doing, he began to make the case for policies rooted in racial equality. This contrasted greatly with the speeches state officials made in previous decades, which justified policies for black Colombians exclusively in the language of cultural difference and protection.

Santos made good on his promise to move toward a law of equal opportunity. About a year and a half later, and after a fraught process of consultation with black communities and political organizations throughout the country, the Minister of the Interior proposed Statutory Bill 125.[61] It called for a shift toward more integrationist policies, including affirmative action for Afro-Colombians in the labor market and higher education. However, much like the 2005 census, the bill straddled the logics of cultural difference and racial equality. Beyond the urban/rural issue, tensions also arose between defining the subject of black rights as individual "Afro-Colombians" (read as urban) versus collective "black communities" (read as rural). The bill itself stated its intention as an attempt "to turn our gaze toward the Afro-Colombian population as bearers of rights . . . who need special protection not only because they are in circumstances of unmistakable vulnerability but because their ethnic and cultural richness is a fundamental part of the Colombian nation." Here, Afro-Colombians' cultural richness ultimately justified affirmative action policies.

However, the legislation also justified itself in the language of economic, political, and social integration. The next sentence of the bill, for example, outlined possible limitations. It stated, "Surely this project will not be sufficient to overcome the historic level of inequality of the Afro-Colombian population and the resulting social, economic, and political *atraso* [lag, backwardness, delayed-ness] of Colombians of African ancestry, but we are sure this will be a step in that direction." The term *atraso* is key here, as it is at odds with much of the discourse of ethno-territorial organizations like PCN that see black rural communities' "*atraso*" as their cultural strength, as it is evidence of their rich, noncapitalist culture, which the state has a responsibility to respect and protect (Escobar 2008). In fact, throughout the bill, the justification for such policies oscillated between a logic of cultural protection and one of racial equality and integration. This duality is also present in the international norms that it invoked. Whereas most legislation for Afro-Colombians only references multicultural norms like ILO Convention 169, this law also cited the Durban Plan of Action as well as the ILO Convention 111 on discrimination.

Beyond the question of what kind of black political subject was being imagined in the bill, there is the actual substance. The legislation did seem to propose a departure from existing Colombian legislation and policies for black communities. Chapter II of the bill outlined, for example, a set of "affirmative action" policies in the area of education. In addition to mandating the "diffusion of ethnic values and the promotion of anti-discrimination," it proposed scholarships for Afro-Colombian students and special funds for "ethnic research." Yet the most radical departure from existing Colombian legislation was Article 10, which proposed quotas, to reach 10 percent by 2024, for Afro-Colombian students in all public universities and technical schools. However, under affirmative action students would not self-identify but instead would require certification that "verified that the candidate belonged to the Black, Afro-Colombian, Raizal, and Palenquera community." The bill specified that the Colombian state, and specifically the Office on Black Communities within the Ministry of the Interior, be responsible for confirming the "authenticity" of these candidates.

This authentication process was similar to the one the University of Valle adopted in 2000. One of the few existing affirmative action programs in Colombia, Univalle reserves 4 percent of university slots for students from black communities.[62] Yet, instead of proving that they are subject to discrimination in employment, housing, and systematically lack access to health care, education, and justice, black students seeking access to the University of Valle through its affirmative action program have to show that they belong to a specific "black community."[63] This criterion was included despite the fact that CADUBHEV, the Afro-Colombian student organization that proposed quotas, had made the case in the language of anti-racism, citing statistics on racial inequality in addition to emphasizing the need for cultural diversity.[64] While the Equal Opportunities Bill also mandated reserving 10 percent of all public and private sector jobs for Afro-Colombians, it did not outline how it would "verify" black community membership in the case of labor markets.

In the end, the bill did not present a radical change in ethno-racial policy in Colombia. In fact, thirty-six of the bill's fifty-seven articles proposed to restructure the Colombian state's institutions to allow for more effective black participation. This emphasis on defining and redefining who represents the "black community" in negotiations with the Colombian state reflects the jockeying for political power within the state and the black movement. As I describe in the next chapter, much discussion about "participation" is a thinly veiled power struggle for access to government contracts, development funds, positions within the state, and old-fashioned bribes. Perhaps because of this, many of the grassroots Afro-Colombian organizations did not officially endorse the bill, in part because it was incubated by a sector within the movement that many activists saw as coopted by the state.

They also maintained their distance because of the international dynamics at play. The Minister of the Interior proposed the bill to congress, but the Intersectorial Commission for the Advancement of the Afro-Colombian Population, which President Álvaro Uribe created in October 2007, originally drafted it. Uribe started the commission—made up of Afro-Colombian members of state advisory commissions, Afro-Colombian congress members, and local politicians—in part to push through the U.S.-Colombia Free Trade Agreement with the "official" endorsement of Colombia's black communities. This unfolded both through regional meetings throughout the country and several lobbying trips to Washington, DC. Thus, while the bill did not directly relate to free trade, its roots were still in the trade agreement. Furthermore, precisely because of the bill's reach, it was hard to imagine it actually passing. It was even less likely that such a law would be fully implemented.

Ultimately, the 2005 census and subsequent anti-racism legislation reveal two things about the nature of the recent, and partial, shift toward racial equality policy in Colombia. First, while explicit discussions of racial discrimination and inequality now occur there, they remain marginalized and subsumed under cultural understandings of the black political subject. Second, the census and the bill underscore how struggles between the Colombian state and different factions within the black movement continue to be embedded in a global political field.

COLOMBIA IS A RACIST COUNTRY!

Beyond policy, Colombian state officials have also begun to develop a discourse of black politics that talks more explicitly about racial inequality and racism. Alongside, and sometimes in place of, the discourse of the "right to difference," state actors have increasingly talked about the "right to equality."[65] This less-tangible shift to a discourse of anti-racism and racial equality was embodied most explicitly in the figure of Colombian vice president Angelino Garzón. In August 2013, Garzón addressed some 900 Afro-Colombian grassroots leaders in a historic national congress in Quibdó marking the twenty-year anniversary of Law 70. Those in the auditorium ranged from black farmers, who had traveled for days by boat, bus, and then plane to reach Quibdó, to black teachers, lawyers, university students, and other professionals, who had flown directly from cities like Bogotá and Cali.

The vice president started his speech by saying, "I'm so happy to be in the folkloric city of Quibdó!" for which he received no applause. However, he began to win over the crowd with his discussion of Afro-Colombians' contributions to the nation. In the charismatic, populist oratorical style he is known for, he said, "Comrades, I've said this before and I think this congress should discuss this. Of course, the law prohibits discrimination and racism in Colombia, but in Colombia, culturally, we are discriminators, we are racists!" The auditorium was overwhelmed with emotion and applause. He continued, "Man, wouldn't it be good for Afro-descendant communities to think about, to discuss having, a quota law? If there are four million people of Afro-descendant, raizal, and palenquero origin in Colombia, why isn't there anything that obligates the national government, the Colombian state, the local and regional government to have an equal proportion of Afro-descendants with responsibilities within the state?" More spirited clapping and shouting followed. He further explained, "If you'll excuse me for repeating this, everyone who governs Colombia has a duty. They have a duty to fight for a politics of social inclusion, to fight against racism, to fight against discrimination!"

The grammar of Garzón's speech was of racial equality. It relied almost exclusively on the idea that black Colombians faced racial discrimination and inequality, which had to be combatted to achieve their full economic, social, and political integration into the nation. This was new language for a Colombian state actor. Garzón could just as easily have couched his speech in the language of cultural protection and ethnic difference his predecessors used. The Colombian state had deeply institutionalized multicultural discourse, and even the black movement had made this discourse its dominant language for talking about the black political struggle. Despite this, Garzón chose to emphasize the right to equality, rather than the right to difference, even when discussing indigenous people. In that auditorium in Quibdó, he seemed to be advising the movement to use a similar language: "For these very reasons, comrades, I think it is only fair, only natural, that this Congress demands—from the national, local, and regional governments, and all of the business leaders in Colombia—more social equity. This [Afro-Colombian] Congress should demand less misery facing the Afro-descendant and black populations in this country. It is only natural." Though, making demands explicitly in the language of racial inclusion and black mobility was anything but "natural" in Colombia at that time. This was particularly so at an important national congress commemorating Law 70, a meeting organized mainly by ethno-territorial organizations like PCN that had defended the right to difference for decades.

As I showed in the last chapter, Cimarrón and other urban-based black organizations that had historically made claims precisely in the language of racial equality had to contend with the ethnicization of blackness in the early 1990s and 2000s. After the 1991 constitution, Law 70, and nearly two decades of legal norms that consecrated a black political subject defined in terms of cultural difference and autonomy, the articulation of policies based on racial equality and integration were not "natural." Instead, many different actors within Colombia's political field still contested these very questions. These debates reflected historic rifts. Urban black sectors often thought about rural blacks and rural poverty as the smoking gun of racial inequality, as precisely the problem to be resolved through social integration and development. In contrast, Colombia's black rural movement defended rural life as an alternative to hegemonic ideas of development. Rather than demand jobs, rural activists demanded the right to traditional forms of mining and farming. Rather than integration, they were articulating a kind of exit.[66] In this sense, the reforms passed under Colombia's multicultural alignment were a direct affront to the integrationist project organizations like Cimarrón advocated.

At the 2013 Quibdó Congress, these tensions were especially pronounced. In the days before Garzón and other high-level state officials arrived at the meeting, the congress of nearly 1,000 leaders met on their own to develop a unified platform with specific demands. I arrived a few days before the congress to help organize some of the material from the pre-congresses held around the country in the previous months and to coordinate a small international delegation that was on its way. During the four-day congress, I participated in two working groups, including the Afro-Urban Working Group. Convening about 100 activists, this group was not organized around a particular issue but rather had an extremely broad and somewhat ambiguous mandate. Leaders in the group focused their discussion on four issues mirroring the thematic working groups: prior consultation, political representation, economic and social development, and the possibility for an autonomous national movement entity. However, much of the discussion was trapped in a kind of pervasive legalism and institutional logic endemic to the Afro-Colombian movement and to Colombia's political field more generally. Black activists in spaces like these commonly fixated on the mechanisms of engagement with the Colombian state rather than on substantive issues.

After hours of discussion, a man in his fifties from the city of Medellín stood up and yelled, "What we [Afro-urbanos] need is a new law!" Fed up with what he saw as an incompatibility between urban issues and existing laws meant for black rural populations, he urged the working group to demand a different route: "What we need is a law for Afro-Colombians in urban areas!" You could feel the tension building in the outdoor patio area that the working group had taken over because "Afro-urbans" were not originally on the Congress agenda. A younger activist organizing with an ethno-territorial organization was visibly annoyed. She fired back immediately "Comrade, I'm sorry but that's absurd, we have Law 70." He lowered his voice and pled with her: "I was born in the city, I was raised in the city, and I do not see myself in Law 70!" In some ways, it is no mystery that Law 70 does not resonate directly with his experiences as someone born and raised in the majority white/*mestizo* city of Medellín. This invisibility of urban blacks was intrinsically tied to the requirements of multicultural citizenship and the political dynamics that led to the inclusion of black communities in the 1991 constitution. However, in meetings like these, the historic memory of the events I discussed in the last chapter was often lost. Rather than acknowledge the limitations of Law 70—that narrowing of black rights that even black rural activists fought against in the early 1990s—ethno-territorial activists often defended Law 70 as a panacea.

This confrontation was one of dozens that occurred on this important anniversary of Law 70. It reflects many unresolved tensions within Colombia's black movement around the nature of the struggle and the possibilities and limitations of the black multicultural subject. Thus, when Vice President Garzón stepped on the stage that day, he was touching on one of the key points of contention within the movement. Even so, the enthusiasm of many of the activists listening to his speech may have revealed that for grassroots activists—rural and urban alike—the language of cultural difference and that of racial equality are not necessarily mutually exclusive. In fact,

Garzón was among the best-received speakers of the entire Quibdó meeting. More importantly, in an auditorium full mostly of black rural activists, his specific mention of racism and the need for integration and equity elicited the most spirited response.

As this moment illustrates, the debates that the leaders of black Colombian organizations engage in around "equality" and "difference" may not actually be as bifurcated in the minds of grassroots activists, or even of ordinary black Colombians. Further, this polarization at the top fails to reflect the ways in which the massive forced displacement of black communities from rural to urban areas muddles the distinctions upon which these different factions of the movement understand themselves. This is perhaps why, as Cárdenas (2012) has noted, AFRODES—an organization that mobilizes around the issues facing displaced Afro-Colombians—has interwoven discourses of ethnic difference and anti-racism so seamlessly (126).

Yet Colombia's ethno-territorial movement's deemphasis of "racism," "anti-racism," and "racial equality" in their platforms—like their more general apprehension about discussing urban issues—was also a reaction to other political dynamics. The vice president's newly found racial consciousness was closely linked to the emergence of what many in Colombia's black movement call the *afro-derecha* (Afro-right). This set of Afro-Colombian individuals and, increasingly, organizations included many with close ties to conservative parties and many who spoke exclusively in the language of black entrepreneurship and social mobility. One of its most important figures was Oscar Gamboa, who was the head of the Presidential Program for the Advancement of the Afro-Colombian Population. He worked very closely with Colombia's presidents and vice presidents, and he was likely behind Garzón's speech in Quibdó. Gamboa, and others active in organizations like Fundación Color—founded in late 2000 with the goal of bringing about "development and the greater integration of the black or afro population into society"—made up a new faction within Colombia's black movement. While they shared a discourse of racial equality with established organizations like Cimarrón, their emphasis on individual rather than collective uplift meant that they never quite aligned.

Colombia's shift toward state discourses of racial equality, integration, and individual black mobility also coincided with the U.S. government's increasing interest in black Colombians.[67] Nevertheless, the efforts of the so-called *afro-derecha* have had one main effect on mainstream political discussions both at home and in the United States: they shifted policy debates toward discussions of racial equality and the need to create the conditions for social mobility for both urban and rural black Colombians. In the end, the *afro-derecha*'s questionable political allegiances—which caused some of them to be incarcerated for ties to paramilitary groups—led to a conflation between struggles for racial equality and *afro-derecha* politics within Colombia's black movement. In this ideological context, struggles for racial equality were often read as inherently conservative, individualist, and counter to the wellbeing of Afro-Colombian communities. Alternatively, the fight for ethno-territorial rights became synonymous with the real grassroots struggle, rather than simply one articulation of it.

The political discourse of factions within Colombia's black movement continued to shift after I officially left the field in 2009. In this period, ethno-territorial organizations like PCN—which had long defined themselves in opposition to urban, integrationist movements—began to articulate a new discourse of anti-racism, which they no longer saw as fundamentally contradictory to discourses of cultural difference and ethnic rights. This shift is best captured in their partnership with Los Andes University to create the Ford Foundation–funded Observatory against Racial Discrimination, as well as their work in founding the Anti-Racist Action Research Network, a regional group of activist-researchers in the United States and Latin America, created in 2010. This shift was not simply discursive but required these organizations to develop new strategies and open up to addressing the myriad of problems facing black populations in Colombia's urban centers. In the city of Buenaventura, PCN also began to do more concerted mobilization around urban dispossession, sometimes working directly with local hip-hop artists to reimagine—both legally and ideologically—collective territoriality in urban space.[68]

The reasons for these transformations were many. First, the forced displacement of millions of Afro-Colombians required ethno-territorial movements to rethink their political platforms. It is no surprise, then, that organizations like the Association of Afro-Colombian Displaced Peoples were instrumental in this shift, having naturally served as bridges between the realities of urban and rural black people and between discourses of ethnic difference and racial equality within the movement. Second, the influx of new young grassroots activists within PCN's ranks—including Francia Marquez, Hamington Valencia, and many others—brought with them a "both and" concept of the black struggle that viewed it as simultaneously rural and urban and about both difference and anti-racism. Finally, in the context of the racial equality alignment, these organizations—among the few grassroots black organizations in the country—were forced to take a political position. If they had not broadened their discourse, they would have had to cede urban space, and the increasing policy debates around racial equality and Afro-Colombians, to the *afro-derecha* without any real contestation.

Another important ingredient to the shift toward racial equality in Colombia was the Ford Foundation. While racial justice had long been a central tenet of the Ford Foundation's philanthropic efforts in the United States, the extent to which this aim was integrated into the portfolios of other regions was largely at the discretion of regional program officers

(Telles 1999). It was under the leadership of Mike Turner in the foundation's Brazil office in the 1980s that Ford began supporting anti-racism efforts and Afro-Brazilian organizations (Lennox 2015). A decade later, sociologist Edward Telles took up much of the work that Turner started when he took the position of human rights program officer in Rio de Janeiro (Telles 1999; Lennox 2015).

It was not until the 2000s that Ford's Andean regional office—housed in Santiago de Chile—began to do similar work on racial justice in Colombia. Also under the guidance of specific program officers like Felipe Aguero, Ford began to support Los Andes University to create the Observatory against Racial Discrimination, conduct research on racial discrimination, engage in legal advocacy, and support the advanced education of Afro-Colombian lawyers working on human rights and social justice.[69] Ford also offered grants to a number of Colombian universities to conduct policy-oriented research on racial discrimination in the labor market, on ethno-racial identity and the census, among other topics. Between 2009 and 2014, the Ford Foundation gave over four million dollars in grants to projects working on indigenous and Afro-Colombian issues, all with the aim of "advancing racial justice and minority rights."[70] The Ford Foundation's support of ethno-territorial organizations like PCN within the specific discourse of racial equality and justice helped to reconfigure the terms of the conversation within the policy community and within the black movement.

This partial and unfinished turn toward a language of anti-racism within the Colombian state underscored the inherent problems with constructing discussions of cultural difference as always against discourses of race. Politics aside, an ethno-territorial movement premised on the idea of protecting cultural difference and maintaining traditional forms of life does not inherently contradict a conception of black Colombians as racialized and thus as suffering from discrimination. However, such projects did oppose a specific kind of racial integration and social mobility project, the brand that urban organizations like Cimarrón, and its more problematic counterparts in the *afro-derecha*, espoused.

Consequently, it may be useful to distinguish between ethnic difference, racial equality, and anti-racism. While it may be difficult to fully reconcile political projects premised on difference and those based on equality, both can be anti-racist insomuch as they understand the problem facing blacks as racism. In this sense, both can potentially offer a path toward liberation that challenges racial hierarchies, albeit it in distinct ways. The realities of contemporary black rural populations in Colombia stem from long histories of state abandonment, capitalist exploitation, dispossession, and the refusal of the Colombian state to guarantee these communities' constitutionally protected rights. While many might see such processes as deeply entangled with processes of racialization, it is only recently that activists working in black rural communities began to emphasize this dimension of the situation. As I discussed in previous chapters, activists in the country's ethno-territorial movement made a strategic decision in the constitutional reform process of the 1990s. As Carlos Rosero of PCN explained:

> Regarding the discourse of racism and racial discrimination, we thought it was valid. It was the discourse of the movement before the one that emerged in the 1990s. We had much discussion and we joined other people who wanted to start a movement in terms of the recognition of specific rights. So instead of talking about racism and racial discrimination, we wanted it to be recognized that we had been over there [in the territories], that we had helped with the construction of this country and that we had a right to territory, identity, and development within the framework we wanted (interview, Carlos Rosero, June 2006).

The idea that a political platform that recognized racism was antithetical to one that defended territory and the right to difference and counterhegemonic development remained in Colombia's political field over the following decades. Nevertheless, activists on the ground in the country's black ethno-territorial movement often understood the problems facing black communities in more complex and overlapping ways. Even as activists with PCN refused to talk about racism—particularly in negotiations with a state that recognized them exclusively in the language of protection of cultural distinction—they often operated with what Scott (1990) calls "hidden transcripts." In their informal discourse, anti-racism and cultural difference were not necessarily so incompatible.

However, one implication of creating a strict dichotomy between "cultural difference" and "racial discrimination" was that for most of the 1990s and 2000s, urban racial equality activists had a de facto monopoly on all (anti)racism talk.[71] Among other things, this meant that when activists like Carlos Rosero faced racial discrimination—as he did when the Bogotá police beat him up while yelling racial slurs–it was largely muted. Indeed, mounting a campaign against state violence and racialized policing in urban areas at that time would have distracted from their more central concerns of territory, political violence, and displacement. When PCN as an organization did begin to talk in the language of racism and anti-racism in the late 2000s, they had many internal discussions around how to develop an anti-racist discourse that did not equate to embracing "racial equality" as integrationist factions of the movement conceived it. Relatedly, they faced an ongoing struggle around how to best incorporate the concerns of urban black populations—discrimination in housing, employment, education, criminal justice, social services, and so on—into their ideological project based on territoriality, anti-capitalism and defending traditional livelihoods.

CONCLUSION

When the Colombian and Brazilian states took up affirmative action and other policies aimed at addressing deep-seated ethno-racial inequalities, they helped propel a shift away from citizenship regimes based in ideas of *mestizaje*. These reforms of the 2000s emerged in the shadow of state multiculturalism. In this chapter, I have argued that—similar to the recognition of multicultural rights for black rural populations just a decade before—racial equality policies happened through the convergence of changes in the domestic and global political fields. More specifically, I maintain that the reorientation of the global ethno-racial field away from a concern exclusively with the plight of indigenous communities and toward a concern for black populations converged with domestic transformations in Colombia and Brazil to create a racial equality alignment. In the context of this alignment, the struggle of urban activists who had been making claims in the language of racial equality for decades became legitimated, as these states institutionalized their demands.[72] Furthermore, in both moments of political field alignment, the action of a relatively small, albeit strategic, group of activists—not a massive movement—ultimately helped bring about these substantive transformations in state discourse and legal institutions.

Still, this is only partially a story about how ethno-racial policies came to pass in Colombia and Brazil. It is also fundamentally about what kind of black political subject has become institutionalized in each case. In the last two chapters, I have shown that whereas the logic of multiculturalism had deeper resonance in Colombia, ideas of racial equality became more deeply entrenched in Brazil's political field. These differences between the two cases complicate the idea that certain ethno-racial policies simply diffused through Latin America, or that they were exported from the United States.

I have argued, instead, that while global political alignments did help to create and legitimate certain types of ethno-racial political subjects, domestic dynamics were especially important in shaping the nature of these policies in Colombia and Brazil. Ultimately, historical imaginaries of race and nation as well as local political articulations determined which discourses of ethno-racial rights had staying power in each case. Whereas many of Colombia's major black organizations came to own—and in some cases even perform—cultural difference, their counterparts in Brazil continued to make demands on the state in the language of racial equality and anti-racism, even after their 1988 constitution enshrined cultural difference. In fact, black Brazilian organizations whose platform included *quilombo* land rights—for example, the Black Cultural Center of Maranhão—never did fully adopt a language of cultural difference. Rather, they understood territorial rights within a broader claim for racial equality. It is no surprise then, that when the Brazilian government launched its national initiative on *quilombo* communities in 2004—Brasil Quilombola—it focused on cultural retention and the demarcation of land alongside access to housing, sanitation, electricity, telecommunication, and roads in *quilombo* communities.[73]

Nevertheless, once these different kinds of black political subjects were institutionalized in each country, a number of new political questions would surface, including how black activists should navigate this new political field and whether these reforms would actually change the lives of ordinary people.

CHAPTER SIX

NAVIGATING THE
ETHNO-RACIAL STATE

In October 2008, I went to Cali for a convening of some 200 black activists from the southwestern region of Colombia. Everyone there represented grassroots black organizations and community councils. Whereas some in attendance were seasoned activists with college degrees and a language of human rights that mirrored that used by international institutions, others were rural community leaders who had traveled hours by boat and then bus. The latter always introduced themselves in relation to the river that ran through their villages: Río Naya, Río Dagua, Río Yurumaguí. The meeting also included long-time activists—like Mario Angulo of PCN, who had been in the movement for three decades—as well as people who had just started black organizations within the previous few years. Over the course of the day, activists raised important issues related to territorial rights, natural resources, escalating violence in black communities, and access to higher education. They also decided which of the leaders in attendance would speak for the movement in official negotiations with the state.

This type of gathering of black leaders was not a new phenomenon in Colombia. However, what was new and particularly distinctive about meetings like the one in Cali was that it happened completely within the logic and patronage of the Colombian state. In this particular event, members of Cali's mayor's cabinet gave the official welcome and launched the day's activities by singing the national anthem, followed by the anthem of the state of Valle. Throughout Colombia, meetings like these, and similar ones I attended in Brazil, not only happened in government buildings but also were convened by high-level government officials, often under the auspices of the state.

Had I conducted this study two decades before, my experience would have been dramatically different. Whereas scholars working on black movements in Colombia and Brazil in the 1970s and 1980s interviewed activists in their homes, churches, schools, and makeshift organizational headquarters, I spent much of my fieldwork in NGO offices, political party headquarters, and government buildings. Likewise, rather than conduct research entirely in the regions where the roots of the contemporary black movements were the deepest—such as Colombia's Pacific coast and cities like São Paulo, Salvador, and Rio de Janeiro in Brazil—I also spent considerable time in the capital cities of Bogotá and Brasília. Indeed, black movement organizations in both countries had moved their offices close to the center of political power, and those that had not often passed through these cities to engage in protest, lobby government officials, and submit paperwork in order to access funding. Furthermore, my frequent visits to government buildings also stemmed from the fact that many of the canonical figures of the black movement in the 1970s and 1980s—including people like Luiza Bairros, Pastor Murillo, Carlos Medeiros, Vilma Reis, and Luiz Alberto—had become state bureaucrats and politicians.

The recognition of black and indigenous rights in Colombia and Brazil came with a plethora of institutions designed to ensure that the state could move beyond symbolic recognition and toward the design, coordination, and implementation of these policies. This set of institutions—made up of local and regional agencies within the state, as well as a number of important consultative bodies, including advisory councils, state-civil society committees, and working groups—make up something I call the "ethno-racial state apparatus." Thus, this recent wave of ethno-racial reforms in Colombia and Brazil not only institutionalized black political subjects into the law but they also created ethno-racial state apparatuses that catalyzed the institutionalization of black movement actors.

In this chapter, I examine how everyday political practices in these new contexts—in which blacks were now legitimated as the subjects of rights and in which a myriad of new state institutions managed ethno-racial issues—have constructed new kinds of black political subjects in Colombia and Brazil. I draw on government documents, interviews, and insights from my ethnographic fieldwork to make sense of how black movement actors in Colombia and Brazil navigated the new political landscape. Analyzing this post-legislation period is important for several reasons. Beyond underscoring the magnitude of the shift in state discourse, these spaces also constitute key sites of contestation both between the state and the black movements in Colombia and Brazil and within the movements themselves. Moreover, how black activists navigate the state and the extent to which they can effectively push for change—from within or from outside the system—has profoundly shaped the politics of implementation in each case.

ABSORPTION, RITUALIZED PARTICIPATION, AND RADICALIZATION

The political landscapes of Colombia and Brazil in the 2000s–2010s could not be more distinct. In the former, President Uribe and his conservative allies institutionalized a culture of *paramilitarismo* within the state and society. In it, the state's counterinsurgency efforts against leftist guerrilla groups were formally about increasing military efforts; informally they created, financed, and supported right-wing, armed illegal paramilitary forces. In this same period, Brazil was not only experiencing a period of relative peace but also the rise of a leftist government. Moreover, the Brazilian state seemed to be developing a more transparent logic of engagement with civil society through the relationships between the Workers' Party (PT) and most of Brazil's social movement sectors. The cornerstone of this shift was Brazil's internationally famous participatory budgeting model of governance.

Despite these major political differences, over the last decades, the patterns of black movement institutionalization in Colombia and Brazil have been remarkably similar. In both countries, states created an ethno-racial state apparatus to manage recent ethno-racial reforms, channel the participation of black activists, and arguably to manage ethno-racial discontent. Yet more than acting as buffers between movements and these states, these ethno-racial institutions have also produced a number of hybrid political actors. Indeed, even as black activists in both countries have taken up positions within these new state bureaucracies, they have continued to think of themselves as "activists within the state." This dynamic of what I call "social movement absorption" has affected the nature of state-movement contestation in both cases.

This process of absorption happened alongside another dynamic that also fundamentally changed the relationship between activists and the Colombian and Brazilian states: "ritualized participation." In his work on the nuclear freeze movement, social movement scholar David Meyer (1993) argued that the institutionalization of dissent often happens through a process of "ritualized participation" in which states provide "a variety of venues for debate on policy issues" while at the same time insulating the policy process from the "undue influence" of social movement actors. The advent of an ethno-racial state apparatus did exactly that. It increased, formalized, and routinized black activists' engagement with the state, particularly through these ethno-racial state apparatuses. These agencies were responsible for coordinating ethno-racial policy, ensuring the participation of black activists, and even convening them. Nevertheless, in neither Colombia nor Brazil did these apparatuses have the power or infrastructure necessary to fulfill their mandates. As such, black activists' participation in these rituals ultimately served to legitimate their respective states' actions and inaction. At the same time, in both countries these different patterns of institutionalization also created further tensions within movements that were already fragmented along regional, ideological, and gender lines.

While Colombian elites commonly boast that their country is one of the oldest democracies in Latin America, for everyone else, democracy existed only in name. Despite the fact that Colombia has one of the most advanced legal systems in the world, the rule of law continues to fall short. Moreover, beyond formal democracy, the actual nature of politics in Colombia has been characterized by violent repression, rampant corruption, and the radical and violent exclusion of the left from mainstream politics (Palacios 2006; Carroll 2011). Despite Colombia's long history of holding elections, instability has manifested in a complex internal conflict—between the Colombian state, leftist guerilla groups, and over the last decades, with paramilitary forces that have been strongly linked to the state's counterinsurgency efforts (Carroll 2011).

In addition to political instability, Colombia's political field was characterized by the heavy influence of international actors, namely the Colombian state's close relationship with the U.S. government. In many ways, the boundary around the political field of Colombia was extremely permeable, especially as the country's military efforts increasingly relied on foreign aid. This was even more true in the 2000s, as Colombia became the third largest recipient of foreign aid from the United States and a key site in the U.S. government's "war against drugs." This was the latest manifestation of a kind of "social control" that the United States has exercised over Colombia" (Mason 2004). The contradictories of such influence were particularly clear in the 2000s under Colombia's Uribe administration. On the one hand, the United States put pressure on Colombia to deal with its internal conflict and drug problem through increased militarization. On the other, U.S. influence prompted the Colombian state to maintain the guise of democracy, including addressing the impunity and systematic human rights violations that governed the political field. This dynamic was an important aspect of the broader political field in which ethno-racial politics in 2000s–2010s Colombia were embedded. As such, it influenced the kinds of relationships black Colombian organizations would have with the state, as well as the outcomes of such engagement.

Formalizing Black Participation in the Colombian State

Law 70 guaranteed "black communities" a host of rights, including the right to collective territory, natural resources, mining, socioeconomic development, and ethnic education. The legislation stated as one of its overarching principles that the state ensures "the participation of black communities and their organizations without detriment to their autonomy in the decisions that affect them as well as all national decisions."[1] The many formal channels the state established to all levels of government—with considerable input from black activists—were meant to ensure such political participation. In order to understand how black activists came to navigate this new context, we must first understand the particularities of these structures.

In total, Law 70 created more than 300 formal spaces for political participation for black communities (Agudelo 1999). In fact, all five substantive chapters of Law 70 included provisions to guarantee the participation of Afro-Colombian communities and their organizations. They also began to register "grassroots organizations" as well as "community councils"—the ethno-territorial organizations that would govern the collective territory of black communities and which would act as "traditional authorities" in these areas—within a state database. While some black rural communities did have preexisting informal local governance structures, community councils codified a particular kind of representational structure that in some ways mirrored the cabildo system for indigenous people (Oslender 2008).

Forming Colombia's ethno-racial state apparatus also involved the creation of the Office on Black Communities, a subdivision of the Ministry of Justice and the Interior. This state agency was created to guarantee the effective exercise of the rights of black communities and to facilitate the implementation of policies related to Law 70.[2] In practice, however, the office often occupied a precarious space between the movement and a Colombian state that showed little interest in implementing Law 70. Since its inception in 1993, former black activists tended to head Colombia's Office on Black Communities, though some of them did not have long trajectories in the movement. When I was in the field, I often saw state actors channel the frustrations of black activists through this office. This occurred despite the fact that the office had little power to craft or implement policies, or to make any decisions related to the big issues affecting black populations, including land titling, illegal mining, development projects, guaranteeing free and informed prior consultation (*consulta previa*), or combating institutional ethno-racial inequality.[3]

In fact, the Office on Black Communities functioned in practice more as a buffer between the Colombian state and the movement (Asher 2009). Afro-Colombian activists were painfully aware of this. While they recognized that the Office on Black Communities was their main interlocutor within the state, they also knew it had considerably less power than it seemed to. For example, Afro-Colombian activist from the Baudó River—Esildo Pacheco—explained that despite the fact that the director of the Office on Black Communities received much of the heat for government policies, he was "simply the Ministry's messenger" (interview, Esildo Pacheco, March 2009). Pacheco explained that the office controlled "absolutely nothing, nothing. It is a public notary and that's it. That needs to change. It needs to be an office that mobilizes things."

The director of the Office on Black Communities himself echoed this in a candid interview. I asked him whether his office was responsible for guaranteeing black communities' right to *consulta previa*, or the right to be consulted on development projects before they are to be implemented. Pastor Murillo clarified that this was the "responsibility of the Ministry of Justice and the Interior, which is headed by the vice minister. . . . This Office on Black Communities lends support in that process" (interview, Pastor Murillo, October 2008).[4] Nevertheless, despite its limited power, the office did serve one important purpose: it officially registered black community councils and grassroots black organizations with the state. This gave the office much more power than was apparent at first glance.

In addition to establishing institutions within the state bureaucracy, Law 70 also created two special seats for black communities in Colombia's lower congressional chamber, and it established advisory commissions at the city, department, and national levels. The most important advisory commission was the High-Level or National Commission on Black Communities. Established through Decree 2248 of 1995, the commission was to consist of high-level state officials from all national ministries—typically at the vice minister level—as well as directors of nearly all national government entities, the two black congressional representatives, and a select group of black activists. The commission was to have an *espacio mixto* that was to include all these actors, as well as an *espacio propio* in which black representatives on the commission were to meet independent of state officials. The purpose of this permanent space for black participation was to "serve as an instance of dialogue between black communities and the National Government with the fundamental goal of monitoring and guaranteeing the implementation of the social, economic, cultural, territorial, and political rights of black communities."[5] This marked the first time in Colombian history that black activists gained this level of engagement with high-level officials within the state at the national level. As a result, these commissions were key points of contention over access and representation within Colombia's black movement.

In figure 6.1, I outline the structure of these advisory commissions on black communities, including their relationship with grassroots social movement organizations and community councils. Some of the not-so-obvious aspects of this structure turn out to be important. While these rules were constantly in flux, between 2006 and 2009 (when I completed most of my fieldwork) there was a relatively straight forward structure. In order to be a commissioner one had to be a representative of a black organization that

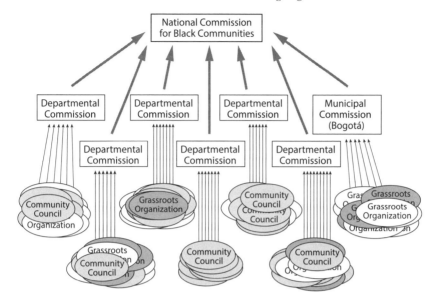

was registered with, and officially recognized by, the Office on Black Communities. To register an organization, one had simply to collect the signatures of fifteen members of the organization, create bylaws, and establish one person to be legally responsible for the organization's bureaucratic matters.[6] It was widely known, however, that one could fulfill the fifteen-signature requirement by simply getting family members to sign.

In 2008, twelve of Colombia's thirty-two departments (or states) had a Departmental Commission on Black Communities.[7] The election for departmental commissioners operated under a one vote per organization system, so whether your organization had the minimum of 15 members or 15,000 members, it still got one vote in the election for departmental commissioners. After the Departmental Commissions were set up, those commissioners chose twenty-seven people among their peers to make up the Comisión Consultiva de Alto Nivel, or the High-Level Advisory Commission.

The fact that this structure established very minimal standards for registering a black organization had two effects. First, it offered incentives for the creation of an infinite number of organizations, which led to the proliferation of small, and often fake, organizations. Second, it discouraged the building of larger grassroots organizations. Whereas before 1993, there were only a handful of Afro-Colombian organizations, by 2008, over 1,500 "grassroots black organizations" and over 350 "community councils" were registered with the Office on Black Communities. In 2009, Pastor Murillo told me that there were at least another 4,000 that had yet to be officially recognized by the government (interview, Pastor Murillo, October 2008).[8]

This was in part because the registry included anything from small cultural groups to community councils to professionalized NGOs working on issues affecting urban black populations. While these organizations also ranged in their level and type of activity, many of them simply did not actually exist in practice. Instead, they were what activists, and even the director himself, called *organizaciones de papel*, paper organizations founded to access to power and state funding.

Whereas some activists took up positions within the advisory commission because they were optimistic about the possibilities for social change within these newly conquered political spaces, others did so looking to benefit personally. This was understandable. The commissions did offer many incentives—both perceived and real—to create paper organizations. In addition to providing the opportunity to represent black populations in negotiations with the government, these coveted spaces within the advisory commissions were a space where individuals could access funding for community projects that existed, but also for projects that did not actually exist. This not only created new cleavages within the movement but also limited activists' ability to pressure the Colombian state to make real reforms.

Whereas the period directly following Law 70 was one marked by a receptive administration, this deteriorated soon after. The land titling process coincided almost perfectly with the exacerbation of violence and internal conflict in precisely the areas where Afro-Colombians and indigenous people had been recently granted rights to land; the violence and conflict posed new threats for these communities. Among other things, serious human rights violations—including massacres, political kidnappings, and the forced displacement of thousands of black families from land recently titled under Law 70—now plagued these populations (Wouters 2001).[9] Thus, much depended on who would actually represent black communities in these spaces of formal engagement with the government. Would the right people be elected to the commission? If so, would they be able to effectively pressure the state to respond to the human rights crisis facing black communities? Because of these lingering questions within Colombia's black movement, elections for commissioners for black communities became battlefields over representation.

Electing "Black Representatives"

On the morning of the election for Bogotá's Advisory Commission on Black Communities in November 2008, I met a group of activists down the street from the hotel where the election was to be held.[10] The leaders that I was with represented different local black organizations and met early to devise their strategy to win the highest number of seats on the commission. I had been invited to these behind-the-scenes meetings because I had helped one of the activists to conduct and analyze a survey on black organizations in Bogotá. He knew I was interested in the advisory commissions. Every fifteen minutes another person—representing another black organization in Bogotá—came into the office vowing to vote for a specific slate of candidates. Other representatives of organizations frantically made calls on their cell phones to finalize the bureaucratic arrangements that would make them eligible to vote absentee. Some of them even borrowed other activists' cell phones, since running out of prepaid *minutos* on their mobile phones was part of everyday life for poor and working-class Colombians. By the time we arrived at the actual voting place about two hours after the election was supposed to start, the group I accompanied knew how many organizations could legally vote, what the different political factions were, and how many votes each of them needed to win.

They were not the only ones who came prepared for this complicated election process. Indeed, almost everyone present had gone through the bureaucracy to register their organizations with the Office on Black Communities, and the overwhelming majority had already formed their political alliances and made backroom deals with each other around the projects they might funnel to allies if they gained a seat on the commission. The meeting was supposed to start around 9 a.m. However, between the morning's negotiations and the disputes over political autonomy and the presence of government officials in the room, the election did not begin until around noon. When it did start, no formal presentation of candidates actually took place. That was unnecessary because the votes had already been determined. Yet the election was still a necessary formality for choosing the incoming commissioners.

The actual voting went on for hours as state officials called each organization up to vote in front of the entire group. The ballot, placed in a large box with a hole in the top, was only technically secret. Most knew who was voting for whom, except for the occasional alliance that congealed in the moments leading up to the vote. Between 150 and 200 people were present at the event, representing eleven slates with a total of seventy candidates for the thirty seats. In this ritual of representation, some individuals voted on behalf of multiple organizations, and other slates were clearly family affairs. More importantly, some legitimate organizations known for their grassroots work in Bogotá were not allowed to vote because the Office on Black Communities did not have them in the official registry. Throughout the day, I heard people complaining that there were too many "one-person organizations," "paper organizations," and "ghost organizations" flooding the election.

Despite this discontent and questioning of legitimacy, the election went on. At the time, blacks represented about 1.5 percent of Bogotá's total population, one of the lowest percentages of blacks among the country's departments.[11] Even so, Bogotá's black movement seemed to be burgeoning there.

Whereas few black organizations existed in the city before Law 70 passed in 1993, by 2006, 80 were registered with the Office on Black Communities. That number had climbed up to 122 by the 2008 election. This increase was likely due to several factors. First, there was a low bar for being officially registered. Second, while opportunism and access to resources were powerful motivations, the proliferation of black movement organizations in the 1990s and 2000s also reflected an awakening of consciousness among black Colombians brought on, in part, by Law 70 itself. Finally, this rise in the number of organizations in cities like Bogotá also reflected the rapidly increasing number of black Colombians displaced from other parts of the country.

Nevertheless, this election made clear that Colombia's complex system of black participation often left newcomers at the margins. That day in Bogotá, many of the commissioners from the previous term were reelected, and many of them subsequently received government contracts related to projects in black communities. More importantly, winning the Bogotá election meant they were also eligible to be part of the National Advisory Commission, which dealt with high-stakes issues that included land reform, large-scale development projects, free trade, and natural resources.

While forming a "grassroots black organization" could easily have been done in a few hours, setting up a black "community council" was a much more difficult task. This was, in part, because such organizations were by definition linked to specific territory. As such, they had to submit a plethora of paperwork, including maps and a community census, to the Office on Black Communities. If they were applying for land titles, they also had to submit paperwork to the various state agencies charged with agrarian reform. Despite this difficulty, community councils still proliferated in rural areas. Some of the increase was predictable, given that very few of these formal territorial organizations existed before Law 70. Further, a community council was the only vehicle through which black Colombians living in rural areas could exercise their right to collective land titles, the extraction of natural resources through traditional means, political autonomy, and alternative development.

However, much of the rapid increase in black community councils, though, came from the division of existing community councils into smaller and smaller units. In the case of Buenaventura in the department of Valle, this trend was particularly marked. The community council of the Rio Naya in Buenaventura was affiliated with The Black Communities' Movement (PCN). It represented roughly 17,000 people and about 100 communities and was organized as one large, unified rural organization that ran the length of the Naya River. Many of the organizations that mobilized black farmers in the period leading up to Law 70 were structured in this manner both in the Chocó and in the Southern Pacific. The Naya community council, then, would receive only one vote in commission elections despite its large size. This was not initially a problem until a new set of black actors began to establish smaller black community councils at the village level, sometimes breaking apart existing councils. As such, the number of votes in commission elections grew exponentially (interview, Mario Angulo, April 2009). If PCN had succumbed to this new structure, Rio Naya's one vote could have been transformed into as many as 100 votes representing each of its different community councils as a separate entity. Yet switching to this disaggregated community council model would have required a dramatic shift in the organizations' ideological principles, not to mention the legal expenses and time. It would also have been nearly impossible to dissolve and reconstitute the community councils, considering that the communities of the Rio Naya were already organized under one legally recognized collective land title. As a result, organizations like PCN, despite their large grassroots base, were severely under-represented on the local, departmental, and national commissions. This was one reason that many grassroots black activists came to see these commissions as sites of cooptation rather than representation. However, because the activists also realized the commissions were the only space in which they could influence the policies aimed at black communities, they continued to engage with them.

Special Seats for Black Communities in Congress

Another motivation for establishing black organizations was congressional representation, a space that would prove equally contentious within Colombia's black movement. Establishing black organizations or community councils enabled individuals to aspire not only to seats on the departmental and national commissions but to the two special seats that Article 66 of Law 70 mandated in the House of Representatives. As was the case with the commissions, candidates for the House seats had to represent a black organization or community council that the state officially recognized. This requirement stopped very few from running. Instead, "black grassroots organizations" were often created and discarded around election cycles (Agudelo 1999). Indeed, while many of these organizations were technically autonomous, traditional political parties often financially backed the campaigns of congressional candidates with few or no ties to the black movement. As a result, many of the black activists I interviewed and spent time with saw these congressional seats, much like the advisory commissions, as plagued with corruption and captured by the state. In 1994, there were only twelve candidates, many representing solid grassroots organizations that had mobilized around Law 70 in the early 1990s. Representatives of recognized black organizations (Zulia Mena and Agustín Valencia) won the first two congressional seats. This quickly began to change when the number of candidates began to multiply. In 2002, 56 people came forward as candidates, followed by 48 in 2006, 170 in 2010, and 77 in 2014.[12] I was doing follow-up fieldwork during the 2010 election, which I thought was the height of the spectacle around these special seats in congress. While there were a number of known black activists on the ballot, the overwhelming majority of candidates had no real ties to the black movement other than their affiliation with an "official" black organization registered with the Office on Black Communities.

The winners of the 2010 election exemplified this. They were both politically connected black professionals from organizations with little connection to the Afro-Colombian movement. One of the winners was Yahir Acuña Cardales, who ran representing Afrovides, an organization he became affiliated with just three weeks before the election. In Acuña's home department, voter turnout increased by a factor of 30, from 1,955 in 2006 to 59,627 in the 2010 special election for black community representatives.[13] The other seat went to Heriberto Arrechea, who was known for his strong ties to Juan Carlos Martínez Sinisterra, a former senator who had renounced his senate seat in 2009 while being investigated by the Constitutional Court for ties to paramilitary groups.[14] The organization Arrechea represented, the Unified Popular Movement (MPU), was neither explicitly nor implicitly an organization that addressed ethno-racial issues. Instead, it was a former political party that had, in the months leading up to the election, lost that status for suspected illegal activities. Members of this banned political party saw an opportunity to seize a couple congressional seats through the special election for black communities.[15]

Directly after the election, I interviewed Rosa Carlina García, then director of the Office on Black Communities. I asked whether the MPU was indeed a grassroots black organization. She took a deep breath and then explained that if the MPU was allowed to run in the special election, they "must have been in the official registry" (interview, Rosa Carlina García, May 2010). When I asked her about the serious charges of corruption in that election, she did not deny them per se. Instead, she responded that in Colombia, election corruption "is not just a black issue" she explained. "This is a more general issue. Any analysis of the national context will show this reflected in every election."

Similar issues emerged in 2014 when the winners of the special seats for black communities also proved to have shady ties to illegal groups. What made matters worse in the minds of many activists was that neither of the elected candidates—with their olive skin and straight black hair common among *mestizo* Colombians—looked particularly black. This was true even if you take into account the slipperiness of ethno-racial categories in Colombia. Nor did they organize around black identity prior to the election. The Ebony Foundation of Colombia (FUNECO), the state-registered black organization that officially backed these candidates, released a press release amid the controversy. In it, they stated that what legitimated the winners of the special seats was their "condition" as "members of black communities," not their "black skin."[16]

This incident demonstrates that, when it came to the question of who legitimately represented black communities, a large gap often existed between the conceptualizations of the state and the black movement. Ultimately, though, the state had the power—as Bourdieu has argued—not only to recognize certain actors and authority, but also more fundamentally, to create them. After public protests and legal mobilization by black organizations, Colombia's Constitutional Court ruled that the election of two people who did not "represent Afro-descendant communities" in the 2014 election had broken the law. The court also mandated that the National Election Council take measures to ensure that this would not happen again. This was subsequently overturned.

Legitimating Bankrupt Spaces for Black Participation

The Afro-Colombian activists who chose to engage with the state and inhabit these institutionalized bodies sometimes did so for personal gain. In other cases, they had altruistic aims, seeking to channel financial resources to the organizations they had created to do meaningful work in communities. This was the case with Orlando Sánchez Lasso, who was one of hundreds of Afro-Colombians who created organizations precisely with the goal of accessing government funding. A compassionate retired city worker who wanted to work with the black community in Yumbo, a small town about an hour outside Cali, Lasso formed AfroYumbo in 2003. He confessed to me that he didn't know much about "black rights" until a friend invited him to a black community meeting some years before. That planted the seed for AfroYumbo. However, Orlando and his fellow organizers quickly figured out that, to access state funding, the group would have to obtain status as an official black organization, form political alliances, and get its members elected to the local advisory commission. He went on:

> If you want your organization to be respected, the recognition of the Ministry of the Interior is fundamental. In many places you go, the first thing they say to organizations is, "Well, I'm sorry, you're not affiliated with the Ministry of the Interior." . . . In our first experience going to the commission meeting, there were many resources that the department gave us, that came from the national government through the department [state government], that came from international funding . . . but we didn't have access to these funds because according to the commissioners at the time, they looked at it like this. . . . We

would go to solicit resources and the first thing they would tell us is, "Awwww, but you guys don't have a commissioner." So from there we started to have issues with [the commissioners] (interview, Orlando Sanchez Lasso, March 2009).

Orlando didn't think it was fair that those without a commissioner could not take advantage of the benefits designated for black communities. Knowing that he had no power to change these dynamics, he began to try to get one or two commissioners elected so that AfroYumbo could have a "voice and vote within the commission" as well as "present projects and exert some influence" (interview, Orlando Lasso, March 2009). Shortly after being officially registered, the organization began to receive funding to work with youth; eventually, Orlando became Yumbo's Coordinator of Ethnic Groups in the Office on Social Well-Being and Participation.

Despite the tight connection between commission participation and state funding, local, departmental, and national commissioners of black communities often said in interviews that they initially joined these commissions because they were important, legally mandated and representative bodies. They saw them as allowing black activists to sit down with high-level government officials and hold them accountable for developing policies to improve the lives of Afro-Colombians on the ground.

Nevertheless, those who defended the advisory commissions also tended to be the most polemic figures within them. This was the case with Rosita Solis—a national commissioner representing the Department of Valle—and one of the most powerful members of the commission. Many of the activists I interviewed referred to Rosita as the quintessential case of *politiquería*, or political manipulation for personal gain.[17] Other activists talked about Rosita and others like her as *traficantes en derechos*, or "rights traffickers," playing on the language of Colombia's infamous drug trade. Shrugging off these critiques, Rosita maintained that the commissions were the only democratic and representative way for black communities to access the state. For her, the commissions were able to sustain direct dialogue with the Colombian state precisely because commissioners were selected through what she saw as a fair and transparent election. This, she argued, gave the commissions a particular kind of legal legitimacy vis-à-vis the state. In my interview with her, she often contrasted this with the unofficial and undemocratic ways in which her critics outside of the commission tended to engage with the Colombian state. She explained, "If you read the functions of the departmental and national commissions, they are a space of a lot of power, a space of inclusion, of negotiation, and consensus building" (interview, Rosita Solis, April 2009).

However, Rosita's view was a rare one, even among commissioners themselves, some of whom actually admitted that the exchange of money and government posts was commonplace within the commissions.[18] When I probed further, asking why the government felt the need to pay off commissioners, one explained that it was often in exchange for their authorization of government development plans and private sector enterprises. In fact, the majority of those I spoke with—including people who were themselves commissioners when I interviewed them—raised serious concerns about corruption as well as the lack of a grassroots base among commissioners.[19] I remember being confused when I saw commissioners yell at government officials in the public meetings between movement actors and the state and then leave with these same officials in government cars and chartered planes. After months of observing these slippery relationships between state actors and activists, I found the idea of the commission as even a semi-autonomous space less plausible.

In this, even well-intentioned commissioners unwittingly participated in what Catholic Priest and activist Padre Egmidio Cuesta called the *mito de la interlocción*, or the "myth of engagement" with the state. In this, activists were duped into feeling like they actually participated. Yet whether they exchanged favors or not, their participation in designated spaces within Colombia's multicultural state apparatus inevitably legitimated the entire enterprise. More specifically, their presence at meetings, signatures on documents, and consultation on government plans often legitimated both state action and inaction. In such a context, a number of activists and organizations decided to distance themselves from these spaces and to insist on a certain level of autonomy.

Demanding Autonomy from the State

In the post–Law 70 period, with struggles over representation, legitimacy, and authenticity centering on the Commissions on Black Communities, and particularly on the National Advisory Commissions, the regional and ideological differences between black Colombian movement actors grew. These differences had always existed, but during this era the divide between organizations close to the state and those that maintained relative political autonomy from it became the most salient cleavage in the movement. The late Afro-Colombian activist Carlos Rua described this as the "black movement over here" and "commissions over there" phenomenon (interview, Carlos Rua, March 2009).

By the mid-2000s, public criticism of the commissions was building. By then, nearly all of Colombia's most respected black organizations had come to the conclusion that the commission structure was completely bankrupt. Many of the activists I spent time with pointed to its lack of financial and political autonomy and charged the black Colombians who occupied the commissions and the special seats in the House of Representatives with rampant *politiquería*. The accusation that commissioners had sold the rights of black communities in exchange for government handouts was both widespread and explicit.[20] I asked activists who began to accuse specific individuals of receiving money from the government if they wanted me to turn off my recorder, and nearly all responded by speaking more loudly and more directly into the microphone. They accused commissioners of—in exchange for money—authorizing development and private sector projects in collective black territories and signing documents stating that local communities had been consulted on things those communities were not aware of.

Some commissioners themselves also raised questions about their effectiveness and transparency. One national commissioner associated with PCN explained:

> Today we are worried about the National Commission because we believe that it hasn't fulfilled its goals, it hasn't served the purpose that we thought it would, and we think that it has turned more into a body that is in the pocket of the government. They insist on saying that they are opening spaces, but in terms of substance, in terms of rights and the positioning of rights for us, I think that it hasn't contributed much because the vision of the government has been to utilize the commission for its projects and for its political interests instead of advancing the recognition of rights (interview, Dionicio Miranda, October 2008).

While the resources that the Colombian state officially allocated to implementing Law 70 were scarce, many sensed that the money that changed hands under the table was abundant. This was not just the sentiment of activists, but it was also the undertone of my conversation with Pastor Murillo, one of the former directors of the Office on Black Communities. He admitted that there were many people who set up fake black organizations (interview, Pastor Murillo, October 2008). For many activists, they did so to *sacar provecho*, or take advantage of their proximity to state officials for their own personal gain: more money, community projects, trips around the country, and government positions.

In the late 2000s, activists argued that if the commissions were to continue at all, they would have to be more accountable to communities and to the movement, which many at the time saw as distinct from the Commission. Mariluz Chaverra, an activist of OBAPO—an organization at the center of the constitutional reform process and the making of Law 70—was one of the many activists pessimistic about these participatory structures. She said:

> A couple of comrades from the Chocó participated in the National Commission, but it's neither here nor there [*ni fu, ni fa*], because they

go there when they are called, they score big, and they don't even come here. It's not like before when they would reach a consensus [with the communities]. Practically nothing happens with the commission, absolutely nothing (interview, Mariluz Chaverra, March 2009).

In the late 2000s, the large grassroots organizations that had been responsible for pressuring the state to adopt Law 70, including PCN and ACIA, were not adequately represented in the department or national commissions. This was due in part to the "one organization, one vote" structure of commission elections and in part to these groups' view that the commissions were bankrupt participatory structures. They decided to launch what was in effect a boycott. Similarly, when I asked one activist from the Association of Displaced Afro-Colombians (AFRODES) whether they were going to participate in the 2009 commission elections, she responded:

Well, AFRODES did participate from 2005 to 2008 in the city-level commission. This November will be the election of the next assembly to elect the new city-level commissioners, and AFRODES has decided not to participate because there are not real conditions to participate in that space. There is not much will on the part of the government (interview, Luz Marina Becerra, February 2009).

Both AFRODES and PCN were among the most effective and respected national black organizations, and both distanced themselves from the commissions in the mid-2000s. In doing so, the two groups challenged the legitimacy of these spaces, while at the same time they ceded the commissions to the very corrupt forces they criticized. These organizations' decision to boycott these national spaces went hand in hand with their strategy to leverage transnational advocacy networks to pressure the state from a more autonomous position than the commissions allowed.

Transnational Leverage and Alternative Engagement with the State

In the 1990s, national organizations like AFRODES, PCN, and Afro-América XXI began to develop direct relationships with international actors. They did this to pressure the Colombian state to comply with Law 70 and to deal with emerging issues facing black communities in Colombia. Indeed, when faced with blockage at home, civil society actors can sometimes leverage the fact that their claims resonate elsewhere, as Keck and Sikkink (1998) argue. This resonance in the international arena can then "echo back" in a dynamic they call the boomerang effect; it then opens up new spaces for issues that domestic politics had formerly marginalized.

Such transnational strategies had been a key feature of black mobilization in both Colombia and Brazil for decades, albeit to different degrees. More specifically in this period, black Colombian organizations started to build solid transnational coalitions with organizations like the Washington Office on Latin America (WOLA), Transafrica Forum, as well as religious organizations and members of the U.S. Congress—the Congressional Black Caucus in particular. The main objective of these efforts was to go around formal structures of political participation in Colombia and raise visibility about human rights violations against black communities. Given the salient role the U.S. government plays within Colombian politics, this leveraging of transnational alliances with state and nonstate actors had been crucial in shaping internal movement dynamics.

Hernán Cortés of PCN explained that his organization began to look to international alliances in the mid-1990s after land titling began which coincided with the intensification of internal conflict precisely in these areas. In such a political context, he asserted: "we need allies, we knew that this government was really scared of international actors at that moment so we began to think first and seek support (respaldo)." For Hernán, the Colombian government was not just susceptible to influence by international actors, but as he put it "scared" of them (interview, Hernán Cortés, February 2009).

Similarly, in the late 1990s, AFRODES began to seek out international alliances to address the intensification of internal displacement among black Colombians, which was directly linked to paramilitary activity and counterinsurgency efforts by the Colombian state. Luz Marina Becerra talked to me about AFRODES's international strategy. She explained that the organization began to do international work though the U.S.-based human rights organization—Witness for Peace—which held a vigil in a church in Colombia and became interested in the work that AFRODEs was doing. A year later, they invited AFRODES leader, Marino Córdoba, to the United States to do a tour of sorts around the country raising visibility about the issue of displacement in black communities. Marino eventually became a political refugee and one of the main linkages of transnational ties between black communities in Colombia and human rights advocates in the United States. Luz Marina explained why such international visibility was important.

> Because we knew that at the level of domestic politics, the rights of Afro-Colombians have historically been violated and they are violated daily, on a permanent basis, and if this doesn't go international, there will be no solution. And the idea behind internationalizing our work and raising visibility about the issues is to seek alliances with international organizations, with churches, with civil society leaders to see how Colombia . . . knowing that these alliances exist, there are other institutions on the other side of the country, who know about the problematic that

we live here, that curb, that check, their actions involving the violation of human rights in black communities. So we believe that this has been important. Also, the support and alliances that we have had with the [Congressional] Black Caucus (interview, Luz Marina Becerra, February 2009).

While these efforts did not always guarantee the end of violence in black communities, they were effective in some regard. As Hernán Cortés explained, by engaging in these transnational networks, organizations like PCN were able to keep activists facing death threats alive (interview, Hernán Cortés, February 2009).

Nevertheless, even as this internationalization gave organizations a kind of external leverage and legitimacy, the more institutionalized sectors of the Afro-Colombian movement like the national commissioners, saw this as directly undermining their own power. In interviews, commissioners often talked about PCN overstepping their boundaries, as having a "monopoly on truth," and believing they were the only legitimate voices in the struggle for black communities. In this sense, PCN's strategy to go international was seen as a way of "sneaking around" the commissions on black communities. As one commissioner put it: "it seems like other movements like PCN, like CNOA go over the head of the commission. They basically replace the commission . . . they do international relations and one person ends up in charge of policies for blacks in this country" (interview, Manuel Emilio Palacios, March 2009).

Many activists with AFRODES, CNOA, and PCN did see their use of transnational strategies as doing precisely that, "going around" both the state and formal spaces for black participation in order to hold both of them accountable to black communities on the ground. Under-represented in official institutionalized spaces, these black organizations made themselves key actors in national debates by linking themselves to international institutions. In the process, they gained external legitimacy and the leverage to pressure the Colombian state from a more autonomous position.

NAVIGATING THE RACIAL EQUALITY STATE APPARATUS IN BRAZIL

Like in Colombia, one of the central demands of black activists in Brazil was that the state create a structure to ensure the implementation of policies related to the promotion of racial equality. Even so, the process through which Brazil's black movement was incorporated into formal politics and state bureaucracies was somewhat distinct. In contrast to Colombia, where black activists gained access to the state through a legal mandate in the chaos of constitutional reform process, the institutionalization of relationships between black activists and the Brazilian state happened through a slow process of absorption spanning more than thirty years. This included their absorption into left and center political parties.

This process began at the very beginning of democratization, when political parties were allowed to operate in Brazil in the 1980s. The same year Brazil's new constitution was approved, black Brazilians active in the Communist Party of Brazil (PCdoB) founded the Union of Blacks for Equality (UNEGRO) which was followed by the foundation of the National Coordinator of Black Entities (CONEN) in 1991. While these organizations are officially independent of political parties—they have maintained for decades that they are autonomous from the PCdoB and the PT, respectively—many in the black movement saw their members as *negros partidarios*, or political party blacks. In practice, UNEGRO and CONEN did seem to function as what one critic called "black arms" of these political parties. All of my interviews with leaders from both organizations took place at their respective political party headquarters. In the case of Flavinho Jorge, one of CONEN's most important leaders, I interviewed him at the PT's Perseu Abramo Foundation, where he was the director. Moreover, 2009 being an election year, I remember the desks of activists from UNEGRO being covered in campaign materials. In the case of UNEGRO in São Paulo, this included pamphlets and posters of well-known Afro-Brazilian PCdoB candidates like TV host José "Netinho" de Paula, who was subsequently elected as a city councilman.[21] In this sense, these organizations' activities, policy positions, funding, and even their physical space signaled what more autonomist activists suggested: that they had deep entanglements with the political parties through which they emerged.

As such, black activists affiliated with these organizations tended to engage with the state through lobbying for specific policies for black populations, and by brokering alliances between the PT and different parties in Congress, and within the bureaucracy. In fact, these black political organizations were at the center of a number of political deals including the more recent negotiations in congress around the Statute of Racial Equality, a point to which I will return. More specifically in the case of black activists organizing within CONEN have also had a monopoly of sorts on the positions within the racial equality apparatus, something that Flavinho Jorge was quite explicit about.

> For CONEN, it was our strategy. In 2002, we had an internal debate within CONEN, and for the first time, we, as a social movement organization, decided to endorse President Luis Inácio Lula da Silva. When Lula won the election, the presence of PT *militantes* that are part of CONEN was really strong in a very transparent way. The main positions in SEPPIR were occupied by leaders of CONEN and the PT . . . That was our strategy (interview, Flávio Jorge Rodrigues da Silva, 2010).

Arguably, this imbrication is precisely what made the racial equality agenda so much more central to the Workers' Party platform than other political parties in Brazil. As Benedita da Silva noted:

Today you have a political party discussing these questions, you have commissions and you have a federal government discussing these questions, introducing racial issues, and the occupation of space by the black intellectual class which was invisible and excluded. The role of the [Workers'] Party was fundamental (interview, Benedita da Silva, Former Senator).

This centrality of racial equality to the PTs platform was also apparent in a televised national debate between presidential candidates in October of 2002. In response to the first question asked of candidates about education, Lula stated that one of the ways he would improve education was by establishing quotas for black people and poor people. In an article, "Lula and Ciro Defend Quotas for Blacks" published in the newspaper *Folha de São Paulo* the day after, they reported Lula's response: "We have to pay our country's debt with black people. We have to increase educational credits for 186,000 students. A country that has money to finance multinational companies has to also have some money for students." This debate at once highlights the centrality of anti-racism in national political debates in this period, but also the and influence of black activists within the Workers' Party.

With the election of President Lula, CONEN leaders gained unprecedented access to the state, and as such, CONEN leaders became the semi-official voices of the black movement within the state. In a statement issued by CONEN in 2010, they said the following: "After the victory of President Lula's election, CONEN became the main center of engagement between the demands of the black movement and the elected government" (CONEN Statement, September 2010). This was possible because many of the leaders were quite influential members within the PT. Flávio Jorge, one of the organization's founders, director of the Workers' Party Foundation (Perseu Abramo) and member of the National Executive Committee in charge of Lula's successful 2002 Presidential campaign is only one example of the entanglements between the PT and CONEN. Other notable cases of this were Afro-Brazilian activist Roque Peixoto, Youth Coordinator of CONEN and member of the PT's National Collective to Combat Racism and Gilberto Leal, former member of the National Executive Committee of the PT and member of the National Coordinating Committee of CONEN. The same entanglement can be found among the ranks of UNEGRO.

These close relationships, though, could be seen as a double-edged sword. On the one hand, it was precisely these ties that helped to bring about the institutionalization of racial equality within Brazilian law and bureaucracy. On the other, this trend toward absorption also came with deep ironies.

Among other things, while the racial equality apparatus was structurally within the Office of the President, it became increasingly clear that its proximity to power did not actually amount to holding power itself.

Absorption into the Racial Equality State Apparatus

By the 2000s, using institutionalized strategies had become the main repertoire of action within Brazil's black movement.[22] In this, both occupying the Brazilian state and engaging with it through formal channels had become normative within this movement, and in nearly every social movement in Brazil. More generally, with the black movement, this was facilitated by the creation of a racial equality apparatus first in the federal government and later at the state level.[23] On March 21, 2003, the International Day for the Elimination of Racial Discrimination, President Lula announced the creation of the Special Secretariat for the Promotion of Racial Equality (SEPPIR), a federal state agency charged with establishing and coordinating initiatives related to racial equality.[24]

This was not the first attempt to institutionalize the goal of racial equality at the federal level. As I discussed briefly in the previous chapter, Cardoso had created the Inter-Ministerial Working Group for the Advancement of the Black Population (GTI) in 1995. The GTI had sought to establish "permanent dialogue with institutions and entities, including black movement organizations, national and international, whose objectives and activities could bring relevant contributions to issues affecting the black population and their development." President Cardoso also created the National Council to Combat Discrimination within the Ministry of Justice. However, neither of these experiences led to the implementation of concrete policies. Also unlike Cardoso's GTI or his National Committee on Durban that were temporary, SEPPIR was created as a permanent federal agency with ministerial status much like the Special Ministry of Fishing and Acuafarming and the Special Secretariat for Policies for Women. While such efforts may have been important in developing a policy agenda for racial equality within the Brazilian state in later decades, the scale of SEPPIR was unprecedented.

The structure of Brazil's racial equality apparatus also borrowed from the experience of a similar institution within the Workers' Party (PT) itself. In the mid-1990s, future president Lula along with black activist and one of the founders of the PT in Pernambuco, Zé de Oliveira and the Afro-Brazilian Senator, Benedita da Silva, proposed the creation of the National Secretariat to Combat Racial Discrimination within the Workers' Party. The goal of this entity was to "guarantee the formation, capacity building, and articulation of black men and women within the PT; contribute to the construction and organization of the party at the state and municipal levels; widen the representation of black men and women in positions of power; and formulate and consolidate efforts to build an anti-racism platform within the PT."[25]

After Lula's election in 2003, a number of black activists who held weight within the PT were called on to be a part of Lula's transitional government.[26] While high-level discussions were already under way within the PT around having a ministry for racial equality, there was still much debate within the transitional government around this. First, there were discussions about if it was necessary, given that the government planned on streamlining a number of social welfare policies across ministries. More importantly, some PT leaders felt that a racial equality ministry would present more political problems for a leftist party that was already seen as lacking the skills necessary to take on the monumental task of running the federal government.

Nevertheless, as CONEN/PT leader Flavinho Jorge explained in an interview, the eventual creation of SEPPIR in 2003 was the result of two factors: Durban and the work of blacks within the PT" (interview, Flavinho Jorge, May 2010). The creation of SEPPIR must be understood as a result of internal arrangements within the PT that involved black *petistas* (PT members) like Flavinho who had worked alongside Lula through his three devastating, unsuccessful presidential campaigns of 1989, 1994, and 1998. As such and as Flavinho noted, Lula had become committed to an anti-racist agenda due to his personal relationships with black comrades within the PT. The structure of SEPPIR was very much reflected these origins. While pressure from black organizations outside of political parties certainly played some role in bringing about SEPPIR, it was largely the internal pressure within the PT that was most important to the creation of Brazil's racial equality apparatus.

Whereas the heads of SEPPIR tended to be members of the PT's rank and file, the lower ranks of the state agency included many black activists. The rise of the PT gave activists unprecedented access to the state apparatus. Ivair Augusto Alves dos Santos was the most quintessential example of the long and difficult history of black activism from within political parties and state institutions in Brazil. A member of the centrist Social Democratic Party of Brazil (PSDB), Ivair worked for decades in different capacities within the state, first as a founder of the Council for the Participation and Development of Blacks in São Paulo and later in the federal government under President Cardoso. He became an influential member of Cardoso's administration, advising him on race issues. Ivair was also central to the GTI in the mid-1990s as well as to preparations for Durban. He was also one of the rare state bureaucrats that continued on after the transition to the Lula administration, where he worked within the Secretariat on Human Rights. I asked Ivair if there were differences in the political climate around ethno-racial issues within the state under Cardoso and Lula. He responded as if the answer was obvious. The differences were "huge!" he explained:

First, they had a lot more people. In my day in the administration of Fernando Cardoso, we had, in government positions, 5 to 10 people, max. They had 50 to 60! It was a colossal difference. In my time [in the government] we couldn't have even imagined that. They had people in different areas with lots of power, power that we didn't even dream to have during the Cardoso period. People outside of the government have no idea how many more influential black people there are than in my day. And the resources they were dealing with, they were way more than we had. The only time we managed a lot of resources was during Durban, something like five or six million *reais* [two million dollars] . . . you can't even compare this [to what they manage under Lula]. They had way more resources and more people to do more effective work (interview, Ivair Augusto Santos, October 2010).

Though, for Ivair, it was not simply the number of Afro-Brazilians within Lula's administration that was new, but the power they had within the party and state apparatus. This power was particularly important since Brazil's presidential system afforded the executive an incredible amount of power in making legislative and presidential reforms (Mainwaring and Shugart 1997). In fact, most of the legislation aimed at racial equality in Brazil has happened through presidential decrees.

When SEPPIR began operations, it employed about forty people and managed a budget of roughly $10 million in 2004. While this budget was in no way sufficient given the agency's expansive mandate, the funds allotted to the agency did steadily increase, doubling to $20 million *reais* in 2008 and to $35 million *reais* in 2010.[27] Among SEPPIR's five objectives was to "promote equality and protect the individual and group rights of the racial and ethnic groups that are affected by discrimination and other forms of intolerance, with an emphasis in the black population" and to "monitor and coordinate the policies of different ministries and government agencies in Brazil to promote racial equality."[28] As such, SEPPIR was not created with the legal mandate to implement policies, making its executive power very limited. Nonetheless, its ministerial status and relationship to the Office of the President—both structural and personal—made it well positioned to push for affirmative action and other policies within the upper echelons of the Brazilian state.

However, in practice, SEPPIR faced both political and infrastructural challenges. While the agency's budget did—as Ivair suggested—far exceed the budget for racial equality initiatives under Lula's predecessor, it was still abysmal. This is particularly clear when you compare it to the two other special secretariats that Lula also created around the same time. Whereas the 2015 budgets of the Special Secretariat of Fishing and Agriculture and the Special Secretariat of Policies for Women were 254 and 182 million *reais*, respectively, SEPPIR's was only 39.5 million *reais*.[29] The latter was the equivalent of just less than 9 million U.S. dollars.[30]

The limitations of SEPPIR's budget and infrastructure were not the only constraints the state agency faced. Even though a special initiative of the president created SEPPIR, the Office of the President housed it, and it had the support of the ruling political party, it lacked the authority and infrastructure to actually implement policies or to effectively pressure other ministries to change their policies. Instead, SEPPIR had to rely on its social capital, endorsement from the president, and political favors, to get its foot in the door at the various federal ministries. Matilde Ribeiro, SEPPIR's first minister, talked about how difficult it was to navigate these power relations within Brazil's state bureaucracy. This struggle was especially acute with bureaucrats within the Ministry of Education, who had shown strong resistance to affirmative action. She explained: "The work of that SEPPIR and the Ministry of Education was disjointed. It wasn't like we were holding hands, doing everything together. So sometimes we would go after things, take the risk, try to do it alone, other times we would go and propose things, which sometimes did lead to action" (interview, Matilde Ribeiro, May 2010).

This predicament was worse at the local level. In addition to SEPPIR, Brazil's racial equality apparatus also consisted of some 600 special coordinators, secretariats and offices on the promotion of racial equality at the state and municipal levels.[31] All of these agencies were officially charged with coordinating public policy implementation with the different secretariats and ministries that made up these various levels of government. Like SEPPIR, these local state institutions did not have the mandate to actually implement policies themselves, and as a result their level of effectiveness depended heavily on the configurations of power within the local political field. Indeed, these state and municipal offices often had even less adequate budgets and more precarious relationships with other local government agencies. In Recife, for example, I remember asking black activists in charge of the local version of SEPPIR what their greatest accomplishments had been. One of the *militantes* in the state cited a series of public meetings they had organized with the Ministry of Education. This was not uncommon, especially at the local level. Rather than a means to an end (for example, policy change, decreasing racial inequality), state-sponsored events had become the end in itself.

Militants in the State

Much like the Office on Black Communities in Colombia, SEPPIR and its local counterparts occupied a buffer space between the state and the black movement. This role as buffer was exacerbated by the fact that activists-turned-bureaucrats in Brazil still tended to identify as "the movement" rather than "the state." This type of blurring of the lines between the state and civil society—and the latter's dependence on the former—was common in a Workers' Party–led Brazilian state (Baiocchi 2003; Baiocchi et al. 2008).

Luiza Bairros's trajectory is particularly illustrative here. Sworn in as the National Minister of the Promotion of Racial Equality of Brazil on January 3, 2011, Luiza had a long history in the black feminist movement in Brazil, and in the mid-1990s was one of the five members of the National Coordinating Committee of the Unified Black Movement (MNU). However, by the mid-1990s Luiza, like many others, left the MNU amid serious internal battles precisely around what relationship the organization should have with political parties and the state (Covin 2006). After attending graduate school in the United States, she took up a position at the United Nations Development Program (UNDP) and taught at the Federal University of Bahia (UFBA).

In the early 2000s, while teaching at UFBA, Luiza was very vocal in her critique of the newly constituted racial equality apparatus. Even after taking up a position as the Secretary for the Promotion of Racial Equality for the State of Bahia (SEPROMI), she questioned the very structure of these agencies. She explained to me that when she was approached to head up SEPROMI in 2008, she didn't respond quickly. "I spoke with some people, but my initial reaction was I didn't want to, no way!" When I asked her why, she said "because I didn't believe [in these institutions]. I was always really close politically to Luiz [Alberto, a congressman with the PT and also formerly of the MNU] and I spoke with him a lot and I knew what kind of situation this was, a really small team, many things to do" (interview, Luiza Bairros, June 2010). Even so, Luiza accepted the position as the head of SEPROMI and only left when she was tapped to be the national Minister of Racial Equality in late 2010. Through all of this, and even as she occupied the state, Luiza insisted in my interview that she was still a *militante* of the black movement.

While Luiza Bairros's trajectory is unique in some ways, it is not unlike that of many Afro-Brazilian activists who started out in radical organizations like the MNU and left to participate in party politics, to form NGOs and/or to take up positions in the Brazilian state. Carlos Medeiros, for example, was one of the founders of the most important black organizations in Rio de Janeiro, the Institute for Research on Black Culture (IPCN). Though when I spoke to him in 2009, some three decades later, he was the Coordinator of Racial Equality of Rio de Janeiro, a local state agency. While Medeiros had taken positions within the Brazilian state a number of times over the previous decades, he still considered his time within the state as temporary. More interestingly, he—like Luiza Bairros—never saw such government positions as compromising his identity as a black *militante*. He explained: "I am a black movement *militante*, and am going to continue being a *militante*. This position, well, I'm going to occupy it for some time, but I am going to continue to be a black *militante*" (interview, Carlos Medeiros, September 2009). In practice, however, this category of "militants in the state" was a complex one writ with many ambiguities, not the least being the fact that these activists-turned-bureaucrats had themselves blurred the lines between "the movement" and "the state."

Transparent but Ritualized Participation in Brazil

For the institutionalized majority within Brazil's black movement, being active in political parties, occupying the state bureaucracy and engaging with state actors through formal channels was—as Edson França of UNEGRO put it—the only site of "real politics" (interview, Edson França, April 2010). While in the 1970s–1990s, this real site of politics had largely been political parties and elected office, in the 2000s and with the PT presidential victory and advent of a racial equality apparatus, it also became the state bureaucracy itself. However, just as in Colombia, this apparatus also consisted of institutionalized spaces for official engagement between the state and organized sectors of the black population. Mandated by Law 10,678 of 2003, the Council for the Promotion of Racial Equality (CNPIR) was the official body within SEPPIR that guaranteed the continued participation of anti-racism activists in the formulation of public policies in Brazil. Their mandate was to "promote, at the national level, policies that promote racial equality, with an emphasis on the black population and other ethnic segments of the Brazilian population."[32] This was part of a larger PT platform of greater civil society participation in budgeting and policy making (Avritzer 2009).

CNPIR was made up of nineteen representatives from federal government agencies, including all of the pertinent ministries as well as nineteen activists from a wide range of civil society sectors including religious communities; representatives from the Jewish, Arab, and Palestinian communities; Gypsy and indigenous peoples; as well as three experts on the situation facing black populations. Unlike the National Commission on Black Communities in Colombia, CNPIR was not a key site of contestation between different social movement actors. This was, in part, because of structural differences in the two bodies created to ensure the political participation of black communities. It was also a reflection of the multiple points of entry that black Brazilian activists had to engage with the state. In addition to CNPIR, black activists participated in innumerous policy-specific councils set up at various levels to institutionalize civil society participation.

In order to be named a national council member, you had to represent a national organization that had the equivalent of 501(c)3 status and that had done work in at least five states in three regions in the country, for at period of at least three years. Among the many documents that organizations had to submit were minutes from their election of their board of directors for the organizations and a report on activities in their last three years.[33] This high bar weeded out the kinds of paper organizations that were so over-represented in Colombia's structures for black participation. It also meant that national organizations strongly associated with political parties, including UNEGRO and CONEN, were often represented in CNPIR. Other national organizations like the National Coordinator of Quilombo CONAQ as well as the Articulation of Black Women were also in CNPIR. This left very few, if any, national black organizations that were not included. In 2008 for example, only twenty-two organizations applied for the nineteen civil society positions within the National Council.[34] At that time, the more radical MNU was the only major national organization that was not part of CNPIR. However, this was not because the organization was not chosen to participate, but rather because they had taken the position to boycott it.[35]

The process was also much more transparent than in Colombia. In 2010, for example, calls for nominations for a new council were advertised on a wide range of civil society list serves. The SEPPIR representative in charge of engaging with civil society through CNPIR also spoke on a number of national TV programs to get the word out and to explain the process.[36] Yet even though CNPIR was not plagued with the same charges of corruption as its Colombian counterpart—the National Advisory Commission on Black Communities—it still had very limited power to pressure the state to make substantive reforms. Instead, they engaged in Brazil's more transparent and less corrupt version of ritualized participation. In it, CNPIR activists were instrumental in the legitimation of the many National Plans for the Promotion of Racial Equality, even as many aspects of the plans were being chipped away, or never enacted. I discuss this in greater detail in the following chapter.

Absorption and State Funding

While CNPIR gave activists privileged access to particular arms of the Brazilian state, and perhaps even state funding, it was by no means their only avenue to engage with the Brazilian state. By the late 2000s, many Afro-Brazilian organizations had also become absorbed into different parts of the local and federal state. This is in part because the PT saw itself, and operated, as the political arm of social movements (Hochstetler 2000). Thus, winning national office with the election of Lula amounted to a colonization of the Brazilian state by civil society. The absorption of social movements into the state also happened through their increasing dependence on state funding.

In fact, nearly every event organized by the black movement that I attended had nicely printed posters typically with a host of logos that read "sponsorship by SEPPIR" or its local and state equivalents. In other cases, it was "Petrobras," "Palmares Cultural Foundation," or "A Brazil for Everyone"—a national campaign that included social policy and the mainstreaming of racial equality—that offered financial support to movement events. Moreover, because I was in Brazil in 2010, an election year, movement events and meetings were constantly postponed, cancelled, reorganized, or downsized, as they were deeply dependent on the fiscal calendar of local and state governments, as well as the political will of politicians and bureaucrats. And while Brazil's black movement was still alarmingly underfunded, most of the funds that organizations had still seemed to come from the state, in some form or another.

The only Afro-Brazilian organizations that were somewhat immune to this trend toward what Baiocchi et al (2008) call "dependent association-alism" were the handful of highly professionalized black NGOs that had garnered significant international funding. As I discussed in the previous chapter, organizations like Geledés and Criola, particularly with the process of organizing around Durban, were able to access international funding in unparalleled ways. As Jurema Werneck of Criola explained, Durban was the first time that many Afro-Brazilian activists were paid to do anti-racism work on a full-time basis (interview, Jurema Werneck, October 2009). Such international funding meant that these organizations did not have to rely on the Brazilian state for daily survival, which in turn afforded them leverage to engage with the state at the same time they were critical of it. As one former high-level official in SEPPIR explained, while many black political organizations had developed dependent and depoliticized relationships with the Brazilian state, this was not the case with some established NGOs.

> The main black movement NGOs don't need SEPPIR in order to engage with the government. They have reached a level that doesn't need that state agency at all. So in reality, when you begin to talk about a relationship between SEPPIR and these institutions, we are talking about a political relationship, in general, and there has even been a distancing from SEPPIR precisely because it is weak (interview, Giovanni Harvey, March 2010).

This relative autonomy of Brazil's major black NGOs was directly related to their ability to access international funding, a reality that activists argued was quickly changing as foundations began to pull funding from Brazil due to the country's improved economic situation (interview, Jurema Werneck, October 2009).

Less professionalized organizations like the MNU never had the same kind of external financial support either from the government or international foundations. And while their costs were relatively low given their less formalized structure, they still needed money to develop community projects, maintain their websites, pay rent, and hold meetings and public events. Yet the more radical branch of the MNU was extremely critical of the cooptation of the movement, which they saw as directly linked to receiving funds from the state. I remember running errands in downtown São Paulo in May of 2010 and bumping into one of the most radical opponents to Brazil's racial equality apparatus. Previously, he explained to me that the MNU refused to receive funding from the state. Nevertheless, when I saw him on the street that day he was on his way to turn in a proposal to the state's Council for the Participation and Development of Blacks for a community project he hoped to do with black youth. What this suggested was that even the most radical arm of Brazil's black movement was still dependent on the state's racial equality apparatus, in some form or another, for its very survival.

Critiquing the Racial Equality Apparatus

Organizations like the MNU—with their radical history and deep suspicions about the state and formal politics—had been on the decline since the 1990s, in part because of the large exodus of activists to political parties and NGOs (Covin 2006). However, in the late 2000s, the organization experienced a revival of sorts with an upswing in membership, the return of old activists to the organization and new involvement by black youth. In the South, the MNU had been at the center of urban *quilombo* organizing, and in Bahia, they were at the forefront of a new convergence of organizing against state violence and the genocide of black communities (Smith 2015). It was in this context that the React or Die movement (Campanha Reaja o Será Morto/a)—a network of community-based organizations that emerged to politicize the deaths of black people and to expose policy brutality, and inequality in Brazil's criminal justice system—was born. While the organization began in 2005 in Salvador, it gained national and international media attention about a decade later with a number of marches against the genocide of black people. While the trend within the larger black movement had been working within state bureaucracies, Reaja was amassing thousands of protestors, first in Salvador, and later in cities across the nation.[37]

Among other things, this revival of radical, grassroots organizing within Brazil's black movement required a rehashing of some of the debates that had crippled organizations like the MNU in the 1990s. The MNU continued to have a substantial contingent within it committed to participating in formal politics and being active in the PT, and those that felt this type of "double militancy" was ineffective and amounted to a cooptation of black movement leaders. Much like the leaders of CONEN and UNEGRO, the more institutionalized sector of the MNU often talked about formal politics as part of the natural evolution of Brazil's black movement. Marta Almeida Filho, one of the most vocal leaders of MNU Pernambuco, best articulated this position. For Marta, institutionalized politics were the only vehicle through which the black movement could actually impact the Brazilian state, and consequently, change the lives of black people on the ground. She maintained "political parties are where [black] militants need to be. In political parties and through laws you can exert pressure, contest power, get funding to be a strong force, to execute [community] projects. That is our responsibility . . . that's what we demand" (interview, Marta Almeida, January 2011). Other leaders in the same city, such as Zé de Oliveira also of the MNU and a founder of the PT, similarly saw formal politics as the way to put the movement's "demands in practice" (interview, Zé de Oliveira, January 2011).

Nevertheless, there were still factions within the MNU, and Brazil's black movement more generally that resisted absorption into the state. More specifically, the near eclipse of the movement—as well as many social movements within the country—by the state had left only a few small sectors to raise questions of political autonomy, each with very distinct relationships with the state. The most vocal critic of black movement institutionalization has been a small sector within the MNU and members of the Collective of Black Entities (CEN). They felt that while the PT-run state had made some undeniable gains with respect to ethno-racial issues, there were still many shortcomings. While these *militantes* were becoming increasingly salient to national debates around anti-racism in Brazil, they were still largely marginalized within the movement as anachronistic or ineffective. To be sure, their calls for political autonomy, particularly from the PT and SEPPIR, often bumped up against the dominant tendency toward movement absorption and ritualized participation.

At key moments in the late 2000s, this more autonomous sector— sometimes in alliance with black NGOs—was crucial in introducing serious questions within the black movement about the effectiveness of working from within the system. They also raised the visibility of serious racial injustices that had never been on the table within the PT or the Brazilian state, like racialized state violence of black people. In contrast to the more autonomous sectors of the black movement in Colombia, these activists felt that rather than being plagued by corruption, institutionalized sectors were simply misguided and subservient to political party agendas. Onir Araújo of the MNU, for example, explained that *negros partidarios* (political party blacks) "really believe that inclusion can be achieved from within the system. Yet what they end up doing is justifying the maintenance of the system itself" (interview, Onir Araújo, MNU, April 2010). Similarly, Marcio Alexandre of CEN, another autonomist organization explained:

> I am not affiliated with any political party. I know where I vote. I'm a leftist guy, but I don't have an affiliation with a political party because

I am civil society, and in my mind, being civil society means having a critical consciousness. You cannot be linked [to political parties] because you lose the capacity to be critical. . . . I'm tired of seeing, I'm ashamed of, the shitload of men or women that fight, yell, talk and make things happen in black movement meetings, yet when they go to their political party meetings they are practically serving coffee. They are over there, completely submissive. That kind of political party doesn't serve me. I don't want a political party like that! (interview, Marcio Alexandre, March 2010).

According to Marcio Alexandre, this subservience had led to an insidious complicity with state inaction. In his view, black organizations that were close to the Workers' Party had enjoyed privileged access to state funding, and in exchange they had to pretend that the government was sufficiently addressing the issue of racial equality. He argued that the biggest challenge facing the black movement was to ensure that such involvement was "sovereign" and that it allow for the "race agenda" to have priority over the "political party agenda."

While in the early years of Lula's administration (2003–2010), these kinds of critiques were seen as bad form, as divisive and as airing the movement's dirty laundry, after Lula's first term and in the context of failed attempts at national legislation for racial equality, these critiques began to gain more sway within the dominant sectors of the black movement. Reginaldo Bispo was one of the most central figures in these internal debates over political autonomy. He was also a prolific critic of the Brazilian state's position on race issues in the few previous years. He was a Trotskyist who had come back from a long hiatus from the MNU to take up the position of national coordinator of the organization. When he returned in the mid-2000s, he did so with the hope of rebuilding an MNU that emphasized a radical autonomy from the state. However, he was met with opposition from within the MNU ranks.

These activists he confronted were dedicated to participating in the PT and taking over *poder público*, or state power. In an open letter to the black movement published and widely distributed, Bispo critiqued this position both within the MNU and the broader movement. With the unabashed prose that he was known for, he maintained that the "love affair" between the Workers' Party and the black movement had ended. He called, instead, for a critical view of the PT administration and argued that Brazil had reached a critical juncture and could no longer remain enchanted by the promise of hope of the PT administration. "We elected the PT and Lula to govern the country hoping for change, above all in the economy, so that they would democratize opportunities for the great masses of excluded people, poor and black people in the country" (interview, Reginaldo Bispo, April 2010).

In his account, there had instead been few advances and "great deception" that required the movement to hold the PT and the state accountable.

Bispo was right, especially in the mid-2000s. Affirmative action policies were under way, but it was due exclusively to legislation at the state and local levels. Indeed, many of the gains at the federal level had been largely symbolic. There was also two more fundamental problems. First, there were many limitations of affirmative action policies to really address systematic and widespread racial inequality, a point I return to in the next chapter. Second, there were many issues that the Workers' Party would simply not touch, like the alarmingly high level of police killings of mostly poor black people in Brazil (Smith 2016).

However, members of CEN, the MNU, and Reaja were not the only ones that critiqued the Brazilian state. Black NGOs too launched public critiques of it. Though while the former largely did so on political grounds, Afro-Brazilian activists working in NGOS had a more technical critique of the state, and particularly of the racial equality apparatus. While SEPPIR officials did ask the most established and professionalized black NGOs like CEERT and Geledés to lend their expertise to the creation of SEPPIR, and the building of the state's new racial equality apparatus, black NGOs took a hands-off approach (interview, Matilde Ribeiro, May 2010). After SEPPIR was created, and its institutional weaknesses became increasingly apparent, activists in these NGOs began to critique the capacity of SEPPIR. To be sure, the problems facing the agency were many. While the agency had ministerial status, its executive power was extremely limited. On the one hand, being housed within the Office of the President made it well positioned to push for and coordinate racial equality policy within the upper echelons of the Brazilian state. On the other, it had no authority to actually design or implement policy as that was left to the substantive ministries of education, labor, health and the like. As a result, the presence of any minister hostile to racial issues undermined racial policy in the country, as was the case with the Minister of Education in the early years.

Black NGOs also argued that SEPPIR lacked competent bureaucrats specializing in racial policies, something that was echoed in my interviews with two people who had worked at SEPPIR. Thus, people like Jurema Werneck of Criola, a black feminist NGO, felt that despite some symbolic advances, Lula's administration had made little progress and there were many structural impediments to the implementation of racial equality policies:

The Brazilian state, the federal government more specifically, has recognized that anti-racism is so important that it created a secretariat with ministerial status. Now there is a minister who is on the same level as the other ministers in the hierarchy, but it is also linked to the president's cabinet. Theoretically it is in the president's cabinet, however, in practice, it doesn't have a structure, it doesn't have qualified personnel, it doesn't have results, it doesn't have anything. Everything they have in terms of results is because civil society pressured for anti-racism (interview, Jurema Werneck, October 2009).

Precisely because of these weaknesses, internationally funded NGOs like Criola and Geledés continued to engage with the state in ways that were not mediated by SEPPIR. They did this by developing relationships with different ministries within the federal government, including pressuring them to adopt policies and consulting them. In some cases, they were subcontracted on the implementation of particular programs, as was the case with the Ministry of Health's Black Health Campaign launched in 2004.[38]

In fact, when I interviewed Jurema was coincidentally the day that Criola was sending out a massive mailing with information on activities throughout the country related to this government. When I asked her about what seemed to be a partnership between the organization and the Ministry of Health, she said emphatically: "No! The definition of this is public policy. It isn't a partnership with the state. It's the state that has to do it. What civil society does is pressure, and in some cases consult . . . one thing is the state, the government, the other is civil society. The State has the obligation [to do this], not us" (interview, Jurema Werneck, October 2009). Yet as I discussed earlier, the roles of the state and civil society were often blurred in practice, especially under a leftist administration that still saw itself as a social movement.

Ultimately, those working in NGOs were more willing than MNU/CEN leaders to consult the government and engage with it in a formal sense, even if they also felt that the role of black organizations was to pressure the state from outside. This position of black NGOs often led radical MNU leaders to critique these largely black women's NGOs as depoliticized in ways that were often gendered. Indeed, implicit in such critiques was the idea that the more male dominated MNU was the only place of real militancy, and the largely woman dominated NGOs were simply professionalized activists, coopted by international funding.

Despite these tensions, black NGOs like Criola did form strategic alliances with the radical sector of the MNU and CEN to challenge the state. They did this at the same time that party-leaning organizations like CONEN and UNEGRO felt strongly that the Lula administration would be more effective if it had the support of the movement. This was the case in November of 2005 when a number of important black NGOs and the radical arm of the MNU refused to participate in the ten-year commemoration of the historic 1995 Zumbí march. They argued that SEPPIR and the Workers' Party were too central to the organizing of this anniversary march for it to have any real political impact. Moreover, because the fate of the PT in the upcoming election was uncertain, they felt it was important to show that they were exerting pressure on the Brazilian state, regardless of which party was in office. Thus, more party-leaning black organizations joined labor unions in support of a SEPPIR-organized march on November 16, while the more autonomist sector held a separate march on November 22. In the latter, organizers banned political party banners and demanded a separate meeting with President Lula in an attempt to demand more substantive racial policies as well as a restructuring of the racial equality apparatus.[39] These kinds of negotiations around how to engage with the state and how to avoid institutionalization are ones that movements everywhere face. However, these questions were further muddled by the fact that the state with which black Brazilian activists were negotiating was a leftist one that had proven itself sympathetic to anti-racism.

CONCLUSION

Despite major differences in the political fields of Colombia and Brazil —as well as radically different paths to institutionalization—the adoption of specific legislation for black populations has reconfigured the relationship between movements and these states in similar ways. First, such legislation led to the construction of an ethno-racial state apparatus designed not only to oversee the implementation of ethno-racial policy but also to guarantee and discipline black movement participation. While Brazil's racial equality apparatus was far better off in terms of structure, mandate, and resources than its Colombian counterpart, both were relatively weak institutions, without the infrastructure or power needed to fulfill their actual mandates. Colombia's multicultural state apparatus was also highly susceptible to corruption.

In both countries, though, the construction of these ethno-racial arms of the state have dramatically reconfigured the relationship between black movements and these institutions through several interrelated dynamics. Participatory structures in both countries simultaneously gave black activists access to the state and at the same time they constrained and disciplined these movements. Among other things, I showed how these ethno-racial state apparatuses have become buffers between movements and the state, how they absorb black activists as they take up positions within the state bureaucracy and become dependent on state funding, and how they create spaces for activists to engage in ritualized participation.

Yet rather than a top-down story of cooptation, I show how black activists in each country continued to have agency. Just as some activists and organizations took up positions within, or engaged formally with, the Colombian and Brazilian states, others refused to become absorbed or to engage in what were often empty rituals of participation. This kind of segmented institutionalization of social movements into the state is not uncommon. As della Porta and Diani (2009) remind us, "the incorporation of one organization can go along with the radicalization of another" (151). Indeed, as the Colombian and Brazilian states increasingly passed legislation aimed at black populations and as they created more and more spaces for black participation, the more radical arms of the black movement in both countries saw these as key sites in the depoliticization, demobilization, and cooptation of their movements. They often concluded that exerting further pressure on the state would require them to maintain their political autonomy. Yet maintaining this ideological position was not always feasible as movements in both Colombia and Brazil depended to some extent on preestablished structures for black participation or on state funding for their basic survival.

What is more, these dynamics created further cleavages in these movements —which were already divided around a number of lines—between those that maintained close relationships with the state and those that kept the state at arms length. In fact, navigating these divisions was one of the most difficult challenges I faced while conducting fieldwork. Much of my time in both Colombia and Brazil involved maintaining some distance from both the more institutionalized black activists and the more radical ones in order to fully understand the array of political practices that made up this new moment in each country. In my mind, the making of black political subjects was fundamentally about both processes of institutionalization and radicalization, just as it also necessarily involved making claims to difference and to equality. Yet maintaining this balance without alienating either faction, or without losing entrée, proved difficult. Activists in both countries constantly challenged me to take a position. My choices of friends, the places I frequented socially, the people with whom I stayed while conducting research in different regions, and who I chose to interview were heavily scrutinized. For activists, these were all political, not methodological or logistical, decisions.[40]

Analyzing these dynamics of black movement institutionalization is important for several reasons. First, they underscore the ways in which the making of black political subjects is ultimately an ongoing political process, rather than one that happens in a single moment or through a specific piece of legislation. Making decisions to register your black organizations with the state, to run as or vote for "black representatives," and to adopt the language of the state or not, are all part of a continual process of making black political subjects in the two countries. Additionally, and as I show in the following chapter, examining these politics of institutionalization also give us a window into how deep such reforms actually go. Indeed, the ways in which black movements in Colombia and Brazil have navigated these newly constituted state apparatuses have had direct implications on whether these states have complied with, restricted, or in rare cases expanded existing legislation.

CHAPTER SEVEN

UNMAKING BLACK POLITICAL SUBJECTS

The adoption of specific policies for black populations in Colombia and Brazil was not simply a policy shift; it amounted instead to a dramatic change in discourse of state institutions as well as a transformation of the way that citizenship was defined in these countries. Nevertheless, it did not naturally follow that these political changes would actually matter in the lives of ordinary people in these countries. In both, ethnoracial legislation had inherent limitations. There was also the notorious gap between laws on paper and actual state practices. As the popular Brazilian adage "There are laws that stick and laws that don't" and the Colombian expression "There are more laws than people" convey, there is widespread skepticism about the ability of legislation to transform daily life in these countries. All this begs the question: to what extent has the adoption of specific policies for black populations translated into real change on the ground?

In this chapter, I analyze the extent to which the two countries have implemented ethno-racial reforms as well as explore the ways in which these policies have changed these societies. In it, I pay special attention to the political conditions that shape these states' decisions to make good on their promises or not. More specifically, I show how implementation has depended heavily on the ways in which activists navigate their domestic political fields, including how they negotiate their newly gained access to the state. It is also profoundly shaped by the emergence of reactionary movements. Indeed, as the dominant classes became increasingly aware of what was at stake with these rights and policies—land, natural resources, seats in congress, and university slots that could maintain or secure one's place within the middle class—they sought to dismantle them, sometimes through violent means. In both Colombia and Brazil, these dynamics of institutionalization and backlash are important to understanding the partial unmaking of black rights, in which black movement gains of the last few decades have remained on paper, or were restricted or undermined entirely.

LETRA MUERTA IN COLOMBIA

The story of black rights in Colombia is at once one of great hope and serious disappointment. Law 70 has five substantive chapters, each focusing on a specific area: land, natural resources, ethnic education, mining, and social/economic development; each was to be implemented through separate pieces of legislation. Yet, despite twenty years of promises by Colombian presidents, ministers, and directors of the Office on Black Communities, the chapters on ethno-education and territory were the only ones that had been seriously institutionalized. Even in those areas, there are still serious limitations, including the fact that less than 10 percent of Colombia's public schools had even adopted the legally mandated curriculum on Afro-Colombian history and culture.[1] In this sense, a number of key provisions in this legislation can be said to be *letra muerta*, or dead law."

The only silver lining has been Colombia's record on land titling of black rural communities, which is impressive, especially when you compare it to Brazil, where efforts to recognize collective titles have largely been crippled. In the mid-1990s, Colombia began to aggressively title indigenous and black territories with help from international institutions. Through their Natural Resource Management Program, the World Bank, and other institutions provided $65 million in loans toward the registering and titling of "minority" communities on Colombia's Pacific Coast.[2] The impact was substantial; as one World Bank publication reported, the funding benefited 497 black communities on the Pacific Coast and 2.36 million hectares of collective land titles.[3] In the same period, the Inter-American Development Bank (IDB) also supported land titling in Colombia through their Land Titling and Registry Modernization program.[4]

More than benevolence or a commitment to social justice or poverty reduction alone, collective titling was necessary for the later expansion of capitalism in these areas. As Goldman (2008) suggests in his work on "green neoliberalism," the demarcation of certain areas as "protected" became a Trojan horse of sorts for the later commodification of land. In the case of ethnic land rights, it was both the environment and culture of traditional communities that needed to be protected. This commodification motive behind such titling was sometimes made explicit. The World Bank, for example, underscored that the goal of the Natural Resource Management Program—which helped to title collective black territories in Colombia— was to "generate the policy, institutional and technical base for future forest management and land titling investments in the Chocó Region."[5] Thereafter, the Colombian state continued to demarcate and title collective territories for black communities on their own. According to the Colombian Institute for Rural Development (INCODER), the state had titled 5.4 million hectares covering 185 black community councils by 2014.[6] These numbers are particularly striking when we consider that this represented 66 percent of the Pacific Coast's 8.3 million hectares of territory.

I had the opportunity to visit some of the rural communities applying for a collective title in March of 2009. They were sprinkled along the upper Atrato River in the department of the Chocó. I had originally traveled to Quibdó to meet a number of long-time activists in the black rural movement including Padre Sterling Londoño, an Afro-Colombian priest and activist that had embraced liberation theology many years before. Padre Sterling saw his friends within the priesthood murdered for their political organizing and he had himself lived through many death threats. In lieu of an interview, he invited me to attend a board meeting of the Regional Community Council of the Popular Peasant Movement of the Atrato River (COCOMOPOCA), an organization that was founded in 1994 just one year after the signing in of Law 70. [7] Padre Sterling explained that the trip to Bagadó would be long, and that we would spend two days with local communities there. We left at seven in the morning in a car that belonged to the Dioceses of Quibdó. After about an hour's drive to the town of Juto, we all got into a small boat that we took upstream for about three hours, stopping in a number of communities along the way, first Lloró, then las Hamacas, and eventually Bagadó. In each town, we picked up someone new, most of them men who had been elected to the board of their respective community councils.

COCOMOPOCA was a regional council that brought together a few dozen community councils representing about 17,500 people. The communities organized under COCOMOPOCA appeared on the surface to be easy cases for land titling. Law 70 stipulated that it recognized the collective territory of "black communities" that resided in the "empty lands located along the riverbanks in rural areas along the Pacific Basin" and who lived according to their "traditional practices of production." The hundreds of families within the territory of COCOMOPOCA easily met these criteria. They were the direct descendants of enslaved Africans brought to work in mining hundreds of years before. They were also situated precisely in the areas that were deemed "empty" or state owned. Equally important was the fact that they also engaged in traditional practices of production, the most important of which were subsistence agriculture and traditional mining. Indeed, on the boat ride to Bagadó that weekend, the Atrato River was peppered with women, men, and children with *bateas*, or large shallow wooden bowls designed to extract gold, platinum, and other precious minerals from the river. While not everyone in these communities lived exclusively off of traditional farming or mining, it was still a critical aspect of their livelihood, as it had been for generations.

Despite being a textbook case of collective multicultural rights, when I visited COCOMOPOCA in 2009 they still did not have a collective land title. The organization had first submitted the necessary paperwork—local

maps, community censuses, proof of their official status as a regional community council, and many other legal documents—to Colombia's National
Institute for Agrarian Reform (INCORA) about a decade before. This was
the first of three national government agencies with which they would deal
during their uphill battle toward legal recognition. In 2003, INCORA was
supplanted by the Colombian Institute for Rural Development (INCODER).
It was then replaced by the National Unit of Lands (UNAT) in 2006, which
was "liquidated" just three years later, at which point INCODER was put
back in charge of land titling.

Navigating this bureaucratic maze required legal expertise, patience,
and resources that many rural black communities in Colombia did not
have. COCOMOPOCA leaders had to meet with government officials
dozens of times in their territory and in the city of Quibdó. In addition,
COCOMOPOCA activists made countless trips to Bogotá, sometimes to
submit documents to bureaucrats who, in some cases, even admitted to having "lost" paperwork at various points along the way.[8] This process also required an arsenal of legal expertise—which was provided by a number of
lawyers who worked in solidarity with the organization—as well as financial
support from organizations like Christian Aid and the Catholic Agency for
Overseas Development.

In the process of applying for state recognition, COCOMOPOCA also lost
a number of leaders to political assassinations and was the constant subject
of death threats. It was this same violence that had prompted many families
within their territory to flee the area. In fact, while the original number of
people included in the collective title of COCOMOPOCA was 30,000, it had
shrunk to 17,000 when it was finally recognized by INCODER.[9] As such, when
the government finally recognized their collective land title, the organization
initiated a return campaign. Moreover, due to the splitting off of some community councils, the territory of COCOMOPOCA was also much smaller than
what the communities had originally demanded from the various government agencies in charge of rural development. It was only after a twelve-year
battle—in September of 2011—that INCODER granted COCOMOPOCA
their collective land title that covered 73,000 hectares and included 2,250 families. To understand why this process took so long, we must move beyond
bureaucratic explanations and beyond the political field, strictly defined, all
together. Instead, we have to examine the economic interests that underlie
such contestations between the state and the rural black movement.

Expanding Capitalism, Delimiting Blackness

By the time COCOMOPOCA's land title came through, much of the
surrounding area was swimming in transnational mining operations,
some with official licenses from Colombia's Ministry of Mines and Energy

and others without. Throughout the process of bureaucratic meandering COCOMOPOCA leaders, much like their counterparts in other parts of the country, were keenly aware that what often looked like administrative hold-ups were actually serious economic interests. Nicolasa Machado was one of COCOMOPOCA's most vocal leaders. She received her political education like many black rural activists in the Catholic Church. I spent a lot of time with her on my trip in 2009 and interviewed her one night in the quarters we shared in the town's monastery. She explained:

> Well, our eternal fight has been with INCORA, then INCODER, then UNAT, and all of that because they have denied our title for 10 years, they have denied us the possibility [of getting a collective title]. And why have they denied it? Because of the interests that the Colombian government has in extractive mining in the Pacific, which is a region with lots of minerals. There are more than twenty minerals that we have here. So the president himself as well as all of his ministries, including the Ministry of Mining, are very interested in mining ex-ploitation here and they have made serious concessions to mining companies. So, from that point of view, it is with these institutions that we have had to fight and with which we have continued to have problems (interview, Nicolasa Machado, March 2009).

Throughout Colombia, the struggle for collective land titles for black com-munities conflicted directly with the interests of local and transnational capital. As a result, leaders often confronted state actors who were not sim-ply inefficient, but rather, who had many incentives to not recognize the constitutional rights of these communities.

The concept of territoriality codified in Law 70 was meant to stave off unfettered capitalist expansion that had for decades threatened the live-lihoods of these communities (Escobar 2008; Asher 2009). Among other things, the legislation vowed to guarantee these communities the rights to traditional forms of livelihood, including ancestral or artisanal mining. Of course, such a project had direct implications for both the profits of transnational capital, and for the Colombian state's development project. In this sense, Law 70 could be understood as an ambitious utopian exper-iment, one that has proved extremely difficult to fully realize. In addition to refusing to implement the legislation, the 2000s saw various attempts to pass legislation that sought to undermine both black and indigenous com-munities' rights to collective territory and natural resources. Among other efforts, this included what would be failed attempts to pass Ley Florestal of 2004 and to modify the country's mining code in 2010.

With these insatiable economic interests came violence. The land titling process on Colombia's Pacific Coast was followed by an unprecedented level of armed conflict in these areas. This violence took the form of forced cultivation of legal and illegal crops, threats against Afro-Colombian leaders and murder (Wouters 2001; AFRODES 2009). The violence also manifested in the form of Afro-Colombians' over-representation in Colombia's internally displaced populations, which at the time of writing this book was one of the largest in the world. Yet while blacks represented about 10 percent of Colombia's population, they were approximately 30 percent of the country's some five million internally displaced peoples. In this, according to AFRODES, between 1995 and 2007, 355,629 of the people that were displaced were from the seventy-five municipalities where Afro-Colombians held collective territories or where they were the majority (AFRODES 2007).[10] So while achieving land titles was a major feat, the ability of these communities to actually enjoy their territorial rights involved the sometimes-deadly task of confronting and fending off such violence.

Returning back to the example of COCOMOPOCA on the Chocó, all elements of this violence and the economic interests that undergirded it, were bubbling underneath the surface. On that visit Bagadó, both illegal and state-sanctioned extractive mining operations that were happening within the demarcated territory of the community councils were numerous. On the boat ride, as I listened to community leaders explain how the river used to be, I counted some twenty-four bulldozers. Many of them were parked and empty at that time during the day. These problems were endemic to what some have characterized as the "mining boom" or "gold rush" in this region.[11] Over the last decade, along the length of the Atrato River and throughout Colombia, transnational companies like Muriel Mining in the Chocó and Antioquia, Gran Colombia Gold in Nariño, and AngloGold Ashanti in Northern Cauca were all operating with mining licenses authorized by the Ministry of Mines and Energy that were in direct violation of Colombia's 1991 constitution and Law 70 (Benavides 2012).

Privatizing natural resources had become a central tenet of Colombia's economic growth and development plan. This aim, to be sure, superseded any desire on the part of state officials to protect the lands and cultures of black communities. This type of mining brought with it armed paramilitary groups that, in conflict with other armed groups, engaged in unparalleled violence in these areas. The community council meeting I attended was actually called to come up with strategies to deal with the problem of illegal mining in the area. Another critical issue was the increasingly entangled relationships between community members who were either coerced at gunpoint or understandably lured by the prospect of extracting in one day what took weeks using traditional methods.

This type of mining threatened these communities beyond the issue of violence. Because it required bulldozers and the use of mercury to better detect where the precious metals were in the river water, this large-scale industrial mining also proved particularly disastrous for the environment.

In this way, it threatened to make small-scale traditional mining unviable, and made the livelihoods of these communities uncertain. While increases in mining operations in these areas were perhaps an inevitable outcome of capitalist expansion, the violence with which they came may be best understood as constituting a backlash against black rights. Rather than blame this violence on Law 70, Carlos Rosero of PCN has called this a new "modality of violence" facing these communities.[12] In it, transnational corporations have sought to undermine already institutionalized black rights to territory and natural resources, often with the complicity of the Colombian state.

Yet while the story of COCOMOPOCA underscores the precariousness of black rights, these communities' location in the "empty lands" of the Pacific Coast meant that they were on much more solid legal footing than communities elsewhere. Since the mid-1990s, many self-identified black communities outside the Pacific Coast as well as in urban areas like Buenaventura found themselves confronting state actors who maintained a narrow definition of "black communities." While Law 70 and related legislation did define black communities in geographically specific ways, there was still a considerable amount of legal ambiguity. For instance, Article 2 of the legislation described "black communities" as those that possess their own culture and who collectively occupy rural territories, rather than define them as residing in specific geographic areas in the country. Similarly, "collective occupation" was defined in the legislation as the "historical and ancestral settlement of black communities in lands developed for collective use for the purpose of subsistence and which develop their traditional production practices."[13]

Nevertheless, by 2014 about 90 percent of the forty-five majority black municipalities in the Pacific had already been collectively titled, while only a handful of collective land titles had been granted to black communities outside of the Pacific.[14] Indeed, despite their best efforts to be legally recognized, black rural communities on the Atlantic Coast and other parts of the country found themselves at the margins of legal definitions of traditional black communities. While bureaucrats certainly had some discretion in the matter, they typically maintained restrictive definitions of black communities. In what follows, I analyze the plight of three communities, each in different parts of the country and each with varying degrees of perceived authenticity as "black communities": La Toma, La Boquilla, and Palenque de San Basilio. This highlights the politics of authenticity that have ensued since the adoption of ethno-racial policies in Colombia.

The Politics of Black Authenticity

Driving a couple of hours south of the city of Cali to the northern part of the state of Cauca, one finds dozens of small black towns: Buenos Aires, Santander de Quilichao, Puerto Tejada, and others. This region of the Norte de Cauca had long been central to the development of Colombia's black ethno-territorial movement and to the political processes that led to Law 70 (Hurtado 2001). Nevertheless, Northern Cauca had a precarious legal standing vis-à-vis black political subjecthood despite the fact that they were widely understood in the regional and national imaginaries as black, and largely identified as such. In fact, many of the families in this region maintained last names like Carabalí, Mandinga, and Lucumí, names that denoted their African ancestry.[15] Nevertheless, these towns were not on the Pacific Coast. Moreover, being near Cali meant that people in these communities did not always engage in traditional forms of production, but instead commuted to Cali and worked in menial jobs there. This proximity to an urban center also made their status as a traditional black community more questionable. This was especially so when they were compared to the remote black communities of the Chocó and the Southern Pacific, which you could access only by boat and through tropical marshlands.

In other respects, communities in this region, like La Toma, could not have been more "traditional." For centuries, they had survived on subsistence farming and small-scale mining in the rivers that ran through the communities. Community leaders often reminded state officials that they were the descendants of Africans who had worked in mining since even before they were enslaved and sent to Colombia. La Toma was also the community in this region from which Francia Marquez Mina—a leader with PCN and the protagonist of a number of documentaries on the Afro-Colombian land struggle—hailed.[16] Francia was also one of my dearest friends in Colombia and invited me to visit her community several times. Despite having set up a community council and submitted the copious amounts of necessary paperwork, INCODER still had not legally recognized La Toma as a traditional black community with the rights to collective territory and natural resources.

What is more, in late 2009, activists from La Toma began to receive eviction notices from the government that said the community had been illegally inhabiting the area, presumably for centuries. At that time, leaders were also experiencing increased violence in the form of death threats, displacements, and murders of leaders. The subtext of these state and nonstate actions was to clear the path for mining companies to enter the area without any fetters. Yet rather than leave, the community took their case to Colombia's Constitutional Court (the equivalent of its Supreme Court), which ruled in their favor.[17] Even without a collective title, the court held that with the exception of small-scale traditional mining, all mining was illegal in La Toma. They also legitimated the community's right to prior consultation before embarking on mining projects, which the Ministry of the Interior had previously tried to restrict only to communities with legal titles. While this legal victory was important, it did not stop mining operators or the Black Eagle paramilitary group from threatening and even murdering a number of local leaders. When another illegal bulldozer showed up in the community, in November 2014 the women of La Toma decided to embark upon a journey of over 3,000 miles to Bogotá. When they arrived, they met with government officials, who refused to do anything about the situation. With no other recourse, they decided to occupy a state building indefinitely.[18]

Whereas violence and the presence of mining companies presented the most serious impediment to territorial rights in communities like La Toma and Colombia's Pacific Coast, on the Atlantic Coast it was real estate and tourist developers. While communities like Boquilla were not situated in a mineral-rich part of the country, they did have the (mis)fortune of sitting on one of the most sought after slices of the city of Cartagena's coastline. While the fishing community of La Boquilla had been there for decades, in the late 1990s, Gloria Sánchez, a local activist, led a group of families in an "invasion" or squatting community on a previously uninhabited part of La Boquilla, establishing the community of Marlinda. In 1999, that community joined the one adjacent, Villa Gloria, to establish the Marlinda Community Council. Just a few months later, in April 2000, the community council applied for a collective title under Law 70.

One afternoon, I sat in La Boquilla in a makeshift restaurant/bar run out of a woman's house just steps away from the beautiful turquoise waters of the Caribbean Sea. This humble fishing community woke up to this every day. I was renting a room in the community and, through a friend, met a community member known as "*El Médico*," or "the Doctor," of La Boquilla. He agreed to a formal interview in which I asked him why La Boquilla had still not been officially recognized as a black community despite nearly a decade of trying. He responded:

> Look, of the fifteen requirements we only fulfilled ten, the other five they have, we didn't. For there to be land titling through Law 70, there has to be a territory that the state makes the decision to assign to the community and say, "since you are black from La Boquilla, take this land." Why can't it be done? It's because before that happened, there was already a political decision made. This land was for the expansion of tourism in Cartagena and the blacks [of La Boquilla] didn't fit into that plan (interview, El Médico, June 2009).

People like El Médico felt strongly that La Boquilla was a "black community," which was an important factor in the legal contestation they had with INCODER. Even so, what was in question was precisely La Boquilla's status as a "black community," as defined by Law 70 and subsequent legislation. At the center of this was not just the question of collective identity, but whether La Boquilla was sufficiently "rural" or "traditional," considering it was technically within the city limits of Cartagena.

Much was also at stake if the people in the community actually identified as black and if they saw themselves in "ethnic" terms. When I asked El Médico what the "requirements" were that the community had not fulfilled, he explained: "It's the cultural stuff. There has to be a black identity, and here we don't have it. It is very poor." I pushed him: "But how can you measure 'black identity'?" He responded as if this were self-evident: "You measure it by the way that people behave, the people's organizational capacity, and their desire to be black, to feel it." El Médico's intuition about how to define a "black community" echoed the way that anthropologists had talked about black communities' fitness for multicultural citizenship in the constitutional reform process decades before. It is that criteria, based in space and in collective identity, that did become enshrined in the Law of Black Communities and in the guidelines for state bureaucrats. Though even if La Boquilla did have a collective identity problem, this issue was inseparable from the material stakes involved in their possible recognition as a black community with the right to collective territory. Indeed, by the 2000s, La Boquilla was already surrounded by luxury condominiums and real estate development companies saw serious potential profits in the community's pristine shoreline.

INCODER did eventually grant La Boquilla their collective title in September 2012. In applying Law 70 to this urban community with questionable legitimacy as a black community and located on the Atlantic Coast, the state arguably set a precedent for other communities to make similar claims. La Boquilla's title was recognized alongside that of Palenque de San Basilio —a community located a couple of hours away—in a public ceremony that included Colombian president Juan Manuel Santos and U.S. president Barack Obama. The U.S. president was visiting as part of the Summit of the Americas held in Cartagena that year. These were historic cases of collective titling because they were the first two communities on the Atlantic Coast to be recognized in this way. Yet whereas the titling of La Boquilla was a surprising concession made by the state, the fate of Palenque was nearly certain. In addition to being one of the first maroon communities in the Americas, Palenque had preserved a number of African-based traditions, including maintaining a creolized language with strong roots in West Central African Bantu languages (Schwegler 2002).[19] Their recognition as culturally distinct was solidified in 2005 when UNESCO recognized the cultural patrimony of the community as a "Masterpiece of the Oral and Intangible Heritage of Humanity." Activists from Palenque had also been central to the struggle for black rights since the early 1990s, and had actually helped to write Law 70. All of this meant that Palenque had perhaps the most plausible claim to multicultural rights than any other community in Colombia.

Nevertheless, what ultimately propelled the Colombian state to recognize Palenque's title was not this cultural or historical authenticity, but rather international factors. USAID had funded many of the costly steps required for Palenque's land titling process, including the completion of surveys, maps, community meetings, and the preparation of legal documentation.[20] More important was the Obama effect, whereby Colombian state officials sought to look as if they were moving forward on ethno-racial policy in the presence of the United States' first black president.[21] If the government had not granted these collective titles, people from Palenque— who had often been called on to provide the colorful cultural content of meetings like the Summit of the Americas because of their strong cultural traditions—threatened to engage in protest against the violation of their constitutional rights, rather than in song and dance.

I cite all of these examples of negotiations over authenticity, land, and resources not because all of them were ultimately success stories. Rather, my intention is to highlight the process through which black rights have become increasingly contested, restricted, and even unmade since the adoption of Law 70. Despite the fact that these communities—COCOMOPOCA, La Boquilla, and Palenque de San Basilio—did all eventually receive a collective land title, their struggles underscore a number of worrisome elements of Colombia's reconfigured political field. Rather than remain marginal to the political field as they were in the 1980s, black rural communities and their leaders were now at the center of it, albeit "without guarantees" as Cárdenas (2012) reminds us. Further, this institutionalization of ethno-racial rights brought with it new kinds of violent economic struggles that were often disguised as legal and bureaucratic in nature. In fact, many of these willful delays in land titling were also camouflaged by talk of fragmentation within the black movement as the cause of holdups.

While COCOMOPOCA had originally consisted of fifty-four community councils, by the time that I visited the upper Atrato, twelve of these councils had broken off from the organization to form a separate one. Their legal advisor was a national commissioner of black communities that many activists had accused of brokering deals between rural black communities and government officials that did not typically lead to collective titling. This was the case with the community of Islas de Rosario, where this same black commissioner was said to be instrumental in convincing the community to usher in a large-scale tourist development project in 2007. The splintering off of these community councils meant that COCOMOPOCA had to resubmit all of the documents that had taken them many years and even greater resources to obtain, this time with only the remaining forty-two community councils. Rather than simply a reflection of local divisions along the Atrato River, this split was undoubtedly motivated by external factors. Some even suggested that government payoffs may have been involved in this case as it was in many others. Of course, I could not verify this. Ultimately though, many of the state officials I spoke to, both formally and informally, suggested that it was the black movement's internal fragmentation that was the true cause of the state's rolling back of black rights rather than the lack of political will and the serious problems with land titling.

Ritualized Participation and the Path That Never Was

The glue that was intended to ensure the full implementation of Law 70 was the institutionalization of black political participation. Given the contestation over land and natural resources that catalyzed black rural mobilization in the first place, throughout the 2000s PCN was at the forefront of movement efforts to pressure the Colombian state not only to ensure participation as defined under Law 70, but also the right to *consulta previa*. Embodied in International Labour Organisation Convention 169 and the UN Declaration on the Rights of Indigenous Peoples, prior consultation is the norm that mandates that governments protect the right to free, prior, and informed consent on all state and private projects that might affect the lives of people in indigenous, and increasingly black, rural communities. However, in the case of Colombia, *consulta previa* had been largely a performative exercise. In it, state officials would meet with leaders, commit to next steps, organize and fund regional and national conferences, and fly black activists around the country to sign on to development plans that would never be implemented, or in some cases, that ran counter to the logic of Law 70. In some instances, state officials used the mere presence of black leaders in meetings as proof that they were legally consulted and agreed to plans.

This precarious state of black rights in Colombia reflects the equally precarious process of black movement incorporation into the Colombian state that I discussed in the previous chapter. Beyond paying off leaders, activists felt that the state had created hundreds of spaces for black participation that were devoid of power and that facilitated state retrenchment. In this, a handful of activists representing themselves through "paper organizations" had colonized most spaces that were initially created to ensure the elaboration and implementation of legislation related to black communities. Given these dynamics, even those Afro-Colombian activists that engaged with the state with more sincere intentions—whether knowingly or not— participated in a dance of ritualized participation (Meyer 1993). In the case of ethno-racial policy in Colombia, the creation of the multiplicity of spaces for the "participation" and "consultation" of black communities had acted not only to institutionalize dissent but also to legitimate the state's rolling back of black rights.

One of the ways that this ritualized participation manifested was through creating discursive constraints on the claims that black activists came to articulate. In going back and forth to Colombia more than a dozen times over the last decade, one of the most consistent things I noticed was a perpetual discussion around the need to find a "path" to the implementation of Law 70. It always seemed strange to me that two decades after the passing of a piece of legislation, rather than promising to actually "ratify" and "implement" its most important chapters—related to natural resources, mining, and development—both state officials and activists continued to talk about finding a "path" to implementation.

The first time I heard this idea was in Tumaco in December of 2008 in a government-sponsored meeting that included nearly 300 people from around the country.[22] Among those in attendance were activists from local rural community councils, urban black organizations, national black organizations of various kinds as well as commissioners for black communities. The goal of the Tumaco meeting was to give these diverse sectors within the black movement an opportunity to dialogue directly with high-level government officials including the ministers of agriculture and of justice. There were many agenda items. First, the government was supposed to set out a roadmap for the full implementation of Law 70. Second, they were to discuss human rights violations against community leaders, and finally to address the serious problems that had emerged mainly in the Southern Pacific around the so-called African Palm. Despite much concern from environmentalists, the Uribe administration in partnership with organizations like USAID made large-scale palm oil (used in food or as biodiesel) the cornerstone of their development project for places like Tumaco. They sought to make Colombia the main exporter of palm oil, a goal that they did eventually realize. However, in 2008 a highly contagious disease had befallen many of the crops in the region, and threatened the state's development plan for Colombia's Pacific.

The Tumaco meeting also happened in a context in which the broader situation facing black rural communities was volatile, to say the least. In some cases, the discussions that happened there were literally matters of life or death, as leaders were facing death threats for defending their territorial rights, with little security from the state. Nevertheless, what ultimately took center stage in Tumaco was a power struggle between different actors within Colombia's black movement. In the weeks before the meeting, the Ministry of the Interior had issued Decree 3770, which was supposed to radically reconfigure the structure of the commissions on black communities and participation more generally. By the time of the Tumaco meeting, the decree had already generated much contention within the movement. The most controversial proposal contained in the decree was to ban the reelection of commissioners. Commissioners were especially concerned, as they hung on fiercely to their monopoly on negotiations with the state. This represented a momentary break in the protocol of engagement with the Colombian state. Rather than commissioners being the only ones privy to discussions with high-level state officials, grassroots leaders as well as activists representing organizations like PCN—which had been pushed out of the commission—were now speaking to these officials directly. For leaders with PCN, this was an opportunity to reseize the commission and establish a more autonomous, less cooptable mode of engagement with the Colombian state. More moments like these would follow.

Their efforts failed after contentious debates in Tumaco and in the weeks following. The decree did not stand up, and the state held elections for black commissioners throughout the country as if nothing had happened. Many of the same people who had been elected in the previous term, including the ones accused of corruption, were reelected. In the department of Valle, where PCN had its strongest grassroots base, the organization won only one of the six seats in the election for departmental commissioners. The Chocó election had a similar outcome. Despite being the largest grassroots organizations in the department, none of the major ethno-territorial organizations were elected to the commission that year. Consequently, following the elections, these organizations issued a public statement protesting the results and charging the elected commissioners of "political manipulations" and "irregularities." They emphasized that in stark contrast to those elected to the commission, they represented a territory of "more than two million hectares" and a "population of nearly 200,000 people."[23]

No path to Law 70 actually came in Tumaco. Nor did it come with the "new" cohort of commissioners. Rather, the Tumaco meeting, like many others before and after it, became a struggle over who would represent the black community in negotiations with the state, rather than what the end point of such negotiations would be. What did come in the wake of Tumaco were more meetings with the same stated objective: to find a path to the elaboration and implementation of Law 70. First was a public hearing I attended in the Senate in Bogotá the year of Law 70's fifteenth anniversary. This was followed by a meeting in Quibdó in August of 2013 in which the vice president of Colombia vowed to implement the remaining chapters of the then-twenty-year-old law by December of that same year. That too came to pass.

Meetings like the one in Tumaco question the very idea that there was, or ever will be, a *ruta*, or route, to the full realization of Law 70. Yet analyzing these events is crucial for understanding the process through which the unmaking of black rights has happened in Colombia. More fundamentally, they underscore the more pervasive logic through which black rights—and black Colombian movement organizations—have become incorporated into the multicultural state apparatus. This logic, of course, has serious implications for the extent to which black Colombians can actually enjoy their constitutionally protected rights. More importantly, in some cases, this has undermined their most basic human right, the right to life.

While economic interests pose serious impediments to the realization of black rights, the cooptation of black leaders through ritualized participation is also an essential ingredient to their unmaking. One of the main agitators at the Tumaco meeting was a leader I will call Teresa.[24] In the month leading up to Tumaco, I had tried desperately to get her side of the story amid accusations that she had received bribes from government officials consistently. When Teresa traveled to Bogotá from the Pacific Coast, she called me to say that she might have some time to meet with me that day. Teresa picked me up at my apartment in Bogotá in a nice car driven by a chauffeur. She whispered to me that she liked the fact that her driver in Bogotá was not only professional, but also white. Given Colombia's implicit racial and regional hierarchy, I assumed that having a white driver from Bogotá was a sign that she had made it. The rest of the day was equally as extravagant. I followed Teresa around as she shopped in the capital city. I had to politely decline a number of gifts she offered me, including candy and nuts from Teresa's favorite imported food store. Throughout all of this, I still hung on to the hope that she would concede me a formal interview.

While an interview never came, after we had lunch in an affluent neighborhood in Bogotá's Zona Norte, I did accompany Teresa as she made her rounds to different government agencies. When we approached the Ministry of Agriculture and Rural Development, I saw armed guards checking official IDs as people entered the building. I mentioned to Teresa, somewhat worried, that I had left my *cédula*, or official ID, at home. She reassured me that it wouldn't be a problem. In fact, we received VIP treatment, bypassing a number of people who stood waiting to be cleared to enter the building. After entering, it was immediately apparent that Teresa was no stranger there. In fact, she had an almost familial relationship with most of the government officials and administrators. "How is your mom doing?" one secretary asked her. "She's recovering, thank God," Teresa responded. After a series of meetings with midlevel government officials, we headed to the office of a higher-up within the ministry. By the time the meeting was over, Teresa had negotiated a community project worth 200,000,000 pesos (or about 150,000 U.S. dollars at the time) for one of the community councils she represented, as well as the promise of a government position for a friend, whose résumé she had brought along. More important, however, was that Teresa had negotiated funding for a number of people she described as "loyal to the government" to participate in the Tumaco meeting I discussed earlier. The point was to stack the deck in favor of the state and to counter the efforts of the black organizations who were "enemies of the state," as Teresa put it.

While allegations of cooptation were widespread, for obvious reasons, it was unusual to witness these kinds of exchanges. In fact, soon after, my access to the most controversial of commissioners would dissipate, as my ties to more autonomist black organizations like PCN made them suspicious of me. This was a rare and rapidly closing window into the kinds of transactions that were likely widespread between government officials and some commissioners for black communities. Any observer of Colombian politics would not be shocked by this story. In fact, I remember telling activists about it, horrified by what I saw; they were unfazed. Moreover, Teresa's interlocutors at the Ministry of Agriculture later came under investigation for corruption by the Constitutional Court; the minister himself was declared a fugitive from the law for funneling subsidies to wealthy families.[25]

It is impossible to understand the outcome of the Tumaco meeting without considering the prior arrangements like the ones that were made that day between Teresa and those working at the Ministry of Agriculture in Bogotá. Teresa was extremely vocal in Tumaco; she and other black leaders spent most of the time questioning the agenda and methodology of the meeting. Their agitation was part of the reason that the government left Tumaco with no meaningful commitments related to Law 70 or otherwise. Yet in the informal interviews I had in Tumaco and later in a meeting in Quibdó in 2013, state officials emphasized how divisions within the black movement had led to a breakdown in negotiations with the state. While movement fragmentation was certainly an impediment to the realization of black rights in Colombia, such fragmentation is best understood as the consequence of state action, rather than the cause of its inaction. In this, formal structures for black participation have acted to legitimate the state's postponement, and in some cases unraveling, of constitutionally recognized rights for black communities.

The extent to which rights on paper have translated into state practices in Colombia is directly linked to how activists negotiate a newly reconfigured political field characterized by rituals of participation, coopted leaders, and powerful capitalist interests in black communities' territories. In this regard, the dynamics of implementation of ethno-racial policy in Brazil were very similar to Colombia. Even so, how the Afro-Brazilian movement became institutionalized, as well as who made up the reactionary movement that threatened ethno-racial policy, was very distinct.

LAWS THAT STICK, LAWS THAT DON'T STICK IN BRAZIL

In contrast to Colombia, ethno-racial policies in Brazil have happened in the context of a much broader expansion of social policy. While much of this was to the credit of the Workers' Party—which took national office with the election of Luiz Inacio da Silva in 2002—secondary enrollment had already increased dramatically under the previous president, Fernando Henrique Cardoso (López-Calva and Lustig 2010). At a time in which nations throughout the Global North and South were shrinking the welfare state, the Brazilian government was expanding it. This included a number of robust national level programs like Fome Zero, a large scale anti-hunger campaign; Bolsa Familia, a cash transfer program that rewards poor families for immunizing their children and keeping them in school; and Saúde para Todos, which substantially expanded access to health care.

Additionally, a number of reforms to higher education, including unprecedented government investment in universities and the creation of programs like PROUNI, which offered tax breaks to private university in exchange for access and scholarships to poor students, had dramatically increased the size of Brazil's higher education sector. The success of these programs was unambiguous. Bolsa Familia alone reduced Brazil's poverty rate by half. When analyzed along with the programs of the previous administration, Brazil saw the percentage of those living in extreme poverty go from 25 percent to 4 percent between 1990 and 2012.[26] Educational attainment at every level also increased over the last decade in the country.[27]

In this same period, racial equality policies also seemed to be expanding, disputing the age-old myth that there is a necessary trade-off between social welfare and policies aimed at ethno-racial inclusion.[28] In addition to affirmative action in universities—which were sprouting up in decentralized form throughout the country—in 2003 President Lula signed Law 10.639, which required all public and private elementary schools to teach African and Afro-Brazilian history and culture.[29] Moreover, under the Workers' Party administration, the Brazilian state also attempted to mainstream racial equality across other policy areas, among them anti-poverty, health, and education policy.

However, this characterization of ethno-racial policy as expanding only holds if we ignore the fact that long before there were quotas in Brazilian universities, the state recognized territorial rights for *quilombo* communities. Thus, when we consider the host of policies targeting Brazil's black population we find that while certain policies have "stuck," others have not. In what follows, I examine the politics of implementation of two specific policy areas: land rights for *quilombos*, and affirmative action in Brazilian universities. In so doing, my intention is not to give a comprehensive account of the implementation of these policies. Rather, as I did in the Colombian case, my goal is to analyze the political processes that shape such implementation, which I argue is at the center of the everyday making of black political subjects in each case. In so doing, I suggest that similar to Colombia, the degree of implementation of ethno-racial policy in Brazil was deeply intertwined with a newly reconfigured political field that was now made up of reactionary movements committed to dismantling both *quilombo* land rights and affirmative action policies.[30]

Ruralista *Backlash and* Quilombo *Rights*

The biggest failure of Brazil's ethno-racial policies has been the titling of *quilombo* land. To date, only one million hectares of land have been titled to *quilombo* communities. To put this number in perspective, this is only a fifth of the amount of land that the Colombian state has titled to black communities despite Brazil's much larger size, its greater number of officially recognized *quilombos*, and its greater state capacity. The degree of *quilombo* titling reflects ongoing debates within the Brazilian state over what a *quilombo* community actually is (French 2009). Are they only communities that are the direct, and provable, descendants of runaway slaves? If former slave owners gave over their property to these communities, did the communities have to know this history? What about cultural traditions—did *quilombos* have to maintain them to qualify for land rights?

Contestation over *quilombo* rights was also intrinsically linked to economic interests in this land. Brazil never quite institutionalized multicultural rights in the same way that the Colombian state did. A few months after the signing of the 1988 constitution, President José Sarney signed a decree creating the Palmares Cultural Foundation. The mandate of this state agency was to promote "the preservation of the cultural, social and values that come from the black influence of Brazilian society."[31] More specifically, Palmares was to organize and promote events related to Brazil's black cultural ancestry and support international exchange and research on black history and culture. It was also charged with identifying and titling *quilombo* territories. Nonetheless, more than a decade after its creation, Palmares had facilitated the titling of very few *quilombos*, and there was still much ambiguity around the very definition of *quilombo*" (Farfán-Santos 2015). In this, and much like in Colombia, anthropological expertise was particularly important in identifying and legitimating *quilombo* communities (French 2009).[32]

After very little movement on the issue of *quilombo* titling, in 2003 President Lula signed a decree that was supposed to help identify, recognize, delimit, demarcate, and title *quilombo* territories in accordance with the country's 1988 constitution. Lula also launched the Brazil Quilombo Program, an initiative that was to help title *quilombo* communities as well as build their infrastructure and implement local development projects and work on issues of citizenship, rights, and participation. Housed in the Special Secretariat for the Promotion of Racial Equality (SEPPIR), Brazil Quilombo was supposed to involve coordination between the Ministry of Agrarian Development, the Ministry of Social Development and Hunger Alleviation, as well as other relevant ministries. However, the lack of a sufficient budget or a real commitment on the part of the substantive ministries curtailed the program's effectiveness. At the dawn of the twenty-fifth anniversary of *quilombo* rights, Brazil's National Institute for Settlement and Agrarian Reform (INCRA) had recognized some 1,360 *quilombos*.[33] Of those, only 193 had received collective titles. The Brazilian state's foot dragging on *quilombo* land titling was deeply tied to underlying economic interests as it was in Colombia.

In April 2010, I visited the Silva Family Quilombo, located in a well-to-do neighborhood in the heart of the city of Porto Alegre, in Brazil's southern city of Rio Grande do Sul. As activists from the *quilombo* told me several times during my visit, their territory was situated in the most expensive square kilometers in the entire city. Indeed, the background of luxury high-rises made the dirt road into the humble *quilombo*, with wooden houses and a huge tree that acted as the community's main plaza, all the more striking. This contrast was reminiscent of the one that I saw between the community of La Boquilla and the surrounding luxury high-rises in Cartagena. Also similar was the fact that real estate developers had been encroaching more and more on the actual territory of the Silva Family Quilombo. In addition, a number of people had come forth to sue members of the *quilombo*, claiming that they were the true owners of the land. However, just months before my visit the community had become Brazil's first urban *quilombo* to receive a land title from the Brazilian government. Local members of the Unified Black Movement (MNU)—along with activists from the community itself—had been at the forefront of this struggle that took over five years. Also like similar cases of collective land rights in Colombia, during that time leaders from the Silva Family Quilombo also received anonymous death threats.

Coincidentally, I had arrived in Porto Alegre just as this other contentious process around *quilombo* territory was unfolding in Bagé, a small town about four hours southwest of Porto Alegre. Onir Araújo, a lawyer and MNU leader, was instrumental in making the legal case for the community of the Silva Family Quilombo.[34] As I was interviewing Onir precisely about the role he had played in that process, our interview was cut short when he received an alarming phone call informing him that white landowners had created a blockade on the road leading to Quilombo de Palmas in Bagé to prevent INCRA from entering. Onir hopped in his jeep, picking up leaders from the Silva Family Quilombo on his way and headed to Bagé.

INCRA had already done an initial study of the Palmas Quilombo that gave the community official recognition as a *quilombo* some five years before this conflict. However, the next stage of land titling required a more detailed study of the area. INCRA officials had planned to do this when local *ruralistas*, or small landowners, blocked the road leading to the *quilombo*. The *ruralistas* also refused to let the attorney general's office enter, which had also been called to mediate the situation. These white *ruralistas* argued that the Palmas Quilombo was actually on their land.

Similarly situated small landowners had done this throughout the country. They feared that when INCRA demarcated the *quilombo*, they would encroach more and more on what they considered to be their land. These battles took the form of frontal confrontations as well as ideological warfare in academic circles and in the popular media. In 2007, for instance, Nelson Ramos Barreto—a journalist and author—published the popular book *The Quilombo Revolution: Race War, Land Confiscation and Urban Collectivism*. As the title suggests, it made the case against *quilombo* land rights.

Precisely because so much was at stake in Bagé in April of 2010, the situation quickly intensified. *Quilombo* leaders feared that things might even turn violent. This all led to an intense standoff that lasted over two weeks. In the end, advocacy on the part of labor and black movement organization led to INCRA calling the federal police, who eventually unblocked the road. This scene of backlash against the territorial rights of *quilombos* was not unlike many I witnessed throughout Colombia. Even so, the actors were different. Instead of mining companies, in Brazil it was white landowners who presented an impediment to these constitutionally protected rights. Also similar to Colombia was the fact that it was only *after* the recognition of *quilombo* rights in 1988 that many political and economic elites came to realize what was actually at stake in these cases.

The Statute of Racial Equality

If the titling of *quilombos* was an uphill battle, affirmative action policies proved to be quite the opposite. By the early 2010s, dozens of Brazil's most prestigious public universities had adopted some form of affirmative action, based on either race, class, or both (Racusen 2009). At that time, 10.5 percent of the country's highly coveted university spaces were reserved under affirmative action, amounting to just under 35,000 students (Paixão et al. 2010). As a result, the number of black and brown students at universities in Brazil had increased substantially. This is remarkable when we consider that at least at first, affirmative action policies had been adopted in a decentralized fashion through decisions made by individual university councils and state legislatures rather than through a federal mandate.

In such a context, the Statute of Racial Equality sought to further institutionalize racial equality policy including affirmative action at the national level and in a more durable way. Initially proposed in 2000 by Afro-Brazilian Senator Paulo Paim with the PT, it proposed to offer "incentives" aimed at increasing the black population's access to education, to accelerate the pace of quilombo land titling, and also to set aside considerable funds to address racial inequality in health, employment, and education.[35] The statute received very little traction within congress when it was first introduced and over the next decade. However, in 2009, the PT took up the issue again, negotiating with a number of political parties in an attempt to draft a version of the statute that could pass. In these negotiations—which involved Paim himself, officials within SEPPIR, black activists in CONEN (PT) and UNEGRO (PCdoB), as well as conservative parties like the Democrats (DEM)—many of the provisions included in the original statute were gutted. Before Brazil's lower chamber voted on the bill in a national public meeting held by SEPPIR, some activists of the MNU refused to support what they called the "Empty Statute." They also voiced their concerns online. As Reginaldo Bispo of the MNU explained to me in an interview:

> When we left Congress, I circulated a report from the meeting over the internet and through the National Council for the Promotion of Racial Equality (CONAPIR) and there was a real revolution, they stopped short of cursing my mother. Because [they said] the position of the MNU was favorable to the Statute and that I had expressed a position that wasn't the official position of the organization, but I was true to the deliberation that we took at the congress (interview, Reginaldo Bispo, MNU).

This provoked a number of activists from NGOs like Geledés and Criola to sit down and analyze closely what had been taken out of the statute at different stages of negotiations between the PT and other political parties. They ultimately joined the MNU in opposing the statute. Jurema Werneck argued that the negotiations around the final statute amounted to the "selling out" of black movements. As Jurema explained:

> To approve the Statute of Racial Equality they had to renounce the entire platform that we had . . . unfortunately other activists didn't really know what they were negotiating. The truth is it wasn't public. They were selling us out to electoral interests. That generated a division within the black movement (interview, Jurema Werneck, October 2009).

Rather than thinking of these negotiations as selling out the movement, CONEN activists close to the process and to the PT defended what they called a "Possible Statute" or the idea that any statute was better than none. On June 17, 2010, after much contention and even name calling over a number of popular black movement e-mail lists, CONEN ultimately took a position somewhat critical of the statute process.[36] In a public statement, they clarified this:

> In response to recent accusations and the questioning of CONEN's position in the 'virtual debate' related to the immediate voting on the

Statute of Racial Equality, and especially given our commitment to seeking out ways to address the concerns of the black population, to eliminating racial inequality and the existing social disparities in Brazil, we are making our position related to the Statute of Racial Equality public. CONEN has supported the approval of the Statute of Racial Equality from the beginning. Considering that CONEN has followed the Statute from the beginning since when Senator Paulo Paim presented it to the National Congress, considering that CONEN understands that the black Brazilian community needs a political and legal instrument that ensures the basic conditions for the development of public policies to promote racial equality, we want to re-affirm our unequivocal need to approve the Statute of Racial Equality in the version *originally* presented to the Senate and in the Chamber of Deputies.[37]

In this statement, CONEN reiterated its position as the main interlocutor between the Brazilian state and the black movement, and as a supporter of the PT. At the same time, they offered a somewhat veiled critique of their party in that they implicitly called on it to halt negotiations with conservative politicians like Demóstenes Torres of the DEM party. Despite these objections, Lula signed a version of the Statute of Racial Equality on July 20 that did not actually further institutionalize affirmative action or *quilombo* land titling.[38] Consequently, CONEN activists refused to attend the public ceremony in which Lula officially sanctioned the statute. During the televised event, President Lula took the opportunity not only to speak about the importance of the statute itself but also to lecture on what he saw as divisions within the black movement. He noted that he was saddened that "people that had accompanied him for over 30 years" were not there to celebrate this "historic day."[39] While he also recognized some of the limitations of the Statute, he was emphatic that addressing racial equality in the country would take some time and that it would require a more "united black movement."[40] Rather than recognize the conflicting interests of many involved in the statute's negotiation in congress, Lula did as presidents in Colombia often had: blame the narrowing of ethno-racial policy on fragmentation within the movement.

More generally, the debate over the statute raised many questions about the possibilities and limitations of institutionalized politics. To what extent were racial equality policies sufficiently institutionalized into the Brazilian state? What would happen if/when the PT lost the presidency? These were precisely the kinds of questions that the more radical, autonomist sector of the Afro-Brazilian movement raised during debates over the statute. In so doing, they were able to shift the debate such that more institutionalized sectors like CONEN took positions that were critical of their party and the Lula administration arguably for the first time ever. Indeed, without the confrontation with MNU leaders, it is not clear if activists with CONEN would have made the plea to withdraw the largely gutted statute from debate in the senate. Perhaps they would have done as many of the accusations of the MNU suggested: quietly take pictures during the signing of an incredibly weakened statute.

In the end, though, the failure of a more robust statute must be situated in larger ideological debates under way in Brazil at the time. This contestation—which played out in universities and in the mainstream media—also heavily shaped these debates. These debates included an emergent reactionary movement against quilombo rights and racial equality policies made up of a loosely connected hodgepodge of actors. Among them were extremely respected intellectuals such as Peter Fry and Yvonne Maggie, both of whom had made their career analyzing questions of race, nation, and culture. It also consisted of strange bedfellows including conservative public intellectuals like Demetrio Magnoli, landowners and new groups like Nação Mestiça, dedicated to defending the rights of mixed people as mixed, as well as the Black Socialist Movement (MNS).[41] It is impossible to understand the politics of implementation of Brazil's racial equality policies without analyzing the emergence of this movement determined to undermine them.

The "Manifesto of the White Elite"

On June 29, 2006, a letter addressed to congress titled "Everyone Has Equal Rights in the Democratic Republic" began to circulate Brazilian newspapers, national and transnational listservs, and the internet. One hundred and fourteen people had signed the letter, including public intellectuals such as renowned social scientist Simon Schwartzman; the Brazilian anthropologist and former first lady of Brazil Ruth Cardoso; as well as one of Brazil's most revered musicians, Caetano Veloso. At the time the letter was released, about a fourth of Brazil's eighty-seven public universities had already adopted some form of affirmative action. Even so, the debates around these policies were intensifying. Brazil's congress was considering voting on the Statute of Racial Equality that I discussed earlier, as well as a Law of Quotas that had also been introduced many years before.[42] Both pieces of legislation proposed to introduce affirmative action at the federal level.

The letter received great visibility when it was published in its entirety in *Folha de São Paulo*, Brazil's largest circulating newspaper. *Folha* also became central to, and emblematic of, the ideological contestation over racial policy in Brazil. It gave a platform to these debates and also became a key actor in them. "Everyone Has Equal Rights in the Democratic Republic" began by invoking Brazil's 1988 constitution: "the principle of political and juridical equality of citizens is the essential foundation of the [Brazilian] republic."

It went on to make the case that the legislation that was on the table would have undermined this equality by introducing privileges that had not previously existed. They warned that if the Statute of Racial Equality or the Law of Quotas were to pass, they would institute a regime where rights were conferred on the basis of *tonalidade*, or "skin tone." The letter ended with an evocation of Martin Luther King, a rhetorical device similar to the one that anti-affirmative action advocates often use in the United States:

> We desire a Brazil in which no one is discriminated against—positively or negatively—for the color of their skin, their sex, their intimate life or their religion, where everyone has access to all public services, where diversity is valued as a lively and inclusive process that involves all humanity, in a future where the word happiness is not just a dream. Ultimately, a place where all people are valued for who they are and what they achieve. Our dream is the dream of Martin Luther King who struggled to live in a nation where people would not be judged by the color of their skin, but for the content of their character.[43]

Black Brazilian activists were deeply familiar with the arguments contained in this public letter. They had long been told that talking about racism was to invent it, to import it, to perpetuate it. In this letter the authors were going a step further in accusing the state, in considering these two pieces of legislation, of doing the same. From their perspective, what was at stake in debates around the Law of Quotas and the Racial Equality Statute was the institutionalization of racism by the Brazilian state.

Soon after the letter was written it began to circulate on the web under the name the "Manifesto of the White Elite," a title that provoked an understandable pushback from its authors. Yet while they saw their intervention as a plea for nonracialism, the unofficial name of the letter was not entirely inaccurate. The majority of the 114 people who signed the letter were professors at elite universities, journalists at top newspapers, and well-off artists. They were indisputably a part of Brazil's elite class. Furthermore, nearly all who signed the letter were socially white, even if we factor in the fact that there is much racial ambiguity in Brazil.

There were, however, a couple of notable exceptions.[44] Members of the Black Socialist Movement (MNS) also signed the letter. In fact, they were chosen to present it to Congress alongside Yvonne Maggie, a Brazilian anthropologist of African-based religion in Brazil and a vocal critic of affirmative action. This decision was likely a strategic one. Goldberg (2009) has noted that "as an end in itself, antiracialism, it turns out for the most part, is whiteness by another name, by other means, with recruitment of people of color to act as public spokespersons for the cause" (22). This decision for MNS to represent the authors of the letter was also one that distorted the nature of the affirmative action debate unfolding at that time. For example, *Folha* published an article titled "The Black Movement Is against Quotas" that reported the meeting held between MNS members, Yvonne Maggie, and the heads of the Brazilian Senate and Lower House. This was problematic for at least two reasons. First, the headline implied that the entire black movement, rather than a single organization, had come out against affirmative action. This was despite the fact that the most visible black organizations in the country—among them the MNU, CONEN, Geledés, and Criola—had all been very public in their support of affirmative action. More grave, however, was the fact that the organization that *Folha* chose to serve as a proxy for the black movement was founded just days before the public letter was written, arguably with the sole goal to legitimate an anti-affirmative action movement made up almost entirely of white elites.[45]

A few days later, on July 3, another document began to circulate titled the "Manifesto in Favor of the Law of Quotas and the Statute of Racial Equality." Much like the letter to which it was responding, among the some 330 people who signed the letter were activists, intellectuals, and artists. It also began in a similar way, by invoking Brazil's legal history:

> Racial inequality in Brazil has strong historical roots. This reality will not be significantly altered with the adoption of specific public policies. The 1891 Constitution facilitated the reproduction of racism by decreeing an equality of citizens that was purely formal. The black population had just been released from a situation of complete exclusion in terms of access to land, education and the labor market, to compete with whites within a new economic reality that was being installed in the country. While they said that everyone was equal according to the letter of the law, various policies that offered differential support and incentives—that might be read today as affirmative action policies—were applied to stimulate the immigration of Europeans to Brazil.[46]

The manifesto went on to justify affirmative action policies as a "leveling" of an unequal playing field, and as a corrective to historic racial discrimination. In addition to publishing the text of this manifesto in favor of affirmative action, *Folha* also published dozens of articles on affirmative action over the following month. The majority of them were against these policies, with titles such as "Official Discrimination" and "The Statute Would Create 'State Racism.'"[47] Though *Folha* did not officially come out against race-based affirmative action until 2014, its coverage left little ambiguity about the newspaper's position on the topic.[48]

More controversial, however, was the position of *Veja*, Brazil's widest circulated magazine and perhaps its more influential. In June of 2007, their cover featured light-brown-skinned identical twins Alex and Alan Teixeira da Cunha, one wearing a white shirt with a white background, and the other standing slightly in front of his brother wearing a black shirt with a black background. The title read "Race Does Not Exist." Both twins had applied to be considered under the affirmative action policy at the University of Brasília (UnB), one of the three Brazilian universities that did not use self-identification as the criteria for admission under affirmative action. Instead, students' applying to be considered under racial quotas at UnB had to be approved by a panel that determined applicants' color. This policy was intended to weed out people who might have otherwise identified as white, but given the incentive of affirmative action, checked the *negro* box. The *Veja* cover explained under the title that "under the quota system, one twin was ruled to be black, while the other was ruled to be white," and inside the magazine was a full article about the Teixeira da Cunha brothers.

More interestingly, in addition to publishing the story on the twins, the edition also featured a large spread of pictures of famous Brazilians. Alongside each picture was a pie chart with each person's "genetic" makeup broken down by percentages.: famous musician Djavan, 65 percent African, 30 percent European, 4.9 percent Amerindian; Olympian gymnast Daiane dos Santos, 40.8 percent European, 39.7 percent African, 19.5 percent Amerindian—to name a few. The point of this exercise, one might conclude, was that all Brazilians were mixed, and as such the idea of discrete racial categories was a fiction. It followed, then, that affirmative action policies made no sense in a Brazilian context.

Nevertheless, all of this rested on the implicit assumption that a strictly biological definition of race was the only possible way that race could be defined. In contrast, UnB's policy, even while it relied on the infamous panel evaluations of racial identification, did not operate with a biological notion of race in mind, but rather a social one aimed at correcting historic racial discrimination.[49] Ironically, what actually made *Veja*'s feature so compelling was its underlying premise: even in the Brazilian context of racial fluidity and ambiguity, all of the people that they chose to feature were considered socially black in Brazil. It was precisely this disconnect between the social and biological race of these famous Brazilians—a gap that may have led people to say "Daiane is only 39.7 percent African?"—that was, in fact, the only reason this was a story at all. Another irony was that by having these famous Brazilians tested for their so-called racial makeup and also by publishing the results, *Veja* had effectively endorsed the idea that races were indeed biological. In fact, it was easy to conclude from the issue that "races" were in fact real and discrete, and Brazilians were made up of a knowable mixture of these clearly identifiable races. Of course, reproducing racialism was the exact opposite of what they intended to do in their famous "Race Does Not Exist" issue.

More generally, many of Brazil's major media outlets had historically been resistant to discussing racial inequality or racism in Brazil (Conceição 2005). When affirmative action policies became increasingly prevalent, the media tended to cover them in ways that revealed some bias, albeit a veiled type. While major Brazilian newspapers tended to publish neutral journalistic pieces on affirmative action, they did this at the same time that they published far more editorials and letters to the editor against these policies (Daflon and Feres Jr. 2012). This often allowed media organizations to maintain the guise of impartiality while controlling the "space of the debate" around affirmative action (Campos et al. 2013). Ultimately, these media debates were important in shaping not only public opinion; they were also the backdrop upon which political struggles around the Law of Quotas and the Statute of Racial Equality transpired.

The prominence of anti-affirmative action articles in Brazilian newspapers was part of a larger reactionary movement. Also central to this movement was the publishing of and promotion around books that also made the case against quotas and all "racialist policies." Two of the most important of this genre were the 2007 volume, *Dangerous Divisions: Racial Policy in Contemporary Brazil*, and Demetrio Magnoli's popular book, *A Drop of Blood: A Genealogy of Racial Thinking*. In September 2009, I attended one of the events along Magnoli's book tour. The book launch was held at the Livraria a Travessa bookstore in one of Rio's chicest malls in the affluent Leblon neighborhood. This was only my second time at this mall because the first time I had gone some years before, a black male Brazilian friend and I were stopped by mall security immediately upon entering. Our bags were "randomly" searched. I had become accustomed to these types of searches by military police and mall security in the affluent Zona Sur region of the city of Rio de Janeiro. For this reason, I had avoided places like Shopping Leblon, especially when accompanied by black male friends, Brazilian or otherwise. I made an exception to attend Magnoli's event for the sake of research. When I arrived, people were already packed in and there was standing room only. I wiggled my way between an older white-haired gentleman standing against the back wall and a cameraman with Band, a conservative news outlet. In addition to Magnoli, the event featured two special guests, Brazilian Yvonne Maggie and British-turned-Brazilian Peter Fry, both prominent anthropologists.

While the event was technically a book launch, it served more as a political platform to further the movement against affirmative action in Brazil. Over the course of the evening, the panelists made many of the usual arguments against quotas: that the policy was a top-down one that did not involve the necessary public debate, that race was a deeply ambiguous phenomenon in Brazil and was not salient in the lives of Brazilians. Much like Gilberto Freyre had done many decades before, the panelists highlighted race mixture both as a testament to the natural racial harmony among Brazilians and as evidence that implementing affirmative action policies would be impossible in Brazil due to such ambiguity.[50] They also argued that racial equality policy had introduced racism into Brazil where it had not previously existed. In so doing, the panelists constantly invoked the United States. Magnoli, for instance, explained that affirmative action policies were not only dangerous, but were imported into Brazil from the United States. Peter Fry echoed this, telling the audience that affirmative action had in fact been widely discredited in the United States precisely because of its inegalitarian nature. Finally, Yvonne Maggie made a more personal appeal speaking on the verge of tears about her experiences while studying at the University of Texas, Austin. There she saw firsthand how racially divided daily life in the United States was. Maggie talked about feeling like she had to choose sides and said that she hoped that Brazil would continue to remain free of such divisions. Though while the audience was convinced by the speakers that day, it was not clear that Brazilian society as a whole was.

Winning and Losing the Ideological Debate

The campaign against affirmative action played out as an ideological debate largely between figures like Maggie, Magnoli, and Fry on the one side, and black activists and their allies on the other. However, these contestations also had real implications on the nature of similar debates happening within political parties and among Brazilian politicians and bureaucrats. On the one hand, the black movement could be said to have won the ideological debate among the Brazilian public and within certain sectors of the state. In the decade leading up to affirmative action, the majority of Brazilians already believed that racism was a problem in the country (Bailey 2009). However, this did not necessarily mean that they supported policies like affirmative action to address it. Even so, in the late 2000s there was increasing evidence that this was the case.[51] In 2006, for example, Datafolha found that 65 percent of Brazilians were in favor of race-based affirmative action, while 87 percent were in favor of class-based quotas. Similarly, seven years later and just as Brazil's Supreme Court considered the landmark affirmative action case, the Brazilian Institute of Public Opinion and Statistics (IBOPE) released results from another nationally representative survey that showed that 64 percent of Brazilians were in favor of race-based affirmative action.[52] This change in the ideological tide was most clear in April 2012, when Brazil's Supreme Court voted unanimously that affirmative action policies were constitutional.

The Supreme Court decision came at a time in which the federal government was also shifting toward a more aggressive stance on racial policy under president Dilma Rousseff and SEPPIR Minister Luiza Bairros.[53] Beyond being more vocal about racism, there were substantive changes in racial policy under this new PT administration. Most notably, in August 2012, Dilma signed the Law of Quotas that had been held up in Congress for over a decade. This was a major feat, considering that professors, including Yvonne Maggie, at Brazil's prestigious federal universities had been among the most vehement opponents to affirmative action. The Law of Quotas required all of the country's fifty-nine federal universities and thirty-eight technical institutes to reserve 50 percent of their seats for poor and working-class students. The law also mandated that these same universities guarantee that the racial makeup of those reserved seats match that of the state where the university was located. While federal universities had until 2016 to comply with this, most of them had already done so by the end of 2012.[54] Beyond higher education, in June 2015, Brazil's Supreme Court approved a resolution reserving 20 percent of all judge positions in Brazil's federal court system (with the exception of the Supreme Court itself) as well as all competitive personnel positions for *negros*.[55]

Yet while affirmative action policies have undeniably transformed state and popular discourse around questions of race and nation in Brazil, it is not yet clear how transformative they have been in material terms. Whereas in 1988, 12.4 percent of whites had some college education, only 3.6 percent of blacks and browns did. This gap actually widened slightly in 2008, when the percentage of college-educated whites increased to 35 percent while that of blacks and browns rose to only 16.4 percent (Paixão et al. 2010). In this sense, the Law of Quotas could radically transform not only the federal university system but also broader patterns of social mobility and racial inequality in ways that more decentralized affirmative action policies had yet to do.

Nonetheless, in some sense, the black movement could be said to have lost the ideological debate over affirmative action. Activists had originally advocated for race-based—not class-based—affirmative action, in part because they realized that quotas for blacks would necessarily mean increasing the percentage of working-class and poor students in Brazilian universities. Yet, the dominant form that affirmative action eventually took across the country and especially with the Law of Quotas, was one that privileged class over race (Htun 2016). Indeed, making public school enrollment the primary requirement for admission under quotas, and race the secondary one, these policies arguably obscured the very real ways in which race might operate independently from class in Brazilian society. In such a framework, the small number of blacks that find themselves in Brazil's middle class, and who send their children to private school, would not qualify for university admission under quotas.

When we analyze affirmative action alongside the case of *quilombo* rights, what we see is that rather than an unmaking of black political subjects, the last few decades of ethno-racial policy in Brazil has been a mixed-bag of laws that have stuck and laws that have not stuck. On the one hand, the territorial rights of *quilombo* communities have been unmade through a process of foot dragging by the Brazilian state, in part because of a backlash by the small landed elite. On the other, affirmative action and other racial equality policies seem to be expanding, particularly under Dilma's administration. The gains of Brazil's 1988 multicultural constitution have been partially supplanted by a racial equality agenda focused more on the realities of urban black populations.

CONCLUSION

In both Colombia and Brazil, ongoing contestation between movements, state officials, and economic actors has sometimes led to the restriction and unmaking of black rights and policies. While there are key differences in how this played out in each country, both Colombian and Brazilian black activists had to navigate profoundly reconfigured political fields as they worked to ensure the implementation of ethno-racial rights. Among other things, this meant negotiating their own newly gained access to the state as well as confronting powerful reactionary movements that have sought to dismantle everything from collective territorial rights to affirmative action. While international dynamics have figured prominently in this book, the role of such international factors in the politics of implementation was uneven. For the most part, debates over implementation between black movements and state actors happened in each country within a relatively insulated realm of national politics. Nevertheless, at key moments international funding and transnational solidarity networks helped pressure states to comply with existing legislation or move toward broader policy reforms.

In recent years, many black organizations in both Colombia and Brazil have changed their mode of operation, spending most of their time fighting against the shrinking of black rights, rather than demanding their expansion. However unintentionally, this move has helped to narrow the discourse of black rights. While in Colombia, ethno-territorial struggles are deeply important, Afro-Colombians also confront other serious problems. To cite just a few examples: systematic racial employment discrimination is widespread in cities throughout the country, as Rodriguez Garavito et al. (forthcoming) found. In addition, according to the 2005 census, black infant mortality rates were double those of nonblack infants, black women lived on average eleven fewer years than nonblack Colombians, and 12.7 percent of them lived in extreme poverty compared to 6.8 percent of whites/ *mestizos* (Garavito et al. 2008). Yet Law 70 was not intended to address these inequalities per se. Indeed, what these statistics underscore is that even if fully implemented, Law 70 would be far from a silver bullet with the power to change the material lives of most black Colombians.

In contrast, Brazil's racial equality apparatus has focused almost exclusively on socioeconomic gaps in higher education and health as well as providing infrastructure and public goods in *quilombo* communities. However, they have not actually guaranteed the territorial rights of those same communities. Furthermore, the emphasis on racial inequality has arguably made invisible other kinds of black movement claims, including those against what Campanha Reaja has for decades termed the "genocide of black people." Within the discursive terrain of the promotion of racial equality, one easily forgets that specific cases of racialized state violence in the city of São Paulo is what propelled the contemporary black movement into existence in the late 1970s (Covin 2006). And much evidence proves that such violence is still endemic in Brazil (Telles 2004; Smith 2016). In this sense, recent racial equality policies in Brazil may have acted to silence more radical claims against racism and oppression and for racial justice just as civil rights did in the United States.

In the end, the making of black political subjects has not only reconfigured the Brazilian and Colombian states' orientation toward ethno-racial issues but it may also have preconfigured the horizons that many black movement actors in these countries imagine. Rather than demanding the many claims that were left out of the legislation passed in the 1990s and 2000s, and rather than constructing new utopias, black movements in Colombia and Brazil have been forced to respond to new threats. Afro-Colombian activist Hernán Cortés perhaps put it best. Discussing the importance of the transnational work that his organization, PCN, does to hold the Colombian government accountable for guaranteeing the basic human rights of black communities, he said, "We know that if we can make a political statement, we calm the dogs. They bark, but they probably won't bite at that moment. [At least] you can postpone the bite" (interview, Hernán Cortés, February 2009).

Yet while already fragile black movements did seem to be on the defensive in both countries, in neither case was it entirely clear who these dogs actually were. Some blamed state actors for their lack of political will, their impulse to restrict, rather than implement or expand black rights. Still others saw institutionalized black activists as a key to the undermining of ethno-racial reforms in Colombia and Brazil. Yet another source of unmaking were the various reactionary movements, some with huge reservoirs of economic, political, and symbolic power. Undoubtedly, it was some combination of these dynamics of retrenchment, institutionalization, and backlash that ultimately kept activists on the defensive, and that led to the partial unmaking of black political subjects in each country.

CHAPTER EIGHT

RETHINKING RACE, RETHINKING MOVEMENTS

I n early 2014, young Brazilians began to flood public spaces, including shopping malls and parks, in something they called *rolês* or *rolezinhos*. The words translate literally to "strolls," but the events were akin to the flash mobs that have become commonplace in the United States in recent years.[1] Unfolding in major cities throughout Brazil, these *rolezinhos* were typically made up of hundreds and sometimes thousands of mostly black and brown youth from favelas and poor neighborhoods. Many of these events did not start off as violent. They instead ranged from less-coordinated *rolezinhos*, where youths simply went to the mall to socialize in big groups, to highly coordinated ones, where they sang and even did large-scale dance choreographies. The Brazilian state response was chilling and included violent repression by the military police. In part to justify their harsh actions, state officials, the police, and mall security also repeatedly portrayed the *rolezinhos* as violent riots of thugs looking for trouble.

Just a year earlier, massive groups of mostly white, middle-class Brazilians had staged protests, and many observers, including the media, noted obvious differences between how the military police treated the mostly brown and black participants of the *rolezinhos* and these previous protestors.[2] As the youth involved in the *rolezinhos* experienced increased state repression, they became more politicized. In São Paulo, for example, after police used rubber bullets and tear gas to break up a *rolezinho*, the event quickly shifted to a protest against racism, classism, and state violence. Black university students and political organizations also joined them with a more explicit message against racial discrimination. As they did so, many malls around the country decided to close their doors in anticipation of these events. For example, one of Brazil's most expensive malls—Shopping JK Iguatemí in São Paulo—closed on January 18, 2014, in fear of the "Flash Mob against Racism," which had already amassed more than 4,000 participants on Facebook.[3]

While these *rolezinhos* were momentary, they marked the first time that the poor nonwhite masses—aided by social media and later by organized black political organizations—engaged in disruptive protest on such a massive scale and in such a creative form. To mediate the situation, President Dilma brought in Minister of Racial Equality Luiza Bairros—herself a long-time black activist before she began working within the state. Bairros departed slightly from the usual script of activists-turned-bureaucrats and spoke candidly in support of the youth, and called out both government officials and mall administrations as "racist." The mass events represented for her an "awakening of black consciousness among the youth," precisely the kind of awakening she and other black Brazilian activists had worked fiercely toward in the 1970s and 1980s. Yet in terms of both their form and their scale, the *rolezinhos* were more an embodiment of what Brazil's black movement was never quite able to achieve in that earlier era, at least not directly: racially conscious mobilization by Brazil's black and brown impoverished masses.

Ultimately, though, the movement may have not needed to do this. In this book, I argue that affirmative action, collective ethnic land titling, the inclusion of black history in public education curricula, and other ethnoracial policies in Colombia and Brazil were not the result of massive black movements. Activists in both countries did engage in some key actions, like the 1995 Zumbí March in Brazil, amassing a considerable number of people to protest against centuries of marginalization. However, these moments were extremely rare. Beyond the question of size, black movements in Colombia and Brazil were not exactly poster children of an effective movement for other reasons. In the period leading up to reform, activists did not have public opinion on their side, and they had few if any powerful allies. They also had very few resources, serious collective identity challenges born out of *mestizaje* ideologies as well as regional and ideological divides.

Yet, despite their limited access to traditional forms of political power, these small black movements in Colombia and Brazil brought about substantial political and social change. Their sustained and tireless work led to important symbolic victories, including recognition that racism existed in their previously colorblind countries and the creation of national holidays like Colombia's National Day of Afro-Colombian Culture and Brazil's Day of Black Consciousness. Their efforts also culminated in material concessions. In Colombia, ethno-racial rights led to the largest agrarian reform in that country's history. In it, about a third of Colombia's national territory became held under collective titles to indigenous or black communities. In Brazil, affirmative action in public education radically transformed the student bodies of the country's most prestigious universities in terms of color and social class. These policy changes were not trivial. Despite the limitations I considered in the last chapter, it is important to underscore the significance of all of this.

These policies also reshaped Colombian and Brazilian societies in a number of other ways. If nothing else, they also punctured the notion, previously taken for granted, that these societies were culturally homogeneous and divided exclusively along class, not ethno-racial, lines. What is more, both states reconfigured their institutions and redefined their citizenship regimes such that black Colombians and Brazilian would now confront the state both as individuals and as the subjects of collective rights. Beyond changes in the law, the adoption of ethno-racial legislation also meant that public debates around race, nation, and inequality—long silenced in these countries—now permeate public school classrooms, newspapers, television, and even taxicabs and street corners. Thus, the politicization of blackness among the masses in Colombia and Brazil more generally—may be best understood as a consequence of these reforms rather than their cause. This inverts the conventional social movement story in which massive social movements push effectively for political changes, which in turn reshape society. It also begs the question: how did these small, under-resourced movements bring about such significant change in the first place?

In this book, I develop a political fields approach in order to make three substantive arguments about the causes and consequences of the shift to ethno-racial legislation in Colombia and Brazil over the last three decades. First, I argue that the interplay between global factors and national political developments—paired with the strategic action of small black movements—best explains why Colombia and Brazil adopted these historic reforms. In this way, my view echoes the work others have done on similarly globally embedded indigenous movements (Brysk 2000; Van Cott 2002; Yashar 2005). Second, I argue that black rights and policies in Colombia and Brazil unfolded in two distinct moments of alignment, each of which corresponded with a different notions of blackness. In both countries, the first alignment led to the institutionalization of an ethnically defined black political subject; a decade later, rather than highlight ethnic difference and autonomy, both states emphasized racial equality and integration. Even so, the political fields of Colombia and Brazil became saturated with these alignments to varying degrees, in ways that mapped onto the way that blackness was imagined and politicized in each case.

The third and final empirical argument I make here is that while there is no doubt that black movements in Colombia and Brazil have both been successful in pressuring the state to make both symbolic and substantive reforms, their struggles have led to only partial victories. Moreover, the shift from *mestizaje* presented new challenges for black movements in each country. Among other things, the creation of spaces for black participation within the state prompted a new kind of institutionalized black politics, which has significantly changed the relationship between black social movement organizations and the state. In this, the absorption of activists into state bureaucracies and through ritualized engagement with the state—as well as the emergence of powerful reactionary movements against ethno-racial legislation—has led to the restriction and unmaking of black rights in both countries.

While Colombia and Brazil are significant cases of ethno-racial and political transformation in their own right, they are especially important when we put them in the broader context of Latin America. Not only were Colombia and Brazil among the first Latin American countries to include blacks in multicultural reforms but they also adopted the region's most comprehensive legislation for this population. As a result, they have often served as models for other regional governments seeking to design their own ethno-racial policies.[4] Thus, understanding how blackness was politicized and institutionalized within the political fields of Colombia and Brazil broadens our understanding of the changing landscape of ethno-racial politics in Latin America more generally.

In this concluding chapter, I want to move away from the specifics of these cases and toward a discussion of their broader theoretical implications. I argue that beyond their regional importance, the making of black political subjects in Colombia and Brazil offers critical insight into two broader fields: the study of social movements and the study of race and ethnicity. This is precisely why I chose to take a comparative approach in the first place. Among other things, this research design afforded me the analytic leverage to draw out the tensions between the different kinds of ethno-racial projects I identify here. It also allows me to think seriously about how different actors, local and global, shape the content and dynamics of ethno-racial struggle as well as rethink what a successful social movement might look like. These lessons, I believe, are relevant not only for Latin Americanists but also for scholars of the United States and elsewhere.

TOWARD A POLITICAL FIELDS APPROACH

Traditional approaches to social movements have a hard time explaining how these small black movements in Colombia and Brazil brought about such monumental political change. I develop the idea that "embedded political fields" and "political field alignments" help to explain this paradox. By "political field," I mean to denote a terrain of struggle defined by material conditions (for example, political elites have relatively more political power and access to the state apparatus than activists) but also by certain symbolic conditions (for example, who has the power to define the rules of the field and the categories of contestation within it). This approach allows me to make three analytic moves that offer lessons beyond this case: (1) broaden the sets of actors we analyze in the study of social movements; (2) examine the role of symbolic power in shaping the terrain of struggle; and (3) consider the global as constitutive of social movement politics today.

Broadening Our Definitions of Political Actors

The first thing that a political fields approach helps us to do is broaden our concept of who counts as a "powerholder"—a term I borrow from Tarrow (1998)—in social movement contestation. In this book I treat movements as embedded in a complex and diffuse set of power relations. Unlike traditional social movement accounts in which state bureaucrats and congressional leaders have, somewhat ironically, become the main protagonists of the story, the narrative that unfolds here features black Colombian and Brazilian activists alongside anthropologists, sociologists, and a range of international actors.[5] As such, state actors are merely one kind of actor in a broader political field, even if we concede that they are particularly powerful ones. In this view, all actors, local and global, can shape the emergence of social movements, the ideological context in which they are embedded, the nature of their struggles, and their effectiveness. Because black movements in Colombia and Brazil did not have the organizational structure, elite allies, favorable public opinion, or ability to mobilize the masses that we once thought were central to social movement success, we must ask what other forms of power—beyond the power of numbers, or the power to disrupt—might compel states to listen to marginalized groups?

The success of black movements in Colombia and Brazil lied in their operation at the intersection of a domestic political field and a global ethnoracial field.[6] These fields included not only a plethora of political actors, including state officials, academic "experts," environmentalists, international human rights advocates, development workers, capitalists, and other social movement actors but also local and global discourses of race, nation, and rights. In fact, only when we situate Colombia and Brazil's black movements of the 1980s–2000s within these overlapping political fields does it become conceivable that these movements defied such incredible odds.

Yet this more diverse array of powerful political actors included not only allies to social movements but also impediments to their success. In chapter 7, for example, I showed how the emergence of reactionary movements against affirmative action in Brazil led to an undoing of certain policies and a reshifting of others. In Colombia, both national and transnational capital critically impeded black rights. The accumulation by dispossession unfolding in black communities throughout Colombia is a chilling reminder that actors beyond the state and political elites should figure more centrally in our analyses.

Taking Symbolic Power Seriously

Broadening the array of actors we examine may also require us to reconsider how we define power itself. More specifically, these cases force us to think more deeply about the role of symbolic power in shaping social movement politics. Put another way, the ideological context in which movements are embedded is not given; it is itself a terrain of struggle over power, meaning, and—more fundamentally—over the very categories of contestation. As such, rather than analyze how social movements draw on, and resonate with, certain preexisting cultural understandings, we should move toward examining how different forms of power—symbolic and material, local and global—are constructed as well as how they shape the conditions and dynamics of social movement contestation.

As I have shown throughout this book, anthropologists, sociologists, and international human rights and development workers within institutions like the International Labour Organisation and the United Nations all played a powerful role in the making of black rights in Latin America. Collectively, they had the symbolic power to set the agenda and the discursive limits of debates around black rights in Colombia and Brazil. By defining power more broadly, we move beyond the question of how movements framed their demands. The struggles that I analyze here were only partly about how black movements framed their issues. More fundamentally, they were about who gets to determine and legitimate particular frames in the first place. In some cases, this symbolic power translated into conventional forms of power as these unconventional actors became directly involved in the drafting of constitutional provisions furthering legislation and authenticating particular communities as the legitimate subjects of rights. Even so, the root of their power as legitimators and authenticators ultimately came from their social and political function as the owners of multicultural knowledge, as the holders of a particular kind of expertise.

Sometimes this symbolic power was tangible, as was the case with the Durban Conference, which propelled previously marginalized voices of anti-racism into the center of mainstream politics. This was also true in negotiations around Colombia's 2005 census, which came on the heels of a series of World Bank–sponsored international meetings on race and census taking. In others, the symbolic weight of ideas of "multiculturalism" circulated in each country's domestic political field in an already externally legitimated form. Without a doubt, the real battle in the late 1980s and early 1990s was not whether Colombia and Brazil would adopt multicultural constitutions or not, but rather whether black populations would be included as the subjects of such reforms.

Global Political Fields and Social Movement Politics

This brings me to my next point, the need to look outward. When one examines a more diverse cast of actors and the role of symbolic power, international and transnational factors are more likely to appear at the center of social movement struggles. In this way, this study joins the call to take more seriously the ways in which international factors profoundly shape the emergence, nature, and outcomes of social movements. With the exception of few important works, the role of international and transnational factors in shaping social movement dynamics has largely been undertheorized.[7] This is due, in great part, to the fact that social movement scholars have typically built their theories from a limited number of cases—namely, the United States and Western Europe.[8] Yet the need to theorize up from other cases may be more necessary than ever if we consider that, until very recently, social movements in the United States seemed to be on the decline at the same time they were on the rise nearly everywhere else on the globe.[9]

The concept of global and national political fields lets us make sense of the varying ways that international actors and discourses matter at different stages of social movement contestation. If we consider domestic political contexts as always embedded in global ones, we begin to recognize that global factors can shape every stage of social movement dynamics, including their emergence, strategies, discourses, and even the nature of their outcomes. Social movements are increasingly subject to, and often adopt, international human rights discourse; they act in fields shaped by geopolitics and have come to depend on funding by international foundations, to survive. By taking seriously these varied international dynamics—while also paying attention to the distinct ways in which they converge with domestic politics—we can analyze more systematically this interplay between these two levels of politics. This, in turn, may give us a better grasp of the conditions under which social movements can bring about significant change.

At this historical moment, social movements are likely to be much more globally embedded than ever before (Keck and Sikkink 1998; Tarrow 2005). This fact makes this type of analysis all the more necessary in both advanced democracies and so-called developing countries. To be sure, the uneven power relations between the Global North and South has meant that international factors have been particularly important in shaping social movement contestation in the latter. It is no surprise, then, that scholars of movements in Latin America—though not always engaging directly with canonical social movement studies—have focused much attention on the global (Alvarez et al. 1998; Brysk 2000; Van Cott 2002; Yashar 2005; Hochstetler and Keck 2007).

In contrast, the role of the international has largely been underplayed in studies of social movements of the United States, in part because the United States has the power to ignore international norms.[10] Yet, the myriad of channels through which the international manifests itself into domestic politics—through the influence of different actors, the dominance of particular language, the work of transnational advocacy networks or geopolitical dynamics—have arguably mattered more in the United States than we once thought.

When we put these many global dynamics at the center of otherwise domestic social movement narratives, we are also likely to find that the patterns of influence are more diverse than we have recognized. For example, we have tended to think of global dynamics and transnational actors as providing "political openings" when domestic political fields were blocked and local powerholders were "deaf" to social movement concerns (Keck and Sikkink 1998). While this "boomerang effect," as Keck and Sikkink (1998) call it, did occur in Colombia and Brazil at times, it was the convergence of domestic and global political openings that catalyzed these countries' adoption of ethno-racial legislation. I found that the alignment—rather than the misalignment—of domestic and global opportunity structures led to political change. However, I do not see this finding as in and of itself providing a generalizable theory of such dynamics. Instead, it suggests that when we take international factors more seriously, our empirical cases will give us further insights into the many ways that domestic and global politics intersect to catalyze or inhibit political change within countries.

A "Long March" View of Social Movements

Finally, this book is a call to widen our temporal lens. In *Contentious Politics*, Tilly and Tarrow (2007) define social movements as a "sustained campaign of claim making, using repeated performances that advertise the claim, based on organizations, networks, traditions, and solidarities that sustain these activities" (8). In so doing, they open up the concept of social movements beyond definitions premised on the size of a movement or defined by actors' use of specific strategies. Rather, they argued that while social movements do often engage in the activities that we have long associated them with (for example, marches, rallies, and demonstrations), they also use more institutionalized strategies, including the creation of "specialized associations, public meetings, public statements, petitions, letter writing, and lobbying" (8). Employing this less restrictive definition of social movements is all the more important when we consider that, increasingly, the same movement actors use disruptive and institutionalized strategies simultaneously, street protest alongside legal mobilization, marches alongside lobbying (Meyer and Tarrow 1998).

This is particularly true in Latin America where many leftist movements have become successful political parties, and where there has been a rise of NGOs that act as political actors. All of this further destabilizes the binary between contentious and formal politics. These changes, among others, signal the need to explore the broad range of strategies that social movement actors use to contest state power and unequal social relations. While black movements in Colombia and Brazil did engage in some rare moments of disruptive action, they centered their contestational strategies on a kind of disruption from within. This included lobbying constituent assembly members amid extremely uneven and power-laden debates around the future of democracy in these countries, as well as writing drafts of legislation and diplomats' statements as Brazilian activists did in Durban.

However, adopting a more flexible understanding of social movements gets us only partway toward understanding how social movements actually bring about political and social change. In Colombia and Brazil, legislation for black populations was only the first step in a long struggle. More generally, it is the nature of political struggle that all victories are likely partial responses to a broader set of social movement demands. However, the cases of Colombia and Brazil reflect a deep chasm between laws on the books and actual state practices. Perhaps because so much social movement theorizing focuses on the United States and Western Europe, we have paid too much attention to the passing of legislation and too little to the politics of their implementation.

The gap between legislation and implementation—which characterizes politics in much of the Global South—makes charting social movements' "long march though the institutions"—as Dutschke called it—all the more necessary. Yet, as Alvarez et al. (1998) rightfully note, the literature on social movements has still largely maintained a "putative eschewal of institutional politics" in the "defense for absolute autonomy" (13). Among other things, this hesitation about analyzing what happens after, in between, and sometimes alongside, cycles of protest has limited how well this literature explains how civil society actually influences state policy (Baiocchi et al. 2008). Thus, even as we adopt broader definitions of social movements, as Tilly and Tarrow (2007) have suggested we do, we need to also move beyond accounts that privilege disruptive tactics above the other strategies that social movements use.

Remedying this tendency requires analytic as well as methodological innovation. I designed this study to do what Baiocchi and Conner (2008) suggest political ethnographies are best equipped to do: offer a "close-up and real-time observation of actors involved in political processes" in ways that can extend the definition of these processes "beyond categories of state, civil society, and social movements" (139). To achieve this redefinition, we must begin and end our empirical analyses of the life cycle of movements at different points in time, a strategy that can reveal a more textured picture of these movements' possibilities and limitations in terms of bringing about real change. In this vein, rather than provide a snapshot of a movement pressuring the state to adopt a singular piece of legislation, this book is fundamentally about the trajectory of black social movements in Colombia and Brazil. I show how black movements pushed effectively for ethno-racial legislation and changes in state institutions but also how these political transformations created new sites of contestation within the two countries' political fields. In this new context, black activists had to make hard decisions about what kind of relationship they wanted with the state. These negotiations have impacted Afro-Brazilian and Afro-Colombian movements' ability to hold the state accountable for implementing existing legislation and for taking on other important issues that have yet to be addressed.

As activists registered their once autonomous organizations with the state, hired and acquired legal expertise, applied for funding, sat on state-civil society councils, and partnered with the ethno-racial state apparatus to organize events and campaigns, they became institutionalized in ways that sometimes facilitated and sometimes undermined their ability to bring about greater substantive change. At the same time, the adoption of specific rights and policies for black populations brought with it new political and ethical concerns. In all of this, the boundaries around the black political subject, as well as its content, continued to be contentious both within and between black political organizations, state institutions, intellectual circles, international agencies, and ultimately among the people meant to inhabit these categories.

The very character of these movements—and other movements around the world—signals the need for social movement scholarship to widen its gaze in all these directions. Only by examining the trajectories of black movements in Colombia and Brazil—that long march through state institutions—can we can truly understand the significance of institutionalizing black political subjects within these countries. And only through such analyses can we also see the unmaking of black political subjects in each case.

RETHINKING ETHNO-RACIAL IDENTITY AND POLITICS

This critical genealogy of the making of black political subjects in Colombia and Brazil also seeks to speak directly to the study of race and ethnicity. More specifically, I hope this work will contribute to the development of new theories of race-making and political change that are not so heavily constrained by thinking about the U.S. case. Among other things, provincializing the United States moves us beyond two latent assumptions: that theories of race in the United States can be extended to the rest of the world; and that the U.S. civil rights and Black Power movements should be the benchmarks from which we define and evaluate black struggle everywhere.[11] Theorizing up from the South will, I believe, simultaneously deepen our understanding of Latin American countries and further our knowledge of ethno-racial politics in the United States and in other countries. To these areas of study, the history of black rights in Colombia and Brazil offers four specific insights. First, it requires us to complicate the idea of Latin America's so-called multicultural turn. Second, it raises important questions about whether there has been, or will be, a "Latin Americanization" of the United States. Third, it forces us to move beyond the idea that U.S. imperialism led to ethno-racial reforms, and the broader politicization of race, in countries like Brazil. Finally, tracing black movements in Colombia and Brazil from political obscurity to the institutionalization of their demands into the law and state institutions underscores the ways in which ethno-racial categories —like other social categories—are politically constructed.

Beyond the Multicultural Turn

As I embarked on fieldwork in Colombia and Brazil, I noticed many ambiguities in the very idea of a black multicultural subject, especially in Brazil. Although nearly all scholarship on ethno-racial reforms in Latin America referred to the multicultural turn as a single shift, a set of cohesive policies, I began to doubt whether all recently adopted ethno-racial policies should be understood as multicultural in nature. The idea that, while the Brazilian nation had already successfully integrated nonwhites in cultural terms, it had failed to fully integrate them economically and politically seemed to be at the core of that country's affirmative action and other racial equality policies. The presumed beneficiaries of Brazil's racial equality were black Brazilians, defined by their experiences of historic and systemic racial discrimination. It was not clear why this should be called multiculturalism. In stark contrast, Colombian activists generally framed black rights as fundamentally about the cultural protection of the country's *grupos étnicos*, a discourse that was rare, especially when it came to black populations, in Brazil.

Thus, I set out to understand not only the process through which ethnoracial policies came about in Colombia and Brazil but also why such different conceptions of blackness became institutionalized in each case. There was no obvious reason for the difference. Both countries developed a form of *mestizaje* nationalism in the early twentieth century; both began to recognize ethno-racial rights in the same period and with a similar language of protecting cultural difference. What is more, state officials in both countries began to talk of racial equality about a decade after adopting multicultural policies. So why did each country ultimately institutionalize blackness in such distinct ways? I came to see that racial equality discourse was prominent in Brazil and multiculturalism discourse prominent in Colombia for two reasons: the way the national imaginaries of each country understood blackness; and the way that black movements in each case seized upon specific moments of national and global political opening.

I argue that moving beyond the idea of a singular multicultural turn allows us to identify both a multicultural alignment and a racial equality alignment. These alignments affected both when each country implemented reform as well as what kinds of claim-making projects those reforms entailed. Even so, the distinction between these alignments is not shorthand for a distinction between "race" and "ethnicity." The idea of groupness based on "race" and groupness based on "ethnic" difference do have distinct academic, social, and political genealogies (Omi and Winant 1986). Nevertheless, social and political practice often lumps both ideas of difference together (Wade 1997). This is because many processes of ethno-racial othering and hierarchization have been, and continue to be, simultaneously about marking "cultural" and "phenotypic" difference. As such, cultural markers are very rarely the sole drivers of "ethnic" exclusion. Rather, meanings attached to perceived phenotypic differences also have a role. For instance, the category of "Muslim" in the United States and around the world is as much about what we tend to think as ethnic and racial difference (Rana 2013).[12]

Then too, the difference between the multicultural and racial equality alignments is not what we understand to be ethnic exclusion—simply a question of black versus indigenous claims-making; neither multicultural nor racial equality claims were inherent to either of these groups in Latin America, or anywhere else. In fact, even suggesting that in the 1990s blacks in certain Latin American countries became "indigenous" or that their claims were "indigenous-like" also runs the risk of obscuring the fact that indigeneity is itself the product of historical and ongoing political constructions. Given the brutal history of colonization, it makes sense that we would naturalize the link between indigenous people and claims to territory and cultural difference. Nevertheless, we cannot forget that contemporary indigenous identity and claims-making are also the products of a parallel story of politicization from peasants to indigenous peoples, just decades before (Yashar 2005).

In this book, I argue that a better way of understanding some of these historical and substantive differences is by thinking about two political field alignments. Whereas 1990s Latin America saw a multicultural alignment in which the law consecrated ideas of ethno-racial rights based on cultural difference, the 2000s marked a shift toward a racial equality alignment in which the goal was to combat racial inequality and bring about racial integration. At the core of the distinction between these two alignments was the type of claims-making project entailed in each. This is perhaps best captured in the language of claims to difference versus claims to equality, respectively.

Beyond these cases, debates around whether equality or difference should be the political aim have been at the center of social movements around the world. The ideological differences between Martin Luther King and Malcolm X were, among other things, about whether the U.S. black movement should struggle to fully integrate into, or to maintain autonomy from, mainstream society and state institutions. This conundrum is not unique to ethno-racial struggles. In fact, feminists have long debated whether women's movements should be about inclusion vis-à-vis difference-blind laws, or whether women should instead fight to maintain some legal distinction (Milkman 1986).[13] In Colombia, debates over the right to equality versus the right to difference were also intrinsically tied to serious questions around whether black Colombians on the country's Pacific Coast would or should embrace or reject hegemonic development and modernization schemes (Escobar 2008).

In highlighting the differences between the logic of multiculturalism and the logic of racial equality, I do not intend to make an argument about which form of rights is better or more liberatory. Rather than give a prescription for what kind of claims black movements in Latin America should make, I have sought simply to analyze the making of these different kinds of black political subjects at the intersection of states, social movement organizations, and international institutions. Claims to equality and difference are both inherently about symbolic recognition and material claims, and both could potentially be conceived of as anti-racist insomuch as they challenge ethno-racial hierarchies.[14]

Those who have suggested that state multiculturalism in Latin America amounts to symbolic performances need simply to look at the often-violent conflicts between capital and the landed elite on the one hand, and indigenous and rural black communities on the other, to see what is at stake in these debates. Likewise, the backlash against affirmative action policies in Brazil attests to the kinds of power relations that racial equality policies actually disrupt. Even if we grant that the logic of racial equality in Brazil does not go far enough toward true racial justice, we must still acknowledge that such policies—especially when they come as part of a larger set of social welfare reforms—could potentially lead to radical transformations in some aspects of social life in Brazil.

What is more, while these alignments were distinct and while they became saturated to different degrees in each country, the discourses they embedded tended to circulate simultaneously in the political fields of Colombia and Brazil. In this way, these two alignments both reflect and (re)produce tensions between political projects based on principles of integration versus autonomy, between ideas of equality and difference, between the material reality of urban and rural blacks, and ultimately between notions of groupness based on the kinds of difference we associate with "race" versus "ethnicity."

Reconsidering the Latin Americanization of the United States

When we compare black rights in Colombia and Brazil with those in the United States, the two regions seem to be trading places (Bonilla-Silva 2002). Indeed, it is hard to ignore the striking parallels between the ideological context of *mestizaje* in Latin American countries throughout most of the twentieth century and the "post-racial" United States of today. Both have prided themselves on racial egalitarianism and fluidity at the same time they have quelled racial critique. Yet, what we learn from Colombia and Brazil is that ambiguity around racial categories was never the same as equality between such categories, either symbolically or materially. Thus, those working to combat racial inequality in a supposedly colorblind United States might learn from the experiences of black activists in Brazil, who have spent most of the twentieth century doing just that.

There are also other comparisons to be drawn between these two regions. Somewhat ironically, just as the U.S. Supreme Court was slowly dismantling affirmative action policies, Brazil's Supreme Court voted unanimously to uphold them. This example suggests that we should pay special attention to questions of history and racial trajectories—to use a term from Omi and Winant (1986)—when comparing racial regimes. When examining "post-raciality" or "colorblind racism" alongside "racial democracy" and *mestizaje*, we should be mindful of what came before each of these. Arriving at a supposedly post-racial state assumes (at least symbolically) that a previous racial moment has somehow been overcome. Yet discourses of *mestizaje* in Latin American countries never came with any admission of a racially unequal moment. Instead, under this ideology, these countries were thought to be inherently egalitarian since their founding. This narrative recast slavery and colonization as benevolent and as cordial. For this very reason, the proliferation of academic discussions on "post-racial Latin America" should give us some pause. While scholars using this language often critique the very notion that Latin America has moved beyond race, the term "colorblind"—which was transposed onto Latin America from the United States—erases the historical particularities of *mestizaje* nationalism. It also may lead us to a mischaracterization of the current moment. With the exception of Brazil, Latin American countries found a way to recognize black and indigenous rights within a logic that did not actually require them to grapple with racial-inequality, racism, or discrimination.

Moreover, as we contemplate the extent to which there has been a "Latin Americanization" of U.S. race relations, we should be careful not to homogenize Latin American countries. This book has demonstrated how nationalist imaginaries and ethno-racial resistance have varied substantially across the region. What is more, black political organizations in Brazil, while sporadic due in part to generalized state repression, were much more developed than in Colombia. Social understandings of race and nation were also distinct in the two cases as was the nature of the ethno-racial reforms that each country embraced. It is precisely for this reason that I contend that the dominant framing of Latin America's diverse set of ethno-racial policy reforms as a multicultural turn may be flawed.

Beyond Cultural Imperialism, toward Global Embeddedness

The nation-making projects in Colombia and Brazil—which involved whitening policies and only later the embrace of racial mixture—were a response to internationally hegemonic "scientific" ideas that linked race with human progress and national development. Nearly a century later, a diverse set of international factors would shape the contestation of these very projects. I have taken on directly the question of whether recent global influences have provided new opportunities for black and indigenous peoples in Latin America or if they have distorted domestic politics.[15] I have also considered whether the story of the politicization of ethno-racial identity, and the adoption of race-based policies, in Latin America is a story of U.S. cultural imperialism.

I tease out such international influence by drawing on interviews with the key actors involved in these political transformations, analyzing the archives for direct and indirect references to international actors, mapping genealogies of a global ethno-racial field, and using discourse analysis to uncover the circulation of ideas of multiculturalism and race. In this, my goal was to challenge simplistic accounts of influence flowing from North to South. The fact that in Brazil—a country that is relatively more powerful than Colombia and less susceptible to U.S. influence—developed ethno-racial policy and discourses that looked more similar to the United States than they did to policies in Colombia significantly challenge one-dimensional accounts of U.S. influence.

I argue that while international factors were very important to the making of black political subjects in Colombia and Brazil over the last few decades, such factors did not always take a singular form, nor did they always follow the trajectories we might have expected. The political field alignment that eventually led to the institutionalization of black rights in Colombia and Brazil necessarily involved both the strategic action of small black movements and the consolidation of a global ethno-racial field. This field—first dedicated to indigenous rights and later to policies for Afro-descendants—did involve U.S. actors like the Ford Foundation, but similar institutions in Latin America and Europe were equally, if not more, important to these developments. Thus, the story of changes in state policy and discourse around race and nation in Latin America was far from a prescripted tale of U.S. imperialism.

Relatedly, while U.S. black movements were a constant reference point for many activists in Brazil and Colombia, these activists' politicization of blackness was not inspired exclusively by ideas about race incubated in the United States. Instead, the locus, nature, and direction of international influence were more dispersed. In fact, urban black activists in 1970s–1980s Colombia and Brazil were just as inspired by anticolonial struggles in South Africa as by U.S. civil rights and the Black Panther Party. Likewise, in Colombia, black peasant movements were as transnational as their urban counterparts, though these peasants' transnationalism was rooted in the Catholic Church and international liberation theology movements. Moreover, the claims that black rural communities in both countries made on their respective states mirrored the international discourse of multiculturalism, human rights, and indigeneity more than they did any discourse of race in the United States. Finally, while affirmative action in Brazil did borrow from similar policies in the United States, in the Brazilian context such policies underwent an intense process of what Merry (2009) calls "vernacularization." In the end, local agents—black activists and their allies in Colombia and Brazil—appropriated international discourses and laws, adapting them to these countries' social contexts and political fields. After much public and private debate, affirmative action policies in Brazil eventually took a hybrid form—they were for "black," "brown," and "indigenous peoples" at the same time as they were for public school students, independent of race. This permutation of affirmative action was meant to ameliorate both race- and class-based inequality simultaneously, as it was also meant to stave off mounting critiques against affirmative action policies.[16]

The international also figured into the making of black rights in Colombia and Brazil through tangible transnational relationships. To be sure, over the last few decades black movements in both countries not only appropriated global discourses of ethnic rights but also received international funding at critical moments. They also leveraged transnational alliances to pressure their states to comply with existing legislation, adopt new reforms, and in some cases, protect the lives of threatened leaders. Geopolitics were also an important part of such transnationalism. As I have shown, the Third World Conference against Racism in Durban offered an unprecedented opening that the Afro-Brazilian movement was only able to leverage effectively because the Brazilian state had invested decades in projecting its image as a racial paradise abroad. If we scan history, we find many examples of the ways in which geopolitics have had a great impact on domestic racial politics. One is the anti-apartheid struggle in South Africa. Likewise, Cold War politics directly impacted the success of the civil rights movement in the United States and black politics in Cuba (Skrentny 2002; Sawyer 2006; Fligstein and McAdam 2012).

In suggesting that ethno-racial struggles are inherently global, my point is not that race means the same thing everywhere, but rather that the construction and deconstruction of ethno-racial categories and hierarchies has never, and arguably will never, begin and end within the boundaries of the nation-state (Goldberg 2002; Hanchard 2003). As Goldberg (2002) suggests, "As much as power was cemented racially in state formations within a global ordering, resistance to any part of the racial ordering of states, affairs and people ultimately has had to assume proportionate global reach" (133). This reality—paired with the increasing globalization of discontent—has meant that local and national ethno-racial struggles are often constituted through complex articulations that involve a plethora of mechanisms and a wide array of transnational actors.[17]

Yet even as we examine these international factors, we must be careful not to obscure the ways in which the agency of black movements, political elites, and ordinary people—as well as local histories and imaginaries—are also deeply important to ethno-racial politics. Only by analyzing domestic politics and history could I make sense of why ideas of racial equality became so entrenched into state and movement discourse in Brazil while ideas of ethnic difference did the same in Colombia. The kind of black politics Colombians and Brazilians engaged in, the strategies they used, the organizational form their movements took, and the types of claims they made reflected the particularities of the national political fields in which they were embedded. Moreover, it would have been impossible to understand the form that black rights took in Colombia without understanding the mobilization of indigenous peoples, the ideological battles between urban and rural black activists, or the regional ways blackness was historically imagined. In this sense, this book is a call to take seriously the articulation of ethno-racial identity and politics as fundamentally both locally and globally constituted.

Interrogating Blackness

Finally, I have also made the case that we need to interrogate, rather than assume, black identity and politics. We have known for some time that race is not simply socially constructed; instead, many of the dynamics that we identify as producing and reproducing ideas of racial difference are specifically political. A myriad of political processes and a combination of state and nonstate actors have proven instrumental to defining and redefining ethno-racial categories. In this sense, contestation within and between activists, bureaucrats, legislators, and even capitalists is as salient to the reproduction of racial hierarchies as are social interactions on the ground.[18] We also know that such political contestation also shapes and is shaped by these everyday social interactions between individuals and groups. This fundamentally political character of processes of racialization is as true in the United States as it is in Latin America. In the former, scholars have shown how categories like "Asian American," "Hispanic," and "Native American" have been constructed in great part through political processes.

Yet when scholars attempt to explain the construction of, and politicization around, these ethno-racial categories in the United States, they often reify the category of "black," perhaps inadvertently so.[19] Rather than interrogate the groupness of blacks in that context or analyze the conditions under which black people in the United States become politicized as blacks, we more often assume that blackness is always, and always has been, a fundamental category of self-making *and* politics. This assumption makes sense given the existence of anti-miscegenation laws, the one-drop rule, Jim Crow, and finally, the general overdeterminacy of race in everyday life in the United States. To be sure, all of this has arguably led to the construction of a category of "black" that is much more neatly bound than other ethno-racial categories in the United States and one that is also more defined than the category "black" in Latin American countries.

Yet while the boundary around blackness may be extremely constrained in a U.S. context, it is not entirely unambiguous either. African Americans—like other socially and politically constructed groups—have undergone processes of consciousness building, politicization, and social negotiations around the boundaries and content of the category. Even the category itself has shifted historically, from "negro," to "black," to "African American." As was also the case with other ethno-racial groups in the United States, the racial formation process involved many steps between racialized oppression and the mobilization of the civil rights and Black Power movements; these steps included cultural mobilization like the move toward "Black Is Beautiful" as well as intense debates within black communities about the terms of inclusion.[20] As such, examining the genealogy of categories like "African American," how collective black identity gets forged and politicized, as well as who it includes and excludes are all significant undertakings. Though, they may be particularly important if we are to understand the emergence of movements like "Black Lives Matter" in recent years.[21] Making sense of these massive protests against anti-black racism in cities around the United

States may require us to ask different questions about collective identity and the politicization of blackness in the United States, rather than assume that it was always already there.[22]

In this sense, the point of departure of this study was precisely what sociological work on black people in the United States has taken for granted. Indeed, when we turn our attention to cases in Latin America, we encounter histories of *mestizaje*, rather than anti-miscegenation, as well as somewhat fluid ethno-racial categories, rather than rigid ones. While this does not preclude the existence of racial hierarchy or fixed meanings associated with blackness, it does necessarily lead us to a more constructivist approach to understanding black identity and politics. As Stuart Hall (1996) reminds us, "Identities are about questions of using the resources of history, language and culture in the process of *becoming* rather than *being*: not 'who we are' or 'where we came from,' so much as what we *might become*, how we have been represented and how that bears on how we might represent ourselves" [emphasis mine] (4). In this view, identity formation is a process that is never quite complete.

In this book, I have taken seriously the idea of becoming black—rather than being black—by examining its political articulation. In so doing, I trace monumental transformations in politics in Colombia and Brazil at the same time that I show the many limitations and ambiguities of this shift. Indeed, as the *rolezinhos* with which I began this chapter suggest, the black political subject that these states institutionalized could never quite contain the multiplicity of black identities on the ground, even if it profoundly shaped those very identities. In the end, what emerged was not a universal black political subject but instead a necessarily partial and unfinished one.

METHODOLOGICAL APPENDIX

This study draws on archival, interview and ethnographic methods. I conducted two years of fieldwork over about eight years, which included eleven months in Colombia starting in the summer of 2006 and between August 2008 and May 2009, as well as seven months in Brazil, between September 2009 and June 2010. I also had follow-up trips to both countries in 2012, 2013, and 2014, totaling just over five months. It is worth noting that before embarking on this project, I worked as a program associate at the Inter-Agency Consultation on Race in Latin America (IAC) in Washington DC, where I met black activists and government officials working on issues of ethno-racial inequality in Latin America, and where I became increasingly interested in understanding why governments in this region had suddenly changed their deeply entrenched discourses of color-blind nationalism to recognize ethnic rights.

My approach to fieldwork was very much an inductive one. Once I was done with fieldwork in Colombia, I had a much better sense of what kinds of people I needed to interview in Brazil. Even so, what themes were most salient, and what kinds of questions I needed to ask came from the particularities of that field. My fieldwork in Brazil also required less time because I was much more familiar with the country, having lived there in 2002 and traveled extensively to the country before starting graduate school. In the end, my findings are based on 111 in-depth interviews with black activists, academics, and government officials, as well as an analysis of archival documents and ethnographic data.

In both Colombia and Brazil, I spent much of my first month getting acquainted with the general political landscape of contemporary black social movement. I did this by working as a volunteer for black organizations in each country, analyzing black movement documents, talking with scholars, and examining newspaper articles from the periods leading up to ethno-racial reforms in Colombia and Brazil. In doing this, I gained a better understanding of the political context in which contemporary black social movements emerged in the two countries as well as a sense of the key actors in these reforms. In this time, I also developed a more extensive list of names of activists and government officials to interview and began to participate in a wide range of events, conduct interviews, collect archival documents, and write extensive field notes. Each interview was different, and was designed in part to triangulate information. The interviews allowed me to better understand the political process from the perspectives of different people involved.

This book is not meant to be a comprehensive study of black movements in Colombia and Brazil. Instead, my aim was more specific: to examine the causes and consequences of the adoption of ethno-racial reforms over the last few decades. I was particularly interested in analyzing the role of the black movement in bringing about these political transformations. Yet, rather than follow individual activists or organizations, I followed the legislation, so to speak. As a result, my analysis leaves out a number of important activists and branches of the black movements of these countries, many with which I spent countless hours and whose work I greatly admire, such as the black student movement in Colombia.

The other shortcoming of this methodological approach is that, at times, my analysis might feel uneven to some readers. For instance, in Brazil I focus quite a bit on the Durban World Conference against Racism and the gender dynamics within Brazil's black movement, in part because there is no way of understanding the making of affirmative action policies without doing so. I have not focused on similar dynamics in Colombia, as they are not as critical to explaining the legislative changes that I seek to understand.

MY MULTIPLE POSITIONALITIES

Aware of the critique that U.S. (black) academics have approached research on race in Brazil with an imperialist eye, I was careful throughout this research project to foreground the language of my interviewees, whether they were activists, academics, or state officials. I believe that my fluency in Portuguese and Spanish, my taking many precautions, and my spending extended amounts of time in each country afforded me the ability to understand many of the nuances of the context that I was analyzing. Though, such rigor and care has not actually shielded previous scholars from such charges. Nevertheless, like all researchers, I have a particular background that informed the way I ask questions and the kind of information I had access to in the field. This meant that I had to negotiate my insider status as black, and my outsider status as a foreign researcher, throughout my time in the field. Often, I oscillated between these two, as my being black meant that activists treated me as part of an imagined African Diaspora, and my status as a young researcher from a foreign elite institution firmly marked me as an outsider. Both identities gave me access to, and allowed me to connect with, different kinds of actors. However, they also presented many challenges.

Whether visiting a mostly black village in Northern Cauca in Colombia, or going dancing in a majority-black hip-hop club in São Paulo, people assumed I was either Colombian or Brazilian. Upon learning that I was from the United States, they often wanted to talk about the connections between African Americans and black people in their own country. Formally educated black activists often talked about how Malcolm X, Martin Luther King, Angela Davis, and Stokely Carmichael had been central sources of inspiration in their own trajectories as activists. Perhaps because I lived in Oakland, California, some of them would even ask me what was going on with the Black Panther Party and if I was active in it. I often had to deliver to them the news about the repression of radical black movements throughout the United States, and the lack of a contemporary black movement on the scale of the 1960s–1970s. From organizational names like the Soweto Study Group, Malcolm X Institute, Angela Davis Foundation, and Barrio Nelson Mandela, to the many symbols of African American and African unity including red, black, and green flags, the connections between the struggles of black people everywhere were often explicit.[1] Consequently, black solidarity and my membership in a larger African Diaspora were also assumed.

In this sense, being black and from the United States gave me a particular insider-outsider status, which allowed me to become very much entrenched in the movements I was studying. I was called on to give presentations on black culture in the United States and the Black Power movement in the United States throughout Colombia and Brazil from events like the National Meeting of Black Students in Colombia, to presentations for grassroots projects in the peripheries of São Paulo. In this, many people, including those I formally interviewed, treated me as a sister, often using the term *hermana* or *irmã*. On one occasion, I interviewed a group of rural black leaders who had recently been forcibly displaced from their collective territory on the Southern Pacific Coast, and who were seeking protection from the Minister of the Interior and Justice in Bogotá. I met them through an Afro-Colombian activist who was from their same region. Before I could ask the first question, the older man in the group told me: "I just wanted to let you know that I would not have let you interview me had you been white." He proceeded to tell me his story of organizing around land rights and alternative development, and how white and *mestizo* people, representing leftist armed groups, murdered community leaders and threatened his life. He felt like he was safe with me, in part, because of my being black.

It was not uncommon that activists talked about us as belonging to the same community. In reality though, my experiences being black from the United States were very different from those of rural Afro-Colombian leaders in almost every way. However, because I spent time with black activists outside their offices, at their homes, and at conferences, social events, meetings, and protests, they knew that I was often treated as they were as a black native (rather than a foreigner). I was denied entrance to nightclubs along with them, was randomly searched along with them, and received much of the racialized and gendered street harassment that black women in both countries experience, particularly in the wealthier and whiter parts of the city. In these many encounters, I was often black before I was "American." Within the black movements in these two countries, I would (somewhat jokingly) refer to myself as a *gringa*; however, my friends and interviewees often felt uncomfortable with such a designation. "You're not a *gringa*!" they would say. There were many reasons it was hard for people to see me as *gringa*, including my ability to speak Spanish/Portuguese. But perhaps most importantly is the fact that *gringa* is at once a national and racial category often used to refer to white foreigners. As a compromise, and careful to not be marked as a fraud pretending to be Afro-Colombian or Afro-Brazilian, I would sometimes refer to myself as afro-*gringa*. While black activists in neither country loved this term, they did find it amusing.

However, my identity as black did not always trump my identity as a privileged researcher from an elite institution in the United States. My affiliations with Berkeley and later with the University of Chicago were understood by most of the college-educated activists and all of the state officials I spoke with. While this gave me access to state officials, it did pose some barriers within the black movement. For some black activists, especially those from organizations that I did not have long-established relationships with, being an academic made me an outsider. This was because black movement organizations in both countries had had previous negative experiences with academics, and were very skeptical of my intentions. This meant that some activists brushed me off and did not allow me to interview them, while others required me to tell them who else I interviewed, what my analysis was so far, and in some cases provide them with copies of their interview transcripts and drafts of publications before they agreed to be interviewed. Both positions were understandable, given the tenuous relationship the black movement had with academics.

In addition to managing my insider status as black and outsider status as a researcher from the United States, I also had to navigate the complex divisions within the black movements in each country. I often felt like I was walking a tightrope or through a minefield. Much of the previous research on black social movements in these countries did not dealt with this directly since it focused mainly on one organization (for example, Covin [2006] on the MNU; Escobar [2008] and Asher [2009] on PCN). In contrast, I set out to map the many different kinds of organizations within the black movement in each country, including those who were largely considered coopted. This meant that activists always questioned my loyalty, allegiances, and intentions. At one meeting in Tumaco, an advisory commissioner I didn't know asked, "Are you here with PCN?"; another activist from Cimarrón whom I had already interviewed responded, "No, she's African American, she's a PhD student." The advisory commissioner pressed on: "That doesn't mean she isn't with PCN." This question was a legitimate one. PCN had been my official affiliation with the Fulbright Fellowship, and had provided me with much of my support system and social networks in Colombia. Nevertheless, my goal was never to write a study of PCN, but of the trajectories of the black movements of Colombia and Brazil, and their relationship with the state and international actors more generally.

This was much harder said than done. In both countries, there were many fault lines within the movement, as one should expect with any movement. Competition over resources, activists leaving organizations to form new ones, and entangled personal lives all made it hard to navigate the political field. What was perhaps the most difficult thing to navigate, though, was the sharp line drawn between activists who had close relationships with the state, and those who preferred to keep the state at arm's length. If I were seen around the city/town with either of these groups, it would raise many questions about whose side I would ultimately take when I wrote up the study.

I was even asked to become an official member of a number of black organizations. I politely declined. As I traveled from city/town to city/town, people would often ask me who I was staying with before agreeing to let me interview them. I remember walking down the street with people I had just interviewed, and then being asked to explain why I was with that person. In the end, where I decided to stay, with whom I decided to eat or go out dancing, were first and foremost political. Though, on a few rare occasions, being an outsider did allow me to refrain from taking a position on the incorporation/autonomy debate.

Now that I have situated myself in this research project, I will discuss some of the specifics of my methods, which included interviews, archival analysis and ethnographic work.

IN-DEPTH INTERVIEWS

Over the course of my time in the field, I conducted fifty-six (56) semi-structured, in-depth interviews in Colombia and fifty-five (55) in Brazil with black activists, scholars, and government officials from many different regions throughout the two countries, as well as several interviews with international development workers. Interviews typically lasted between one to two hours, though a few were much longer. My interviews with government officials tended to be thirty to forty-five minutes. While I did have a more general interview schedule for each country, I rarely used it. Instead, each interview was tailored to the person being interviewed based on a number of factors like when they entered the field. For black activists, I asked different questions based on the length and nature of their trajectory within the movement, my knowledge of their participation in specific organizations and historical events, and especially in the case of Brazil, if they had ever occupied a position within the state. There were some common threads in my interviews with activists that are worthy of mention. All of my interviews with black activists started with questions about where they grew up followed by questions about how they came to be interested in political activism. After these questions, my interviews roughly covered the following topics:

- History in the movement
- Organizational history
- Strategies and agenda in the period leading up to reforms
- Strategies in the period following reforms
- Evaluation of legislation and their implementation
- Relationships with the state over time
- Relationships with international actors

Interviewing activists—who consistently evaluate the political context in which they are acting and who often have complex analyses of society—made things both easier and harder for me to develop my own analysis. This is why the idea of me as "researcher," and black activists as "research subjects" never quite held true. Instead, everyone I interviewed had their own complex analyses of what political factors led to recent changes in state policies, as well as the political dynamics at play during my time in the field. The arguments I make in this book were heavily informed by these activists' analyses, though not entirely. My ethnographic work also was crucial for contextualizing these interviews. I am infinitely grateful for their many insights and have tried my best to cite them respectfully.

ETHNOGRAPHIC FIELDWORK

In addition to conducting interviews, my life in the field consisted of attending events organized by black organizations, including conferences, internal meetings, protests, marches, and meetings with government officials. I also attended a number of key events organized by the state, including the Public Hearing on Law 70 in commemoration of the twenty-year anniversary of the law, held in the Colombian Senate, as well as a Public Hearing on Affirmative Action in the Supreme Court of Brazil right before they decided unanimously that affirmative action policies did not violate the constitution. In participating in these events, and conducting thousands of informal interviews, I gained a better understanding of the relationships among black movement actors and between them, the state, and international actors. I wrote extensive field notes almost every day I was in the field, which included both descriptive accounts and preliminary analysis. Additionally, I wrote notes on my first impressions of the formal interviews I conducted in order to make sure they were contextualized.

Originally setting out to understand why the Brazilian and Colombian states adopted specific legislation and policies for black populations meant that the scope of my project was national. This decision did not come without pitfalls. At times, I had to sacrifice local cultural and political specificities for the sake of crafting a more macro narrative around the making of black political subjects in the two countries. In this sense, my approach to ethnography was by no means traditional. While some might call it "multi-sited," I prefer to think of it as a political ethnography in which I chose a substantive, rather than a geographic space as my "field site," so to speak. Thus, instead of embedding myself in a specific city or neighborhood, I embedded myself within a national field of political relations, one where blackness was being politicized and institutionalized within the state. In Brazil, I spent roughly six months in Rio, three months in São Paulo, one month in Salvador da Bahia, and a week in each of the following cities: Brasília (Goiás), Recife (Pernambuco), Porto Alegre (Rio Grande do Sul), and São Luiz (Maranhão). In Colombia, I spent most of my time between Bogotá and Cali. I also made several trips to towns in Northern Cauca and spent about two weeks in the cities of Quibdó, Buenaventura, Medellín, and between Cartagena and Santa Marta. I also traveled quite frequently to participate in regional and national meetings of black movement organizations, but also ones where movement and state actors converged, and sometimes collided. It is also important to note that because activists hoping to engage with the state at the national level did travel to Bogotá and Brasília, I also was able to interview quite a few people from the regions that I did not visit. As such, my research is much better suited to understand the dynamics of black organizing at the national level rather than the local level.

Additionally, in taking this bird's-eye view of these movements, I do not focus too much on subregional variation. After spending time in both countries, and reading the works of Kim Butler, Paulina Alberto, and Peter Wade, I know that region matters quite a bit in the ideology and dynamics of black movements. However, I had to sacrifice some of these regional specificities in order to tell a broader, national-level story about ethno-racial politics unfolding in these cases. I realize that not everyone will be satisfied with this macro approach.

ARCHIVAL ANALYSIS

Finally, I collected many government and black movement organization documents over the course of my research too numerous to actually be included in this study. However, I do rely on these archival documents to support some of the arguments I make in chapters 3 and 4 of this book. In Colombia, I collected and analyzed over 600 pages of primary government and organizational documents from 1991 to 1994. The most central of these documents were the minutes of the National Constituent Assembly sessions related to ethno-racial legislation and the text of Provisional Article 55. Law 70 was drafted by the Special Commission on Black Communities, which included policymakers, black activists, and academics. I also analyzed the transcripts of this commission. Much of my archival analysis centers on the minutes from these sessions, as they highlight the debate between different key actors. Because of a lack of documentation, I did not analyze many civil society sources from this period. I was able, however, to find some correspondence with Afro-Colombian organizations through the National Library and the Colombian Institute of Anthropology and History.

For Brazil, I also collected many documents that did not end up being central to the narrative I crafted in this book. However, I do rely heavily on government documents in my discussion of ethno-racial provisions in Brazil's 1988 constitution in chapter 4. All of the archives from the National Constituent Assembly—including official transcripts of the Subcommission on Blacks, Indigenous Peoples, the Disabled, and Minorities; transcripts from the plenaries; and related newspaper articles from the period—were archived on the website of Brazil's Senate. I also analyzed a combination of newspapers, government documents, and archives from international institutions to analyze the shift from racial democracy to affirmative action. This meant examining national and international newspaper articles on anti-racism and affirmative action policies in Brazil beginning in 2000 and up until the adoption of the first affirmative action policies in government posts in 2001, and in public universities in 2002. Because this analysis—as well as my interviews with activists and government officials—underscored the centrality of the Durban Conference in this shift, I turned my attention there. In order to make the arguments I make in chapter 5, I draw heavily on both newspaper articles and official UN statements made by Brazilian diplomats related to anti-racism and discrimination from 1978–2002. I also paid special attention to the period leading up to the Third World Conference against Racism in 2001 and the regional preparatory meeting held in Santiago de Chile a year earlier. In order to piece together my narrative on the contemporary period, and supplement my ethnographic data, I also analyzed legislative decrees related to affirmative action and policies promoting racial equality in Brazil, and a small number of documents produced by the Ministry for the Promotion of Racial Equality (SEPPIR). These government documents were crucial for understanding exactly how black movement demands, and activists themselves, have been formally incorporated into the state apparatus.

ANALYZING THE DATA

More specifically, I took an interpretive approach in analyzing these many different kinds of data including my interview transcripts, field notes, and archival documents. I used Tams Analyzer, and when I got more research funds NVivo, qualitative software to organize my data, draw out themes, and see patterns in the data. This approach is in contrast to other ways of using such software to quantify qualitative data. Instead, I developed an initial coding scheme, which acted as the point of departure for my analysis. My original interpretive coding scheme focused on three themes: (1) ethno-racial terminology used in these debates and legislation, (2) how different sides of the debate justified their positions around adopting specific policies for black populations, and (3) the different actors involved in these debates. The coding scheme was designed to answer the following subquestions: What was the political context under which ethno-racial legislation was passed in Colombia and Brazil? What was at stake in these debates? Who were the major actors involved? What were the justifications for and against this legislation? What role did black activists play? The codes included "race," "ethnicity," "culture," "identity," "international actors," "academics," "environmentalists," "leftist groups," "individual vs. collective rights," "lobbying," "transnational alliances," "funding/lack of resources," "movement divisions," "external leverage" and "political instability." For the period following these changes, I developed a coding scheme through an equally inductive process. The most important broad categories of codes that emerged from the data "movement fragmentation," "relationships with the state," "authenticity and political representation," "the grassroots," "cooptation," "funding," "political autonomy," and "transnational alliances." I analyzed all data in Spanish/Portuguese and translated text into English only when I used direct quotes.

NOTES

CHAPTER ONE: POLITICAL FIELD ALIGNMENTS

1. Though this is hard to verify, both Turner (2002) and Sabóia and Porto (2001) have made this claim. The co-author of the latter article, Gilberto Sabóia, was one of the key diplomats representing the Brazilian delegation to Durban. It is also likely that these accounts actually claim that Brazil was the largest delegation *after* the South African delegation.

2. The political category activists used at the time was *negro*, which was meant to include both *pretos* (black people) and *pardos* (brown or mixed-race people). While this conception of a group that includes both blacks and browns has increasingly gained traction in Brazil, there are still many gaps between activists' use of the term and the way ordinary people understand such categories in Brazil (Nobles 2000; Telles 2004; Bailey 2009; Loveman 2014).

3. Speech by Fernando Henrique Cardoso, December 19, 2001.

4. See Alberto (2011) for discussion on state repression and black movements throughout twentieth-century Brazil.

5. I believe that such immersion can happen not only in contemporary political processes but also in historical ones. This approaches the idea of ethnography as a sensibility, as an interpretive exercise, rather than exclusively as a technique like participant observation (Wedeen 2013).

6. See Giugni (1998), Giugni and Yamasaki (2009).

7. See Greene (2003), Hooker (2005), Hale (2007), Rahier (2012), and Loveman (2014) for accounts that outline a singular shift to multicultural, multi-ethnic state policies.

8. This is very different from the experiences of U.S.-based academics who did their work in earlier periods in which racial critique was still heavily silenced and unpopular (Degler 1971; Hanchard 1993; Winddance Twine 1998).

9. It is important to note that this contrast holds only if we consider the United States pre-1960s (and particularly the U.S. South) or South Africa pre-1990s. See Hernandez (forthcoming) for a discussion of the politics of comparison.

10. Brazilian Diplomat, Committee on the Elimination of All Forms of Racial Discrimination, 1978.

11. Colombian diplomat, Committee on the Elimination of All Forms of Racial Discrimination, 1984.

12. Though, as many scholars have noted, formal inclusion did not shield non-whites from de facto political and economic exclusion. Sawyer (2006) refers to this phenomenon as "inclusionary discrimination." The exceptions to this

pattern are the countries that were under U.S. occupation, in which U.S. officials implemented Jim Crow–like policies. These countries included Costa Rica (Purcell 1993); Panama (Priestley 2008); the U.S. territory of Puerto Rico (Findlay 1999); and Cuba (De la Fuente 2001) during specific periods.

13. See Quijano (2000).

14. Previously, many Latin American states had only included a question, usually on language aimed at estimating the size of the indigenous population (Loveman 2014).

15. Throuogut most of the twentieth century, Brazil and Cuba were the only Latin American countries to consistently collect ethno-racial data on Afro-descendants. Due to pressure from international agencies such as the World Bank and the Economic Commision on Latin America and the Caribbean —as well as mobilization by black political organizations—by the 2010 round of the census, eleven countries included a question aimed at counting their Afro-descendant population (del Popolo 2008; Loveman 2014). On that same census, seventeen out of nineteen countries in Latin America counted their indigenous populations.

16. See Hanchard (1994) and Marx (1994).

17. Scholars have analyzed the influence of a number of global processes, including the diffusion of global multicultural norms like UN declarations and conventions on indigenous rights (Van Cott 2000; Kymlicka 2007) as well as transnational activism (Brysk 2000; Htun 2004; Telles 2004) in the making of ethno-racial rights in Latin America.

18. Scholars have found that these international factors have been deeply important to policy changes around the world (Keck and Sikkink 1998; True and Mintrom 2001; Tarrow 2005; Tsutsui and Shin 2008; Ayoub 2013).

19. The work of scholars from a number of disciplines profoundly challenge Bourdieu and Wacquant's (1999) argument that U.S. academics and foundations nearly single-handedly imported U.S. "folk notions of race" into Brazil. Historians Paulina Alberto and Amilcar Pereira, for instance, have examined black mobilization in the early twentieth century, where they found that categories like *homens de cor*, or "men of color," were common in that period. Similarly, ethnographic works on contemporary Brazil have argued that, in fact, race is not only salient in everyday lives of ordinary Brazilians, but they also often understand their society as being structured around racial inequality and racism (Twine 1998; Sheriff 2001). This finding has also been echoed in the survey data. For example, the DataFolha 1995 survey found that the overwhelming majority of Brazilians (in Rio de Janeiro) believed that racial prejudice was a problem in their country (Guimarães 2002; Bailey 2009).

20. These accounts emphasized the strength and autonomy of black movements in the region and contrasted slightly from earlier scholarship, which argued that black movements had piggybacked on indigenous mobilization (Van Cott 2006).

21. See Gamson (1990); Burnstein et al. (1995); Giugni (1998); Snow and Cress (2000); or Amenta et al. (2010) for a discussion of what factors shape social movement outcomes.

22. I should note that many authors use the term "Afro-descendant" to refer to

people who identify as black as well as those that identify as *mulato/pardo*. Even so, people who identify as *pardo* or brown in Brazil do not necessarily understand themselves as Afro-descendant. Also, this is in terms of absolute numbers, not proportion of the population. The United States has the second largest such population.

23. Starting with the 1993 National Census, official government estimates of the Afro-Colombian population have ranged from 1.5 percent to 26 percent. The 10.6 percent figure is based on the 2005 census, which used a broad definition of Afro-Colombian (including those who self-classified as "negro," "mulato," "raizal," "palenquero" or "Afrocolombiano"). *Raizal* refers to the population from the islands of San Andrés, Providencia, and Santa Catalina and who are the descendants of West Indian migrants. *Palenquero* refers to people from Palenque de San Basilio, a maroon community on Colombia's Atlantic coast. Black movement actors have disputed this 10.6 percent on methodological grounds and instead defend a 26 percent figure, which was also used by state officials before 2005. The number comes from an official government planning document (CONPES 3169 of 2002) that estimated the size of the Afro-Colombian population to be 10.5 million people, though the document's methodology was unclear.

24. The countries that recognized the rights of certain groups in the black population are Nicaragua (1987); Brazil (1988); Colombia (1991); Ecuador (1998); Guatemala (1998); and Bolivia (2009), primarily through constitutional reform processes. Honduras (1991) has passed multicultural legislation not through constitutional recognition (Anderson 2008).

25. While *quilombo* translates best to "maroon," or escaped slave communities, it is often understood as a broader category of black rural communities. For more on the ambiguity around, and contestation over, who is included in this category see French (2009) and Farfán-Santos (2015).

26. With few exceptions, the literature on black political struggle as well as the study of policies for these populations has been limited to analyses of specific black communities rather than including within or cross-country comparisons.

27. This is known in these countries and internationally as the "right to prior consultation." It is recognized in both countries, legally, and in the case of Colombia, has been further legitimated through Constitutional Court rulings.

28. See Htun (2014) for an in-depth discussion of these special seats.

29. This fetishizing of the spectacular, disruptive, and even dangerous aspect of social movements is also pronounced in the social movement literature.

30. It is important to note, however, that Jasper (2012) strategically avoids the term "fields" because, as he argues, field approaches often conflate actors within the field, whom he calls "players within an arena," and the arena or field itself. I agree that this happens, but I do not believe this is necessarily the case. Instead, I see a fields approach as a way of recognizing the entanglements between "structure" and "agency," between "fields" and "actors," such that structure can be deeply internalized at the same time that actors create that very structure.

31. See Comaroff (1995); Brysk (2000); Hale (2002); Hanchard (2003); Sawyer (2005); Paschel and Sawyer (2008); and Pereira (2013) for similar analyses.

32. Also see Guidry et al. (2001); Khagram et al. (2002); Khagram (2004); Bandy and Smith (2005); and Friedman (2009).
33. This aspect of social movements was largely undertheorized in earlier research on social movements, in part because these studies overwhelmingly focused on social movements in the United States and Western Europe.
34. While I discuss these as they are relevant to my cases, what I have in mind here in terms of mechanisms are Keck and Sikkink's idea of "boomerangs," Sally Engle Merry's "vernacularization," and Tarrow's "externalization." Some examples of specific transnational actors are found in Tarrow's idea of "rooted cosmopolitans" and Keck and Sikkink's "transnational advocacy networks" and "global policy networks."
35. Fligstein and McAdam's (2012) offer a similar conception of fields that borrows from Bourdieu and organizational theory, but which is not explicit about transnational processes.
36. Of course, domestic transformations could have resulted in the articulation of black movements and the adoption of policies for black populations. However, this was rare. In fact, Cuba may be the only country in which the adoption of racial equality policies was initiated through domestic politics. While these policies were passed in the context of the 1959 internal revolution, Sawyer (2005) notes that Castro's racial policies must be understood as inherently geopolitical, as the Cuban leader was trying to show that his regime was morally superior to the racial atrocities of the United States.
37. This idea of alignment differs from Keck and Sikkink's argument about the role of transnational politics in local political struggles (1998). They argue that when faced with political blockages at home, domestic political movements are able to leverage the fact that their claims resonate elsewhere. This resonance in the international arena can then "echo back" like a boomerang, opening new spaces for issues that had formerly been marginalized in domestic politics. I found, instead, that ethno-racial reforms typically happened when there was a kind of convergence in political openings at the domestic and international levels.
38. Also see Ng'weno (2007a) and Greene (2007).
39. Both urban and rural blacks in Colombia and Brazil were, in fact, the products of dual processes of assimilation and cultural resistance that had taken place over centuries.
40. Among other limitations, this idea obscured the very real ways that indigenous peoples are also the victims of systemic racial discrimination. There is also a parallel here in terms of the study of ethnicity in Latin America (read indigeneity) and race (read blackness) (Wade 1997).
41. The right to free, informed, and prior consent around development and private sector projects before they are approved.
42. This stems in part from the fact that most of the literature on the making of multicultural rights has focused primarily on indigenous rights. See Brysk (2000); Sieder (2002); Hale (2002); Warren and Jackson (2005); Yashar (2005); Rappaport (2005); Langer and Muñoz (2003); and Postero (2006). When scholars have turned toward the specific examination of black inclusion in multi-

cultural reforms, they have rarely done so with a comparative lens. Hooker (2005); Wade (2013); and Loveman (2014) are some notable exceptions.

43. Barbary and Urrea (2004) estimate that 71.5 percent of Afro-Colombians are in urban areas. The Brazil figures come from estimates I did using the data from a 2005 Brazilian Institute of Geography and Statistics (IBGE) government survey.

44. The question of where blackness fit into nationalist imaginaries is itself the result of earlier periods of articulation.

45. The idea that Brazilians use an infinite number of racial/color categories is somewhat overblown. Many scholars and journalists cite a 1976 survey in which a sample of Brazilians responded with 135 different answers to an open-ended racial identity question. As Telles (2004) noted, however, the overwhelming majority (95 percent) of these respondents used only six categories. For a discussion on the distinction between racial/color categories in Brazil, see Sheriff (2001).

46. I have chosen to pursue that interest in other work. See Paschel (2013) and Telles and Paschel (2014) for the first published pieces along these lines.

47. While the terms "Afro-descendant," "Afro-Colombian," and "Afro-Brazilian" may seem akin to the famous one-drop rule governing black racial identity in the United States, the state officials, activists, intellectuals, and international development experts with whom I spoke used these terms to refer specifically to a category that included blacks and *mulatos/pardos*.

48. There is also a more pragmatic question of flow, which does, in some cases make the use "Afro-Colombian" or "Afro-Brazilian" preferable.

49. I should note, however, that when I returned to both Colombia and Brazil for follow-up research trips in 2012–2014, the abbreviated term "afro" had taken hold more firmly as a descriptive category, both within movements and society more generally. In Brazil, this term has a much longer history within cultural movements like the *blocos afros* that emerged in Bahia in the 1970s.

50. Scholars have pointed out that while *negro* has been used by the contemporary black movement in Brazil, as well as institutionalized into new state policies, it is still not widely used by ordinary people (Nobles 2000; Burdick 1998a, 1998b; Telles 2004). While this is certainly true, my sense while in the field was that this was also rapidly changing due to the prominence of the word in popular culture, from television to music to newspapers.

51. Loveman (2014) and many others also employ this term.

52. See Wacquant (1997), Wade (1997) or Hattam (2007) for a similar critique of this analytic distinction.

CHAPTER TWO: MAKING *MESTIZAJES*

1. For a discussion of this, see Stepan (1991); Skidmore (1993); and De la Fuente (2001).

2. See Wright (1990) for discussion of Venezuela; Barrow and Priestley (2008) for Panama; Freyre (1933) and Skidmore (1974) for Brazil; Wade (1993) or Sanders (2004) for Colombia.

3. Helg (1990) argues that in Cuba, the adoption of policies to attract white immigrants was a response to the real threat of annexation to the United States. She adds that such a racist whitening logic was not always economically rational, nor was it always consistent with elite visions of the nation.

4. There is still an active debate around this among Latin Americanists. While some see *mestizaje* projects as a clear rupture from whitening, others see continuity between these two nationalist projects.

5. Argentina (Andrews 1980) and Costa Rica (Palmer 1993), for example, did not develop the idea of a *mestizo* nation, but rather of a white nation.

6. Skidmore (1993) argues that Latin American countries often were competing for the same would-be immigrants. Incentives in the way of subsidies helped to make certain places more attractive to them.

7. Though, as Telles (2004) notes, since the Brazilian state did not include a racial question on the 1910 or 1930 census, it is hard to know this for sure. He argues that the exclusion of the racial question was probably, in part, to downplay Brazil's racial composition (31).

8. Borges (1993) also notes that some even considered Rodrigues mulatto. This makes sense when we consider that within Brazil there are drastic differences in racial classification by region. As such, many people who might be considered white in the Northeast would likely be seen as some version of nonwhite in the Southeast or South (9).

9. Beyond being a public intellectual of sorts, Freyre's ideas, especially those laid out in his work *Masters and Slaves*, indirectly shaped state policies. The first director of the Brazilian Institute of Historic and Geographic Patrimony, for instance, was one of Freyre's close friends and supported him while he labored through writing *Masters and Slaves*. Skidmore (2002, 16).

10. While this may have been because of the different disposition of Brazilian elites, it could be argued that it was impossible for them to ignore Brazil's sizable nonwhite population. Brazil's 1890 census, for example, identified 14.6 percent of Brazilians as black and 32.4 percent as *mulato/pardo*. By 1940, the nonwhite population had decreased substantially, but it was still over 35 percent of the population (Andrews 2004, 155). This is much bigger than the black and *mulato* population of Brazil's neighboring countries in the same period.

11. One example of this is in his discussion of food. He holds that "in Bahia and Pernambuco the pokeka was deliciously Africanized, or, better, Brazilianized, in the form of the moqueca of the Big House kitchens" (Freyre 1986, 179).

12. Interestingly, Freyre argued that the actual stock of Africans who went to Brazil was superior to those who went elsewhere in the Americas: "it is the anthropo-cultural and historico-social aspects of African life that seem to us to indicate that Brazil benefited from a better type of colonist from the 'dark continent' than did the other countries of America" (306).

13. *Courier* V(8–9), August–September, 1952.

14. Also see Loveman (2014) for a more in-depth discussion of these debates.

15. This contrasts with Colombia, which developed a more regional and aggregated version of *mestizaje* (Wade 1993), and Cuba, which developed the idea of racial fraternity (Ferrer 1999).

16. Document written by Freyre in 1945, page 5; available at www.fgf.org.br (accessed September 10, 2014).

17. In Mexico and Colombia, for example, *mestizaje* emphasized the bringing together of cultures rather than literal mixture through sex and intermarriage, though that also is not entirely absent from those variants.

18. Caldwell (2007) underscores how racial democracy was inherently about the self-realization of a particular national subject: white elite men.

19. A number of U.S.-based historians including Frank Tannenbaum endorsed this view, arguing that slavery in Brazil was not particularly harsh, especially when compared to slavery in the United States. Indeed, the United States was the perpetual shadow case for those with favorable views of race in Brazil.

20. While manumission typically refers to slave owners freeing the enslaved people they owned, in many Latin American countries manumission happened through enslaved people saving up money to buy themselves freedom, or freed people buying them out of slavery (Andrews 2000).

21. These are not the only two important regimes; however, they were ones where racial concerns were institutionalized in ways that left a paper trail. See Alberto (2011) for a more in-depth discussion of these periods as well as the interim ones.

22. It is important to note that these thinkers also held positions within the state apparatus. Vasconcelos, for example, served as minister of education from 1920–1924, and Gilberto Freyre served in various capacities, formal and informal, within local and national government.

23. Vargas's political career was defined by three additional military coups: one in 1937, which initiated his more repressive regime of the Estado Novo; the coup of 1945, which removed him from office; and in 1954, after being democratically elected as president, he committed suicide as the military made their way to the presidential palace to undertake another coup (Levine 1998).

24. Capoeira, a Brazilian martial art developed by enslaved Africans in the country, for example, was outlawed through a statute passed in 1890 (Andrews 2004).

25. While this agency was not technically a Ministry of Culture, it in many ways served that function (Williams 2001).

26. Despite growing support throughout the country, the Brazilian Black Front had been unsuccessful at electoral politics at the local level in São Paulo, where they had their strongest place (Andrews—blacks and whites in SP).

27. Banco de la República—Departamento de Investigaciones Económicas, "Explicaciones al Cartograma No. 14," in *Atlas de Economía Colombiana*, vol. 2 (Bogotá: Imprenta del Banco de la República, 1960), map 14.

28. Analyzing data from the 1778 census, Uribe (1963) shows that while enslaved Africans worked in a number of industries including carpentry and transportation, around 50 percent were sent immediately to mining centers.

29. From Orlando Melo, "Etnia, region y nacion: el fluctuante discurso de la identidad," *Memorias del Simposio Identidad Étnica, Identidad Regional, Identidad Nacional* (Bogotá: COLCIENCIAS, 1989), 27–28; Cited in Castillo (2007).

30. Cited in Marco Palacios and Frank Safford, *Colombia: país fragmentado, sociedad dividida: su historia* (Bogotá: Editorial Norma, 2002), 138.

31. While the Colombian state did not collect ethno-racial data through most of the twentieth century, the 1912 census reported the black population at 10.2 percent, and in 1918, 9.3 percent (Smith 1966).

32. The government-released document Conpes 3310 estimates the Afro-Colombian population in the Chocó at 85 percent. This would mean that over one-third of the national Afro-Colombian population is in this one department (state).

33. Restrepo (2007) traces this back to the early part of twentieth century, and shows how ideas (not just geography) construct these regions in racialized ways.

34. Or if my English accent was apparent, they often asked what part of Colombia my parents were from.

35. Interestingly, many *Chocoanos* (people from the Chocó) just assumed I was *Chocoana*. They would often say to me, "hola paisana," an affectionate greeting for people presumed to be from one's region.

36. Chaves and Zambrano (2006) have an interesting analysis of *mestizaje* and the tension between distinction and mixture in Colombia.

37. Under the López de Mesa presidency in the 1930s, the Comisión de Cultura Aldeana y Rural Colombiana was also created with a mandate to increase the cultural resources and activities of the rural areas, but the agency was terminated after only six months of existence (Helg 2001, 153). This is just one example of many of the challenges in state capacity that López de Mesa faced in institutionalizing his nationalist vision.

38. The disparaging of Brazil's Northeast as backward exists alongside and often in tension with prevalent discourses of the region as the core of Brazil's collective identity and national pride. This ambivalence is similar to the way that blackness has figured into Cuban nationalism (Sawyer 2005).

CHAPTER THREE: BLACK MOVEMENTS IN COLORBLIND FIELDS

1. In Colombia, there is no socioeconomic data that disaggregates people who identify as *mulato* from those that identify as *negro*, making it hard to know how people who identify in these categories compare on these measures. However, Wade (1993) has noted that, at least on the symbolic level, *mulatos* do indeed occupy an intermediate status in Colombian society, even if that status is fraught and questioned from below (320).

2. This is not to say that there have not been key moments of state repression against black movements. See Sawyer (2006) or De la Fuente (2001) for a discussion of the 1912 massacre of the Partido Independiente de Color, or Alberto (2011) for an analysis of the surveillance and demobilization of Brazil's black movement under Vargas and then later under its military regime.

3. While Marx did not use this exact terminology, he did make this analytic distinction throughout his work. For example, in *The Poverty of Philosophy*, Marx (1963) explains: "Economic conditions had first transformed the mass of the

people of the country into workers. The combination of capital has created for this mass a common situation, common interests. This mass is thus already a class as against capital, but not yet for itself. In the struggle, of which we have noted only a few phases, this mass becomes united, and constitutes itself as a class for itself. The interests it defends become class interests. But the struggle of class against class is a political struggle" (125).

4. For a discussion of the political trajectory and ideology of Serra, see Fusté (forthcoming). For an analysis of Córdoba, see Wade (1993) or Rausch (2003).

5. See Hall (1980); Collins (1999); Stoler (2002); Cohen (1999); and McClintock (2013). While people do not typically think about Hall as an intersectionality theorist, some of his work was trying to theorize the intersection between race, class, and nation. Hall (1980), for example, avoids both racial and economic reductionism by calling for analyses that treat the object of inquiry as a "complex articulated structure" (320).

6. So while the concept of "class-for-itself" is a useful one here, it needs some revision if it is to elucidate the dynamics of ethno-racial struggle. Hall (1986) notes this in his analysis of Gramsci's relevance for the study of race. In it he critiques both Marx's and Gramsci's treatment of class-consciousness as "non-contradictory" and "homogeneous." He argues that because of this assumption that identity is singular, Marxist analyses have a hard time grappling with the reality of "working class racism."

7. I do not mean this to even gesture at a comprehensive genealogy of black movements in this case, as I believe that such a task better suited for historians. See Alberto (2011) and Pereira (2013) for amazing, in-depth analyses and the black movement in Brazil. For more in-depth histories of the black movement in Colombia, see Agudelo (2005) and Castillo (2007).

8. This also poses a challenge for the prevalent idea among scholars that "identity politics" is something outside of material struggles.

9. Brazil also had an unusually high amount of slave rebellions as well as high rates of maroonage (Andrews 2004).

10. Vargas was deposed by a military coup the year after the Black Experimental Theatre (TEN) was founded and the political context in which it emerged was still volatile.

11. With this distinction, I do not mean to suggest that culture is not political, but rather that these organizations mobilized formally around a kind of culture that was not explicitly politicized.

12. It is worth noting that Flavinho is of a medium-light brown complexion. He explained that when he tried to go to a black movement meeting, they denied him entrance because he was considered white by the movement. In another project, I am exploring the boundaries around the category "black" within the black Brazilian movement over the course of the twentieth century.

13. These regional differences in the kind of black movements that emerged have historical roots (Butler 1998; Alberto 2011).

14. A year later, the organization dropped the "against racial discrimination" from its name (Covin 2006).

15. Also taken from the MNU's mission statement and interviews with activists.
16. I found that while black Brazilian activists were, on average, more educated and better off than the broader nonwhite population, the overwhelming majority grew up in poor families. The ones that did go to college were the first in their families to do so. Activists Carlos Medeiros and Amauri Mendes Vilma Reis and Suelí Carneiro and Luiza Bairros all obtained their master's and doctoral degrees much later in life than their white counterparts in the university.
17. Hamilton left the organization to form the React or Die Movement, an organization that has mobilized for a decade against racialized state violence within and outside the prison system.
18. Martins (2004) and Johnson (2008) both give a comprehensive account of how black activist and congressman with the Democratic Labor Party (PDT)(1983–1987) Abdias do Nascimento as well as Benedita da Silva of the PT (1996) proposed multiple pieces of affirmative action legislation, none of which passed.
19. Paraphrased from the cartilha S.O.S. Racismo of Maria Mulher.
20. Available at http://www.casadeculturadamulhernegra.org.br/quem-somos/ (accessed August 8, 2014).
21. Rather than understand the role of international foundations as importing a foreign "logic of race," as Bourdieu and Wacquant (1999) assert, I see foundations like Ford, the Inter-American Foundation, and others as catalyzing the NGO-ization of a black Brazilian movement that was very much under way at least since the 1970s, and arguably since the 1910s, as we see in Alberto (2011).
22. Other scholars have made similar arguments about the political use of culture being a possible impediment to mobilizing the nonwhite masses (Burdick 1998; Telles 1999). Telles (1999) maintained that despite structural constraints to black mobilization, "Afro-Brazilian leaders seeking to mobilize the masses of blacks and browns may succeed by appealing to their common history of oppression and their similar socioeconomic status, at least in Brazil's more developed regions. Efforts to build a common ethnicity that focus only on cultural differences such as religion are not likely to succeed, as past experiences have shown" (Telles 1999, 95). Similarly, Burdick (1998) argues that the emphasis on African-based religion (Candomblé) by middle-class black activists effectively marginalized the working-class, Christian black masses.
23. Many black activists consider this event—which included activists and intellectuals from throughout Latin America and the Caribbean—the beginning of a transnational Afro-Latin American movement (Davis et al. 2011).
24. Proceedings from the event.
25. Wade (1998) also notes that Smith-Córdoba used a more North American conception of blackness than a Latin American one, which he argues contributed to the lack of resonance among the people he was targeting.
26. Later in the interview, Juan de Dios mentioned that some black rural Colombians had become professionals through programs designed to professionalize teachers. Becoming professionalized, he argued, had converted them to "normal Colombians."
27. In addition, Cimarrón also faced the challenge of being confused with an arm of the leftist guerilla group, the Revolutionary Armed Forces of Colombia

(FARC), which went by the same name. While I often heard people say that these two groups indeed had ties, Cimarrón denied the connection. In September 1994, after the FARC blew up a bus in Tadó, Chocó the organization issued a statement clarifying that they had no connection to the guerilla group ("Cimarrón no es subversivo," *El Tiempo*, September 3, 1994).

28. Taken from a document titled "S.O.S." issued by Chocó-based organizations OBAPO, ACADESAN, ACIA, and Organización Regional Embera-Wounaan (OREWA) in the early 1990s.

29. In my interviews with activists who were involved in ACIA and OBAPO, they often recast these initial years in the language of cultural difference and the need to protect black culture; at the time, the goal of such organizing was not always marked in ethno-racial terms.

30. This analysis of whitening as a strategy of survival is similar to the one Peter Wade makes in his 1993 work.

31. Peter Wade has used this term for some time, and formally developed it in Wade (2014).

32. This echoes the discourse around the U.S. Occupy Movement (2012–2013), which was charged by many with provoking "class warfare."

33. "Racist Carnival Group Hits a Low Note," *A Tarde*, February 1974.

34. It is important to note that black rural organizations mobilizing around land did not face a similar pushback because, as I will discuss in the following chapter, they did not articulate their claims in the language of race or anti-racism until later.

35. In her work on independence wars in late eighteenth-century Colombia, Lasso (2007) analyzes the sedition cases in which nonwhites were accused of enmity toward whites. She argues that "these cases illuminate how the explicit expression of racial grievances became a mark of unpatriotic divisiveness" (13).

36. Sawyer (2006) found this to be the case for Afro-Cubans as well.

37. This resembles Dawson's (1994) idea of linked fate among African Americans across class and other cleavages, only on a global scale.

38. While these same activists were aware of the plight of black political organizations in other parts of Latin America, Africa and the United States were much more important references for black activists in Colombia and Brazil in the 1970s and 1980s. This particular view of a hemispheric blackness only seems to have emerged in the 2000s. The one exception to this is the regional work that the Catholic church did beginning in the mid-1980s with the Pastoral Afroamericana (Restrepo 2004).

39. Wade (1995); Hanchard (2000); and Sawyer (2005) all make similar arguments.

40. Scholars of social movements might argue that this simply suggests either a lack of collective identity among blacks or the appropriate frames to resonate with potential followers (Snow and Benford 1988). I believe that these perspectives obscure the deeper dynamics of symbolic power that create the very conditions of possibility for the legitimate deployment of particular frames. It makes sense, instead, to view this as Bourdieu does, as a question of power, which has the capacity to make particular kinds of political struggles illegible and illegitimate.

CHAPTER FOUR: THE MULTICULTURAL ALIGNMENT

1. Constituents discussed these concerns as well as environmental issues heavily as it related to indigenous rights.
2. By 2007, 29.9 percent of the national territory of Colombia was titled under *resguardos*, or collective territory of indigenous peoples, and 4.13 percent in the form of collective titles to black communities. Figures taken from 2007 Departamento Administrativo Nacional de Estadística publication titled "Una nación multicultural, su diversidad étnica."
3. This soccer term translates literally to "huge goal" but is typically used to refer to exceptional and unexpected goals.
4. While Brazil's inclusion of indigenous and black rural rights actually preceded the ILO 169, scholars have argued that earlier international treaties weighed heavily on political elites minds in drafting it (Valle Evangelista 2004).
5. The UN also later created three new permanent mechanisms to address indigenous rights: the Special Mechanism on the Rights of Indigenous Peoples (2007), the Special Rapporteur on the Rights of Indigenous Peoples (2001), and the United Nations Permanent Forum on Indigenous Issues (2002).
6. See Goldman (2005) for a critique of land titling by the World Bank.
7. Quote by Robert Goodland, colleague of Sandy Davis and quoted in a piece by Jorge E. Uquillas titled "Remembrance of Our Friend, Sandy Davis."
8. Davis also wrote the book *Victims of the Miracle*, which highlighted how development projects had been having devastating consequences on indigenous peoples.
9. Quotation from Robert Goodland, a colleague of Davis at the World Bank, as cited by Jorge E. Uquillas (2011), "Remembrance of Our Friend, Sandy Davis," *Journal of the Society for the Anthropology of Lowland South America* 9(2): 1–3.
10. This departs a bit from Bourdieu, who saw the state as the primary repository of symbolic power and who did not center his analysis on how transnational processes shape state power.
11. Much of the text from the Colombia section of this chapter was previously published. See Paschel (2010).
12. See Linz and Stepan (2011) for a critique of the limited nature of this initial democratization effort.
13. After Afonso Arinos, the judge that was the president of the commission.
14. *Jornal de Brasilia*, Brasilia, September 4, 1985.
15. Available at http://www2.camara.gov.br/atividade-legislativa/legislacao/Consti tuicoes_Brasileiras/constituicao-cidada/constituintes (accessed January 4, 2016).
16. *Folha de São Paulo*, São Paulo, August 31, 1986, p. 8.
17. It is remarkable how similar Abdias's proposal in 1986 is to the legislation that the Brazilian state adopted some two decades later.
18. MNU declaration dated August 26–27, 1986.
19. Ibid.
20. This highly racialized, classed, and gendered expression literally translates to "foot in the kitchen." It references enslaved women working in kitchens in the colonial period and means that one has some African/black ancestry. Even while this declaration may have deterred some of this kind of discussion,

a number of white ANC members did emphasize their own black/African blood in discussing racial policies.

21. Their emphasis on racial justice reforms alongside broad social welfare policies was reminiscent of the kind of demands the Black Panther Party in the United States had made just a decade earlier with their 10-point program.

22. The other two subcommissions under Social Order were the Subcommission on Health, Safety, and the Environment and the Subcommission on Workers and Public Sector Employees,

23. Subcommission transcript, April 22, 1987. The term he used was "secondary piano," though "second fiddler" is a more fitting translation.

24. Subcommission transcript, April 28, 1987.

25. Subcommission transcript, April 9, 1987.

26. Ibid.

27. However, this role was also because of the strong relationship between the Pan-Indigenous movement that emerged in Latin America in the 1970s and an increasingly politicized group of anthropologists. In fact, As Brysk (2000) and others have suggested, the contemporary indigenous movement in Latin America is often traced back to 1971 meeting of radical indigenist anthropologists in Barbados (64).

28. Subcommission transcripts, April 23, 1987.

29. Ibid.

30. I could not find one academic reference on this either in English or in Portuguese.

31. Roughly translated as the "black masses." The term *criolo* was historically used in Brazil to refer to blacks born in Brazil and came to be used in a derogatory way (Graden 2006). It has since been reappropriated by activists and people on the ground (for example, the Rio-based black feminist organization Criola).

32. Subcommission transcripts, April 28, 1987.

33. Ibid.

34. Subcommission transcripts, May 4, 1987.

35. It is not clear if he was referring only to quotas for black Brazilians, or for other groups. Also, he did not specify in what area these quotas might be (that is, education, labor market, and so on).

36. Subcommission transcripts, May 4, 1987.

37. Ibid.

38. Subcommission transcripts, April 28, 1987.

39. While Congresswoman Silva did go on to propose affirmative action legislation after the National Constituent Assembly, she was not the person who proposed these within the subcommission, at least not officially. Even so, being the only Afro-Brazilian member of the subcommission likely made her the immediate target of such critique.

40. Subcommission transcripts, April 28, 1987.

41. Ibid.

42. Palmares was founded by escaped enslaved people in the early seventeenth century and lasted nearly a hundred years before being destroyed by Portuguese military forces in 1694.

43. This idea of *quilombismo* was perhaps best elaborated by Abdias do Nascimento

in his 1980 work, *Quilombismo* (Arruti 2000). One sees a similar ideological development of the concept Cimarrónaje by Juan de Dios the founder the Afro-Colombian organization, Cimarrón.

44. For the black movement, and sometimes for the state, the idea of maroon communities is sometimes used interchangeably with black rural communities more generally.

45. There is a serious tension in Carneiro da Cunha's plea. ILO Convention 107 on Indigenous and Tribal Populations was an integrationist policy that, while it sought to protect traditional groups, subscribed to the idea that they would disappear with modernization. It was replaced in 1989 with Convention 169, which is more in line with the San José Declaration. It was just on the horizon as Brazil adopted its new constitution in 1988.

46. Carneiro da Cunha, "A questão indigena na constituinte," *Folha de São Paulo,* May 5, 1987.

47. This demand was more specifically a reaction to the apartheid regime in South Africa. It was in the original list of demands made by the black movement in their August declaration. Despite being defended vehemently by Benedita da Silva in the plenary, it did not pass. The constitution did include anti-racism as one of a number of principles of their diplomatic relations.

48. The word "equality" appears twelve times in the constitution.

49. Hooker (2005) challenges this claim in her work on black rights in Latin America more generally.

50. Taken from Brazil's 1988 constitution.

51. This included ninety-seven articles that mandated separate policies to be implemented.

52. While the 1988 constitution criminalized racism, the harsher penalty for discrimination happened with the passing of Law 7.716, also known as Lei Caó after the Afro-Brazilian congressman Carlos Alberto de Oliveira who proposed it. The law made discrimination based on race, color, ethnicity, religion, or national origin an unbailable crime with a sentence of 1 to 5 years in jail and a fine.

53. This idea was consistent with the way that Afro-Colombians had historically been conceived of vis-à-vis the state. Since the abolition of slavery in 1851, the Colombian state had maintained colorblind policies while at the same time reproducing regional hierarchies that kept Afro-Colombians marginalized and invisible in the nationalist imaginary. In contrast, the Colombian government had set aside *resguardos*, or semi-autonomous collective territories, to protect indigenous peoples under a corporatist political model very much influenced by colonial law, and which conferred these rights on the basis of indigenous people inhabiting the territory prior to state formation (Padilla 1996; Van Cott 1996).

54. Carlos Rosero, now of PCN, was a candidate, as was Juan de Dios Mosquera, who was included low in the ranks of the M-19 list. Also, while indigenous representatives and others such as ANC member Fals Borda did mention Afro-Colombians in their statements and proposals on ethnic rights, most discussions in the ANC still centered exclusively on indigenous populations.

55. A number of Afro-Colombians from the Pacific Coast also went to Bogotá

with Birry to develop and lobby for what would become Provisional Article 55 (interview, OBAPO leaders, July 2006).

56. It is not clear if these sit-ins were actually illegal demonstrations. They occupied the Embassy of Haiti in Bogotá and a church, two places that may have been amenable to black Colombian activists.

57. Interviews with Zulia Mena and Libia Grueso revealed that such action was not without costs. Many of the Afro-Colombians who lobbied Congress and ANC members during the constitutional reform process used their personal resources to make trips back and forth to Bogotá.

58. Activist Libia Grueso contended, "We had originally put urban areas, inter-Andean valleys, coastal areas, and fluvial zones. All of these [black communities] were discriminated against, and we had all of them in the first draft of the Provisional Article" (interview, Grueso, July 2006). In many of the minutes from the special commission that developed Law 70, this broader definition was also being used.

59. Representatives from the Colombian National Institute of Agrarian Reform were particularly concerned about how to title land in zones where Afro-Colombians lived alongside *mestizo* and indigenous populations.

60. In the letter addressed to the vice minister, they demanded basic funding, including per diems and honorariums to allow for Afro-Colombian commissioners to travel and attend regular meetings.

61. He added that this is not just an academic or conceptual resistance but that ICAN has political, cultural, and economic allegiances that also contributed to this position.

62. While there were four subcommissions within the Special Commission—Territory and Natural Resources, Development, Cultural Identity, and a Financial/Operational subcommission—the question of ethnicity and cultural identity was by no means limited to the cultural identity commission and in many ways was seen as the transversal issue needed to advance the proposals in all of the subcommissions.

63. Brysk (2000) gave a similar geneology of the Pan-Indigenous movement when she traced it back to a 1971 meeting in Barbados in which a group of "dissident anthropologists" pledged to "promote indigenous self-determination and enter politics to save endangered cultures" (18).

64. In this period, to the extent that they could obtain financial support, Afro-Colombians also focused on raising the visibility of AT55 among the grassroots black community and constructing the proposal for Law 70 through this process.

65. While there were attempts to expand the idea of blackness outside rural areas of the Pacific Coast, both actions by activists in the special commission aimed at socializing the Provisional Article 55 and constructing Law 70 from the grassroots were mostly in rural areas of the Pacific Coast, reproducing the notion that this law was for a specific kind of blackness.

66. There was also discussion of urban black populations, though such discussions were often limited to urban populations on the Pacific Coast, with Quibdó and Buenaventura being the most-cited examples of black communities that

were urban but that also preserved black culture and had to be included in Law 70, albeit using different legal provisions.

67. Anthropologists working on black mobilization in Colombia have taken very different positions in this regard. While Arocha (1992) and Escobar (2008) tend to highlight the cultural particularities of black communities in Colombia, Restrepo (2013) takes a more radical constructivist approach, analyzing the ethnicization of blackness in Colombia in the early 1990s.

68. See Escobar (2008) for a deeper discussion of how Colombia's ethno-territorial movement has challenged hegemonic development models.

69. I am not the first to challenge these accounts (Wade 1998; Restrepo 2004; Hooker 2005; Ng'weno 2007b; French 2009; Asher 2009). Van Cott revised her initial formulation and included an analysis of black rights in her book on multicultural constitutionalism (2002).

CHAPTER FIVE: THE RACIAL EQUALITY ALIGNMENT

1. See Barbary and Urrea (2004); Hooker (2005); and Ng'weno (2007a).

2. While Brazilians do think of their regions as culturally distinct, the boundaries around each region tend not to be as rigidly drawn. While Bahia, and the Northeast more generally, may be the region associated with African culture, all of Brazil is imagined as having a piece of Bahia in it.

3. In full disclosure, I worked at the Inter-Agency Consultation on Race in Latin America for two years as a program associate before starting my PhD program at Berkeley.

4. Facing a number of fundraising problems, as well as issues of diminished interest in black populations by some donor institutions, the IAC was disbanded in 2007.

5. Precisely because of this, there is no direct point of comparison with the Brazilian case. As such, while in Colombia, I focus on the ongoing struggle to expand state definitions of the black political subject outside rural areas on the Pacific Coast, whereas my Brazil discussion focuses specifically on affirmative action and the mainstreaming of racial equality in Brazil's social policy.

6. The National Executive Commission of the march included Black Pastoral Agents (APN's), Cenarab, Center for Popular Movements, CGT, Rural Black Communities, the Central Workers' Union (CUT), Union Force, the Forum, National Black Entities, the Black Women's Forum, the Unified Black Movement, the Movement for Reparations, the Comunidades Negras Rurais, the Coordinator of Black Entities (CONEN), Black Union for Equality (UNEGRO), and Grucon.

7. Taken from text of Decree 4.886, available at http://www.jusbrasil.com.br/leg islacao/98187/decreto-4886-03 (accessed January 4, 2016).

8. Ibid.

9. While I had a series of questions about the Durban Conference on my interview schedule, in most cases, interviewees mentioned Durban before I had the chance to.

10. While scholars have also made this argument, they offer very little in the way of explaining why Durban was so important (Htun 2004; Telles 2004).

11. Hellwig (1992) does argue that Dubois later changed his position on this.

12. The UN Convention on the Elimination of all Forms of Racial Discrimination (CERD) was not adopted until 1965, and the Committee on the Elimination of all forms of Racial Discrimination had not yet been created.

13. This study was actually Cardoso's entrée into the study of race relations. He was a student of Fernandes, and as a result of this study, Cardoso wrote a number of works books on racial inequality in São Paulo.

14. August to September 1952 of UNESCO magazine, *Courier*.

15. This was the case in many of the UN records I analyzed.

16. Official UN record of the 54th session, 22nd meeting, October 25, 1999, document A/C.3/54/SR.22.

17. Official UN record, October 18, 1991. Emphasis mine. It is not clear in the translation of this statement to English (by UN officials), if the Brazilian representative meant to say that they had to deal with this in the past, or if they still had to confront it in the present.

18. Official UN record of the 43rd session, 12th meeting on CERD, October 18, 1988, document A/C.3/43/SR.A2.

19. Official UN record of the 54th session, 22nd meeting, October 25, 1999, document A/C.3/54/SR.22.

20. In a cursory search of newspaper articles printed about Brazil in the English language media in April 2000, I found dozens of articles on these events.

21. Taken from the UN "Report of the Latin American and Caribbean Regional Seminar of Experts on Economic, Social and Legal Measures to Combat Racism with Particular Reference to Vulnerable Groups." The word "Afro-Latino" was likely a mistranslation.

22. Taken from the Santiago Declaration.

23. September 8, 2000, Presidential Decree, Brazil.

24. In addition, after the Durban Conference, Roland was chosen by the UN to be one of the five eminent experts charged with monitoring Durban follow-up around the world.

25. The main funder was the Ford Foundation, but they also received funding from other donors.

26. I counted the names of activists from recognizable black women's organizations on the official declaration (dated September 28, 1993) accessed in the archives of *Criola*.

27. Some of the black women activists at Beijing were Nilza Iraci and Sueli Carneiro of Geledés. Wania Santanna was also there. Other organizations that participated in the preparatory meetings for Beijing in Brazil did not participate in the actual conference because they refused to receive money from USAID, who sponsored much of the Brazil civil society participation (informal interview with Lucia Xavier of Criola).

28. Taken from the Articulação de Organizações de Mulheres Negras publication, "Construindo a Equidade: Estratégia para implementação de políticas públicas para a superação das desigualdades de género e raça para as mulheres negras."

29. Canada and Israel also boycotted the conference. There were also some conflicts

over classifying slavery a crime against humanity and the language of reparations.

30. Sabóia and Porto (2001) note that while the majority of these were black Brazilian activists, not all of them were.

31. Activists wrote much of the text of the Santiago document from Brazil and throughout Latin America.

32. See Htun (2002) and Telles (2004) for a discussion of the Itamaraty program. The program within the Ministry of Agriculture and the National Institute of Colonization and Agrarian Reform (INCRA) referenced racism and the Durban Conference, but it instituted a gender-based quota exclusively; available at http://www.incra.gov.br/sites/default/files/uploads/institucionall/legislacao--/portarias/portarias-de-2001/portaria_mda33_080301.pdf (accessed October 1, 2015).

33. I discuss the role of black Brazilians in the Workers' Party in implementing racial equality policy in the following chapter.

34. Anthropologist Bettina Ng'weno (2007a, 2007b) has analyzed some of these tensions, including the tentative shift to understandings of blacks defined in terms of race in Colombia in Constitutional Court rulings.

35. The Department of National Planning issued a policy document in 2002 estimating the black population at 26 percent, a number still widely used by Afro-Colombian activists and some government officials. See "Social Policy Document 3169: Policy for the Afro-Colombian Population."

36. In contrast, nine of the eleven censuses have included a question aimed at counting the indigenous population (Barbary and Urrea 2004; Mosquera et al. 2009).

37. CONPES 3310, Departamento Nacional de Planeación, República de Colombia, October 2005.

38. National Development Plan of Colombia (2002–2006).

39. Taken from a press release issued by the Inter-American Development Bank (IDB) on November 18, 2000.

40. Departamento Administrativo Nacional de Estadística (DANE) document titled "Talleres regionales dirigidos a los grupos étnicos. La información estadística del Censo General 2005 y su pertinência en la planeación del desarrollo local y regional."

41. Public letter from coalition of Afro-Colombian organizations sent to President Uribe, October 14, 2004.

42. The coalition included the National Afro-Colombian Conference (CNA), the Black Communities' Movement (PCN), the National Cimarrón Movement, the Association of Mayors from Cities with an Afro-descendant Population (AMUNAFRO), the Federation of Cities from the Pacific Coast (FEDEMPACIFICO), the Association of Black Community Organizations (ORCONE), the Kambiri National Network of Afro-Colombian Women, and the National Network of Afro-Colombian Youth, Students and Organizations.

43. Public letter from the coalition sent to President Uribe, October 14, 2004.

44. Ibid.

45. PCN (2006), and letter to President Uribe dated October 14, 2004.

46. See "Insumos para el análisis de las barreras que impiden el avance de la po-

blación negra, afrocolombiana, palenquera y raizal," Departamento Nacional de Planeación, República de Colombia, government document published August 15, 2008.

47. Transcribed from the official video; available at http://comminit.com/global/node/310299 (accessed August 2, 2011). Translations by author.

48. In my informal conversations with some of the activists at the forefront of this campaign, it did not seem like they were consciously drawing on U.S. notions of race, though it is quite possible that this was happening subconsciously. Indeed, some of the urban black organizations and activists involved in the campaign were very directly inspired by the U.S. civil rights movement. This, paired with the concern with ensuring a larger count of the black Colombian population, likely led to this more expansive definition.

49. Taken from the census form; available at www.dane.gov.co (accessed January 6, 2016).

50. I heard the term several times while in the field to refer to *mestizo* Colombians. Afro-Colombian activist Leonardo Reales also spoke about such *mestizo* normativity at the 2014 Afro-Latino Forum Conference in New York City.

51. The category *indio*, or "indigenous," might be an exception here.

52. Taken from undated Departamento Administrativo Nacional de Estadística (DANE) document titled "La visibilización estadística de los grupos étnicos colombianos" (46); available at https://www.dane.gov.co/files/censo2005/etnia/sys/visibilidad_estadistica_etnicos.pdf (accessed January 4, 2016).

53. While Afro-Colombian activists argued for the inclusion of this term because *moreno* is used synonymously with "black" in some regions, DANE officials refused to include it because the ambiguity of the term (Estupiñan 2006).

54. There were some important culturalist definitions of blackness and black struggle emerging out of Brazil's Northeast and mainly through religious practices (Alberto 2011). I do not mean to ignore these, I just want to suggest that blackness as defined by color/phenotype and by experiences with discrimination was the dominant current in Brazil's black movement and broader political field, since at least the turn of the twentieth century.

55. This was circulated on Facebook and e-mail at the time, but was also available at http://vimeo.com/5212659 (accessed November 11, 2014).

56. This is different from the Observatory for Racial Discrimination, a joint initiative of Los Andes University's Program on Global Justice and Human Rights, The Center for the Study of Rights, Justic and Society (Dejusticia) and the Black Communities Movement (PCN). It is housed at Los Andes in Bogotá.

57. Taken from the website of the OCDR; available at http://observatoriocdr.gov.co/index.php/quienes-somos (accessed September 15, 2014).

58. Law 1482, adopted November 20, 2011.

59. The official name is the Independent Movement of Absolute Renovation.

60. The name in Spanish is Día de la Afrocolombianidad, which translates literally to Day of Afro-Colombianness. The holiday was passed by Congress on December 27, 2001.

61. The official name of the bill is the Participation and Representation for Black Communities and Afro-Colombians Bill, but it is popularly known as the Equal Opportunities Bill. This right to prior consultation and consent is one

of the main principles of ILO Convention 169, and became institutionalized for black communities in the late 1990s in Colombia. It mandates that black communities are adequately informed about, and consent to, any major policy or development project that might affect their lives.

62. Students can receive benefits if they prove to be from one of the following areas: the Pacific basin, the rivers of the Pacific, the rural river zones, San Andrés, Providencia or Santa Catalina, or "other regions in the rest of the country with Afro-descendant settlements." Taken from Resolución No. 038, Consejo Superior, Universidad del Valle (May 13, 2010).

63. Barbary and Urrea (2004); Rodríguez Garavito et al. (2008); and Viáfara and Urrea (2009) have all shown persistent ethno-racial inequalities in Colombia.

64. Analysis of Colectivo Afro descendientes pro Derechos Humanos Univalle Benkos Vive (CADHUBEV) proposal: "Propuesta Académica para la Asignación de Cupos a las Comunidades Afrocolombianas en la Universidades Públicas y Privadas y Sus Sedes y Privadas y Sus Sedes Seccionales y Regionales."

65. For an example of this see a press release of the Ministry of the Interior available at https://www.mininterior.gov.co/sala-de-prensa/noticias/colombia-presenta -avances-para-garantizar-el-derecho-la-igualdad-y-enfrentar-cualquier-forma -de-discriminacion#sthash.L1eIZ6gc.dpuf (accessed October 5, 2015) .

66. It is important to note that there is an ongoing debate around characterizing Colombia's black ethno-territorial movement as anti-capitalist and anti-development. See debate between Escobar (2008) and Asher (2009).

67. In 2010, the U.S. Department of State launched an official program, the U.S.-Colombia Action Plan on Racial and Ethnic Equality, modeled on a similar bilateral initiative with the Brazilian government. Whereas the latter was built atop a strong legal, bureaucratic, and discursive infrastructure dedicated to racial equality, the former has been much more fragile and disembedded from political practice in Colombia. There are a few forthcoming works that examine the complexities of these transnational relationships between black Colombians and Washington, DC, including Pedro Cortes's work and Tatiana Alfonso Sierra's MA thesis on transnational Afro-Colombian activism.

68. The most interesting iteration of this is the Marcando Territorio mobilizations.

69. See Ford Foundation Grant Database; available at https://www.fordfounda tion.org/work/our-grants/grants-database (accessed January 3, 2016).

70. Language taken directly from the "primary intiative tab" of the Grants Database; available at https://www.fordfoundation.org/work/our-grants/grants-da tabase (accessed January 3, 2016).

71. It is important to note that PCN, like any organization, was made up of a diverse array of people. While some PCN leaders did not talk explicitly about racism, others leaders did. This was the case with PCN activists like Dionicio Miranda on the Atlantic Coast, who had a discourse of "cultural racism," and who linked the experiences of marginalization of rural black populations with that of racial discrimination in urban areas (inteview, Dionicio Miranda, October 2008).

72. I should also note that in neither case did this happen through Congress, but rather through the executive, a fact that complicates the traditional idea that have centered political parties and favorable public opinion.

73. Taken from SEPPIR'S website; available at http://www.seppir.gov.br/comuni
    dades-tradicionais/programa-brasil-quilombola (accessed September 5, 2015).

CHAPTER SIX: NAVIGATING THE ETHNO-RACIAL STATE

1. Taken from the text of Law 70.
2. This was previously called the Office on Ethnic Affairs, in which there was
   a division on indigenous peoples and one on black communities. Over the
   course of the nineteenth and twentieth centuries, there were a number of previous agencies to govern indigenous peoples in Colombia (Wade 1997).
3. The discourse of blackness institutionalized into state structures through Law
   70 further complicates how the Afro-Colombian movement engages with the
   state today.
4. While the Office on Black Communities was never thought to be a particularly powerful state institution, it was seen as losing power and legitimacy over
   time, especially as some national commissioners have gone recently around
   the office to directly negotiate with the government at the ministry level and
   with the offices of the president and vice president.
5. Text of Decree 2248 of 1995.
6. Taken from untitled and undated document written by the Office on Black
   Communities.
7. Under Law 70, any department can set up a commission on black communities if there are officially registered black organizations in that department.
   Since 2008, a number of departments have set up their own commissions. In
   addition, the city of Bogotá now has a city-level commission.
8. While the Office on Black Communities was never thought to be a particularly powerful state institution, it was seen as losing power and legitimacy over
   time, especially as some national commissioners had gone around the office
   to directly negotiate with the government at the ministry level and with the
   offices of the president and vice president.
9. This violence must be situated in the ongoing civil war, or internal conflict,
   which started in the 1960s with a number of insurgent leftist groups. However,
   it is important to note that before the late 1990s, many of the rural majority–
   Afro-Colombian areas were relatively far outside the intense fighting between
   armed groups.
10. At that time, Bogotá was the only city to have its own advisory commission.
    Elsewhere it was at the department, or state, level.
11. Figure from 2005 Census and reported in the 2007 Departamento Adminis-
    trativo Nacional de Estadística publication titled "Una nación multicultural,
    su diversidad étnica."
12. Registraduria Nacional del Estado Civil, Colombia; available at http://www
    .registraduria.gov.co. It is also important to note that Carlos Rosero (PCN)
    and Juan de Dios Mosquera (Cimarrón), two of the most known black activists
    of national organizations have both run for these special seats in Congress on
    several occasions since 1994, and neither has won.

13. *El Tiempo* article, "Votos De Afros En Valle Y Sucre Se Multiplicaron Hasta 30 Veces," published March 21, 2010, reported this figure and suggested that such a drastic increase had raised many flags about possible corruption. The article also reported that in Juan Carlos Martínez Sinisterra's department of Valle, the figure increased from 18,107 to 58,806.

14. See *El Espectador* article titled "Juan Carlos Martínez presentó renuncia a su curul en el Senado," March 14, 2014.

15. See Htun (2015) for a more in-depth discussion of the problems with ethnic political representation in Colombia.

16. See *El Espectador* article titled "Nuevos representantes de negritudes se defienden," March 14, 2014. Eight different cases went to Colombia's Constitutional Court charging that their election was illegal. Eventually, the court decided that they were elected legally and that they represented the "Afrodescendant community."

17. This is not an endorsement of this view of Rosita as corrupt. Rosita herself vehemently denied this idea, citing all of the government contracts and international funding her adversaries within the black movement also have received.

18. I have chosen not to name them here for ethical reasons. Though I should note that many of them prefaced this by saying they were not directly involved in such corruption.

19. Some commissioners also cited incompetency and the lack of political and financial autonomy of the commission from the state as other problems that hamper the effectiveness of the National Commission.

20. During my fieldwork, it was also clear that Afro-Colombian activists were able to take advantage of bureaucratic holes, the demise and creation of different agencies, and personal relationships with government officials to advance their own personal interests or those of their organizations/movements. Activists in the commissions, particularly the National Commission, are best positioned, and many think are more likely, to take advantage of these things.

21. When Netinho became the subject of an investigation over alleged corruption in 2011, UNEGRO was the first organization to publicly defend him.

22. When Tilly (1998) initially wrote about social movement strategies, he talked about "repertoires of contention," focusing exclusively on disruptive protest; in his later work, Tilly (2008), he included a wider range of action that those without traditional forms of power take. Given the importance of lobbying, legal mobilization, and other institutionalized or bureaucratic strategies, I prefer to use the term "repertoires of action" rather than "repertoires of contention."

23. There had been local state agencies to address racial inequality—including the State of São Paulo's Council for Black Development and Participation created in 1984 as well as similar agencies in Minas Gerais and Rio Grande do Sul—that preceded these federal efforts in the 2000s.

24. Interviews with Flavinho Jorge and Matilde Ribeiro, SEPPIR's first Minister, both suggested that while there were discussions of having a ministry before Lula took office, there were many doubts that this would actually happen. This was especially the case since Lula, early on in his presidency, was accused of excessive government expansion since he had already created two new spe-

cial secretariats with ministry status: Ministry of Fishing and Agriculture and the Special Secretary of Policy for Women.

25. Taken from Workers' Party website; available at http://www.pt.org.br/secretaria /combate-ao-racismo/ (accessed January 6, 2016).

26. This included Flavinho Jorge (director of the Perseu Abramo Foundation), Matilde Ribeiro, the first minister of SEPPIR, and Matevs Chagas.

27. Taken from SEPPIR's website; available at http://www.seppir.gov.br (accessed January 6, 2016).

28. Ibid.

29. Portal Orçamento Senado Federal available at http://www12.senado.gov.br/ orcamento/documentos/loa/2015/elaboracao/parecer-preliminar/relatorio-pre liminar/view (accessed September 28, 2015).

30. On October 2, 2015, President Dilma Rousseff announced the closing of SEPPIR along with seven other federal ministries. While formally closed, its functions were set to continue on as part of a new joint ministry along with those of the Special Secretariat for Policies for Women and the Secretariat for Human Rights.

31. Press release by the Brazilian government titled "STF abre debate sobre cotas raciais nas universidades," published on March 3, 2010.

32. Text taken from Law 10,678 of 2003.

33. Taken from text of call for nominations for the 2010 CNPIR.

34. Available at http://www.portaldaigualdade.gov.br/apoiproj (accessed September 9, 2015).

35. They were represented on subsequent councils.

36. See https://www.youtube.com/watch?v=M3KZUP_RdDY (accessed September 11, 2015).

37. Smith (2016) offers a thorough analysis of the Campanha Reaja movement, including an examination of marches that drew thousands of people throughout Brazil against the extermination of black people.

38. Though this relationship has changed with the naming of Luiza Bairros, a former activist with strong ties to the black women's movement in Brazil, as Minister of Racial Equality.

39. The demands of the two marches were not very distinct, nor was the actual profile of those in attendance (Heringer 2006).

40. For a more detailed discussion, please see the methodological appendix. I should note that previous research on black social movements in these countries had not dealt with this problem directly since they have focused mainly on one organization, or on a faction within a broader movement. Some examples include Covin (2006) on the Unified Black Movement, which as he notes is more of an organization than a movement. Also see Escobar (2008) and Asher (2009), on the Black Communities' Movement (PCN), as well as Restrepo (2004) and Cárdenas (2012), which study several organizations within the ethno-territorial faction of Colombia's black movement.

CHAPTER SEVEN: UNMAKING BLACK POLITICAL SUBJECTS

1. Figure taken from a report issued by the National Council of Planning titled "Reflexión para la Planeación Balance General del Plan Nacional de Desarrollo 2006–2010."
2. Taken from World Bank website; available at http://www.worldbank.org/pro jects/P006868/natural-resource-management-program?lang=en (accessed November 25, 2014).
3. 2002 World Bank Report titled "Titulación territorios Comunales afro-colombianos e Indígenas Costa Pacífica de Colombia."
4. Available at http://www.iadb.org/en/projects/project-description-title,1303.html ?id=CO0157 (accessed January 4, 2016).
5. Taken from the project abstract; available at http://www.worldbank.org/proj ects/P006868/natural-resource-management-program?lang=en (accessed October 19, 2014).
6. Available at http://www.incoder.gov.co/portal/default.aspx (accessed September 15, 2015).
7. The original name of the organization was OPOCA.
8. Presentation given by Sandra Martínez from Univalle on October 19, 2014, at the National University of Colombia in Bogotá for the Cátedra Manuel Ancízar.
9. A number of factors contributed to this. In addition to forced displacement, many left because of the economic and legal precariousness they were facing. The size of the land title that COCOMOPOCA was given also reflects the fact that twelve community councils broke off to establish a separate territorial organization, something I discuss later in this chapter.
10. These are based on official statistics from the Subdirección de Atención a Población Desplazada de Acción Social—Sistema de información de Población Desplazada (SIPOD).
11. See 2008 FEDESARROLLO report titled "La minería en Colombia: Impacto socioeconómico y fiscal," written by Mauricio Cárdenas and Mauricio Reina; available at http://www.fedesarrollo.org.co/wp-content/uploads/2011/08/La-min er%C3%ADa-en-Colombia-Informe-de-Fedesarrollo-2008.pdf (accessed January 5, 2016).
12. Informal discussion with Carlos Rosero.
13. Chapter 1 of Law 70 (1993).
14. Taken from the 2006 "Plan Nacional de Desarrollo. 2006–2010. Tomo II. Estado Comunitario: desarrollo para todos" of Colombia's Departamento Nacional de Planeación (DNP); available at https://colaboracion.dnp.gov.co/CDT/PND/PND_Tomo_2.pdf (accessed January 4, 2016).
15. I found this out talking with people, asking them their names, but also looking through a local phonebook. In a detailed study of this phenomenon, Tamayo (1993) found that there were fifty-six different last names given to enslaved Africans in Colombia during the colonial period that were meant to denote their ethnic group, or the port from which they were purchased.
16. The two documentaries are the independently produced *La Toma*, directed by Paola Mendoza, and the Colombia documentary of the PBS *War We Are Living* series.

17. See Order 1045-A of 2010.
18. Taken from statements released by women marchers.
19. Palenque was founded sometime in the late sixteenth century as a runaway slave society.
20. This happened through their Afro-Colombian and Indigenous Program.
21. It is important to note that Obama and his administration had been directly involved in a number of issues around Afro-Colombian politics. When he was a senator, one of the first speeches he gave on the senate floor was a call for solidarity with Afro-Colombian communities. Additionally, during his first election campaign, he promised to not sign the free trade agreement between the United States and Colombia unless the Colombian government addressed issues with labor and ethnic rights. However, Obama ultimately signed the agreement without those protections. See Washington Office on Latin America statement released on April 10, 2012, titled "Obama Poised to Give Presidential Seal of Approval to Gross Labor Rights Violations in Colombia."
22. I participated in the actual meeting as well as the three-day pre-meeting with PCN activists.
23. Taken from denuncia dated September 18, 2009.
24. I have decided to use a pseudonym here because of the sensitivity of the issue. Also, even while Teresa never agreed to a formal interview, she knew that I was writing an academic book.
25. After being put on preventive detention, Andrés Felipe "Uribito" Arias Leiva, former minister of agriculture, was declared a fugitive of the law. He was sentenced to 17 years in prison.
26. Available at http://www.ipea.gov.br/agencia/images/stories/PDFs/comunicado/120925_comunicadodoipea155_v5.pdf (accessed October 1, 2015).
27. Ibid.
28. See Banting and Kymlicka (2006) for a critique of this zero-sum argument.
29. The education system was not only the main vehicle through which race and class stratification was perpetuated in Brazil, but also the most central arm of the state in the production and diffusion of racial democracy ideologies. As such, textbooks typically highlighted racial mixture as the strength of the nation, while at the same time marginalizing Afro-Brazilians from history (Munanga and Gomes 2005). There have been many impediments to implementation, including intense debates within the Ministry of Education between some who support the legislation and others that believe it has actually introduced racism into Brazilian schools (Moura et al. 2009; Silva Souza and Souza Pereira 2013; Gomes and de Jesus 2013).
30. There has been a similar backlash to health policies like the "Health of the Black Population" campaign organized by the Ministry of Education on the grounds that it was introducing biological ideas about race into Brazil. See Maggie et al. (2007) for a critique of these policies, and Caldwell (forthcoming) for an examination of the politics of their implementation.
31. Text of Law 7.668 of August 22, 1988.
32. It is also worth mentioning that the *quilombo* movement emerged largely after the 1988 constitution and The National Coordinator of Quilombos (CONAQ), for example, was created in 1996.

33. It is important to note that this number does not include the many communities still fighting for official recognition as *quilombos*.
34. The *quilombo* struggle has become an important part of the MNU's revitalization, particularly in the southern part of the country.
35. Text of the original Statute of Racial Equality; available at http://www.plan alto.gov.br/ccivil_03/_Ato2007-2010/2010/Lei/L12288.htm (accessed November 21, 2015).
36. I am a member of these listservs and was able to see the conversation unfold in real time.
37. Statement titled "CONEN: Posicionamento Político sobre o Estatuto da Igualdade Racial," published on June 22, 2010; available at http://arquivo.geledes .org.br/areas-de-atuacao/questao-racial/afrobrasileiros-e-suas-lutas/6189-co nen-posicionamento-politico-sobre-o-estatuto-da-igualdade-racial (accessed December 28, 2015).
38. In fact, the final statute called for a decentralized approach to affirmative action, which was precisely the opposite of its original intention.
39. Available at http://www.youtube.com/results?search_query=san%C3%A7% C3%A3o+do+estatuto+de+igualdade+racial&aq=f (accessed October 4, 2015).
40. Ibid.
41. Nação Mestiça is a fascinating case. The organization denounces all of the racial policies adopted by the Workers' Party because they argue they have created an apartheid in Brazil and amount to discrimination against, and encourage the ethnic cleansing of, mixed people. Yet, rather than call for a return to colorblind policies, they have demanded that the state recognize the specific rights of mixed people in a number of areas, including as the original owners of land. The organization has a grassroots following in the Northeast of the country, and has been at the center of anti-affirmative action efforts as well as campaigns against the land rights of *quilombo* and indigenous communities.
42. It is important to remember that this was not the first time that a federal affirmative action law was proposed. Afro-Brazilian congresswoman Benedita da Silva proposed Bill 433 of 1993, which proposed to "institutionalize the minimum quota for racial/ethnic populations that are socially discriminated against in higher education" (Martins 2004; Johnson 2008).
43. Text from letter.
44. This included the Macaense Movement of Black Cultures in the state of Rio de Janeiro, Aurélio Carlos Marques de Moura, president of the Afro-Brazilian Cultural Association Ibó de Zambi and the Black Socialist Movement.
45. The Black Socialist Movement (MNS) was founded May 13, 2006. It is also worth noting that the majority of the Afro-Brazilian activists that I interviewed had long histories in different kinds of socialist movements. This included those who were part of clandestine socialist organizations in the 1970s who went on to found the PT as well as others who remained Trotskyist and who refused to be incorporated into party politics (that is, Reginaldo Bispo of the MNU). However, none of them were members of the MSN, nor did they consider it a legitimate black movement organization.
46. Text of letter.

47. In another project, I compiled all articles on race in Folha between 1990 and 2013. This analysis comes from that project.

48. In 2014, *Folha* launched the "What Folha Thinks" campaign, which made their position on a number of contentious political debates clear, among them gay marriage, abortion, capital punishment, and the mandatory vote in Brazil. They declared their support of class-based quotas, as well as their position against color or race-based affirmative action in print as well as through online videos.

49. Text of UnB quotas policy.

50. It is worth noting that despite all of the talk about racial mixture and ambiguity in Brazil, with the exception of myself and a representative from the Black Socialist Movement, everyone in the audience would have been read as unambiguously white, a difficult task to accomplish in Brazil. This was also true of the panelists. Peter Fry is a white Englishman who has lived in Brazil for years. Both Maggie and Magnoli's non-Portuguese last names suggest they are, in part, the descendants of Europeans that came to Brazil after the colonial period.

51. It is important to remember that the debate around affirmative action may have been particularly polarizing because rather than a point system, the majority of policies were based on a quota system that reserved a specific percentage of seats to students based on race or class or both. This information was taken from the Grupo de Estudos Multidisciplinares da Ação Afirmativa (GEMAA), which has a comprehensive map with information on all university affirmative action policies in Brazil; available at http://gemaa.iesp.uerj.br/dados/mapa-das-acoes-afirmativas.html (accessed October 28, 2014).

52. They asked respondents their opinion on affirmative action based on color, attending public school, or income. Much like in the 2006 Datafolha survey, the support for class-based affirmative action was higher (77 percent). Only 16 percent of Brazilians overall were against all forms of quotas, though this percentage increased substantially when they look specifically at wealthy Brazilians. Results taken from IBOPE website; available at http://www.ibope.com.br/pt-br/noticias/Paginas/62-dos-brasileiros-sao-favoraveis-a-cotas-em-univ ersidades-publicas.aspx (accessed October 28, 2014).

53. Luiza was the first person in that position with deep roots in the black movement. In contrast, previous ministers had been leaders within the Workers' Party, rather than within the black movement, which made them particularly vulnerable to critiques from the movement.

54. Information taken from GEMAA; available at http://gemaa.iesp.uerj.br/dados/mapa-das-acoes-afirmativas.html (accessed November 22, 2015).

55. Available at http://www1.folha.uol.com.br/poder/2015/06/1639980-cnj-fixa-co ta-de-20-para-negros-em-concurso-para-juiz-e-servidores-dos-tribunais.shtml (accessed January 6, 2015).

CHAPTER EIGHT: RETHINKING RACE, RETHINKING MOVEMENTS

1. Like Brazil's *rolezinhos*, flash mobs in the United States ranged from innocent to violent gatherings of young people.

2. I found a number of political cartoons in Brazil's major newspapers that high-lighted the racial dimensions of the policing of the *rolezinhos* compared to earlier protests.

3. Available at http://sao-paulo.estadao.com.br/noticias/geral,shopping-de-luxo -de-sp-fecha-as-portas-apos-protesto-em-apoio-a-rolezinhos,1120043 (accessed January 6, 2015).

4. The Ministry for the Promotion of Racial Equality in Brazil, for example, has consulted with governments throughout Latin America on institutional de-sign. In addition, the inclusion of black rights in Colombia's most recent con-stitution (1991) and later with the Law of Black Communities (1993) served as a template for the inclusion of blacks in Ecuador's multicultural constitution some years later.

5. I am thinking here of political process approaches like McAdam (2010). For a critique of these state-centered accounts of social movements, see Goodwin and Jasper (1999) or Morris (2000).

6. While Ray (2000) does not explicitly conceptualize a global political field around women's rights, international actors and discourses were very impor-tant to explaining the differences in the political culture of her Bombay and Calcutta cases.

7. There are some important exceptions, including Keck and Sikkink (1998); Tarrow (2005); and Tsutsui and Shin (2008). There is also a robust literature on the translation of international human rights law and discourse into local struggles—for example, Merry (2009)—however, this has largely remained a separate literature from the social movement literature within sociology.

8. Some of the canonical texts in the field include Morris (1986); Tarrow (1994); Della Porta and Diani (1999); Benford and Snow (2000); Ferree (2002); McAdam et al. (2003); and Tilly and Tarrow (2007).

9. This included the emergence of the far-right Tea Party movement, the Occupy movement that began in 2011, and the Black Lives Matter movement, which emerged a few years later in protest of the murders of Mike Brown, Rekia Boyd, Tamir Rice, Eric Garner, and many other black men and women by the police.

10. More recently, there has been a revising of previous accounts. For example, prominent social movement scholar Doug McAdam has called for a rethink-ing of the role that global factors played in his canonical study of the U.S. civil rights movement (McAdam 2010; Fligstein and McAdam 2012).

11. I borrow the term "provincialize" from postcolonial theorist Dipesh Chakra-barty.

12. It is precisely for this reason that I have opted for using the term "ethno-racial" throughout this book.

13. To be fair, some feminist theorists have sought to unsettle this very dichotomy (Fraser 1995).

14. Indigenous movements are an interesting example of the ways in which dis-courses of cultural difference can be married with an anti-racist/anti-colonial discourse. The compatibility between anti-racism and claims to cultural dif-ference gets lost when we confuse state multiculturalism—which was not ex-

plicitly about racism or subverting power relations—for the demands of indigenous and black communities.

15. See Van Cott (2000); Hanchard (2003); Htun (2004); Kymlicka (2007); and Paschel (2010) in the former camp, and Bourdieu and Wacquant (1999); Maggie and Fry (2004); Castro-Gomez and Restrepo (2008); and Magnoli (2009) in the latter.

16. Before the 2012 Law of Quotas, there was another level of vernacularization that happened at the local level, as different universities and different states within the country institutionalized different racial categories; available at http://gemaa.iesp.uerj.br/dados/mapa-das-acoes-afirmativas.html (accessed January 6, 2016) .

17. This is similar to the perspective advocated by Fitzgerald and Cook-Martín (2014) and Loveman (2014), both of which analyze similar race and nation-making processes in Latin America, albeit in earlier periods.

18. See Espiritu (1993); Nagel (1994); Hattam (2007); Beltrán (2010); and Mora (2014) for an analysis of political contestation over ethno-racial categories. See Mora (2014) for an analysis of how media elites—among many other actors—helped to construct and solidify the category "Hispanic" in the United States.

19. Nobles (2000) and Daniels (2009) are notable exceptions. Okamoto and Mora (2014) move toward an approach that looks at the construction of blackness using a panethnicity lens.

20. Historians and African American Studies scholars have contributed much more in this area.

21. Black Lives Matter is a national movement of activists from throughout the United States, which emerged in the wake of the 2013 acquittal of George Zimmerman, the man who killed African American teen Trayvon Martin. Founded by Alicia Garza, Patrisse Cullors, and Opal Tometti, Black Lives Matter began as a hashtag on Twitter and gained momentum with the upsurge in public cases of police killings of black men, women, girls, and boys. By 2015, it was a very visible national network of activists led mainly by black youth, with a decentralized and nonhierarchical structure.

22. Political scientist Michael Dawson's concept of "linked fate"—which attempts to understand and measure how class shapes African Americans' sense of collective identity and political behavior—moves us in this direction.

METHODOLOGICAL APPENDIX

1. For a discussion of these transnational political circulations, see Pereira (2013) on Brazil; Sawyer (2005) on Cuba; and Wade (1995) on Colombia.

REFERENCES

Agudelo, Carlos. 2005. *Retos del multiculturalismo en Colombia: Política y poblaciones negras*. Medellín: La Carreta Social Editores.

———. 2004. "La Constitución Política de 1991 y la inclusión ambigua de las poblaciones negras." In *Utopia para los excluidos: El multiculturalismo en Africa y América Latina*, edited by Jaime Arocha. Bogotá: Facultad de Ciencias Humanas, Universidad Nacional de Colombia, 179–204.

———. 1999. "Política y organización de poblaciones negras en Colombia." Working Paper Number 39. Cali: Universidad del Valle, Facultad de Ciencias Sociales y Económicas.

Alberti, Verena, and Amilcar Pereira. 2007. *Histórias do movimento negro no Brasil: depoimentos ao CPDOC*. São Paulo: Fundação Getulio Vargas CPDOC.

———. 2006. "A defesa das cotas como estratégia política do movimento negro contemporâneo." *Estudos Históricos* 1(37): 143–166.

Alberto, Paulina. 2011. *Terms of Inclusion: Black Intellectuals in Twentieth-Century Brazil*. Chapel Hill: University of North Carolina Press.

Alvarez, Sonia E. 1999. "Advocating Feminism: The Latin American Feminist NGO 'Boom.'" *International Feminist Journal of Politics* 1(2): 181–209.

———. 1990. *Engendering Democracy in Brazil: Women's Movements in Politics*. Princeton, NJ: Princeton University Press.

Alvarez, Sonia E., with Evelina Dagnino and Arturo Escobar, eds. 1998. *Cultures of Politics, Politics of Culture: Re-visioning Latin American Social Movements*. Boulder, CO: Westview Press.

Alves dos Santos, Ivair Augusto. 2006. *O movimento negro eo Estado (1983–1987): o caso do Conselho de Participação e Desenvolvimento da Comunidade Negra no Governo de São Paulo*. São Paulo: Imprensa Oficial.

Amenta, Edwin, Neal Caren, Elizabeth Chiarello, and Yang Su. 2010. "The Political Consequences of Social Movements." *Annual Review of Sociology* 36: 287–307.

Anaya, S. James. 2004. *Indigenous Peoples in International Law*. New York: Oxford University Press.

Anderson, Mark. 2007. "When Afro Becomes (Like) Indigenous: Garifuna and Afro-Indigenous Politics in Honduras." *Journal of Latin American and Caribbean Anthropology* 12(2): 384–413.

Andrews, George Reid. 2004. *Afro-Latin America, 1800–2000s*. New York: Oxford University Press.

———. 1991. *Blacks & Whites in São Paulo, Brazil, 1888–1988*. Madison: University of Wisconsin Press.

Appelbaum, Nancy P. 2003. *Muddied Waters: Race, Region, and Local History in Colombia, 1846–1948*. Durham, NC: Duke University Press.

Arocha, Jaime. 1998. "Inclusion of Afro-Colombians: Unreachable National Goal?" *Latin American Perspectives* 25: 70–89.

Arruti, José Maurício Andion. 2000. "Direitos étnicos no Brasil e na Colômbia: notas comparativas sobre hibridização, segmentação e mobilização política de índios e negros." *Horizontes antropológicos* 6(14): 93–123.

Asher, Kiran. 2007. "Ser y Tener: Black Women's Activism, Development, and Ethnicity in the Pacific Lowlands of Colombia." *Feminist Studies* 33(1): 11–37.

———. 2009. *Black and Green: Afro-Colombians, Development, and Nature in the Pacific Lowlands.* Durham, NC: Duke University Press.

Association of Displaced Afro-Colombians and Global Rights (AFRODES). 2009. "Life in the Face of Adversity: The Human Rights Situation of Internally Displaced Afro-Colombian Women." Bogotá: AFRODES.

Avritzer, Leonardo. 2009. *Democracy and the Public Space in Latin America.* Princeton, NJ: Princeton University Press.

Auyero, Javier. 2006. "Introductory Note to Politics under the Microscope: Special Issue on Political Ethnography I." *Qualitative Sociology* 29(3): 257–259.

Ayoub, Phillip M. 2013. "Cooperative Transnationalism in Contemporary Europe: Europeanization and Political Opportunities for LGBT Mobilization in the European Union." *European Political Science Review* 5(2): 279–310.

Azevedo, Celia Maria Marinho de. 1987. *Onda negra, medo branco: o negro no imaginário das elites—século XIX.* São Paulo: Annablume.

Baer, Werner. 1964. "Regional Inequality and Economic Growth in Brazil." *Economic Development and Cultural Change* 7(3): 268–285.

Bailey, Stanley. 2009. *Legacies of Race: Identities, Attitudes, and Politics in Brazil.* Palo Alto, CA: Stanford University Press.

Baiocchi, Gianpaolo, and Brian Conner. 2008. "The Ethnos in the Polis: Political Ethnography as a Mode of Inquiry." *Sociology Compass* 2(1): 139–155.

Baiocchi, Gianpaolo, with Patrick Heller and Marcelo K. Silva. 2008. "Making Space for Civil Society: Institutional Reform and Local Democracy in Brazil." *Social Forces* 86(3): 911–936.

Bandy, Joe, and Jackie Smith, eds. 2005. *Coalitions across Borders: Transnational Protest and the Neoliberal Order.* Lanham, MD: Rowman & Littlefield.

Banting, Keith, and Will Kymlicka, eds. 2006. *Multiculturalism and the Welfare State: Recognition and Redistribution in Contemporary Democracies: Recognition and Redistribution in Contemporary Democracies.* New York: Oxford University Press.

Barbary, Olivier, and Fernando Urrea, eds. 2004. *Gente Negra en Colombia: Dinámica Sociopolíticas en Cali y el Pacífico.* Cali: Conciencias Editora.

Bastide, Roger. 1971. *As religiões africanas no Brasil: Contribuição a uma sociologia das interpretações de civilizações.* São Paulo: Livraria Pioneira Editôra, Editôra da Universidade de São Paulo.

Beltrán, Cristina. 2010. *The Trouble with Unity: Latino Politics and the Creation of Identity.* New York: Oxford University Press.

Benford, Robert D., and David A. Snow. 2000. "Framing Processes and Social Movements: An Overview and Assessment." *Annual Review of Sociology* 26: 611–639.

Bernardo Gomes, Lilian Cristina. 2009. "Justiça Seja Feita: Direito Quilombola ao Território." Doctoral Thesis, Political Science Department, Federal University of Minas Gerais.

Bonilla-Silva, Eduardo. 2009. *Racism without Racists: Color-Blind Racism and the Persistence of Racial Inequality in America*. Lanham, MD: Rowman & Littlefield Publishers.

———. 2002. "We Are All Americans!: The Latin Americanization of Racial Stratification in the USA." *Race and Society* 5(1): 3–16.

Borges, Dain. "'Puffy, Ugly, Slothful and Inert': Degeneration in Brazilian Social Thought, 1880–1940." *Journal of Latin American Studies* 25(2): 235–256.

Bourdieu, Pierre. 1991. *Language & Symbolic Power*. Cambridge, MA: Harvard University Press.

———. 1977. *Outline of a Theory of Practice*. Vol. 16. New York: Cambridge University Press.

Bourdieu, Pierre, with Loïc Wacquant. 1999. "On the Cunning of Imperialist Reason." *Theory, Culture & Society* 16(1): 41–58.

Brubaker, Rogers, and Frederick Cooper. 2000. "Beyond 'Identity.'" *Theory and Society* 29: 1–47.

Brysk, Alison. *From Tribal Village to Global Village: Indian Rights and International Relations in Latin America*. Palo Alto, CA: Stanford University Press.

Burdick, John. 1998. *Blessed Anastácia: Women, Race, and Popular Christianity in Brazil*. New York: Routledge.

Burstein, Paul, Rachel L. Einwohner, and Jocelyn A. Hollander. 1995. "The Success of Political Movements: A Bargaining Perspective." In *The Politics of Social Protest: Comparative Perspectives on States and Social Movements*, edited by J. Craig Jenkins and Bert Klandermans. Minneapolis: University of Minnesota Press, 275–295.

Butler, Kim. 1998. *Freedoms Given, Freedoms Won: Afro-Brazilians in Post-Abolition São Paulo and Salvador*. New Brunswick, NJ: Rutgers University Press.

Caldwell, Kia. 2007. *Negras in Brazil: Re-envisioning Black Women, Citizenship, and the Politics of Identity*. New Brunswick, NJ: Rutgers University Press.

Campos, Luiz Augusto, João Feres Júnior, and Verônica Toste Daflon. 2013. "Administrando o debate público: O Globo e a controvérsia em torno das cotas raciais." *Revista Brasileira de Ciência Política* 11: 7–31.

Cárdenas, Mauricio, and Carolina Mejía. 2006. "Migraciones internacionales en Colombia: ¿qué sabemos?" *Documentos de Trabajo* 30.

Cárdenas, Roosbelinda. 2012. "Multicultural Politics for Afro-Colombians: An Articulation 'Without Guarantees.'" In *Black Social Movements in Latin America: From Monocultural Mestizaje to Multiculturalism*, edited by Jean Muteba Rahier. New York: Palgrave Macmillan, 113–134.

Cardoso Simões Pires, Antônio Liberac. 2006. *As Associações dos Homens de Cor e a Imprensa Negra Paulista: Movimientos Negros, Cultura e Política no Brasil Republicano (1915–1945)*. Belo Horizonte, Brazil: Fundação Universidade Federal do Tocantins.

Carneiro, Sueli. 2003. "Mulheres em movimento." *Estudos avançados* 17(49): 117–133.

Carrigan, Ana. 2009. *El Palacio de Justicia: Una tragedia colombiana*. Bogotá: Icono Editorial.

Carroll, Leah. 2011. *Violent Democratization, Social Movements, Elites, and Politics in Colombia's Rural War Zones, 1984–2008*. Notre Dame, IN: University of Notre Dame Press.

Carvalho, José Alberto Magno de, Charles H. Wood, and Flávia Cristina Drumond

Andrade. 2004. "Estimating the Stability of Census-Based Racial/Ethnic Classifications: The Case of Brazil." *Population Studies* 58(3): 331–343.

Castillo, Luis Carlos. 2007. *Etnicidad y Nación. El desafío de la diversidad en Colombia*. Cali: Universidad del Valle.

Castro-Gómez, Santiago, and Eduardo Restrepo. 2008. "Introducción: Colombianidad, población y diferencia." In *Genealogías de la colombianidad. Formaciones discursivas y tecnologías de gobierno en los siglos XIX y XX*, edited by Santiago Castro-Gómez and Eduardo Restrepo. Bogotá: Editorial Pontificia Universidad Javeriana,11–40.

Centeno, Miguel Angel. 2002. *Blood and Debt: War and the Nation-State in Latin America*. University Park: Pennsylvania State Press.

Centeno, Miguel Angel, and Agustin E. Ferraro, eds. 2013. *State and Nation Making in Latin America and Spain: Republics of the Possible*. New York: Cambridge University Press.

Chakrabarty, Dipesh. *Provincializing Europe: Postcolonial Thought and Historical Difference*. Princeton, NJ: Princeton University Press, 2009.

Chaves, Margarita, and Marta Zambrano. 2006. "From *Blanqueamiento* to *Reindigenización*: Paradoxes of *Mestizaje* and Multiculturalism in Contemporary Colombia." *Revista Europea de Estudios Latinoamericanos y del Caribe/European Review of Latin American and Caribbean Studies* 80: 5–23.

Clemens, Elizabeth. 1997. *The People's Lobby: Organizational Innovation and the Rise of Interest Group Politics in the United States, 1890–1925*. Chicago: University of Chicago Press.

Cohen, Cathy J. 1999. *The Boundaries of Blackness: AIDS and the Breakdown of Black Politics*. Chicago: University of Chicago Press.

Collins, Patricia Hill. 1999. *Black Feminist Thought: Knowledge, Consciousness, and the Politics of Empowerment*. New York: Routledge.

Comaroff, Jean. 2005. "The End of History, Again? Pursuing the Past in the Postcolony." In *Postcolonial Studies and Beyond*, edited by Ania Loomba, Suvir Kaul, Matti Bunzl, Antoinette Burton, and Jed Esty. Durham, NC: Duke University, 126–144.

Comaroff, John L. 1995. "Ethnicity, Nationalism, and the Politics of Difference in an Age of Revolution." *International Studies in Global Change* 7: 243–276.

Conceição, Fernando. 2005. *Como fazer amor com um negro sem se cansar: e outros textos para debate contemporãaneo da luta anti-racista no Brasil*. Rio de Janeiro: Terceira Margem.

Contins, Márcia. 2005. *Lideranças Negras*. Rio de Janeiro: Aeroplano.

Covin, David. 2006. *The Unified Black Movement in Brazil, 1978–2002*. Jefferson, NC: McFarland & Co.

Cress, Daniel M., and David A. Snow. 2000. "The Outcomes of Homeless Mobilization: The Influence of Organization, Disruption, Political Mediation, and Framing." *American Journal of Sociology* 105(4): 1063–1104.

Daflon, Verônica Toste, and João Feres Jr. 2012. "Ação afirmativa na revista Veja: estratégias editoriais e o enquadramento do debate público." *Revista Compolitica* 2(2): 65–91.

Dagnino, Evelina. 1998. "Culture, Citizenship and Democracy: Changing Discourses and Practices of the Latin American Left." In *Cultures of Politics/Politics of Cultures: Revisioning Latin American Social Movements*, edited by Sonia Alvarez, Evelina Dagnino, and Arturo Escobar. Boulder, CO: Westview Press, 33–63.

Daniel, G. Reginald. 2010. *Race and Multiraciality in Brazil and the United States: Converging Paths?* University Park: Pennsylvania State Press.

da Silva Souza, Florentina, and Leticia Maria da Souza Pereira. 2013. "Implementação da Lei 10.639/2003: mapeando embates e percalços." *Educar em Revista* 47: 51–65.

Davis, Darien, Tianna Paschel, and Judith Morrison. 2011. "Pan-Afro-Latin African Americanism Revisited: Legacies and Lessons for Transnational Alliances in the New Millennium." In *Re-Examining the Black Atlantic: Afro-Descendants and Development*, edited by Bernd Reiter. East Lansing, MI: Michigan State University Press.

de Friedemann, Nina S. 1974. *Minería, descendencia y orfebrería artesanal. Litoral pacífico.* Bogotá: Universidad Nacional de Colombia.

de Friedemann, Nina S., and Jaime Arocha. 1988. *De sol a sol: génesis, transformación y presencia de los negros en Colombia.* Bogotá: Planeta.

———. 1982. *Herederos del jaguar y la anaconda.* Bogotá: Carlos Valencia Editores.

de Friedemann, Nina S., and Carlos Patiño Roselli. 1983. *Lengua y sociedad en el Palenque de San Basilio.* Vol. 66. Bogotá: Instituto Caro y Cuervo.

Degler, Carl. 1971. *Neither Black nor White: Slavery and Race Relations in Brazil and the United States.* Madison: University of Wisconsin Press.

de la Fuente, Alejandro. 2001. *A Nation for All: Race, Inequality and Politics in Twentieth-Century Cuba.* Chapel Hill: University of North Carolina Press.

della Porta, Donatella, and Mario Diani. 1999. *Social Movements: An Introduction.* Oxford, UK: John Wiley & Sons.

del Popolo, Fabiana. 2008. *Los pueblos indígenas y afrodescendientes en las fuentes de datos: experiencias en América Latina.* Santiago de Chile: United Nations.

Dersso, Solomon A. 2010. *Perspectives on the Rights of Minorities and Indigenous Peoples in Africa.* Pretoria, South Africa: Pretoria University Law Press.

dos Santos, Marcio André. 2009. "Política Negra e Democracia no Brasil Contemporâneo: Reflexões Sobre os Movimentos Negros." In *Caminhos Convergentes: Estado e Sociedade na Superação das Desigualdades Raciais no Brasil*, edited by Marline de Paula and Rosana Heringer. Rio de Janeiro: Fundação Heinrich Böll e ActionAid Brasil, 227–258.

Dugas, John. 1993. "El desarrollo de la Asamblea Nacional Constituyente." In *La Constitución Política de 1991: ¿Un pacto político viable?*, edited by John Dugas. Bogotá: Universidad de los Andes, 15–44.

Dwyer, Augusta. 1990. *Into the Amazon: The Struggle for the Rain Forest.* San Francisco: Sierra Club Books.

Escobar, Arturo. 2008. *Territories of Difference: Place, Movements, Life, Redes.* Durham, NC: Duke University Press.

———. 2003. "Displacement, Development, and Modernity in the Colombian Pacific." *International Social Science Journal* 55(1): 157–167.

Espiritu, Yen. 1993. *Asian American Panethnicity: Bridging Institutions and Identities.* Philadelphia: Temple University Press.

Estupiñan, Juan Pablo. 2006. "Afrocolombianos y el censo 2005." *Revista de Información Básica* 1: 56–69.

Evans, Peter. 2000. "Fighting Marginalization with Transnational Networks: Counter-Hegemonic Globalization." *Contemporary Sociology* 29(1): 230–241.

Farfán-Santos, Elizabeth. 2015. "'Fraudulent' Identities: The Politics of Defining Quilombo Descendants in Brazil." *Journal of Latin American and Caribbean Anthropology* 20(1): 110–132.

Felice, William F. 1996. *Taking Suffering Seriously: The Importance of Collective Human Rights*. Albany: State University of New York Press.

Fernandes, Rubem Cesar. 1994. *Privado Porem Publico: O Terceiro Setor na America Latina*. Rio de Janeiro: Relome-Dumara.

Ferree, Myra Marx. 2002. *Shaping Abortion Discourse: Democracy and the Public Sphere in Germany and the United States*. Cambridge, UK: Cambridge University Press.

Ferrer, Ada. 1999. *Insurgent Cuba: Race, Nation, and Revolution, 1868–1898*. Chapel Hill: University of North Carolina Press.

Findlay, Eileen. 1999. *Imposing Decency: The Politics of Sexuality and Race in Puerto Rico, 1870–1920*. Durham, NC: Duke University Press.

Fitzgerald, David Scott, and David Cook-Martín. 2014. *Culling the Masses*. Cambridge, MA: Harvard University Press.

Fligstein, Neil, and Doug McAdam. 2012. *A Theory of Fields*. New York: Oxford University Press.

Fraser, Nancy. 1995. "Recognition or Redistribution? A Critical Reading of Iris Young's Justice and the Politics of Difference." *Journal of Political Philosophy* 3(2): 166–180.

French, Jan Hoffman. 2009. *Legalizing Identities: Becoming Black or Indian in Brazil's Northeast*. Chapel Hill: University of North Carolina Press.

Freyre, Gilberto. 1986 (1933). *The Masters and the Slaves: A Study in the Development of Brazilian Civilization*. Berkeley: University of California Press.

Friedman, Eli. 2009. "External Pressure and Local Mobilization: Transnational Activism and the Emergence of the Chinese Labor Movement." *Mobilization: An International Quarterly* 14(2): 199–218.

Fusté, José I. "Translating Negroes into *Negros*: Rafael Serra's Trans-American Entanglements between Black Cuban Racial and Imperial Subalternity, 1895–1909." In *Afro-Latinos in Movement: Critical Approaches to Blackness and Transnationalism in the Americas*, edited by Petra Rivera-Rideau, Jennifer Jones, and Tianna S. Paschel. New York: Palgrave Macmillan.

Gamson, William A. 1990. *The Strategy of Social Protest*, 2d ed. Belmont, CA: Wadsworth.

Gamson, William A., and David Meyer. 1996. "Framing Political Opportunity." In *Comparative Perspectives on Social Movements*, edited by Doug McAdam, John McCarthy, and Mayer Zald. New York: Cambridge University Press, 275–290.

Giugni, Marco G. 1998. "Was It Worth the Effort? The Outcomes and Consequences of Social Movements." *Annual Review of Sociology* 24: 371–393.

Giugni, Marco, and Sakura Yamasaki. 2009. "The Policy Impact of Social Movements: A Replication through Qualitative Comparative Analysis." *Mobilization: An International Quarterly* 14(4): 467–484.

Goldberg, David Theo. 2002. *The Racial State*. Malden, MA: Blackwell Publishers.

Goldman, Michael. 2005. *Imperial Nature: The World Bank and Struggles for Social Justice in the Age of Globalization*. New Haven, CT: Yale University Press.

Gomes, Nilma Lino, and Rodrigo Ednilson de Jesus. 2013. "As práticas pedagógicas de trabalho com relações étnico-raciais na escola na perspectiva de Lei 10.639/2003: desafios para a política educacional e indagações para a pesquisa." *Educar em Revista, Curitiba, Brasil* 47: 19–33.

Gonzalez, Lélia, and Carlos Alfredo Hasenbalg. 1982. *Lugar de negro*. Rio de Janeiro: Editora Marco Zero.

Goodwin, Jeff, and James M. Jasper. 1999. "Caught in a Winding, Snarling Vine: The Structural Bias of Political Process Theory." *Sociological Forum* 14(1): 27–54.

Graden, Dale Torston. 2006. *From Slavery to Freedom in Brazil: Bahia, 1835–1900*. Albuquerque: University of New Mexico Press.

Green, John. 2000. "Left Liberalism and Race in the Evolution of Colombian Popular National Identity." *Americas* 57: 95–124.

Greene, Shane. 2007. "Introduction: On Race, Roots/Routes, and Sovereignty in Latin America's Afro-Indigenous Multiculturalisms." *Journal of Latin American and Caribbean Anthropology* 12(2): 329–355.

Grueso, Libia. 2000. "El proceso organizativo de comunidades negras en el pacífico surcolombiano." Master's Thesis, Department of Political Studies, Pontificia Universidad Javeriana, Colombia.

Grueso, Libia, with Arturo Escobar and Carlos Rosero. 1998. "The Process of Black Community Organization in the Southern Pacific Coast Region of Colombia." In *Cultures of Politics/Politics of Cultures: Revisioning Latin American Social Movements*, edited by Arturo Escobar, Evelyn Dagnino, and Sonia Alvarez. Boulder, CO: Westview Press, 196–219.

Guerreiro, Almerinda. 2000. *A trama dos tambores: a música afro-pop de Salvador*. São Paulo: Editora 34.

Guidry, John A., Michael Kennedy, and Mayer Zald, eds. 2001. *Globalizations and Social Movements: Culture, Power, and the Transnational Public Sphere*. Ann Arbor: University of Michigan Press.

Guimarães, Antonio Sérgio Alfredo. 2001. "Racial Inequalities, Black Protest and Public Policies in Brazil." Conference paper for Third World Conference against Racism, Durban, South Africa.

Hale, Charles R. 2002. "Does Multiculturalism Menace? Governance, Cultural Rights and the Politics of Identity in Guatemala." *Journal of Latin American Studies* 43: 485–524.

Hall, Gillette, and Harry Anthony Patrinos, eds. *Indigenous Peoples, Poverty, and Human Development in Latin America*. New York: Palgrave Macmillan, 2006.

Hall, Stuart. 1996. "Who Needs 'Identity'?" In *Questions of Cultural Identity*, edited by Stuart Hall and Paul du Gay. London: Sage Publications, 1–17.

———. 1986. "On Postmodernism and Articulation." In *Stuart Hall: Critical Dialogues in Cultural Studies*, edited by David Morley and Kuan-Hsing Chen. New York: Routledge, 131–150.

Hamilton, Charles, and Kwame Ture. 2011. *Black Power: Politics of Liberation in America*. New York: Vintage.

Hanchard, Michael. 2003. "Acts of Misrecognition: Transnational Black Politics, Anti-imperialism and the Ethnocentrisms of Pierre Bourdieu and Loïc Wacquant." *Theory, Culture & Society* 20(4): 5–29.

———. 1994. *Orpheus and Power: The Movimento Negro of Rio de Janeiro and São Paulo, Brazil, 1945–1988*. Princeton, NJ: Princeton University Press.

Harris, Marvin. 1956. *Town and Country in Brazil*. New York: Columbia University Press.

Hasenbalg, Carlos Alfredo. 1979. *Discriminação e desigualdades raciais no Brasil*. Rio de Janeiro: Graal.

Hasenbalg, Carlos Alfredo, and Nelson do Valle Silva. 1988. *Estrutura social, mobilidade e raça*. Rio de Janeiro: Instituto Universitário de Pesquisas do Rio de Janeiro.

Hattam, Victoria. 2007. *In the Shadow of Race: Jews, Latinos, and Immigrant Politics in the United States*. Chicago: University of Chicago Press.

Helg, Aline. 2004. *Liberty and Equality in Caribbean Colombia, 1770–1835*. Chapel Hill: University of North Carolina Press.

———. 2001. *La educación en Colombia, 1918–1957: una historia social, económica y política*. Bogotá: Universidad Pedagógica Nacional.

———. 1990. "Race in Argentina and Cuba, 1880–1930: Theory, Policies, and Popular Reaction." In *The Idea of Race in Latin America: 1870–1940*, edited by Richard Graham. Austin: University of Texas Press, 37–69.

Hellwig, David J., ed. 1992. *African American Reflections on Brazil's Racial Paradise*. Philadelphia: Temple University Press.

Heringer, Rosana. 2006. "II-Participação e posicionamento politico." In *Zumbí + 10 /2005: O perfildos participantes*, edited by José da Silva, Sales Augusto dos Santos, Rosana Heringer, and Osmundo Pinho. Rio de Janeiro: Programa Políticas da Cor na Educação Brasileira.

Hernandez, Tanya Kateri. Forthcoming. "Inventing the United States in the Latin American Myth of Racial Democracy Mestizaje: What Do We Compare When We Compare?" *Latin American and Caribbean Ethnic Studies* 11(2).

Hochstetler, Kathryn. 2000. "Democratizing Pressures from Below? Social Movements in the New Brazilian Democracy." In *Democratic Brazil: Actors, Institutions, and Processes*, edited by Peter R. Kingstone and Timothy Joseph Power. Pittsburgh: University of Pittsburgh Press, 167–184.

Hoetink, Herman. 1967. *Caribbean Race Relations*. London: Oxford University Press.

Holston, James. 2008. *Insurgent Citizenship: Disjunctions of Democracy and Modernity in Brazil*. Princeton, NJ: Princeton University Press.

Hooker, Juliet. 2005. "Indigenous Inclusion/Black Exclusion: Race, Ethnicity and Multicultural Citizenship in Latin America." *Journal of Latin American Studies* 37(2): 285–310.

Htun, Mala. 2016. *Inclusion without Representation: Gender Quotas and Ethnic Reservations*. New York, NY: Cambridge University Press.

Hurtado, Teodora. 2001. "La protesta social en el Norte del Cauca y el surgimiento de la movilización étnica afrocolombiana." In *Acción colectiva, Estado y etnicidad en el Pacifico colombiano*, edited by Pardo Mauricio. Bogotá: Colciencias, Instituto Colombiano de Antropología e Historia.

Institute of Applied Economic Research (IPEA). 2014. *Planejamento, Orçamento e a Promoção da Igualdade Racial: Reflexões sobre os planos plurianuais 2004–2007 e 2008–2011*. Brasília: IPEA.

Jackson, Jean E., and Kay B. Warren. 2005. "Indigenous Movements in Latin America, 1992–2004: Controversies, Ironies, New Directions." *Annual Review of Anthropology* 34: 549–573.

Jasper, James. 2012. "Introduction: From Political Opportunity Structures to Strategic Interaction." In J. Goodwin and J. Jasper, *Contention in Context: Political Opportunities and the Emergence of Protest*. Palo Alto, CA: Stanford University Press, 1–32.

Johnson III, Ollie A. 2008. "Afro-Brazilians Politics: White Supremacy, Black Struggle, and Affirmative Action." In *Democratic Brazil Revisited*, edited by Peter R. Kingstone and Timothy J. Power. Pittsburgh: University of Pittsburgh Press, 209–230.

———. 1998. "Racial Representation and Brazilian Politics: Black Members of the National Congress, 1983–1999." *Journal of Interamerican Studies and World Affairs* 40(4): 97–118.

Kay, Tamara. 2005. "Labor Transnationalism and Global Governance: The Impact of NAFTA on Transnational Labor Relationships in North America." *American Journal of Sociology* 111(3): 715–756.

Keck, Margaret, and Kathryn Sikkink. 1998. *Activists beyond Borders: Advocacy Networks in International Politics*. Ithaca, NY: Cornell University Press.

Kelley, Robin D. G. 1994. *Race Rebels: Culture, Politics and the Black Working Class*. New York: Free Press.

Khagram, Sanjeev. 2004. *Dams and Development: Transnational Struggles for Water and Power*. Ithaca, NY: Cornell University Press.

Khittel, Stefan. 2001. "Usos de la historia y la historiografía por parte de las ONG y OB de las comunidades negras en el Chocó." In *Acción colectiva, Estado y etnicidad en el Pacífico colombiano*, edited by Mauricio Pardo. Bogotá: Colciencias-ICANH, 71–94.

Koopmans, Ruud, and Paul Statham. 1999. "Ethnic and Civic Conceptions of Nationhood and the Differential Success of the Extreme Right in Germany and Italy." In *How Social Movements Matter*, edited by Marco Giugni, Doug McAdam, and Charles Tilly. Minneapolis: University of Minnesota Press, 225–251.

Kymlicka, Will. 2007. *Multicultural Odysseys: Navigating the New International Politics of Diversity*. New York: Oxford University Press.

Lacerda, Rosane. 2008. *Os povos indígenas na Constituinte: 1987–1988*. Brasília: Conselho Indigenista Missionário.

Langer, Erick, and Elena Muñoz. 2003. *Contemporary Indigenous Movements in Latin America*. Wilmington, DE: Scholarly Resources.

Lasso, Marixa. 2007. "Un mito republicano de armonía racial: raza y patriotismo en Colombia, 1810–1812." *Revista de Estudios Sociales* 27: 32–45.

Lavalle, Adrian Gurza, and Natália S. Bueno. 2011. "Waves of Change within Civil Society in Latin America Mexico City and São Paulo." *Politics & Society* 39(3): 415–450.

Leite, Correia José. 1992. *E disse o velho militante José Correia Leite*. São Paulo: Secretaria Municipal de Cultura, Brasil.

Lennox, Corrine. 2015. "The Role of International Actors in Norm Emergence: Supporting Afro-Descendants' Rights in Latin America." In *International Approaches to Governing Ethnic Diversity*, edited by Jane Bouden and Will Kymlicka. Oxford, UK: Oxford University Press, 128–168.

Levine, Robert M. 1998. *Father of the Poor?: Vargas and His Era*. Cambridge, UK: Cambridge University Press.

Linz, Juan J., and Alfred Stepan. 2011. *Problems of Democratic Transition and Consolidation: Southern Europe, South America, and Post-Communist Europe*. Baltimore, MD: Johns Hopkins University Press.

López-Calva, Luis Felipe, and Nora Lustig, eds. 2010. *Declining Inequality in Latin America: A Decade of Progress?* Washington, DC: Brookings Institution Press.

Loveman, Mara. 2014. *National Colors: Racial Classification and the State in Latin America*. New York: Oxford University Press.

———. 2009. "The Race to Progress: Census-Taking and Nation-Making in Brazil." *Hispanic American Historical Review* 89(3): 435–470.

———. 1999. "Making 'Race' and Nation in the United States, South Africa, and Brazil: Taking Making Seriously." *Theory and Society* 28(6): 903–927.

Loveman, Mara, and Jeronimo O. Muniz. 2007. "How Puerto Rico Became White: Boundary Dynamics and Intercensus Racial Reclassification." *American Sociological Review* 72(6): 915–939.

Lukács, Georg, and György Lukács. 1971. *History and Class Consciousness: Studies in Marxist Dialectics*. Vol. 215. Cambridge: Massachusetts Institute of Technology Press.

Luna, Francisco Vidal, and Herbert S. Klein. 2014. *The Economic and Social History of Brazil since 1889*. New York: Cambridge University Press.

Maggie, Yvonne, and Peter Fry. 2004. "A reserva de vagas para negros nas universidade brasileiras." *Estudos Avançados* 18(50): 67–80.

Magnoli, Demétrio. 2009. *Uma gota de sangue: história do pensamento racial*. São Paulo: Contexto.

Mainwaring, Scott, and Matthew Soberg Shugart. 1997. *Presidentialism and Democracy in Latin America*. New York: Cambridge University Press.

Martins, Sergio da Silva, Carlos Alberto Medeiros, and Elisa Larkin Nascimento. 2004. "Paving Paradise: The Road from 'Racial Democracy' to Affirmative Action in Brazil." *Journal of Black Studies* 34(6): 787–816.

Marx, Anthony. 1998. *Making Race and Nation: A Comparison of the United States, South Africa, and Brazil*. New York: Cambridge University Press.

Mason, Ann. 2004. "Colombia's Conflict and Theories of World Politics." Contemporary Conflicts Series, Social Science Research Council. Available at http://conconflicts.ssrc.org/andes/mason/ (accessed January 23, 2016).

McAdam, Doug. 2010. *Political Process and the Development of Black Insurgency, 1930–1970*. Chicago: University of Chicago Press.

McAdam, Doug, Sidney Tarrow, and Charles Tilly. 2001. *Dynamics of Contention*. Cambridge, UK: Cambridge University Press.

McCammon, Holly J., Courtney Sanders Muse, Harmony D. Newman, and Teresa M. Terrell. 2007. "Movement Framing and Discursive Opportunity Structures: The Political Successes of the U.S. Women's Jury Movements." *American Sociological Review* 72(5): 725–749.

McClintock, Anne. 2013. *Imperial Leather: Race, Gender, and Sexuality in the Colonial Contest*. New York: Routledge.

Melo, Jairo. 2015. "The Intersection of Race, Class, and Ethnicity in Agrarian Inequalities, Identities, and the Social Resistance of Peasants in Colombia." *Current Sociology* 63: 1017–1036.

Merry, Sally Engle. 2009. *Human Rights and Gender Violence: Translating International Law into Local Justice.* Chicago: University of Chicago Press.

Meyer, David S. 1993. "Institutionalizing Dissent: The United States Structure of Political Opportunity and the End of the Nuclear Freeze Movement." *Sociological Forum* 8(2): 157–179.

Meyer, David S., and Sidney Tarrow, eds. 1998. *The Social Movement Society: Contentious Politics for a New Century.* Lanham, MD: Rowman & Littlefield.

Milkman, Ruth. 1986. "Women's History and the Sears Case." *Feminist Studies* 12(2): 375–400.

Mitchell, Michael. 1998. "Blacks and Abertura Democratica." In *Blackness in Latin America and the Caribbean: Eastern South America and the Caribbean.* Bloomington: Indiana University Press, 75–98.

Mora, G. Cristina. 2014. *Making Hispanics: How Activists, Bureaucrats, and Media Constructed a New American.* Chicago: University of Chicago Press.

Morris, Aldon. 2000. "Reflections on Social Movement Theory: Criticisms and Proposals." *Contemporary Sociology* 29(3): 445–454.

Mosquera, Sergio A. 2004. *La Gente Negra en la Legislación Colonial.* Bogotá: Editorial Lealon.

Mosquera Rosero-Labbé, Claudia, and Ruby Esther León Díaz. 2009. "Acciones Afirmativas en Colombia: entre paradojas y superposiciones de lógicas políticas y académicas." In *Acciones afirmativas y ciudadanía diferenciada étnico-racial negra, afrocolombiana, palenquera y raizal: Entre bicentenerios de las independecias y Constitución Política de 1991,* edited by Claudia Mosquera Rosero and Ruby Esther León Díaz. Bogotá: Universidad Nacional de Colombia, Facultad de Ciencias Humanas, Centro de Estudios Sociales, i–xxvi.

Moura, Ana Carolina, M.L.S. Braga, and Eliane Veras Soares. 2009. "A Lei 10.639/03: da luta política à implementação." *Agenda Social* 3(2): 78–120.

Munanga, Kabengele, and Nilma Gomes. 2005. *Para Entender o Negro no Brasil de Hoje: História, realidades, problemas e Caminhos.* São Paulo: Global.

Múnera, Alfonso. 2005. *Fronteras imaginadas. La construcción de las razas y de la geografía en el Siglo XIX colombiano.* Bogotá: Editorial Planeta.

Murray Li, Tania. 2000. "Articulating Indigenous Identity in Indonesia: Resource Politics and the Tribal Slot." *Comparative Studies in Society and History* 42(1): 149–179.

Nagel, Joanne. 1994. "Constructing Ethnicity: Creating and Recreating Ethnic Identity and Culture." *Social Problems* 41:152–176.

Ng'weno, Bettina. 2007a. "Can Ethnicity Replace Race? Afro-Colombians, Indigeneity and the Colombian Multicultural State." *Journal of Latin American and Caribbean Anthropology* 12(2): 414–440.

———. 2007b. *Turf Wars: Territory and Citizenship in the Contemporary State.* Palo Alto, CA: Stanford University Press.

Nobles, Melissa. 2000. *Shades of Citizenship: Race and the Census in Modern Politics.* Palo Alto, CA: Stanford University Press.

Okamoto, Dina, and G. Cristina Mora. 2014. "Panethnicity." *Annual Review of Sociology* 40(1): 219–239.

Omi, Michael, and Howard Winant. 1989. *Racial Formation in the United States from the 1960s to the 1980s.* New York: Routledge.

Oslender, Ulrich. 2008. *Comunidades negras y espacio en el Pacífico Colombiano: Hacia un giro geográfico en el estudio de los movimientos sociales.* Bogotá: Instituto Colombiano de Antropología e Historia/Universidad Colegio Mayor de Cundinamarca, Universidad del Cauca. Colombia.

Paixão, Marcelo, Irene Rosseto, Rabiana Montovanele, and Luiz M. Carvano. 2010. *Relatório Anual das Desigualdades Raciais no Brasil 2009–2010: Constituição Cidadã, seguridade social e seus efeitos sobre as assimetrias de cor ou raça.* Rio de Janeiro: Editora Garamond Ltda.

Palacios, Marco. 2006. *Between Legitimacy and Violence: A History of Colombia, 1875–2002.* Durham, NC: Duke University Press.

Palmer, Steven. 1993. "Getting to Know the Unknown Soldier: Official Nationalism in Liberal Costa Rica, 1880–1900." *Journal of Latin American Studies* 25(1): 45–72.

Paschel, Tianna S. 2013. "'The Beautiful Faces of My Black People': Race, Ethnicity, and the Politics of Colombia's 2005 Census." *Ethnic and Racial Studies* 36(10): 1544–1563.

———. 2010. "The Right to Difference: Explaining Colombia's Shift from Color Blindness to the Law of Black Communities." *American Journal of Sociology* 116(3): 729–69.

Paschel, Tianna S., with Mark Sawyer. 2008. "Contesting Politics as Usual: Black Social Movements, Globalization, and Race Policy in Latin America." *SOULS: A Critical Journal of Black Politics, Society and Culture* 10(3): 197–214.

Pedrosa, Alvaro, et al. 1996. "Movimiento negro, identidad y territorio: entrevista con la Organización de Comunidades Negras." In *Pacífico: ¿desarrollo o diversidad? Estado, capital y movimientos sociales en el Pacífico colombiano*, edited by Arturo Escobar and Alvaro Pedrosa. Bogotá: CEREC, 245–265.

Pereira, Amilcar. 2013. *O Mundo Negro: Relações raciais e a constituição do Movimento Negro contemporâneo no Brasil.* Rio de Janeiro: Pallas.

Perry, Keisha-Khan Y. 2013. *Black Women against the Land Grab: The Fight for Racial Justice in Brazil.* Minneapolis: University of Minnesota Press.

Pierson, Donald. 1942. *Negroes in Brazil: A Study of Race Contact at Bahia.* Chicago: University of Chicago Press.

Piven, Frances Fox, and Richard A. Cloward. 1977. *Poor People's Movements: Why They Succeed, How They Fail.* Washington, DC: Brookings Institution Press.

Postero, Nancy Grey, and León Zamosc. 2006. "The Struggle for Indigenous Rights in Latin America." *Journal of Latin American Anthropology* 11(1): 208–210.

Priestley, George, and Alberto Barrow. 2008. "The Black Movement in Panamá: A Historical and Political Interpretation, 1994–2004." *SOULS: A Critical Journal of Black Politics, Culture, and Society* 10(3): 227–255.

Proceso de Comunidades Negras (PCN). 2006. *Y el Chocolate espeso: Evaluacion del censo general y la pregunta de autoreconocimiento étnico entre afrocolombianos.* Bogotá: Proceso de Comunidades Negras.

Purcell, Trevor W. 1993. *Banana Fallout: Class, Color, and Culture among West Indians in Costa Rica.* Los Angeles: Center for Afro-American Studies, University of California.

Quijano, Aníbal. 2000. "Coloniality of Power and Eurocentrism in Latin America." *International Sociology* 15(2): 215–232.

Racusen, Seth. 2010. "Fictions of Identity and Brazilian Affirmative Action." *National Black Law Journal* 21(3).

Rahier, Jean Muteba, ed. 2012. *Black Social Movements in Latin America: From Monocultural Mestizaje to Multiculturalism*. New York: Palgrave Macmillan.

Rana, Junaid. 2011. "The Language of Terror: Panic, Peril, Racism." In *State of White Supremacy: Racism, Governance, and the United States*, edited by Moon-Kie Jung, João Costa Vargas, and Eduardo Bonilla-Silva. Palo Alto, CA: Stanford University Press.

Rappaport, Joanne. 2005. *Intercultural Utopias: Public Intellectuals, Cultural Experimentation, and Ethnic Dialogue in Colombia*. Durham, NC: Duke University Press.

Rausch, Jane M. 2000. "Diego Luis Cordoba and the Emergence of Afro-Colombian Identity in the Mid-Twentieth Century." *Secolas Annals* 32: 51–65.

Ray, Raka. 1999. *Fields of Protest: Women's Movements in India*. Minneapolis: University of Minnesota Press.

Restrepo, Eduardo. 2013. *Etnización de la negridad: la invención de las "comunidades negras" como grupo étnico en Colombia*. Popayán, Colombia: Universidad del Cauca.

———. 2007. "Imágenes del 'negro' y nociones de raza en Colombia a principios del siglo XX." *Revista de Estudios Sociales* 27: 46–61.

———. 2004. "Ethnicization of Blackness in Colombia: Toward De-Racializing Theoretical and Political Imagination." *Cultural Studies* 18: 698–715.

———. 2001. "Imaginando comunidad negra: Etnografía de la etnización de las poblaciones negras en el Pacífico sur colombiano." In *Acción colectiva, Estado y etnicidad en el Pacífico colombiano*, edited by Mauricio Pardo. Bogotá: Instituto Colombiano de Antropología e Historia Colciencias, 41–70.

Restrepo, Eduardo, with Santiago Castro-Gómez. 2008. "Colombianidad, población y diferencia." In *Genealogías de la colombianidad: Formaciones discursivas y tecnologias de gobierno en los siglos XIX y XX*, edited by Santiago Castro-Gómez and Eduardo Restrepo. Bogotá: Pontifica Universidad Javeriana, 10–32.

Ribeiro, M. 1995. "Mulheres negras brasileiras: de Bertioga e Beijing." *Revista Estudos Feministas* 2: 446–457.

Rivera, Luz Ángela Herrera, Martha Cecilia García Velandia, Sergio Andrés Coronado, Alejandro Cadena Benavides, Margareth A. Figueroa Garzón, and Andrés Yepes. 2012. *Minería, conflictos sociales y violación de derechos humanos en Colombia*. Bogotá: Centro de Investigación y Educación Popular / Programa por la Paz.

Rodrigues, Cristiano Santos. 2014. "Reforma constitucional, políticas públicas e desigualdades raciais no Brasil e Colômbia: Um (breve) apontamento analítico." *Revista de História Comparada* 8(1): 236–274.

Rodrigues, Cristiano Santos, and Marco Aurélio Maximo Prado. 2010. "Movimento de mulheres negras: trajetória política, práticas mobilizatórias e articulações com o Estado brasileiro." *Psicologia & Sociedade* 22 (3): 445–456.

Rodriguez, Clara E. 2000. *Changing Race: Latinos, the Census, and the History of Ethnicity in the United States*. New York: New York University Press.

Rodríguez Garavito, César, Tatiana Alfonso Sierra, and Isabel Cavelier Adarve. 2008. *The Right Not to Be Discriminated Against: The First Report on Racial Discrimination and the Rights of the Afro-Colombian Population*. Bogotá: Universidad Los Andes.

Sabóia, Gilberto Vergne, and Alexandre Jose Porto. 2001. "A Conferencia Mundial de Durban e o Brasil." In *Direitos Humanos: Atualização do Debate*. Brasília: Ministerio das Relações Exteriores, 21–26.

Sánchez, Enrique, and García, Paola. 2006. *Más allá de los promedios: afrodescendientes en América Latina. Los afrocolombianos*. Washington, DC: World Bank.

Sánchez, Enrique, and Roldán, Roque. 2002. *Titulación de los Territorios Comunales Afrocolombianos e Indígenas en la Costa Pacífica de Colombia*. Washington, DC: Banco Mundial.

Sánchez, Enrique, Roque Roldán, and María Fernanda Sánchez. 1993. *Los pueblos indígenas y negros en la Constitución Política de Colombia de 1991*. Bogotá: Disloque editores.

Sanders, James. 2004. *Contentious Republicans: Popular Politics, Race, and Class in Nineteenth-Century Colombia*. Durham, NC: Duke University Press.

Sawyer, Mark. 2006. *Racial Politics in Post-Revolutionary Cuba*. New York: Cambridge University Press.

Schatz, Edward, ed. 2013. *Political Ethnography: What Immersion Contributes to the Study of Power*. Chicago: University of Chicago Press.

Schwartz, Stuart B. 1974. "The Manumission of Slaves in Colonial Brazil: Bahia, 1684–1745." *Hispanic American Historical Review* 54: 603–635.

Schwegler, Armin. 2002. "On the (African) Origins of Palenquero Subject Pronouns." *Diachronica* 19(2): 273–332.

Scott, David. 2004. *Conscripts of Modernity: The Tragedy of Colonial Enlightenment*. Durham, NC: Duke University Press.

Scott, James C. 1990. *Domination and the Arts of Resistance: Hidden Transcripts*. New Haven, CT: Yale University Press.

Scott, Joan W. 1988. "Deconstructing Equality-versus-Difference: Or, the Uses of Poststructuralist Theory for Feminism." *Feminist Studies* 14(1): 32–50.

Sheriff, Robin E. 2001. *Dreaming Equality: Color, Race, and Racism in Urban Brazil*. New Brunswick, NJ: Rutgers University Press.

Sieder, Rachel, ed. 2002. *Multiculturalism in Latin America*. New York: Palgrave Macmillan.

Skidmore, Thomas. 2002. "Raízes de Gilberto Freyre." *Journal of Latin American Studies* 34(1): 1–20.

———. 1999. *Brazil: Five Centuries of Change*. Oxford, UK: Oxford University Press.

———. 1993. *Black into White: Race and Nationality in Brazilian Thought*. Oxford, UK: Oxford University Press.

———. 1990. *The Politics of Military Rule in Brazil, 1964–1985*. Oxford, UK: Oxford University Press.

Skrentny, John D. 2002. *The Minority Rights Revolution*. Cambridge, MA: Belknap Press, Harvard University Press.

Sloan, Ariel. 2007. "Black Identity Formation as Racial Politics in São Luis, Maranhão, Brazil." Unpublished manuscript.

Smith, Christen A. 2016. *Afro-Paradise: Blackness, Violence and Performance in Brazil*. Champaign: University of Illinois Press.

———. 2013. "Strange Fruit: Brazil, Necropolitics, and the Transnational Resonance of Torture and Death." *SOULS: A Critical Journal of Black Politics, Culture, and Society* 15(3): 177–198.

Smith, Sandra Susan, and Jennifer Anne Meri Jones. 2011. "Intraracial Harassment on Campus: Explaining Between-and-within-Group Differences." *Ethnic and Racial Studies* 34(9): 1567–1593.

Smith, T. Lynn. 1996. "The Racial Composition of the Population of Colombia." *Journal of Inter-American Studies* 8(2): 212–235.

Snow, David A., and Robert D. Benford. 1988. "Ideology, Frame Resonance, and Participant Mobilization." *International Social Movement Research* 1: 197–217.

Snow, David A., E. Burke Rochford Jr., Steven K. Worden, and Robert D. Benford. 1986. "Frame Alignment Processes, Micromobilization and Movement Participation." *American Sociological Review* 51: 464–481.

Stepan, Nancy Leys. 1991. *The Hour of Eugenics: Race, Gender, and Nation in Latin America*. Ithaca, NY: Cornell University Press.

Stolcke, Verena. 1989. *Marriage, Class, and Color in Nineteenth-Century Cuba: A Study of Racial Attitudes and Sexual Values in a Slave Society*. Ann Arbor: University of Michigan Press.

Stoler, Ann Laura. 2002. *Carnal Knowledge and Imperial Power: Race and the Intimate in Colonial Rule*. Berkeley: University of California Press.

Sue, Christina A. 2013. *Land of the Cosmic Race: Race Mixture, Racism, and Blackness in Mexico*. New York: Oxford University Press.

Sue, Christina, and Tanya Golash-Boza. 2013. "'It Was Only a Joke': How Racial Humour Fuels Colour-blind Ideologies in Mexico and Peru." *Ethnic and Racial Studies* 36(10): 1582–1598.

Tamayo, Jorge. 1993. *Las gentes del Choco*, edited by Pablo Leyva, Colombia Pacifico: Tomo II.

Tannenbaum, Frank. 1947. *Slave and Citizen*. New York: Alfred A. Knopf.

Tarrow, Sidney. 2005. *The New Transnational Activism*. Cambridge, UK: Cambridge University Press.

———. 1998. *Power in Movement: Social Movements, Collective Action, and Politics*. New York: Cambridge University Press.

Taylor, Verta. 1989. "Social Movement Continuity: The Women's Movement in Abeyance." *American Sociological Review* 54(5): 761–775.

Telles, Edward. 2007. "Race and Ethnicity and Latin America's United Nations Millennium Development Goals." *Latin American and Caribbean Ethnic Studies* 2(2): 185–200.

———. 2004. *Race in Another America: The Significance of Skin Color in Brazil*. Princeton, NJ: Princeton University Press.

———. 1999. "Ethnic Boundaries and Political Mobilization among African Brazilians: Comparisons with the U.S. Case." In *Racial Politics in Contemporary Brazil*, edited by Michael Hanchard. Durham, NC: Duke University Press, 82–97.

Telles, Edward, and Tianna Paschel. 2014. "Who Is Black, White, or Mixed Race in Latin America? How Skin Color, Status and Nation Shape Racial Classification in Latin America." *American Journal of Sociology* 120(3): 1–45.

Tilly, Charles. 1999. "From Interactions to Outcomes in Social Movements." In *How Social Movements Matter*, edited by Marco Giugni, Doug McAdam, and Charles Tilly. Minneapolis: University of Minnesota Press, 253–270.

Tilly, Charles, and Sidney Tarrow. 2007. *Contentious Politics*. Boulder, CO: Paradigm Publishers.

Treviño González, Mónica. 2009. "Opportunities and Challenges for the Afro-Brazilian Movement." In *Brazil's New Racial Politics*, edited by Bernd Reiter and Gladys L. Mitchell. Boulder, CO: Lynne Rienner Publishers, 123–140.

True, Jacqui, and Michael Mintrom. 2001. "Transnational Networks and Policy Diffusion: The Case of Gender Mainstreaming." *International Studies Quarterly* 45(1): 27–57.

Tsutsui, Kiyoteru, and Hwa-Ji Shin. 2008. "Global Norms, Local Activism and Social Movement Outcomes: Global Human Rights and Resident Koreans in Japan." *Social Problems* 55(3): 391–418.

Turner, Michael J. 2002. "The Road to Durban—and Back." *NACLA Report on the Americas* 35(6): 31–35.

Uribe, Jaime Jaramillo. 1963. "Esclavos y señores en la sociedad colombiana del siglo XVIII." *Anuario Colombiano de Historia Social y de la Cultura* 1(1): 5–76.

Valle Evangelista, Carlos Augusto. 2004. "Direitos indígenas: o debate na Constituinte de 1988." Master's Thesis, Universidade Federal do Rio de Janeiro.

Van Cott, Donna Lee. 2006. "Multiculturalism versus Neoliberalism in Latin America." In *Multiculturalism and the Welfare State: Recognition and Redistribution in Contemporary Democracies*, edited by Keith Banting and Will Kymlicka. Oxford, UK: Oxford University Press, 272–296.

———. 2002. "Constitutional Reform in the Andes: Redefining Indigenous-State Relation." In *Multiculturalism in Latin America: Indigenous Rights, Diversity and Democracy*, edited by Rachel Sieder. New York: Palgrave Macmillan, 45–73.

———. 2000. *The Friendly Liquidation of the Past: The Politics of Diversity in Latin America*. Pittsburgh: University of Pittsburgh Press.

———. 1996. "Unity through Diversity: Ethnic Politics and Democratic Deepening in Colombia." *Nationalism and Ethnic Politics* 2(4): 523–549.

Viáfara, Carlos, Fernando Urrea-Giraldo, and Juan Byron Correa Fonnegra. 2009. "Desigualdades sociodemográficas y socioeconómicas, mercado laboral y discriminación étnico-racial en Colombia: análisis estadístico como sustento de acciones afirmativas a favor de la población afrocolombiana." In *Acciones Afirmativas y ciudadanía diferenciada étnico-racial negra, afrocolombiana, palenquera y raizal: entre bicentenarios de las independencias y constitución de 1991*, edited by Claudia Mosquera Rosero Labbé and Ruby León Díaz. Bogotá: Universidad Nacional de Colombia, Facultad de Ciencias Humanas, 153–346.

Viveros Vigoya, Mara. 2016. "Social Mobility, Whiteness and Whitening in Colombia." *Journal of Latin American and Caribbean Anthropology* 20(3): 496–512.

Wacquant, Loic. 1997. "For an Analytic of Racial Domination." *Political Power and Social Theory* 11(1): 221–234.

Wade, Peter. 2014. *Mestizo Genomics: Race Mixture, Nation, and Science in Latin America*. Edited by Carlos López Beltrán, Eduardo Restrepo, and Ricardo Ventura Santos. Durham, NC: Duke University Press.

———. 2013. "Blackness, Indigeneity, Multiculturalism and Genomics in Brazil, Colombia and Mexico." *Journal of Latin American Studies* 45(2): 205–233.

———. 2009. "Defining Blackness in Colombia." *Journal de la Société des Américanistes* 95(1): 165–184.

———. 2005. "Rethinking Mestizaje: Ideology and Lived Experience." *Journal of Latin American Studies* 37(2): 239–257.

———. 2003. "Repensando el *mestizaje*." *Revista Colombiana de Antropología* 39: 273–296.

———. 2000. *Music, Race, and Nation: Música Tropical in Colombia*. Chicago: University of Chicago Press.

———. 1998. "The Cultural Politics of Blackness in Colombia." In *Central America and Northern and Western South America*, volume 1 of *Blackness in Latin America and the Caribbean: Social Dynamics and Cultural Transformations*, edited by Norman E. Whitten Jr. and Arlene Torres. Bloomington: Indiana University Press, 311–334.

———. 1997. *Race and Ethnicity in Latin America*. London: Pluto.

———. 1993. *Blackness and Race Mixture: The Dynamics of Racial Identity in Colombia*. Baltimore, MD: Johns Hopkins University Press.

Wedeen, Lisa. 2013. "Ethnography as Interpretive Exercise." In *Political Ethnography: What Immersion Contributes to the Study of Power*, edited by Edward Schatz. Chicago: University of Chicago Press, 75–94.

Williams, Daryle. 2001. *Culture Wars in Brazil: The First Vargas Regime, 1930–1945*. Durham, NC: Duke University Press.

Williams, Robert A. 1990. "Encounters on the Frontiers of International Human Rights Law: Redefining the Terms of Indigenous Peoples' Survival in the World." *Duke Law Journal* 4: 660–704.

Winant, Howard. 2001. *The World Is a Ghetto: Race and Democracy since World War II*. New York: Basic Books.

Winddance Twine, France. 1998. *Racism in a Racial Democracy: The Maintenance of White Supremacy in Brazil*. New Brunswick, NJ: Rutgers University Press.

Wouters, M. 2001. "Ethnic Rights under Threat: The Black Peasant Movement against Armed Group's Pressure in the Chocó, Colombia." *Bulletin of Latin American Research* 20 (4): 498–519.

Wright, Michelle. 2004. *Becoming Black: Creating Identity in the African Diaspora*. Durham, NC: Duke University Press.

Wright, Winthrop R. 1990. *Café con Leche: Race, Class, and National Image in Venezuela*. Austin: University of Texas Press.

Yashar, Deborah. 2005. *Contesting Citizenship in Latin America: The Rise of Indigenous Movements and the Postliberal Challenge*. New York: Cambridge University Press.

———. 1999. "Democracy, Indigenous Movements, and the Postliberal Challenge in Latin America." *World Politics* 52: 76–104.

ACKNOWLEDGMENTS

L ike any project of this magnitude, this book reflects the support, work, contributions, and patience of many people. When I took my first job in the Department of Political Science at the University of Chicago, I did so knowing that this book would very much be a product of that place. This book is the result of years of critical dialogue with my generous colleagues at U of C. I would especially like to thank Cathy Cohen for her generous feedback on this work, as well as her mentorship and friendship over the years. She not only offered me her time and brilliance, she also showed me what intellectual rigor and a deep commitment to political struggles and to family looks like in practice. I would also like to thank Bernard Harcourt for his friendship and mentorship and for convincing me, almost single-handedly, that the University of Chicago was the best place for me at the time. It indeed was. I am also deeply appreciative of the feedback I received from Michael Dawson, Dan Slater, Lisa Wedeen, Stan Markus, Iza Hussin, Alberto Simpser, Monika Nalepa, Ben Lessing, Mike Albertus, and Paul Staniland. They always met me where I was, and pushed me on substantive, not disciplinary, grounds. I am also thankful for the many other intellectual spaces from which I benefited at Chicago, among them the Workshop in Latin America and the Caribbean, the Race and Racial Ideologies Workshop and the Comparative Politics Workshop. My life in Chicago would have been extremely unbalanced were it not for the friendships of Micere Keels, Adrienne Brown, Rachel Jean-Baptiste, Gina Samuels, Kristen Schilt, Forest Stuart, Chase Joynt, Meghan Morris, Sylvia Zamora, Jasmine Johnson and Josh Begley, who all, in their different ways, sustained me both personally and intellectually throughout my time there.

I would also like to thank Meagan Levinson—my editor at Princeton University Press—for believing in this book, and for approaching the entire project with the eye of a thoughtful curator. I am also grateful for the feedback I received from anonymous reviewers as well as the extensive comments from Peter Wade, Michèle Lamont, David Theo Goldberg, and César Rodríguez, all of whom took a few days out of their lives to attend my book workshop in May 2014. A heartfelt thanks is also in order to Charlie Hale and Mara Loveman, who read every page of the manuscript and gave me page-by-page edits. While the generosity of all of these individuals made this a more interesting book, I also realize that I may not have fully addressed all of their concerns. Indeed, some of their provocations will be the source of many intellectual debates to come. I welcome them. Additionally, I would like to thank Ruth Homrighaus and Kathleen Kearns, who both provided exceptional editing at different stages of this book's development.

This book originally began as a dissertation in the Department of Sociology at UC Berkeley. It still bears the mark of my time there, where everyone had the intellectual audacity to engage with work beyond their subfields, and beyond their geographic areas. I would first like to thank the chair of my dissertation committee, Peter Evans. His constant encouragement and confidence in my work from the very beginning afforded me lots of autonomy to develop my own ideas, and to take unexpected turns in my research and professional journey. He was a model for what generous mentorship looks like, and through his own work, inspired me to make my work relevant beyond the ivory towers.

This book would also not have been possible without the unwavering support, guidance, and critical feedback of my other dissertation committee members at Berkeley. They each brought unique expertise in the different substantive areas to which this book speaks. Sandra Smith was not only a committee member but also a mentor and dear friend throughout my time at Berkeley. I thank her deeply for her sincerity and for never requiring me to leave my personal life at the door. Raka Ray was also a believer in this project from the beginning. Her work on women's movements in India was also particularly inspiring for the present study. I am also deeply appreciative for Taeku Lee, who used his razor-sharp ability to ask just the right question at the right time. All of them were critical for the development of the dissertation that became this book.

Beyond my committee at Berkeley, I relied on a broader intellectual community. In this vein, I'd like to thank Marcel Paret, Heidi Sarabia, Trevor Gardner, Dawn Dow, Abigail Andrews, Simon Morfit, Juan Herrera, Dan Buch, Eli Friedman, Ryan Centner, Hana Brown, and Kimberly Hoang, who were all generous and gave me critical feedback on my work time and time again. Shannon Gleeson and Ruha Benjamin were my intellectual big sisters at Berkeley. They were generous with their time and helped me navigate the idiosyncrasies of this profession. I'm also thankful for the Department of African American Studies, which was my second intellectual home. They also were the main supporter of the Afro-Latino Working Group—a group I co-founded with Petra Rivera-Rideau, Vielka Cecilia Hoy, Jennifer Jones, Ryan Rideau, and Rebecca Bodenheimer—and which was so critical to my formation as a scholar. It was through those conversations that I was forced to think about the issues I cared about in more interdisciplinary ways, and where I was able to meet scholars of Afro-Latin America from around the country. Kara Young and Margo Mahan not only offered feedback on this book at various stages, they were my family in the Bay Area. I will also be grateful for the kind of work-life balance we achieved together, especially in Petrolia. I was also privileged to have many friends outside of academia. All of the beautiful dancers, drummers, and singers of Emesé at the Malonga Arts Center in Oakland always kept me grounded throughout the emotional rollercoaster of graduate school, at the same time that they lifted me up.

Just a few months before I finished this book, I found myself at Berkeley again, this time as a faculty member in the Department of African American Studies. My engagement with my new colleagues during the visit and my first year on campus was crucial for developing a more sophisticated way of thinking about the relationships between black identity, consciousness, and politicization. I would especially like to thank Ula Taylor, Brandi Wilkins Catanese, Darieck Scott, Nikki Jones, Leigh Raiford, Na'ilah Nasir, Jovan Lewis, Stephen Small, and Chi Elliot for all of their feedback and support over the last year.

Yet while this book is very much a product of the Berkeley, the University of Chicago, and Berkeley again, I was also privileged to have a host of mentors and interlocutors outside of these institutions who also contributed to this book project and to my intellectual development overall. First, I would also like to give my sincerest thanks to Edward Telles, who while an official member of my dissertation committee, was actually much more than that. Over the last decade and a half, I have (somewhat) jokingly referred to him as my intellectual *padrino*. It makes sense. I've known him since I was an undergrad at UCLA and he is the reason I became a sociologist. He made me realize before it was too late that my political commitments, and the many things that intrigued me in my travels to Latin America, could actually be the basis of my research and my career. Mark Sawyer also deserves special mention. Mark was convinced that I was capable of doing this many years before I was myself convinced. He was a mentor, friend, and colleague throughout every stage of my career and I am extremely grateful for his support and encouragement. He was incredibly generous, egalitarian, and feminist in all of the collaborations upon which we embarked, including co-authored publications. If this were more common in academia, it would be an entirely different place. Much love and much respect to you Mark!

I also benefited greatly from having a larger global community of colleagues and mentors with whom I engaged throughout this project, including Chris Zepeda-Millán, Gianpaolo Baiocchi, Isar Goudreau, Charlie Hale, Emiko Saldivar, Sonia Alvarez, Michèle Lamont, Amilcar Perreira, Rosana Heringer, Mala Htun, Luisa Schwartzman, Judith Morrison, Tanya Golash-Boza, Anthony Dest, Cristiano Rodrigues, Eduardo Bonilla-Silva, Ollie Johnson, Michael Hanchard, Graziella Morães Dias da Silva, Ann Orloff, Patrick Heller, Antônio Sérgio Guimarães, Mario Small, Roosbelinda Cárdenas,

Barbara Ransby, Miriam Jiménez-Román, Tukufu Zuberi, Hector Perla, Juan Flores, Celia Lacayo, Peter Wade, Christina Sue, Tony Chen, Tanya Kateri Hernandez, Erica Simmons, Agustín Lao-Montes, and Cristina Mora. I am thankful for them as I am for Keisha-Khan Perry, Juliet Hooker, and Christen Smith, who all not only engaged deeply with my work, but also took on the role of informal mentors/sisters to me. Thank you.

Ultimately, though, this book would not have been possible without the generosity and contributions of the many black activists, government officials, and academics in Colombia and Brazil who took out time to allow me to interview them, provided me with information, and allowed me to tag along to many events and meetings. They were much more than research "subjects" or "participants." Each one of them, through their own complex analyses of race and politics, contributed to both descriptive and conceptual aspects of this book. I am deeply grateful to, and humbled by, them. While these some one hundred people are too numerous to name, there were a few individuals who were especially important during my time in the field who deserve special mention.

Francia Marquez, Carlos Rosero, Charo Mina Rojas, Daniel Garcés Carabalí, Konty Bikila Cifuentes, Mario Angulo, Libia Grueso, and Hamington Valencia of Proceso de Comunidades (PCN) were extremely generous with their time and support. They opened up their homes, archives and hearts to me, and I would like to express my gratitude to all of them. Carlos, in particular, took me under his wing and was patient with me throughout this process. His courage and humility also served as a constant reminder of what was at stake in these struggles, and why I embarked on this journey to begin with. I would also like to thank many others in Colombia: Rossih Amira Martínez, Aiden Salgado Cassiani, Juan de Dios Mosquera, Iván Alberto Vergara Sinisterra, Zulia Mena, Sergio Mosquera, Claudia Mosquera, and Rudecindo Castro, all of whom were incredibly generous with their time, but also helped me contact many others in their organizations and networks to interview. Eduardo Restrepo shared archives with me and helped me to refine my research question early on in my journey. Thank you to César Rodríguez, who provided me with a beautiful workspace and intellectual home at the Observatorio de Discriminación Racial, while Cleo and Leo of Tambores de Eleggua Dance Company taught me the subtleties of cumbia and were my family in Bogotá. Mil gracias.

In Brazil, I would like to thank all of the activists who allowed me to interview them. I'd like to especially thank Samoury Mugabe, who was extremely generous with his time as well as Ailton Pinheiro, who would stay up with me for hours discussing questions of political autonomy, reparations, and justice. Adriana Batista, Flávio Jorge, Carlos Medeiros, Jurema Werneck, Reginaldo Bispo, and Marta Almeida, all introduced me to many people I would later interview. Lucení dos Santos Ferreira helped me comb through critical archives at Criola's office. Angela Paiva at PUC gave me an intellectual home and kept me from being deported. Thank you also to Marcio André and Amilcar Pereira for the many *bate papos* we had about black politics in Brazil and in the larger African Diaspora.

Anyone who has written a book will know that having ideas is only half the battle. Books are also enterprises that require a great deal of technical skill, administrative expertise, and money. In this regard, I am infinitely indebted to Elsa Tranter, Carolyn Clark, and Belinda Kuo White at Berkeley as well as Kimberly Schafer, Penny Pivoriunas, Katherine Hamaguchi, and Fione Dukes at the University of Chicago. They ran the whole operation that made this book possible and they also tolerated my infamous lack of organization. A number of other people also lent their skills and knowledge to this project, including Leydi Chivito in Colombia, Luciana dos Santos Reis, and Luciane Reis in Brazil, who transcribed my interviews, as well as Gabriel Kitamura and Alejandra Vasquez, Yaniv Kleinman, Alysia Mann Carey, Jaime Sánchez, and Yuna Blajer de la Garza, who were all excellent research assistants. I am also grateful for the financial support of the Ford Foundation, the Andrew W. Mellon Foundation, and the Fulbright Commission, as well as support from various institutions at the University of Chicago and the University of California—Berkeley, which allowed me to buy necessary equipment, make trips to Colombia and Brazil, and hire research assistants as well as editors.

Last but not least, I would like to acknowledge the most important people in my life: my family. I am grateful for my mom, Pamela Paschel, for her love and support over the years. She always made sure that education was a top priority, even amid all the challenges we faced. I am also infinitely indebted to my sister, Crystal, who always found a way to encourage and help me even as she juggled a million things, among them her career as a math teacher, motherhood, and many adversities. When I left my business matters in shambles to head to South America, Crystal saved me from going hungry, from missing flights, and from possibly going to jail as a result of unpaid parking tickets. I love you! I am also grateful for my hermanita Brittany and to my little brother Bryson who both supported me from near and far. Finally, I would like to thank my niece Nakaiyah "Papaya" Paschel-Mason, who is the main reason I maintained my sanity while writing this book. I would like to thank her for her silliness, her clever sense of humor, our impromptu dance parties, and for the many songs she composed on the fly and allowed me to accompany with off-key background vocals and simplistic beats. She also reminded me that being a professor and researcher also means being a teacher, a simple but often forgotten fact.

Thank you all for making me, and this book, possible.

INDEX

Note: Page numbers in *italics* indicate figures; those with a *t* indicate tables.